ARMED MILITIAS OF SOUTH ASIA

THE COMPARATIVE POLITICS
AND INTERNATIONAL STUDIES SERIES

Series editor, Christophe Jaffrelot

This series consists of translations of noteworthy manuscripts and publications in the social sciences emanating from the foremost French researchers of Sciences Po, Paris.

The focus of the series is the transformation of politics and society by transnational and domestic factors–globalisation, migration and the post-bipolar balance of power on the one hand, and ethnicity and religion on the other. States are more permeable to external influence than ever before and this phenomenon is accelerating processes of social and political change the world over. In seeking to understand and interpret these transformations, this series gives priority to social trends from below as much as to the interventions of state and non-state actors.

LAURENT GAYER
CHRISTOPHE JAFFRELOT
Editors

Armed Militias of South Asia

Fundamentalists, Maoists and Separatists

Translated by
Cynthia Schoch, Gregory Elliott and Roger Leverdier

Exclusively distributed in South Asia by

ƒOUNDATION
B ◉ ◉ K S

New Delhi • Bangalore
Mumbai • Kolkata
Chennai • Hyderabad

First published in the United Kingdom in 2009 by
C. Hurst & Co. (Publishers) Ltd.,
41 Great Russell Street, London, WC1B 3PL
© Laurent Gayer and Christophe Jaffrelot 2009
All rights reserved. Printed in India

The right of Laurent Gayer and Christophe Jaffrelot to be identified
as the editors of this publication is asserted by them in accordance
with the Copyright, Designs and Patents Act, 1988.

A Cataloguing-in-Publication data record for this book
is available from the British Library.

ISBN
978-1-85065-977-8 *paperback*

www.hurstpub.co.uk

CONTENTS

THE CONTRIBUTORS

MARIAM ABOU ZAHAB, a researcher specialising in Pakistan, teaches at Sciences Po and at the Institut National des Langues et Civilisations Orientales (Inalco), both in Paris. Her research focuses on Shiism, sectarianism and jihadi groups in Pakistan, and also on Pashtun society and the tribal areas of Pakistan. She has carried out extensive fieldwork in Pakistan and has published articles in various journals and edited volumes.

AMELIE BLOM is part of the Visiting Faculty in Political Sociology at Lahore University of Management Sciences (School of Humanities, Social Sciences and Law) and a researcher associated with the French Agence Nationale de la Recherche. She is also co-editor of the *South Asia Multidisciplinary Academic Journal* (http://samaj.revues.org). She is a co-editor of the recently published *The Enigma of Islamist Violence* (Hurst, 2007). Her research focuses on patterns of social and political activism in the name of Islam in Pakistan.

GILLES BOQUERAT is research associate at the Centre for the Study of India and South Asia (Centre d'Etudes de l'Inde et de l'Asie du Sud, CEIAS, EHESS-CNRS, Paris) and at the ISSI (Institute of Strategic Studies of Islamabad).

JEREMIE CODRON is a PhD candidate at Sciences Po-CERI (Centre de Recherches et d'Etudes Internationales), working on Islamist movements and national issues in Bangladesh.

RENAUD EGRETEAU holds degrees in Oriental Studies and a PhD in Political Science from Sciences Po, Paris (2006). He is the author of *Wooing the Generals—India's New Burma Policy* (New Delhi, Authorspress, 2003) and has been focusing his academic research on Burma's political landscape, India's Asian policies and instability in India's North-Eastern States.

LAURENT GAYER obtained his PhD in Political Science from Sciences Po Paris in 2004. His thesis focused on the issue of the internationalisation of Sikh and Mohajir nationalisms. He is a researcher in political sociology at the

CNRS, affiliated with CURAPP (Centre universitaire de recherches sur l'action publique et le politique). He is also a research associate at the Centre for the Study of India and South Asia (Centre d'Etudes de l'Inde et de l'Asie du Sud, CEIAS, EHESS-CNRS, Paris). He is currently working on the individual trajectories of male and female recruits of the Sikh movement for Khalistan and on the history of violence in Karachi.

CHRISTOPHE JAFFRELOT was Director of CERI (Centre d'Etudes et de Recherches Internationales) at Sciences Po (Paris) from 2000 to 2009. He is Senior Research Fellow at the CNRS (Centre National de la Recherche Scientifique) and teaches South Asian politics and history at Sciences Po. His most significant publications are *The Hindu Nationalist Movement and Indian Politics, 1925 to the 1990s*, London, Hurst/New York, Columbia University Press/New Delhi, Penguin India, 1996 and 1999; *India's Silent Revolution. The Rise of the Low Castes in North India*, New York/London/Delhi, Columbia University Press/Hurst/Permanent Black, 2003; and *Dr Ambedkar and Untouchability. Analysing and Fighting Caste*, London, Hurst/New York, Columbia University Press/New Delhi, Permanent Black. He has also edited *Pakistan, Nationalism without a Nation?*, Delhi, Manohar, 2002 and co-edited with T. Blom Hansen, *The BJP and the Compulsions of Politics in India*, Delhi, Oxford University Press, 2001.

NICOLAS JAOUL is a researcher in anthropology at the CNRS, affiliated with IRIS (Institut de Recherche Interdisciplinaire sur les Enjeux Sociaux, EHESS). His comparative ethnographic approach focuses on the politics of the poor by comparing Dalits according to their various ideological movements (Hindu nationalists, Gandhians, Dalits, Ambedkarists, Maoists). He is interested in political iconography and hagiography and more particularly in the political use of statues.

MARIE LECOMTE-TILOUINE is a senior researcher in Social Anthropology at the CNRS (UPR 299, Milieux, Société et Cultures en Himalaya), Villejuif, France, and teaches at the Institut National des Langues Orientales, Paris. She recently published *Hindu Kingship, Ethnic Revival, and Maoist Rebellion in Nepal*, Oxford University Press, 2008, and edited the volume *Bards and Mediums. History, Culture and Politics in the Central Himalayan Kingdoms*, Almora Book Depot, forthcoming 2009. She is now coordinating an ANR programme on the history and anthropology of the People's War in Nepal.

CHRIS SMITH is associate fellow at the International Security Programme, Chatham House, London. Previously a Senior Fellow at the International Policy Research Institute, Kings College, Director of the Institute's Centre for South Asia Studies, and a MacArthur Foundation Research and Writing Fellow, Dr Smith is a specialist in the areas of technology and organised crime, conflict and insurgency in Sri Lanka, and security sector reform.

LIST OF MAPS

ACRONYMS

ABPS	Akhil Bharatiya Pratinidhi Sabha (Pan-Indian RSS Representatives Committee)
ABSDF	All Burma Student Democratic Front
ABVP	Akhil Bharatiya Vidyarthi Parishad (All India Students Council)
AHAB	Ahl-e-Hadith Andolon Bangladesh (Bangladesh Ahl-e-Hadith Movement)
AISSF	All India Sikh Students Federation
AJK	Azad Jammu and Kashmir
AL	Awami League
ALA	Arakan Liberation Army
ALP	Arakan Liberation Party
ANNA	All Nepal Nationalities Association
APHC	All Parties Hurriyat Conference
ARIF	Arakan Rohingya Islamic Front
ARNO	Arakan Rohingya National Organisation
BJP	Bharatiya Janata Party
BPKS	Bihar Pradesh Kisan Sabha (Bihar peasant organisation)
BNP	Bangladesh Nationalist Party
BSF	Border Security Force
CCOMPOSA	Coordination Committee of Maoist Parties and Organisations of South Asia
CFA	Cease-Fire Agreement
CIA	Chin Independence Army
CID	Central Investigation Department
CNA	Chin National Army
CNF	Chin National Front
CPB	Communist Party of Burma
CPI	Communist Party of India
CPI-M	Communist Party of India-Marxist
CPI-ML	Communist Party of India-Marxist-Leninist
CPNP	Communist Party of Nepal

CPN-M	Communist Party of Nepal-Marxist
CPN-UML	Communist Party of Nepal-United Marxist-Leninist
DAB	Democratic Alliance of Burma
DKBA	Democratic Karen Buddhist Army
ERFCC	Ethnic and Regional Fronts Coordination Committee
HM	Hizb-ul-Mujahidin (Mujahidin Party/Party of the Warriors of God)
HUJI	Harkat-ul-Jihad al-Islami (Movement for an Islamic Holy War)
ICG	International Crisis Group
ISGA	Interim Self-Governing Authority
IJT	Islami Jamiat-i-Tulaba (Islamic Student Organisation)
IOJ	Islami Oikyo Jote (Islamic United Front)
IPF	Indian People's Front
IPKF	Indian Peace Keeping Force
ISI	Inter-Services Intelligence
JD-U	Janata Dal (United) (People's Party)
JeM	Jaish-e-Muhammad
JHU	Jathika Hela Urumaya (National Heritage Party)
JI	Jamaat-i-islami (Islamic organisation)
JI-AJK	JI-Azad Jammu and Kashmir
JI-JK	JI-Jammu and Kashmir
JI-P	JI-Pakistan
JKLF	Jammu and Kashmir Liberation Front
JMB	Jama'at-ul Mujahidin Bangladesh (Party of the Mujahidi of Bangladesh)
JMJB	Jagrata Muslim Janata Bangladesh (Awakened Muslim Masses of Bangladesh)
JTA	Jamiat-i-Tulaba-i-Arabiya (Organisation of Arab students)
JUH	Jamiat-e Ulema-e Hind (Organisation of Indian Islamic Scholars)
JUI	Jamiat-e Ulema-e Islam (Assembly of Islamic Clergy)
JVP	Janatha Vimukhti Peramuna (People's Liberation Front)
KCF	Khalistan Commando Force
KIA	Kachin Independence Army
KIO	Kachin Independence Organisation
KNDA	Karenni National Defence Army
KNF	Khambuwan National Front
KNLA	Karen National Liberation Army
KNO	Karenni National Organisation
KNPP	Karenni National Progressive Party
KNU	Karen National Union
LeJ	Lashkar-e Jhangvi (Jhangvi's Army)
LeT	Lashkar-e-Tayyebah
LLF	Limbuwan Liberation Front

LTTE	Liberation Tigers of Tamil Eelam
MCC	Maoist Communist Centre
MILF	Moro Islamic Liberation Front
MIP	Millat-e Islamia Pakistan (Islamic Nation of Pakistan)
MIS	Military Intelligence Service
MKSS	Mazdur Kisan Sangram Samiti (Worker-Peasant Struggle Council)
MLO	Muslim Liberation Organisation
MMA	Muttahida Majlis-e Amal (United Council of Action)
MNDAA	Myanmar National Democratic Alliance Army
MPRF	Madhesi People's Rights Forum
MQM	Mohajir Qaumi Movement (Mohajir National Movement), renamed Muttahida Qaumi Movement (United National Movement) in 1997
MTA	Mong Tai Army
NAP	National Awami Party
NCGUB	National Coalition Government of the Union of Burma
NDA	New Democratic Army
NDAA	National Democratic Alliance Army
NDF	National Democratic Front
NEFEN	Nepal Federation of Nationalities (Nepal Janajati Mahasangh)
NEFIN	Nepal Federation of Indigenous Nationalities
NMSP	New Mon State Party
NRC	Nepal Rashtriya Congress
NSCN	National Socialist Council of Nagaland
NUFA	National United Front of Arakan
NUPA	National United Party of Arakan
NWFP	North West Frontier Province
OBC	Other Backward Classes
PLOTE	People's Liberation Organisation of Tamil Eelam
PML	Pakistan Muslim League
POLSAN	Political Science Association of Nepal
POTA	Prevention of Terrorist Activities Act
PPP	Pakistan People's Party
PSLO/A	Palaung State Liberation Organisation Army
PWG	People's War Group
RAW	Research and Analysis Wing
RIF	Rohingya Independent Force
RJD	Rashtriya Janata Dal (National People's Party)
RPF	Rohingya Patriotic Front
RSO	Rohingya Solidarity Organisation
RSS	Rashtriya Swayamsevak Sangh (National Volunteer's Union)
SAD	Shiromani Akali Dal (Army of the Faithful)

SGPC	Shiromani Gurduwara Prabandhak Committee (Committee of Shrine Management)
SLORC	State Law and Order Restoration Council
SNA	Shan National Army
SNUF	Shan National United Front
SPDC	State Peace and Development Council
SSA	Shan State Army
SSIA	Shan State Independence Army
SSP	Sipah-e Sahaba Pakistan (Army of the Prophet's Companions)
SUA	Shan Unity Army
SURA	Shan United Revolutionary Army
TELO	Tamil Eelam Liberation Organisation
TJP	Tehrik-e Jaafriya Pakistan (Pakistan Jafarite Movement)
TNA	Tamil National Army
TNFJ	Tehrik-e Nifaz-e Fiqh-e Jaafriya (Movement for the use of Jafarite jurisprudence)
TULF	Tamil United Liberation Front
ULFA	United Liberation Front of Assam
UNP	United National Party
UPFN	United People's Front of Nepal
URPC	United Revolutionary People's Council
USDA	Union Solidarity and Development Association
UWSA	United Wa State Army
VKA	Vanavasi Kalyan Ashram (Tribal Welfare Ashram)

Map 1: South Asia

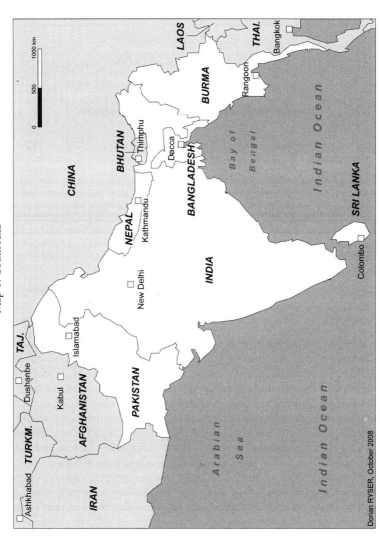

INTRODUCTION

Laurent Gayer and Christophe Jaffrelot

Ethnic and religious conflicts threaten to tear apart more societies today than any other issue. These conflicts rise out of identity movements that construe an enemy "other" and characterise themselves as nationalists even though they are based on exclusionist agendas. Since these movements do not adhere to democratic norms they seek to achieve their goals through private armies or militias [...] Militias comprise unemployed youth who are given a purpose by virtue of arms and a free mandate, and they function as an underground sword arm for political parties or movements [...] The intention is to militarise civil society by militarising religion, culture and people through the creation of militias.

Anuradha M. Chenoy, "Militia Mentality", *The Times of India*,
17 September 2002.

Although not indicated in the preceding lines, the societies Anuradha M. Chenoy refers to are those of South Asia. The proliferation of militias in this part of the world is indeed a factor in the notable rise in violence in the region over the past thirty years. In every South Asian country, one finds incidents of pitched battles between armed groups and riots pitting paramilitary forces—self-proclaimed avant-gardes of ethnic communities—against one another, as well as forms of cultural repression and social pressure that seek to control the behaviour of "deviants". Before becoming physical, violence can be symbolic—it can be exercised on minds as much as on bodies.

Militias are defined, here, as organisations perpetrating violence—physical or psychological—on behalf of a cause, an ideology or a programme. They may be in the form of small groups or fully-fledged private armies. They may use techniques similar to terrorist groups, but they differ from them in one aspect at least and that is their work on society in order to gain grassroots support.

However, the nature of the phenomenon varies not only according to the country but also within one and the same country, depending on the objectives pursued. Contrary to what the quotation of A.M. Chenoy might lead one to think, nationalist movements alone do not explain the processes discussed here. In the present introduction to the phenomenon we will therefore first examine the extent of it, and then devote the second part to attempting a typology that hopes to clarify the terms of the debate.

But the crux of the problem lies elsewhere, even doubly elsewhere. First, it has to do with the ability of such movements to recruit young people in growing numbers. Doubtless, the idleness and the search for status mentioned by A.M. Chenoy are important factors for the lumpen elements that make up the militias' ranks. But a more thorough sociological analysis is needed to understand the appeal a militia career holds for these young people. Such an examination should also include investigation of their perceptions and their violent practices in society.

Besides, it is somewhat shortsighted to be satisfied with the privatisation of violence as an explanation. It suggests that militias operate without any connection whatsoever with the official public sphere. Yet they do maintain relations with institutional political forces and even the state—by default or intentionally, depending on the case at hand. Even more, these militias can take part in their own way in state formation, and this is true in both authoritarian and democratic frameworks.[1]

A region at the grasp of military violence

The number of casualties is one indication of the rise in irregular armed groups in South Asia: more than 80,000 deaths in Sri Lanka after 25 years of civil war pitting a highly militarised separatist movement, the Liberation Tigers of Tamil Eelam (LTTE), against the army; at least 40,000 deaths in Kashmir after twenty years of similar conflict, in which Pakistan-based jihadist groups are also involved; about 30,000 deaths in Punjab in the conflict between Sikh separatist groups and Indian security forces between 1984 and 1995; approximately 10,000 deaths in ten years of civil war in Nepal (1996–2006); and a comparable number of victims in riots between Hindus and Muslims in India[2] since the Ayodhya movement developed in the early 1980s, when Hindu nationalists began demanding restitution of the site on which the first Great Mughal had had a mosque built in that Uttar Pradesh city, but which the Hindus consider to be the birthplace of Lord Ram. Starting in 1984, Hindu nationalist activism took a particularly aggressive turn and degenerated into anti-Muslim provocations that would lead to recurrent and massive outbreaks of violence. The riots in Bhagalpur in 1989 and in Gujarat in 2002 alone left one thousand and two thousand dead respectively. Violence between Sunnis and Shias has been responsible for the death of 4,000 people in Pakistan since 1990, whereas urban conflicts in Karachi have claimed nearly 10,000 lives since 1985, as many as those killed by the Burmese junta since the democratic movement was crushed in 1988. Islamist violence in Bangladesh is much less deadly by comparison, taking less than one hundred lives since jihadist organisations started their terror campaign in 1999. The Maoist insurgency that India has been facing since the late 1960s was also until recently relatively less bloody, but this situation is likely to change, especially in Chhattisgarh since the creation of an anti-Naxalite militia, Salwa Judum ("Peace Mission"), in 2005. The annual number of victims in this conflict is now closer to a thousand, and according to Prime Minister Manmohan Singh's address to the Nation on August 15, 2006, the Maoist insurgency represents the major threat for India's national security, whereas in the Kashmiri revolt, the number of victims has been steadily decreasing since 2001.[3]

Despite the resolution of some conflicts (Punjab since 1995; Nepal since 2006, though things may change with the resignation of Prime Minister Prachanda in May 2009) and the lowered intensity of others (Nagaland, Burma, Kashmir) in recent years, since the 1990s there has been an overall rise in the level of violence, coupled with its geographic extension. In India, Maoists insurgents continue to expand their field of action, which now affects 12 of the 28 states that comprise India.[4] In Bangladesh, the wave of attacks on 17 August 2005 (400 bombs exploded practically simultaneously throughout the country) demonstrated the nationwide ambition of jihadist organisations, which after focusing for long on their local base decided to attack society and the political system on a larger scale. In Pakistan, Karachi has faced renewed incidents of urban violence since 2007,[5] and two new conflicts pitting irregular combatants against security forces have blossomed in recent years in the Pashtun belt and in Baluchistan. In these areas, the central government has only nominal authority, and in the "tribal areas" as well as the North-West Frontier Province (NWFP) the local Taliban are currently emerging as a parallel power. And in Sri Lanka, the death of Prabhakaran and the decimation of the LTTE does not mean that the Tamils may not take arms again.

An attempt at typology

South Asia's militia movements take root in a wide variety of rationales. But it is more difficult than it might first appear to identify the distinctive feature on which to build a typology.

Initially, it would seem possible to distinguish roughly between paramilitary groups touting an ethno-nationalistic ideology from Maoist-inspired revolutionary groups. This distinction contains some relevance but does not apply systematically. On close examination, for instance, the Maobadi in Nepal turn out to represent mainly certain tribes to the exclusion of others, as Gilles Boquérat demonstrates in this volume. As for the Indian Naxalites, they are riven by caste issues, since their rank and file—and sometimes even their cadres—are recruited mainly among Dalits, as Nicolas Jaoul shows in the chapter he devotes to the Naxalites in Bihar, one of the Indian bastions of South Asian Maoism. Although caste and class (and tribe and class) largely overlap in the Indo-Nepalese world, the fact is that beyond revolutionary ideology, the "subtext" is often an identitarian one in the case of both the Maobadi and the Naxalites. Maoist cadres themselves may contribute to this ethnicisation of the Revolution by locating the roots of their "class war" in ethnically specific forms of oppression, as shown by Marie Lecomte-Tilouine in her chapter.

Another "sorting key" that can be derived from the analysis contrasts emancipation movements with those that aim, on the contrary, to exercise social control. Many of the conflicts in South Asia in fact originate from people's aspiration to self-determination, as among the Tamils in Sri Lanka, the Sikhs and Kashmiris in India or tribes in the peripheral areas of Burma. But a number of national liberation movements are also movements of national oppression. Until their military defeat in May 2009, the LTTE were an example, striving as they did to regiment their community by using the most brutal forms of control to carry out their war against the Sri Lankan government, as Chris Smith shows in his chapter. As for the Kashmir insurrection, today it is led by Islamist movements such as the Hizb ul-Mujahidin (HM)—studied here by Amélie Blom—whose agenda is not to work toward Kashmir's independence but to have its Indian portion attached to Pakistan in the name of a militant version of Islam. As Laurent Gayer shows, the Sikh insurgent groups that made their appearance in India's Punjab in the second half of the 1980s were emanations of religious militias that had surfaced in the province in the late 1970s. And even if these armed groups were formed to liberate Punjab from India's yoke, some of them mainly sought to impose a strict orthopraxy on the Sikh community.

In this light, the LTTE, the HM and the Khalistani guerrilla movement are less clearly demarcated from movements that have a more or less explicit goal of exercising control over society in the name of religion. This third and final category is the best represented in South Asia. No religious community that has any critical mass escapes this type of movement. In Pakistan, the re-Islamisation of society has given rise to constant escalation and fuels so-called sectarian conflicts (between Sunnis and Shias), as Mariam Abou Zahab demonstrates in her chapter. In Bangladesh, the shadow of the Razakar militias which collaborated with the Pakistani "occupiers" during the 1971 liberation war still looms. The Jama'at-e-Islami student front has served as a model for others, but the aim of Bangladesh Islamist radicals is no longer only to fight against the heretics of the Ahmadiyya sect:[6] Jérémie Codron explains that it sees the whole of society as justifying a domestic *jihad*. As for the Hindu nationalist militias, even if the Muslim (and Christian) Other was for a long time their sole target, they have recently begun attacking their fellow Hindus, as shown by the acts of violence perpetrated by the Bajrang Dal studied by Christophe Jaffrelot, aiming to keep the majority community "on the right path".

Tracing militia careers

Despite their ideological and strategic divergences, South Asian militias share a common feature in their recruitment. Their militants are usually young, sometimes only adolescents; the enrolment of children is more rare although it has existed, as in the LTTE's case. Here like elsewhere, the militant rank and file is recruited primarily among the unschooled or educated but unemployed youth, whose futures are compromised particularly because of discrimination and economic underdevelopment.[7] And if militias attract young people who have few prospects for the future, it is first of all because they offer a career. Like the notion of a "terrorist career" analysed by Romain Bertrand in his study on the social and ideological trajectory of the Indonesian jihadist Imam Samudra,[8] the notion of a "militia career" can be understood in two ways. First, what might be considered its common meaning is the acquisition of marketable skills that earn both material and symbolic rewards. But in the perspective of symbolic interactionism, the notion of "career" can also be taken to mean a course of objective personal development with subjective consequences.[9] In this second meaning, the notion of a "militia career" thus refers to the sequence of events leading up to enrolment in an irregular armed group and sustaining or, on the contrary, moderating this commitment through the years.[10]

This career-oriented approach has the advantage of "not confining the analysis to determinants of militancy but of considering how the involvement process fits in with the life cycle".[11] That is the approach adopted here in a more or less explicit manner by most of the contributors, attuned to the individual combatant trajectories and how they fit into specific social, political and institutional contexts. An approach in terms of career or trajectory in fact implies incorporating "biographical time" into "social time", that is, into evolutions in society, the political system and social movements.[12] In other words, narrowing the focus onto the individual does not rule out a need to analyse the political arena, the structures of (de)mobilisation, the specific costs and rewards of each militant experience, the sociological density (the nature and intensity of collective bonds), or the ideological links between an individual and his organisation.

Indeed, individual factors (personal motivations or predispositions) informing these commitments in their early stage cannot be divorced either from the social context of such decisions—by embracing the career of militants, youngsters become part of a group—or from the process that such a career implies regarding ideology. At first, new recruits may well join a movement for other reasons than its ideology, but gradually they subscribe at least to some of its ideas and become part of a tradition—some movements' history goes back several decades and comprises their own world view, legends and myths.

Ideology is not defined here merely in political terms but also in a Weberian perspective as a network of significations making sense of the world. As Clifford Geertz suggested years ago:

It is a confluence of sociopsychological strain and the absence of cultural resources by means of which to make sense of the strain, each exacerbating the other, that sets the stage for the rise of systematic (political, moral, or economic) ideologies. And it is, in turn, the attempt of ideologies to render otherwise incomprehensible social situations meaningful, to so construe them as to make it possible to act purposefully within them, that accounts both for the ideologies' highly figurative nature and for the intensity with which, once accepted, they are held.[13]

This approach applies to nationalist ideologies—especially in their ethnic garb,[14] though it retains its heuristic power in the case of other ideologies, revolutionary or ethno-religious for example, such as those propagated by the movements under review in the present volume.

As Amélie Blom points out in her study on the Pakistani *mujahidin*[15] and Laurent Gayer in his work on the Sikh insurgent movement in the years 1984–95,[16] the three ideal-types of militants that Farhad Khosrokhavar identified in revolutionary Iran[17] can also be found in South Asia. The first are the "martyropaths", guided by a self-annihilating death wish that attests to an unshakeable belief in the justness of the cause defended or, on the contrary, to disillusion and a sense of failure.[18] As many of the case studies gathered here show, Islam does not have a monopoly on voluntary death in combat and in South Asia, the Sikh insurgents in Punjab and the Hindu Tamils of the LTTE have been spurred on by the same desire for martyrdom as the jihadist combatants in Kashmir. The strategic use of voluntary death is not specific to religious organisations either, as can be seen in the glorification of martyrdom by Nepalese Maoists,[19] and in the LTTE's "sacrificial ideology" and the logistics that enable it to be carried out.[20]

In addition to the "martyropath", another style of militant is the "game-player". Beyond the moral gratification that comes with conducting a just, even "holy" war, young militants find in the organisation a counter-society that allows them to indulge in risk behaviour that involves putting their own life on the line.[21] The militia is not only a disciplinary institution that exercises strict social control over its militants and society. It is also a "game-playing community" whose members find themselves joined by the "feeling of being 'apart together' in an exceptional situation".[22] And if this dangerous game includes a share of risk, the militants who take part in it derive both private and collective pleasure from it. Oskar Verkaaik's research into the Mohajir nationalist movement in Hyderabad (Sindh) well illustrates the "fun" dimension of this "high-risk activism",[23] emphasising particularly the "euphoric" nature of the violence carried out by the Mohajir Qaumi Movement (MQM) militants.[24]

South Asia's militias count among their ranks, lastly, a certain number of "opportunists", guided by designs of material development and symbolic recognition.[25] These private armies enable their members to achieve prestige. Often they are also paid a salary, which allows them to take part in practices of accumulation that, as they become widespread, transform the militias into "enterprises of violence", that is, into organisations "acting to convert organized force (or violence) into money or other market resources, and this in a permanent fashion".[26]

The militia is primarily a man's world. But that does not mean women are absent. In some cases they participate actively in armed struggle, as in Sri Lanka and Nepal, where the guerrilla movements' female numbers approached those of male militants.[27] In India, several hundred, or maybe even several thousand women fight in the ranks of the Maoist movement, which has some exclusively female battalions, like the National Park Dalam in Andhra Pradesh, commanded by a former doctor, Nirmala Akka.[28] Some women also fought in the Sikh guerrilla movement, whereas the Hindu nationalist movement founded exclusively female offshoots.[29] On the other hand, women were for a long time excluded from jihadist movements, in contrast to other areas of the world (Palestine, Chechnya). In Kashmir, the Dukhtaran-e-Millat (Daughters of the Nation) have formed a female Islamist militia outfit that supported the call for *azadi* (independence) and Islamisation of the public sphere put forward by nationalist and Islamist forces, but for long they—and their male relatives—opposed the recruitment of women by jihadist organisations.[30] Recent developments however suggest that at least some jihadist organisations in the region have started opening their ranks to women. In Kashmir, Pakistan based militant groups have started recruiting female fighters. In Bangladesh, the Jama'at-ul Mujahidin has formed exclusively female units. In Pakistan, female students from the Red Mosque in Islamabad organised themselves as a militia in early 2007 to put up resistance against the city's urban renewal campaign (which planned to demolish religious buildings not complying with the building code), and then to impose their radical interpretation of Islam in the heart of Pakistan's capital. But to date, none of these burqa-clad activists ever picked up a gun and incidents of female suicide attacks remain unknown among South Asian Muslims.

Most South Asian women combatants seem to be professing a form of "martial feminism", to use Peter Schalk's expression regarding the LTTE female militants.[31] Though the influence of ideology should not be neglected, these women may also be prompted to leave their family homes to escape domestic violence, forced marriages or land tenure conflicts, as is indicated by the journalist Li Onesto's interviews with the Nepalese female Maoist combatants[32] and, in the case of the Indian female Naxalites, the survey recently published in the Indian magazine *The Week*.[33] Maoist or separatist cadres often reinforce this martial brand of feminism by propagating new conceptions of gender roles in the context of war, as shown by Marie Lecomte-Tilouine in her chapter. As regards Hindu nationalists, in addition to the Durga Vahini of the Sangh Parivar dealt with by Christophe Jaffrelot in this volume, a special mention must be made of the female wing of the Shiv Sena studied by Atreyee Sen, who convincingly argues that "poor women in the slums of Mumbai who supported the political right were not Hindu fundamentalist women passively mobilised by a party into the ascendant nationalist wave".[34] They had their "own rationale for supporting the pan-Indian cause of Hindutva, which was related to their growing aspiration to maintain links with rural women [those of their family with whom they did not have much left in common except religion], legitimise female militancy in their localities and carve out a visible public role for women".[35]

Emancipation via militias nevertheless has limits. These organisations, in South Asia, systematically subordinate the "liberation" of women to the larger goals of the people's struggle, and nothing guarantees that the relative emancipation attained by female combatants in wartime will translate into a genuine reassessment of gender roles after the guns fall silent.[36] Moreover, these militias practice strict sexual control over their militants of both genders by often obliging women to take husbands in the militia[37] and severely punishing extramarital affairs. This militia moral order not only proceeds from ideological motives focusing on preservation of the patriarchal order in the militia counter-society, it also contains a strategic dimension. Control of the militants' sexuality has prophylactic virtues, since it aims to prevent romantic conflicts from breaking out that could jeopardise the unity of the movement. These partisan marriages also serve as a tool for collective radicalisation in the sense meant by Gilles Dorronsoro and Olivier Grojean:[38] they contribute to the advent of a counter-society by isolating the combatants from their original background, as the anthropologist Judith Pettigrew has shown in the case of the Maobadi.[39]

Militia-state connections

In theory, the development of militias in South Asia challenges the state's fundamental role as guardian of the social and political order. Weber's definition of the state in this regard remains as relevant as ever in gauging the impact of social violence: "A compulsory political organization with continuous operations [...] will be called a 'state' insofar as its administrative staff successfully upholds the claim to the monopoly of the legitimate use of force in the enforcement of its order".[40] If the state is characterised by the fact that it dispenses legitimate violence, it is because it has control over the bureaucracy and police forces. This monopolisation is the very basis of state building, as Norbert Elias has shown so well in a more dynamic approach than Weber's.[41] For him, the "civilizing process" rests in fact on a scientific law which he calls a "monopolistic law", according to which, when the relationship between several entities is one of competition, they have no other choice than to get along, because a merely defensive attitude would condemn them to disappear as the most vulnerable of them are absorbed by the most powerful. This creates a "center for crystallization" triggering the "monopoly mechanism" that ends up concentrating power within a single centre.[42]

In South Asia, the proliferation of paramilitary movements, militias and other private armies chips away at a pillar of the modern state as the Mughals had conceived it—to take a historical view—and especially as the British shaped it. And this all the more so since in many cases, these same movements were spawned in reaction to state policies. Maoism developed in Nepal against a monarchy full of contempt for the people, and in India after the expectations of the peasants regarding land reform were disappointed. The LTTE has prospered thanks to a context of discrimination towards the Tamil minority by the Sinhalese authorities, and the Kashmiri insurgency has done the same in reaction to New Delhi's centralising authoritarianism—a scenario that is also found with the Sikhs in Punjab. As for Shia militancy in Pakistan—

against which Sunni sectarianism has (re)formed—it is largely the result of General Zia's policy of Islamisation.

The fact that militias rise up against the state does not however mean that they develop without having any ties with it whatsoever. Actually, the state is involved in the militia phenomenon everywhere. It is actively so when it arms activists according to a purely instrumental logic. In Kashmir, the Pakistani army literally subcontracted out to the guerrillas, offering them the necessary logistic support to "bleed India". In Burma, the junta delegates the quashing of ethnic uprisings to the militias that it arms. In Indian Punjab, New Delhi backed the rise of the most radical Sikhs so as better to combat the moderates whom the authorities saw as more dangerous for the control of that province. Elsewhere the state has proved more discreet but just as effective. In Bangladesh, some militias have taken advantage of the government's complicit non-intervention, and the Bajrang Dal, a Hindu nationalist militia, enjoyed similar complacency from the Indian authorities when the Bharatiya Janata Party (Indian People's Party, BJP), a related party, was in power.

Ideological affinities alone do not always explain this approach. The state can also find it convenient to entrust maintenance of social and/or cultural order to private armies. Militias then become arms of the state by "outsourcing" their policing.[43] In the rural areas of Bihar, private armies such as the Ranvir Sena have been formed by upper castes to contain the development of Naxalism. The link with the state is even more obvious in Chhattisgarh, where the Salwa Judum militia which, like its Maoist adversaries, mainly recruits among the tribal populations, was created out of nothing by the state government and trained by the local police.[44] In Bangladesh, Islamist militias served the state in similar fashion by hunting down communist opponents on campuses or in rural areas. Beyond that, militias can impose themselves as security forces independently of any state backing. In Pakistan, the Sipah-e Sahaba Pakistan (Army of the Prophet, SSP) has served as a security force for the Jhang business owners' association and arbitrates in conflicts between neighbours. In these cases, militias take over from the state in order to perform some of its functions and sometimes even become states within the state.

It should nevertheless be pointed out that these cases of state support for irregular armed groups never involve the state in its entirety, but rather local law enforcement agencies and "secret bureaucracies",[45] whose capacity for exploiting militias is not limitless. Militants have their own agendas which may vary from one individual to the next,[46] and they can gain room for manoeuvre by finding other patrons or securing ever greater resources. This is how the jihadist movements active in Kashmir have acquired considerable autonomy with respect to Pakistani state actors that sponsored them for a long time. Furthermore, international constraints should not be underestimated. Foreign diplomatic and/or financial pressure from multilateral bodies or individual countries can oblige a state to put down militias perceived as troublemakers undermining their stability or that of their region. Thus General Musharraf's Pakistan, under pressure from the United States, had no choice but to tackle the Islamist groups tied to Al-Qaeda networks or involved in the *jihad* in Indian Kashmir. The external variable can however sometimes work in favour of militias. In many cases, they actually obtain foreign support, as in the case of Saudi Arabia's funding of the Pakistani and Bangladeshi Islamists or donations made to the LTTE by expatriate Tamils.

Even if they jeopardise the state's monopoly on legitimate violence, militias nevertheless participate in the process of state formation in the sense meant by Bruce Berman and John Lonsdale. Those authors make an important distinction between the formation of the state as a social institution and the construction of the state as an administrative apparatus.[47] Reasoning solely in terms of state-building, as many analyses are wont to do, tends to reduce state histories to their foundational period and the actions of official agents. Berman and Lonsdale's analysis, on the other hand, has the merit of examining state trajectories over the long term, integrating the role of private actors.[48] As they point out regarding the case of Kenya, societies always crash the gates of the state formation process through techniques contributing to the "vulgarization of power", which involve appropriating public authority to private ends.[49] This approach has obvious heuristic virtues for analysing militias in South Asia and their relationship to the state. It helps to qualify the anti-state nature of these private armies and considers their contribution to state formation in the region from two different angles and in two opposite directions: outsourcing of violence to society by certain state actors, and enhancement of such state patronage to political or economic ends by violence entrepreneurs. Even when militia violence is turned against state servants or symbols, it partakes of state formation in that through these actions, the dissenting militants attempt to "form the state for themselves", to use Berman and Lonsdale's terms regarding Kenyan social groups that subvert the process of colonial state formation by their geographic mobility and their modes of assembly and later their political mobilisation.[50]

Militias only truly undermine the foundations of the state when they set up parallel governments such as the LTTE had in Sri Lanka—a state within the state in the literal sense—until the "final" war of Spring 2009, the Karens' movement in Burma, and the Maobadi in Nepal until they joined the government and began laying down their weapons. But the notion of parallel government covers a wide array of contrasting situations, ranging from "liberated zones" (of the Naxalites in Bihar and the Nepalese Maoists) and inviolable territories controlled by Burmese militias to the moral dictatorship observed in the villages of Bangladesh dominated by the Jagrata Muslim Janata or the Jama'at-ul Mujahidin. These configurations provide examples not of state formation but of counter-state formation, increasingly referred to in the literature as "guerrilla governance".[51]

The often-mentioned "criminalisation" of guerrillas and militia groups does not necessarily work against these plans to form a state. The spread of predatory practices that often accompanies the development of militia organisations can certainly contribute to alienating the movement's grassroots base;

11

this is suggested in particular by the case of Indian Punjab, where the rural population, at first in favour of the young "rebels" (*kharku*), turned against them when their extortion practices became unbearable and the armed groups turned out to be more factors of insecurity than providers of security. But what the Punjab example implicitly reveals is the key to success for militias hoping to form a counter-state: the ability to ensure the protection of their social base against abuses perpetrated by the state, but also against their own violence, in exchange for the moral and material support of this same population.[52]

The criminalisation of militias thus goes well beyond mere recourse to illegal means of financing. It involves setting up extortion schemes that are both an instrument of social control and a means of extracting economic benefits. Along with Charles Tilly, we might make the hypothesis that the criminalisation process constitutes the first step toward state formation, the protection/retribution scheme being at the basis of state-making.[53] The success of any state-building enterprise, however, lies in the legitimacy of the violence done and the effectiveness of the protection function assumed by the actor aspiring to a monopoly over the use of force, an element of Weber's standard definition often neglected. A militia's capacity to form a parallel state thus depends on its military capabilities as much as the extent of its popular support, which varies according to what its social base estimates the cost of protection to be and the latter's ability to break free of this imposed protection.

The difficulty of fieldwork

Each of the studies collected here is the product of fieldwork conducted in circumstances that were often difficult. This difficulty first lies in the conditions in which contact with the militias can be made. They systematically cloak their activities in a certain degree of secrecy, even when they operate legally. Only after a painstaking effort to approach them—which involves establishing relations of trust with organisation members or peripheral actors in contact with them (activists involved in the armed groups' legal fronts, journalists, human rights activists, etc.)—is it possible to penetrate this opaque world. This entails a degree of risk, especially when the field is a war zone such as in Nepal, Kashmir or Sri Lanka. Aside from the physical risk involved in such situations of armed conflict, they do not necessarily lend themselves to rigorous sociological investigation. In a civil war situation, an observer declaring his or her impartiality has virtually no place. Such persons are always suspect in the eyes of the belligerents, and the information they sometimes consent to give is closer to propaganda or "ethnographic seduction"[54] than an objective account.[55]

One of the best ways to overcome this obstacle of stereotypical discourse strongly biased by an organisation's official rhetoric is to investigate militant trajectories by questioning combatants about their social and ideological background. It is through personal, even private considerations that militia phenomena should be approached, even if it is essential then to work up to the meso-organisational level and later to the macrostructural level of political opportunity. As we suggested earlier, the concept of "career" is probably the most apt to describe this movement that "allows one to move back and forth between the personal and the public, between the self and its significant society".[56] This concept moreover offers the advantage of integrating the contingency effects inherent in any social trajectory that pertain to the actor's socio-economic status, his or her web of relations, or those incidents along the way that can prove to be decisive in an individual's life and the idea he has of himself and his social environment. As Erving Goffman points out, it is through "case histories" that these "career contingences" are best revealed, especially when they affect the "private experience of self".[57]

It is probably in their twilight moments that militias best lend themselves to sociological study, in that the decrease in the level of violence and a degree of hindsight can loosen militants' tongues, which were previously restrained by the threat of repression from either the state or the militia organisations themselves. Although it is always preferable to study phenomena of political violence after the fact, such a position is unfortunately not always possible to take. When conflicts endure, several generations of militants emerge and the veterans of the first generation are often in a better position to exert a critical eye on their personal involvement and their organisation's trajectory, even if hindsight also has a disadvantage: militants have a tendency to adopt a teleological viewpoint on their involvement, taking it out of its historical context and reinterpreting it in light of the outcome.[58] The contributors to this volume have striven to overcome all these obstacles during the work meetings that preceded this book, which were held in the framework of CERI's South Asia monitoring group.[59]

BIBLIOGRAPHY

Books

Bayart, Jean-François (ed.), *La Réinvention du capitalisme*, Paris, Fayard, 1994.
———— *La Greffe de l'État*, Paris, Fayard, 1996.
Berman, Bruce and John Lonsdale, *Unhappy Valley. Conflict in Kenya and Africa*, vol. 1, *State and Class*, vol. 2, *Violence and Ethnicity*, London, James Currey, 1992.
Crettiez, Xavier, *Violence et nationalisme*, Paris, Odile Jacob, 2006.
Dewerpe, Alain, *Espion. Une anthropologie politique du secret d'État contemporain*, Paris, Gallimard, 1994.
Elias, Norbert, *The Civilizing Process. Sociogenetic and Psychogenetic Investigations*, Oxford, Blackwell, 2000 [1939].
Geertz, Clifford, *The Interpretation of Culture*, New York, Basic Books, 1973.
Goffman, Erving, *Asylums. Essays on the Social Situation of Mental Patients and Other Inmates*, Anchor Books, Doubleday, New York, 1961.
Hugues, Everett, *Men and their Work*, Glencoe (Ill.), The Free Press, 1958.

Huizinga, Johan, *Homo Ludens. A Study of the Play Element in Culture*, Boston (Mass.), The Beacon Press, 1955 [1ˢᵗ ed. 1950].

Jaffrelot, Christophe, *The Hindu Nationalist Movement and Indian Politics*, London, Hurst/New York, Columbia University Press/Delhi, Penguin, 1996.

Le Breton, David, *Conduites à risques*, Paris, PUF, 2002.

Machanda, Rita (ed.), *Women, War and Peace in South Asia. Beyond Victimhood to Agency*, Delhi, Sage, 2001

Onesto, Li, *Dispatches from the People's War in Nepal*, London/Ann Arbor (Mich.)/ Chicago (Ill.), Pluto Press/Insight Press, 2005.

Pratten, David and Atreyee Sen (eds), *Global Vigilantes*, London, Hurst, 2007.

Verkaaik, Oskar, *Migrants and Militants. Fun and Urban Violence in Pakistan*, Princeton University Press, 2004.

Weber (Max), *Economy and Society. An Outline of Interpretive Sociology*, University of California Press, 1978 [1914].

Articles and chapters in edited volumes

Agrikoliansky, Eric, "Carrières militantes et vocations à la morale: les militants de la LDH dans les années 1980," *Revue Française de Science Politique*, 51 (1–2), 2001: 27–46.

Bertrand, Romain, "'Plus près d'Allah': l'itinéraire social et idéologique d'Imam Samudra," in Annie Collovald and Brigitte Gaïti (eds), *La Démocratie aux extrêmes. Sur la radicalisation politique*, Paris, La Dispute, 2006: 201–22.

Blom, Amélie, "Kashmiri Suicide Bombers: 'Martyrs' of a Lost Cause," in Amélie Blom, Laetitia Bucaille and Luis Martinez (eds), *The Enigma of Islamist Violence*, London, Hurst, 2007: 71–87.

Bozarslan, Hamit, "La figure du martyr chez les Kurdes," in Catherine Mayeur-Jaouen (ed.), *Saints et héros du Moyen-Orient contemporain*, Paris, Maisonneuve & Larose, 2002: 335–47.

Collovald, Annie and Brigitte Gaiti, "Questions sur la radicalisation politique," in Annie Collovald and Brigitte Gaïti (eds), *La Démocratie aux extrêmes. Sur la radicalisation politique*, Paris, La Dispute, 2006: 201–22.

Davis, Diane E. and Anthony W. Pereira, "Contemporary Challenges and Historical Reflections on the Studies of Militaries, States, and Politics," in Diane E. Davis and Anthony W. Pereira (eds), *Irregular Armed Forces and their Role in Politics and State Formation*, Cambridge University Press, 2003: 3–34.

Dobry, Michel, "'Penser = classer?' Interview with André Loetz, Gérard Noiriel and Philippe Olivera," *Genèses*, 59, 2005: 151–65.

Dorronsoro, Gilles and Olivier Grojean, "Engagement militant et phénomènes de radicalisation chez les Kurdes de Turquie," *European Journal of Turkish Studies*, 2004, available online at the following URL: *http://www.ejts.org*

Fillieule, Olivier, "Propositions pour une analyse processuelle de l'engagement individuel," *Revue Française de Science Politique*, 51 (1), 2001: 199–215.

——— "Temps biographique, temps social et variabilités des rétributions," in Olivier Fillieule (ed.), *Le Désengagement militant*, Paris, Belin, 2005: 17–47.

Gayer, Laurent, "Le jeu de l'amour': trajectoires sacrificielles et usages stratégiques des martyrs dans le mouvement sikh pour le Khalistan," *Cultures & Conflits*, 63, 2006: 113–33.

Jaffrelot, Christophe, "For a Theory of Nationalism", in Alain Dieckhoff and Christophe Jaffrelot (eds), *Revisiting Nationalism. Theories and Processes*, London, Hurst/ New York, Palgrave, 2005: 10–61.

INTRODUCTION

Kasfir, Nelson, "Guerrilla Governance: Patterns and Explanations," Paper presented to the Seminar in Order, Conflict &Violence,Yale University, 29 October 2008, accessible at: *http://www.yale.edu/macmillan/ocvprogram/papers/Patterns&Explan23.10.8.pdf*

Khosrokhavar, Farhad, "Le modèle Bassidji," *Cultures & Conflits*, 29–30, 1998, pp. 59–118.

Lecomte-Tilouine, Marie, "'Kill One He Becomes One Hundred': Martyrdom as Generative Sacrifice in the Nepal People's War," *Social Analysis*, 50 (1), Spring 2006: 51–72.

McAdam, Doug, "Recruitment to High-Risk Activism: the Case of Freedom Summer," *American Journal of Sociology*, 92 (1), 1986: 64–90.

Pettigrew, Judith and Sara Shneiderman, "Women and the Maobadi: Ideology and Agency in Nepal's Maoist Movement," *Himal*, January 2004, available online at the following URL: *http://www.himalmag.com*

Robben, Antonius C.G.M., "Seduction and Persuasion: The Politics of Truth and Emotion Among Victims and Perpetrators of Violence," in Antonius C.G.M. Robben and Carolyn Nordstrom (eds), *Fieldwork Under Fire. Contemporary Studies of Violence and Culture*, Berkeley (Calif.), University of California Press, 1996: 81–103.

Robinson, Geoffrey, "People's War: Militias in East Timor and Indonesia," *South East Asia Research*, 9 (3), 2001: 271–318.

Schalk, Peter, "Resistance and Martyrdom in the Process of State Formation in Tamililam," in Joyce Pettigrew (ed.), *Martyrdom and Political Resistance. Essays from Asia and Europe*, Amsterdam University Press, 1997: 61–83.

Sen, Atreyee, *Shiv Sena Women. Violence and Communalism in a Bombay Slum*, London, Hurst, 2007.

Shah, Alpa, "Markets of Protection: the 'Terrorist' Maoist Movement and the State in Jharkand, India," Critique of Anthropology, 26(3), 2006, pp. 297–314.

Thapa, Majushree, "Girls in the War," *Himal*, Kathmandu, June 2003, available online at: *http://www.himalmag.com*

Tilly, Charles, "War Making and State Making as Organized Crime," in Peter Evans, Dietrich Rueschmeyer and Theda Skocpol (eds), *Bringing the State Back In*, Cambridge University Press, 1985: 169–91.

Volkov,Vadim, "Les entreprises de violence dans la Russie post-communiste," *Politix*, 13 (49), 2000: 57–75.

NOTES

1. Diane E. Davis and Anthony W. Pereira consider this phenomenon in "Contemporary Challenges and Historical Reflections on the Studies of Militaries, States, and Politics," in Diane E. Davis and Anthony W. Pereira (eds) (2003), p. 9.
2. This figure does not include the 1,000 persons or so who have been killed over the same period by terrorist attacks due to Pakistan-based jihadist movements such as Laskar-e-Taiba or local Islamists such as the Indian Mujahidin. In this book, as mentioned above, we focus on militias and not on terrorist groups, though the frontier between the two may become blurred when the former use the same tactics as the latter.
3. The number of victims in the Kashmiri conflict has dropped spectacularly since 2001: whereas 4,507 dead were counted in 2001, this figure fell to 3,022 in 2002, 2,542 in 2003, 1,810 in 2004, 1,732 in 2005, 1,116 in 2006 and 777 in 2007;

cf. Kanchan Lakshman, "India: Darkness and Light," *South Asia Intelligence Review*, 5 (25), 1 January 2007. See also by the same author, "Jammu and Kashmir: Respite from a Proxy War," *South Asia Intelligence Review*, 6 (30), 4 February 2008.

4. R. Prasannan, "Maoist Threat, More Hype Than Real?" *The Week* (Kochi), 11 June 2006, p. 24.

5. Clashes occurred in the city between armed Mohajir, Sindhi and Pashtun activists on 12 and 13 May 2007, which claimed some forty victims. And between 29 November and 1 December 2008 the city witnessed its largest and bloodiest episode of Mohajir-Pashtun violence since the mid-1980s, which claimed 48 lives.

6. The Ahmadiyya movement developed in India in the late 19th century. Although its members view themselves as Muslims, the movement is considered heretical by the Sunni religious authorities because of the way the sect's founder is worshipped. This movement has been proscribed in Pakistan since 1974, and Bangladeshi Islamists would like to see a similar ban in their country.

7. We will see through several of the chapters in this book, however, that this assertion must be qualified and militias movements can also attract members from the dominant classes or castes, although in smaller numbers.

8. Romain Bertrand, (2006), pp. 201–22.

9. Everett Hughes (1958); Erving Goffman (1961).

10. We borrow this understanding of "careers" as "sequential analytical modes of social behavior" from Eric Agrikoliansky (2001).

11. Olivier Fillieule (2001), p. 214.

12. Olivier Fillieule (2005), pp. 17–47.

13. Clifford Geertz (1973), p. 220.

14. See Christophe Jaffrelot, "For a Theory of Nationalism," (2005), pp. 10–61.

15. Amélie Blom (2007), pp. 71–87.

16. Laurent Gayer (2006), pp. 113–33.

17. Farhad Khosrokhavar (1998), pp. 59–118.

18. As Amélie Blom shows in the case of the Pakistani *mujahidin*, martyrdom can be an admission of military or political failure; cf. Amélie Blom (2007).

19. Marie Lecomte-Tilouine (2006), pp. 51–72.

20. Peter Schalk (1997), p. 67.

21. David Le Breton (2002), p. 10, cited by Hamit Bozarslan, "La figure du martyr chez les Kurdes," in Catherine Mayeur-Jaouen (ed.) (2002), p. 347.

22. Johan Huizinga (1955 [1st ed. 1950]), pp. 3–12.

23. Doug McAdam (1986), pp. 64–90.

24. Oskar Verkaaik (2004).

25. Regarding ambitions of "material development" and "symbolic recognition" among actors of violence in the context of identitarian conflicts, cf. Xavier Crettiez (2006), pp. 172 ff.

26. Vadim Volkov (2000), p. 57.

27. In the case of Nepal, the Maoist leadership has always claimed that women made up one-third of the guerrilla members, but the figure would appear to be much lower; cf. Majushree Thapa (2003).

28. "Nirmala Akka MBBS," *The Week*, 11 June 2006, p. 20.

29. See the chapters devoted to women's affiliates of the Sangh Parivar in Christophe Jaffrelot (ed.), *Sangh Parivar. A Reader*, Delhi, Oxford University Press, 2006.

30. Rita Machanda, "Guns and Burqa: Women in the Kashmir Conflict," in Rita Machanda (ed.) (2001), pp. 42–101.

31. Peter Schalk (1997), pp. 69 ff.

32. Li Onesto (2005).
33. "Killer Women," *The Week*, 11 June 2006, especially Kanhaiah Bhelari, "I Have Killed Five; I Will Murder One Hundred," p. 23.
34. Atreyee Sen, *Shiv Sena Women* (2007), p. 41.
35. Ibid. p. 23.
36. For a balanced assessment of the "emancipation by the gun" thesis, from a Sri Lankan perspective, see Darini Rajasingham-Senanayake, "Ambivalent Empowerment: The Tragedy of Tamil Women in Conflict," in Rita Machanda (ed.) (2001), pp. 102–30.
37. This rule would appear to be less observed among the Indian Naxalites than among the Maobadis and especially among the Sikhs, where marriage with a member of the guerrilla movement was a prerequisite to the recruitment of female combatants. For the account of a single female Naxalite combatant who uses the demands of her mission to justify her voluntary celibacy and sexual abstinence, see Kanhaiah Bhelari, "I Have Killed Five…", art. cit.
38. Gilles Dorronsoro and Olivier Grojean (2004), available at http://www.ejts.org/
39. Judith Pettigrew and Sara Shneiderman (2004).
40. Max Weber (1978) [1914], p. 54.
41. Norbert Elias (2000) [1939]), pp. 257–68.
42. Ibid.
43. Helene Maria Kyed, "State Vigilantes and Political Community on the Margins in Post-War Mozambique," in David Pratten and Atreyee Sen (eds) (2007), p. 412.
44. "Fact Finding Report on the Salwa Judum, Dantewara District," press release from the People's Union for Civil Liberties (PUCL), 2 December 2005, available at http://www.pucl.org.
45. Alain Dewerpe (1994).
46. Regarding the variety of motivations for joining a pro-Indonesian militia in Eastern Timor in the late 1990s, cf. Geoffrey Robinson (2001), pp. 271–318.
47. Bruce Berman and John Lonsdale (1992).
48. In France, Jean-François Bayart was the first researcher to grasp the epistemic possibilities of the paradigmatic shift suggested by Berman and Lonsdale and integrate it into the work of his research team, the Groupe d'Analyse des Trajectoires du Politique at the Centre d'Etudes et de Recherches Internationales (CERI); see in particular the volumes he has edited: *La Réinvention du capitalisme*, Paris, Fayard, 1994 and *La Greffe de l'État*, Paris, Fayard, 1996.
49. Bruce Berman and John Lonsdale (2006), vol. 1, pp. 36–8.
50. Ibid., p. 38.
51. Nelson Kasfir (2008), accessible at the following address: http://www.yale.edu/macmillan/ocvprogram/papers/Patterns&Explan23.10.8.pdf
52. Alpa Shah, 2006, pp. 297–314.
53. Charles Tilly (1985), pp. 169–91.
54. Antonius C.G.M. Robben (1996), p. 83.
55. Naturally there is no such thing as a perfectly objective account, as the theorists of "oral histories" have taught us. Beyond idiosyncratic twists, such accounts are oriented by their speech context, which may sometimes be more conducive to freer and less ideologically- or emotionally-loaded discourse.
56. Erving Goffman (1961), p. 127.
57. Ibid., pp. 88–189 [Eng 133–4].
58. As Annie Collovald and Brigitte Gaïti point out, research into political mobilisation implies "recreating the conditions experienced by the actors of not knowing

what happened next," as Michel Dobry suggested before them by recommending that the "outcome be put aside"; cf. Annie Collovald and Brigitte Gaïti, "Questions sur la radicalisation politique" (2006), p. 30 and Michel Dobry (2005), p. 158.

59. Since 2004, this group has been a prime locus of collective analysis for French researchers working on South Asia, and in particular PhD and postdoctoral research students, to whom it offers funding for fieldwork.

Map 2: India

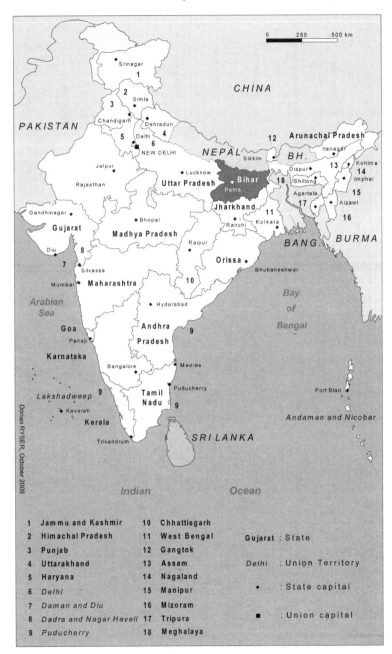

1	Jammu and Kashmir	10	Chhattisgarh
2	Himachal Pradesh	11	West Bengal
3	Punjab	12	Gangtok
4	Uttarakhand	13	Assam
5	Haryana	14	Nagaland
6	Delhi	15	Manipur
7	Daman and Diu	16	Mizoram
8	Dadra and Nagar Haveli	17	Tripura
9	Puducherry	18	Meghalaya

Gujarat : State

Delhi : Union Territory

◆ : State capital

■ : Union capital

Map 3: Districts of Bihar

NEPAL

UTTAR
PRADESH

JHARKHAND

WEST
BENGAL

Paschim
Champaran

Purba
Champaran

Sitamarhi

1

Gopalganj

Siwan

Saran

Madhubani

Muzaffarpur

Darbhanga

Vaishali

Bhojpur

Buxar

Bhabhua

Kaimur

Rohtas

PATNA

Jehanabad

Nalanda

Aurangabad

Gaya

Nawada

Samastipur

6

4

3

Supaul

Saharsa

2

Khagaria

5

Jamui

Araria

Purnia

Katihar

Bhagalpur

Banka

Kishan Ganj

1 Sheohar

2 Madhepura

3 Sheikhpura

4 Lakhisarai

5 Munger

6 Begusarai

Dorian RYSER, October 2008

1

NAXALISM IN BIHAR

FROM BULLET TO BALLOT

Nicolas Jaoul

Four decades of Marxist-Leninist armed revolt in India have nourished internal discussion among the Maoist insurgents (the Naxalites) about the contradictions induced by the decision to take up arms. Naxalites define rural Indian society as a mixture of feudalism and capitalism, and view the Indian state as still today being influenced by its colonial heritage. But how can an underground armed struggle against the state be reconciled with a mass movement of the most unprivileged, among whom the movement has its base? On several occasions, the strategic emphasis on popular support has led these revolutionaries to question the effectiveness of their initial strategy of seizing power through armed struggle, as opposed to merely providing armed protection to the poor peasantry's class struggles, an option that has always been more popular among their peasant base but has been stigmatised as "revisionism" by the more orthodox factions. This question has in fact been a central ideological issue in the many splits and re-formations that have marked the history of the movement.

The issue of "bourgeois democracy" adopted after independence has become the main bone of contention. Whereas the moderate faction believes that the democratic system can be used strategically as an institutional framework on which to build a mass movement, the advocates of the founder's Maoist line stress the risk of becoming absorbed into parliamentarism (or what they stigmatise as "parliamentary cretinism") and that the "bourgeois institutions" should, on the contrary, be boycotted since they merely represent an instrument of domination and legitimation of the ruling class.

In India's northern states, and particularly in Bihar, one of the Naxalites' historic strongholds, a democratisation process has nevertheless taken place over the past 20 years, enabling a new political elite to emerge out of the lower castes and Dalits[1] (their main social base) and provide a sense of democratic assertion.[2] In this state of 83 million inhabitants, the most backward in India in terms of per capita income[3] and literacy,[4] the arrival in power of Laloo Prasad Yadav[5] represented a symbolic revenge of the plebeian castes ("*Bahujan*") over the upper castes. However, his policies only aggravated problems of underdevelopment, corruption and violence. According to a National Sample Survey study published in 2006, 32.5% of the population in Bihar lives beneath the poverty threshold, compared with a national average of 22.1%.[6] However absurd it may seem, this state, the poorest of India in all respects, is also the one that benefits the least from central government financial aid, with a per capita expenditure of less than half the national average.[7]

In Bihar, as in other neglected areas of the country, scepticism among the underprivileged has reached a critical threshold, as the progress of the Naxalites in the poorest areas of the country during the last decade testifies. Their experience among the poor Bihar peasantry thus offers a new perspective on the evolving ways in which underprivileged populations relate to Indian institutions. While it sticks to its Naxalite legacy as a political identity, the moderate faction, which has now adopted legal means of struggle and forsaken clandestinity, embodies a demanding conception of democracy. It has resolved to stake its bets on people's attachment to this form of government and on the possibilities it offers for a radical democratic movement of the unprivileged. The more orthodox Naxalites, on the other hand, seem more determined than ever to confront the Indian state militarily. Yet as recent anthropological studies have pointed out, in their strongholds, their clandestine power generates forms of mediation with the local authorities that seem to play against the class interests and emancipatory aspirations of the underprivileged.

Naxalbari and Indian Communism

Although the Communist Party of India (CPI) actually came round to parliamentarism with the very first elections in 1952, heated internal theoretical debates have persisted on which attitude to adopt towards "bourgeois" democracy, its revolutionary strategy and even its position on the rivalry between China and the USSR.[8] In 1964, the CPI finally split into a "leftwing" faction in favour of the Chinese model (and a revolutionary strategy for the most radical of them) and a "rightwing" faction loyal to the CPSU and closer to the Congress party, which itself gradually moved closer to Moscow. Supporters of Mao, who had adopted an antipatriotic stance during the Chinese-Indian war in 1962, then founded the CPI (Marxist) (CPI (M)). In 1967, the CPI and the CPI (M) became part of a government alliance in Bengal with a dissident faction of the Congress party. The Naxalite movement emerged out of this experience in government, through an initiative of the radical fringe of the CPI (M), opposing such an alliance with a "bourgeois" party and deeming the situation conducive to a peasant insurgency. Counting on the difficulties their party would face in putting down a peasant revolt, and considering that the agrarian reform planned by the new government, however modest, was likely to pull the rug out from under the revolutionary communists, the CPI (M) radicals attempted to put into operation a Maoist strategy of encircling towns with armed peasants. The opportunity was supplied by a rural conflict in the Naxalbari region (Siliguri district, near Darjeeling) pitting Santhal tribal labourers against upper caste landowners, as well as a strike on one of the region's tea plantations. Charu Mazumdar (1918–72), a communist militant from the landed aristocracy of this same district, Kanu Sanyal (born in 1932), who had become his right-hand man after their meeting during the Tebagha peasant revolt in the late 1940s, and Jangal Santhal, a peasant leader of tribal stock, led the uprising.

The insurgents formed peasant committees, encouraging members to put into effect the land redistribution announced by the government and arm themselves against possible repression. Thus began the Naxalbari uprising, with land occupation and establishment of parallel administrations. Although the tribes were poorly organised and their arsenal rudimentary (flails, sickles, spears, bows and arrows, etc.), they managed to take the landowners by surprise and make off with firearms. The conflict took a murderous turn, particularly after a police shootout in May 1967 that left nine dead among the tribal population, including six women and two children.

Students in Calcutta sided with the peasants, while violent clashes between the latter and landowners multiplied. On 28 June 1967 Radio Beijing backed the revolt, baptising it "Spring Thunder". It only lasted 52 days and was crushed in violence that left some 20 dead. News of Naxalbari echoed throughout all of India in intellectual circles and filtered into the poor peasantry, whose living standards had scarcely improved since independence. In the autumn of 1967 Charu Mazumdar turned the revolt into a national symbol when he declared, "hundreds of Naxalbaris are smouldering... Naxalbari has not died and it will never die".[9] As for the CPI (M), it decided to exclude the rebels and those supporting them within the party, thus provoking the second major split in Indian communism three years after the first one.

In 1969 the CPI (Marxist-Leninist) (CPI (ML)), an underground party, was formed with Mazumdar as its leader. He planned to make the politicised elements of the poor peasantry responsible for leading the guerrilla activity, ruling out from the start the fastidious task of politicising the masses or leading agrarian revolts. Such eagerness is not devoid of a form of Messianism: convinced of the redeeming virtues of insurgency for the people, he in fact believed he could disregard such basic givens as religion, caste and peasant mentalities.[10] Any idea of negotiating with the "bourgeois state" was moreover labelled "revisionist". His statements could sometimes be extremely violent: "He who has not dipped his hand in the blood of class enemies can hardly be called a communist".[11]

The CPI (ML) programme adopted in Calcutta in 1970 expounded a strategy of military control and power takeover in several small areas. These "liberated zones" were to implement land reform and other popular measures so as to forge an alternative political model and form the embryo of the future "people's democratic state".[12]

In August 1970, reacting to the nationwide spate of political murders targeting the police, certain CPI (M) activists as well as businessmen and informants, Prime Minister Indira Gandhi declared her firm determination to put an end to this uprising. In the spring of 1972, most Naxalite leaders were behind bars. Nearly 8,500 underground activists had been arrested, including 4,000 in Bengal, 2,000 in Bihar and 1,400 in Andhra Pradesh.[13]

As soon as it ventured into the field, the party strategy was called into question. In that regard, the party has followed an evolution similar to the Maoist Communist Centre (MCC), a group that had gone underground before it and which, without renouncing armed struggle, stressed the importance of not yielding to a military rationale.[14] This organisation, whose foothold is primarily in the forests of Andhra Pradesh where it dispensed the political education of tribal villagers, believed it was important to take root in the class struggle of the underprivileged; the phase of armed struggle should only be triggered once the people had been strongly politicised.[15]

The first splits took place within the CPI (ML) in the early 1970s. Having doubts about the effectiveness of armed struggle in response to the repression sweeping down on the movement, dissidents turned towards a mass movement and struggles authorised by the Constitution (participation in elections, demonstrations, court battles to enforce laws in favour of the poor, etc.).

Establishing Naxalism in Bihar

Before Naxalism appeared, Bihar had already been rent by a half-century of agrarian struggle. These militant movements were however limited to mobilising tenant farmers, leaving day labourers on the fringe.[16] After independence, the abolition of the *zamindari* system[17] enabled former tenant farmers to acquire property, whereas the former day labourers formed a class of landless peasants or marginal smallholders.

The Naxalites first appeared in Bihar in the late 1960s, by addressing this extremely poor and exploited category. The first uprising, harshly repressed in April 1968, took place in the vicinity of Musahari (Muzzafarpur district); there, under the leadership of a villager who had migrated to Calcutta and had returned with the idea to lead the revolt, six "class enemies" were murdered. The second outbreak came from Bhojpur district, where Naxalism latched onto the lower caste and Dalit revolt against the humiliations inflicted by the upper castes. Jagdish Mahto and Rameshwar Ahir, respectively a secondary school science teacher in the district headquarters and an ex-convict, both belonging to lower castes[18] and both from the village of Ekwari, went to Calcutta to enlist Charu Mazumdar's support.[19] Joined by Bengali militants sent by Mazumdar, they formed the first CPI (ML) militia in 1971. Between 1971 and 1977, the Bhojpur district unit of the CPI (ML) was made up of 50 squads of five to eight members, themselves primarily composed of Dalits and party ideologues. In this district alone, the Naxalites murdered 90 large landowners during the same period. During the day they took refuge in Dalit hamlets, where they held political meetings at night.

The party soon realised that its local recruitment capacity was dependent on its ability to address popular concerns such as land redistribution, wage increases, and the protection of Dalit women from sexual exploitation by the upper castes. The armed squads were rapidly brought by their social base into protecting agrarian struggles and repressing local tyrants. The popular tribunals (*jan adalat*) that they held in the villages passed sentences ranging from beheading or amputation of a limb to mere public apology, sometimes accompanied by symbolic humiliation of an upper caste class enemy, such as a Dalit slapping the offender in the face with his sandal.

Such acceptance by the party of the local population's demands, mentalities and modes of functioning proved its effectiveness during the State of Emergency from 1975 to 1977, when the police manhunt for Naxalites was thwarted by complicity in Dalit hamlets. A Bhojpur police report estimated for instance that the Naxalites enjoyed the support of 80% of the landless peasants,[20] which explains the stubborn resistance of some hamlets to the army.

At the end of the Emergency period, the released Naxalite political prisoners reestablished their presence in the most dispossessed areas of the country, albeit in a fragmentary and disorganised manner, under the leadership of different organisations (MCC and various factions of the CPI (ML)). In Bihar, the movement attracted former student activists of the major protest movement led by the socialist J.P. Narayan against Indira Gandhi, advocating a Gandhian "total revolution". These new recruits, unhappy with their movement's merger into the Janata Party (an electoral coalition carved out of the main opposition parties after the State of Emergency), saw in the Naxalite movement a radicalism that suited their aspiration for social justice and their rejection of electoral politics.[21] Naxalism in Bihar was thus no longer confined to the poor peasantry; it now managed to recruit among local intellectuals. Its student wings enabled the movement to renew its cadres and enjoy a capital of sympathy among intellectual circles and the middle classes in Patna. During my fieldwork in Patna, I realised that even today, many former activists continue to extend support to the cause and provide assistance in one way or another to their former comrades (who can even be their own relatives) even if they have formally resigned their membership. Whether in the rural proletariat or in the urban intellectual class, the movement can thus be considered as deeply entrenched in Bihar society.

After the Emergency, the Naxalite movement in Bihar was divided into three main groups that can be placed on a scale ranging from the far left to the ultra-left.[22] The CPI (ML) (Liberation), which derives its name from the original CPI (ML) press organ, was led by the historic CPI (ML) leader from the Bhojpur stronghold (where Ekwari is located), Vinod Mishra. Starting in 1977, a "rectification movement" was developed internally to draw lessons from the past and emphasise the strategic importance of agrarian struggle over a solely military strategy. The point was to count on the support of the poor peasantry, which had proven essential in countering repression. From the early 1980s, the party gradually entered legality.

The CPI (ML) Unity Organisation was formed in 1978 by activists who settled in the neighbouring district of Jehanabad as soon as they had got out of prison. After founding a peasant union, the Mazdur Kisan Sangram Samiti (Committee for Proletarian Peasant Struggle, MKSS),[23] in 1983 they merged with another faction under the new name of CPI (ML) Party Unity (Party Unity). At odds with the new moderate line of Vinod Mishra, they defined themselves as a "third way"[24] by attempting to combine development of an underground party for armed struggle and that of a mass movement, particularly on the agrarian front where they were intensely active. However, as soon as the party gained a foothold in Jehanabad district, the poor peasants made it clear that they wished to get hold of weapons[25] and exhorted the party to murder certain oppressive landowners.[26] In 1998, Party Unity merged with the CPI (ML) People's War Group (PWG) in Andhra Pradesh and Jharkhand, and again edged towards Charu Mazumdar's strategy advocating armed confrontation with the state.

Finally, in 1979, the MCC decided to concentrate on Bihar, even though its historic stronghold was in Andhra Pradesh. As soon as it was founded in October 1969, it established a base in the districts of Hazaribagh and Gaya[27] before spreading to the districts of Aurangabad and Jehanabad as well as Jharkhand, the South Bihar tribal area, which since the year 2000 has formed a separate state. Although the MCC originally distinguished itself from the CPI (ML), criticising its militarism and advocating politicisation of the masses, it went totally underground itself. Its legal organisations remained atrophied until they vanished totally after a ban in 1994.[28]

These three organisations were run by carefully selected cadres that constituted "the party" (the popular appellation for the organisations' executive head), who defined a political line, centralised authority and preserved its underground nature (with the exception of the CPI (ML) Liberation which became a mass party and acquired legal status in the early 1990s). Peasants approached local branches of mass organisations with requests, which their representatives drafted into a petition sent to the party authorities. Bela Bhatia points out that these documents are similar in form to those received by the local administration and that "the Naxalite parties are also known in some areas as *Lal Sarkar* (red government)".[29]

The action of these three parties is characterised, however, by increased mediation between the agrarian organisations and local administrative authorities. The MKSS, Party Unity's agrarian front, thus plays such a role in the seven districts of "Central Bihar"[30] where it has a foothold. Its relentless struggles to enforce the minimum wages set by law, as well as seizure of land exceeding the ceiling of land that could legally be owned, helped it win certain noteworthy battles, leading for instance to the legalisation of its "illegal" or *de facto* redistributions of land (which ought to have been done by the state). Its armed force serves to impose measures that are legal in essence and that are later negotiated by the party with the authorities in order to make them official. Paradoxically, "illegitimate" Naxalite violence thus helps to restore the rule of law, at least as concerns agrarian laws infringed by dominant local figures. Through such practices, Party Unity has imposed its local authority and gathered considerable popular support.

As for the MCC, it rules out any such mediation with the local authorities.[31] In the villages under its control, called "free zones", it replaces state authority with revolutionary peasant committees (Krantikari Kisan Samiti), which confiscate weapons and harvests from large landowners as well as landed properties exceeding the legal ceiling. It redistributes the seized land mainly to landless peasants, while keeping a portion of it to produce seed stock for the community. The MCC also imposes a boycott of legal taxes, levying its own revolutionary tax, and is even supposed to have founded a few schools.[32] It should also be noted that, through their militias, these three organisations have managed to rid their strongholds of armed gangs that had imposed an arbitrary order (sometimes with police complicity) since the 1960s.[33] It was only after a successful struggle against these armed gangs that Party Unity managed to gain a foothold in the district of Jehanabad in the late 1970s.[34]

Liberation on the other hand evolved towards an open form of complementarity with government institutions, which has not prevented it from maintaining its criticism of the state. It concentrated its action systematically on the implementation of unheeded government measures. An example was the redistribution of what was known as "surplus" communal land, i.e. land acquired by towns in accordance with the law of 1961 placing a ceiling on farm size of 6 ha of irrigated land,[35] which the "20–point programme" to fight poverty passed in 1976 by the central government usually failed to implement owing to local administrations' inertia.[36] In July 1979, a national party conference was organised in Bhojpur district to officialise this new strategy. It was decided at the time to count on people's mobilisation via mass organisations. The party thus performed its historic turnaround towards legality and successively founded the Bihar Pradesh Kisan Sabha (BPKS) in 1981[37] and the Indian People's Front (IPF) in 1982, the latter being in charge of attempting to win elected office. Run in reality by Liberation, which thus intended to broaden its popular base, it grouped 250 organisations spread over the country, most of them communist but also including progressive organisations supporting social and economic justice. The IPF fielded candidates in Bihar state elections for the first time in 1985. In the national elections of 1989 Rameshwar Prasad, former BPKS secretary general, who was the party's candidate in its Bhojpur stronghold, was elected MP for the Ara constituency. Hailing from a poor family (his father was a day labourer in a brick factory) and of lower caste (Koeri, an OBC community made mostly of sharecroppers), he was the first Naxalite to enter the Indian parliament. In 1989 and

1990, the IPF organised rallies in Patna and Delhi. It was disbanded in 1994 by the CPI (ML) (Liberation), which wished to establish its own name in the political landscape.[38] The election commission recognised the party in 1995, thereby making it eligible to participate in elections as the CPI (ML)

In December 1992, during the Calcutta conference, Vinod Mishra officially announced Liberation's passage to legality and called for the creation of a confederation of communist parties. He justified this transition as a temporary phase enabling proletarian struggles to enjoy parliamentary support before the final "decisive battle" (armed proletarian revolution), which remained to him the only possible way to achieve communism. This vague promise of a final hour of triumph, indicative of a desire to maintain a Naxalite identity despite the evolution toward parliamentary communism, was however not enough to dissuade many party militia members who were wanted by the police from joining Party Unity, all the more so since the party had failed to address the question of amnesty for its armed militants.

Far from achieving the hoped-for electoral breakthrough, Liberation was faced with competition in its Bihar stronghold from the populist Laloo Prasad Yadav, who won the political leadership of the state in 1990, as well as Dalit mobilisation from Ram Vilas Paswan, a Dalit politician who obtained a ministerial portfolio in V.P. Singh's central government. Rameshwar Prasad lost his national parliamentary seat in the early elections of 1991, while the number of the party's members of the provincial state assembly stagnated, going from seven in 1990 to six in 1995 and 2000 and back to seven in 2005.[39] The party's difficult expansion can be explained by the mobilisation of the poor peasantry along a caste rationale which favoured the party in power (Laloo Prasad Yadav's Rashtriya Janata Dal, RJD), either directly or indirectly through the interplay of alliances. In the 2004 national elections the Dalit leader Ram Vilas Paswan thus enabled the RJD to consolidate its victory (29 out of 40 seats won), by handing him the votes of the Dusadh community to which he belonged (according to the 2001 census, the community made up 30% of the Bihar Dalit population, or 5% of the state's total population).[40] The Bahujan Samaj Party, which also mobilised the Dalits by playing on caste allegiances and making headway in the neighbouring state of Uttar Pradesh, particularly thanks to the unconditional support of the Chamar caste,[41] garnered 3.58% of the votes cast in Bihar, one-third more than Liberation, which lost some ground with 2.41%.[42] Although these various competitors on the election market of underprivileged politics hampered Liberation's electoral growth, its ability to maintain its presence attests to the solidity of its base in its strongholds.

Biased and counterproductive state repression

In 1985 the Bihar government set up its first coordinated police operation, "Operation Task Force", aiming to "flush out" the six districts where Naxalites had a strong presence. The strategy implied that the Naxalites could be chased from Bihar, which assumed a distinction between activists and the poor peasantry. But as searches and arrest followed in succession in the villages, the Naxalite organisations counted on popular resistance and coordinated action. A major protest rally called by the IPF and the MKSS, despite its being banned, drew 40,000 people in the town of Jehanabad on 4 October 1985. "Class violence" claimed 121 casualties between 1976 and 1985, 74 victims in the year 1986 alone. From that day on, the increase in massacres prompted the central government to react. More precisely, it intervened in the wake of the Arwal massacre of April 1986 during which 24 poor peasants were killed by police fire as they were protesting against a civil servant's illegal occupation of public land. Although the superintendent of police had given orders to fire into the crowd without warning, having deliberately blocked all the emergency exits, the Chief Minister of Bihar declared that the victims were merely "thugs, antisocial elements and extremists". He refused to visit the site of the massacre on the pretence that it would demoralise the "brave police forces".[43] The central government then organised "Operation Rakshak" ("security") which involved deploying the paramilitary Border Security Force in seven districts of Central Bihar. As a counterpart to this repressive aspect, the three districts most affected by Naxalite violence (Jehanabad, Aurangabad and Gaya, the strongholds of MCC and Party Unity) benefited from "Operation Siddhartha" (named after the Buddha, whose enlightenment happened in this area), which involved injecting 700 million rupees into development projects as well as land distribution. But the programme only attained one-fifth of its land redistribution objectives, while police camps in the villages were a burden and an additional source of harassment for the poor.[44] The troops were in fact billeted in primary schools and public health centres, preventing them from functioning, while privileged relations came to be established between police and upper caste villagers to the detriment of the poor. These operations were thus rendered ineffectual and were diverted in a way that reflected the connivance between the Indian state and local elites, and so eventually generated even more bitterness among the Naxalites' social base.

Unified demonstrations against police harassment, such as the one in Patna on 10 March 1989 in which over 100,000 poor peasants took part, confirm that repression only heightened the people's sense of injustice that fuels Naxalite mobilisation.

The Arwal massacre also played a decisive role in the radicalisation of Party Unity. Dr Vynian, a moderate from the JP movement leading the MKSS since 1977, was thus marginalised in favour of Arvind, a young grassroots leader from the Kurmi caste (OBC), who advocated militarisation. The effects of such police presence were moreover hardly convincing, because class violence remained high after 1987 (237 casualties from 1987 to 1995 inclusive, with a sharp rise in deaths caused by police as of 1991). Police action was in fact limited to suppressing Naxalites, whereas class violence was mainly perpetrated by landowner militias. Figures given by Prakash Louis show that between 1976 and 2001, two-thirds of the victims of massacres died at the hands of landowner militias, whereas the Naxalites were only responsible for over 50 deaths, the rest being attributed to the police.[45] From 1996 until the decline of the main militia (Ranvir Sena) and the belated arrest of its leader in 2002, this violence set records: 421 victims between 1996 and 2001.

Naxalites versus landowners: the spiral of violence

Landowners were behind the massacres of Dalit agricultural labourers that started in the second half of the 1970s. In 1977, there were 14 dead in Belchi and in 1980, 14 dead in Pipra, two villages located in the district of Patna, the capital of Bihar. These massacres drew attention from the national media and main opposition parties, which seemed primarily interested in the opportunity to destabilise their opponents in power.[46] The violence, up to then mainly perpetrated by thugs hired by large landowners, became organised in systematic fashion in 1979 with the formation of militias intended to dissuade the poor peasants from supporting the Naxalites. The first of these landowner militias was the Kunwar Sena ("Kunwar Army"), formed by upper caste Rajput landowners in Bhojpur district, and the Kisan Suraksha Samiti ("Peasant Safety Committee"), formed by Kurmi landowners (an OBC caste) in several districts. This latter militia, which recruited its thugs from armed gangs, was renamed Bhumi Sena ("Land Army") in the early 1980s. In 1981, it perpetrated several massacres including the one in Pipra that received wide media coverage following Indira Gandhi's visit. The perpetrators of these massacres received informal support from the main state-based political parties, especially regional Congress-I officials, even though Indira Gandhi, who created an uproar over the massacres, was the head of their party. Local leaders from various parties (Congress-I, BJP, Lok Dal) even took part openly in the officially banned armed procession of 3,000 men that this militia organised in October 1981 in a rural area of Patna district.[47] Despite its efforts to assert its authority over all the Kurmis, this militia was unable to secure the support of the poorest fringes of its own caste, which supported the MKSS.

Thirteen militias were thus formed by both lower caste (Kurmi, Yadav, Koeri) and upper caste (Rajput, Bhumihar) landowners between 1979 and 1994. Like the Bhumi Sena, these militias claimed to be caste organisations, thus attempting to form a social base that defence of large landowner interests alone did not secure. The issue for them was to promote infra-caste, vertical caste solidarity at the expense of horizontal, inter-caste class solidarity which was promoted by the Naxalites. The names they chose testify to this legitimation endeavour, invoking as they did mythical folk heroes such as Kunwar, Lorik or Ranvir. By drawing on the register of local folklore, they thus attempt to appear as popular "sons of the soil" reacting to the Naxalites as intruders from outside who upset the region's so-called "social peace".[48]

Founded in 1995 by Bhumihars in the Bhojpur district, the Ranvir Sena is the most recent and the most powerful of these landowner militias. The Bhumihars form a prosperous dominant caste of Brahminical status (although the Maithila Brahmins from northern Bihar challenge this claim).[49] In the

Bhojpur district divisions of Sahar and Udwantnagar where Ranvir Sena leaders hail from, Bhumihar prosperity is due to an irrigation system that has improved crop yields, while their numerical importance lends them a hegemony that has yet to be challenged. Ranvir Sena's initial aim was to combat CPI (ML (Liberation)'s local presence, which directly threatened Bhumihar economic interests. Their Brahmin status prohibits them from farming the land themselves because of Brahminical ritual pollution taboos. Their dependence on day labourers explains the economic threat that the Naxalite agrarian organisations pose to them. Having managed to enlist the entire caste (except for a few intellectuals who support the Naxalites) as well as landowners from other castes, Ranvir Sena has gradually spread to eight districts of central Bihar. Its fighters are paid and their families given financial compensation in the event of their death. Like the CPI (ML) (Liberation), which it tries to imitate so as better to combat it, Ranvir Sena has built a network of legal organisations, notably a women's branch and a social arm, the purpose of which is to organise charity work among Bhumihars. It even fielded candidates in the 1999 elections. Between 1995 and 2000, it perpetrated 27 massacres that left a total of 263 dead, mainly in the districts of Bhojpur and Jehanabad. When he was finally arrested in 2002, Brahmeshwar Singh, the militia's leader, assumed responsibility for these massacres, which are reported to have purposely targeted children and pregnant women in order to check Dalit population growth.[50] The largest of them took place (in chronological order) in Bathani Tola (Bhojpur district, 11 July 1996, 22 dead), Lakshmanpur Bathe (Jehanabad district, 1 December 1997, 58 dead), Shankar Bigha (Jehanabad district, 10 February 1999, 23 dead) and Myanpur (Aurangabad district, 16 June 2000, 35 dead).[51]

During its sixth annual conference in 1997, the CPI (ML) (Liberation) expressed regret at not having sought to militarily destroy the Ranvir Sena and having allowed it to develop, thereby echoing a wider popular sentiment in the affected areas. Other Naxalite groups in areas of influence where the militia also struck criticised Liberation for this as well, since the militia was able to develop mainly in CPI (ML) Liberation areas, where the lack of military vigilance facilitated its growth and further geographical expansion.[52] During the previous decade, Liberation and Party Unity in fact had managed to crush the Bhumi Sena (in 1985) by selectively killing its leaders and by organising labour boycotts targeted against landowners that backed it.[53] As for the MCC, it advocated a policy of systematic and amplified retaliation ("four lives for every one") that it inaugurated in 1987 in Dalelcha Baghauria (Aurangabad district) with the murder of 42 men and women of large landholding families. This was followed by another massacre in Senari in 1999 (Jehanabad district, 35 dead).[54]

In 1998, Party Unity drew conclusions from the massacres perpetrated by the Ranvir Sena in its areas of influence, especially Jehanabad, and leaned toward militarisation at the expense of its agrarian union work. It adopted the name "People's War" after merging with the CPI (ML) People's War Group

(PWG), an armed group active in the forests of neighbouring Jharkhand as well as Andhra Pradesh. Through contacts made with the Tamil Tigers in Sri Lanka (LTTE), the PWG had managed to acquire modern weapons and training in the handling of explosives.[55] The former Party Unity in Bihar thus managed partly to modernise its weaponry, which was previously at best as rudimentary as that of the police, whose guns it was in the habit of seizing during attacks (particularly the robust but archaic one-round 303 carbine used by the colonial police). The CPI (ML) (Liberation) for its part found itself considerably weakened in the wake of Ranvir Sena's Dalit massacres in the mid-1990s.

The national and international wave of indignation sparked by the Lakshmanpur Bathe massacre prompted the Bihar government to set up the Amir Das commission, charged with investigating ties between the Ranvir Sena and local politicians of various parties (RJD, BJP, JD-U and Congress) as well as one of the national BJP leaders, Murli Manohar Joshi.[56] This belated reaction did not, however, prevent Ranvir Sena from continuing its massacres, and certain clues indicate police connivance, according to the CPI (ML) (Liberation) leadership.[57] After the Shankar Bigha and Narayanpur massacres the Bihar police, sharply criticised by human rights organisations and the national media, finally began arresting some Ranvir Sena organisers. Nevertheless, out of 54 people arrested to curb militia violence, only 14 were Ranvir Sena members, as opposed to 40 Naxalites. In August 2002, the arrest of the Ranvir Sena chief Brameshwar Singh finally put an end to the dreaded militia, which then fell prey to internal rivalries. As former Ranvir Sena members told me in the course of fieldwork carried out in Ekwari in March 2005, the decline can also be explained by the financial cost, all the more so since those participating in or backing it had their farms systematically boycotted by the labour force, some having been ruined as a consequence.

Official repression of the Ranvir Sena has nevertheless remained limited. Some ministers in the current coalition government led by Nitish Kumar were implicated by the Amir Das commission; however, the commission's mandate expired in 2006 and despite not having submitted its report, was not extended.[58]

Intra-Naxalite violence and its lessons

On top of landowner militia violence, violent clashes began to occur in 1995 between various Naxalite factions. These were at first due to rivalries between the MCC and Party Unity and battles for territorial influence. In 1997, confrontations between these two organisations left 60 dead, accounting for one-third of their total casualties. The inability of these organisations to put a stop to this violence despite repeated condemnations from their central committees reflects a certain assumption of autonomy by local activists and even a loss of political control over them. The use of violence to extend territorial influence or keep control over it in the face of rival incursions is a practice that villagers condemn. Villagers with whom I discussed the issue claimed that such attacks in which the poor were pitted against one another were unworthy of the Naxalites, who they believed had become "contaminated" by the local "feudal" mentality, an ironic statement that reformulated the Naxalites' own criticism of rural mentalities' "backwardness".[59]

In 1998, the merger of Party Unity and PWG at the national level, which gave rise to People's War, and then the gradual rapprochement of this new group with the MCC, helped to restore a semblance of peace, even if it was always precarious and conflictual relations continued between local outfits. In January 2000 the MCC called its activists in Bihar to declare a unilateral cease-fire with People's War. This group urged its militants to do the same two months later. This truce was sealed in June 2001 during a Coordination Committee of Maoist Parties and Organisations of South Asia (CCOMPOSA) international conference. On 24 August 2001, after a two-day meeting, the two central committees published a common pamphlet in Hindi addressing their cadres and activists in Bihar, calling on their militants to put an end to their fratricidal clashes, even envisaging a military rapprochement for periodic operations in Bihar and Jharkhand.[60] Such a trend was moreover encouraged by new repressive legislation passed in December 2001 by the central government, the Prevention of Terrorist Activities Act (POTA), since the inclusion of People's War among banned outfits forced it to go underground and thus encouraged its merger with the MCC.[61]

Such underground unity, however, turned against the CPI (ML) (Liberation), whose elected officials at the village level, most of them Dalits having won seats in the 2001 municipal elections, became the target of the underground Naxalites.[62] The CPI (ML) (Liberation) denounced the criminal drift of its Naxalite adversaries who thus targeted elected officials from the poor peasant movement.[63] In November 2004, I participated in a protest march through the fields, from Jehanabad's CPI (ML) (Liberation) party office to Isse Bigha village, organised to denounce the murder of one of its Panchayat (village council) elected members by People's War and to prove that its mass movement remained popular and psychologically strong despite the military intimidation. Interestingly, in the violence perpetrated against CPI (ML) (Liberation) by People's War in 2004 there is some evidence of connivance between the latter organisation and the party in power (Laloo Prasad Yadav's RJD). On the night of 18 August 2004 five Liberation activists, including two Panchayat elected officials and three local officials from various fronts of the party, were murdered in their sleep at the party headquarters in Paliganj (Patna district). People's War activists claimed the massacre and threatened to strike again. Following CPI (ML) (Liberation)'s statewide mass mobilisation to denounce the attack, the police undertook an operation and found a People's War squad commander hiding inside the home of the local RJD Member of Parliament, Dinanath Yadav. The RJD reacted by temporarily excluding the MP, and the government had the local police official transferred, which in both cases amounted to acknowledging collusion between the party in power and the banned organisation. An article in CPI (ML) (Liberation)'s monthly, *Liberation*, accused People's War of acting as the armed wing of the party in power, quoting an expression (which the author claimed was a popular local saying, thus lending it the status of a "well-known truth") stigmatising this duplicity: "*din mein RJD, raat mein PWG*" ("RJD by the day, PWG by the night").[64] CPI (ML) Liberation also denounced the fact that the public authorities arrested only one of the 22 suspects for the Paliganj massacre and that searches, rather than being directed towards People's War's zones of influence, were conducted in CPI (ML) (Liberation) villages.[65]

If true, this collusion between People's War and the RJD could be explained by the fact that CPI (ML) (Liberation) positions itself both as an election contender and as a champion of the poor peasantry, prompting convergent hostility from its Naxalite rivals and electoral opponents, and making an objective alliance between them possible. In support of this, Liberation asserted that in the national elections, People's War and the MCC issued their ballot boycott instructions selectively in favour of "bourgeois" parties, whereas according to the CPI (ML) (Liberation) they concentrated their attacks on its own activists, premises and vehicles in the constituencies of Jehanabad, Aurangabad and Ara, thus seeking to intimidate its voters. Confirming this interpretation, Prakash Singh claims in his book that this group's selective approach to election boycotting enabled the RJD to remain in power in 1995.[66]

Moreover, caste networks were instrumental in fostering such collusion between the party in power and the underground Naxalite outfits. A study conducted by the ADRI, an independent research institute in Patna on the various Naxalite organisations in Bihar, has shown that beyond their ideological differences, their caste makeup differs. In particular, a Kurmi advantage was noted in the People's War state committee as well as a clear majority of Yadavs in that of the MCC, which may help account for complicity with the party in power from 1990 to 2005, which is also strongly dominated by the Yadavs.[67]

OBC domination within these two organisations is the result of strategies adopted to secure the support of the poor and middle peasantry from these castes, particularly to counter the influence within the castes of landowners and their militias, such as the Yadav Lorik Sena or the Kurmi Bhumi Sena. MKSS farm workers for instance boycotted the farms of large Kurmi landowners that backed the Bhumi Sena, while medium-sized farm owners of this caste were systematically spared. The testimonial of a PWG squad commander in Jehanabad district, quoted in George Kunnath's article, moreover confirms this pro-Kurmi evolution at the expense of Dalit interests.[68] Likewise, as noted by Prakash Louis, the MCC asked farm workers to accept lower wages from employers in this category than what they demanded of large landholders, encouraging them to work mainly for the former out of "class solidarity".[69]

A Patna police officer who confided in me under cover of anonymity pointed out that Yadav militia members of the MCC came from underprivileged fringes of the caste, whereas RJD militants were usually better off. Caste solidarity among them fostered arrangements between the party in power and the underground organisation. At the time of my fieldwork, the MCC apparently refrained both from going against the interests of Yadav landowners and from carrying out their instructions to boycott elections in villages that voted RJD. In exchange, the underground activists enjoyed a certain degree of protection from within the party in power. Although other testimonials converge towards this caste explanation, the temptation to use caste as a variable that would account for everything pertaining to Bihar (as an archetype of the archaic caste-ridden society, as if the rest of India was not like that) should be avoided. Unless it is placed in context, caste can explain everything and nothing at the same time. The inability of Kurmi and Yadav landowner militias to impose a caste rationale in answer to the Naxalite class rationale in fact reveals the composite nature of rural society in Bihar, where class logics and party affiliations can come into play while overlapping with caste networks. It is also important to investigate the changes in the nature of local power, which reveal such links between a party in power and underground organisations.

For local elected officials in constituencies where the MCC and People's War possess influence, it can be useful to act as mediators between the higher authorities of the provincial state and the Naxalite leaders, given the local authority based on fear (but sometimes also prestige and charisma) and the nuisance capacity that the latter enjoy. Government contractors are especially in need of such mediation given that they are systematically obliged to pay Naxalites a commission, or else their works are systematically blown up. The MCC and People's War moreover tended to create restrictions on such development works, especially roads that might facilitate police access into their strongholds. These armed groups thus tend to maintain conditions of underdevelopment that are favourable to their underground power. As shown by Alpa Shah in the case of neighbouring Jharkand, for local elected officials such contacts are useful to ensure the smooth functioning of their constituency and can lead to implicit forms of local power sharing.[70]

From this standpoint, local Naxalite power carries the permanent temptation to reach arrangements with dominant interests. Party Unity/People's War tribunals have for instance managed to establish a parallel legal authority by settling certain disputes effectively (given the slowness of the official legal system). Bela Bhatia thus notes, "Sometimes individuals simply join the Naxalite movement as a shortcut to local power".[71] To understand such collusion one must realise the local importance of weapons, which enable individuals and groups to assert their power and prestige.[72] In 1980, the Kurmi youth in Jehanabad district joined Party Unity (or rather its predecessor, Unity Organisation) as it viewed that organisation's updated arsenal (following a large theft of arms from the police) as a source of power and prestige.[71] According to a well informed Patna journalist who sympathises with the Naxalite cause but criticises its criminal drift, individuals from the wealthy peasantry, particularly Bhumihars, often simulate an ideological allegiance in order to join Naxalite groups for as long as it takes to carry out plans for murder, sometimes in their own caste, by having personal enemies labelled "class enemies". Once the deed is done, they leave the Naxalites to join landowner militias or act as police informers to be cleared of their crimes. A lawyer in Patna who fought Naxalite cases in the Patna court notes that, conversely, it has happened that former members of the Bhumi Sena, a Kurmi landowner militia, switch over to People's War, attracted by its military superiority in the Jehanabad district. According to the same source, Naxalite militias have also started recruiting delinquents wanted by the police, offering them a hideout and some degree of protection, as a means of increasing their numbers. These converging testimonials show that the violence exceeds the political context and that militias can offer a refuge for ordinary crime.

What mass radicalism in a context of violence?

CPI (ML) (Liberation)'s English-language mouthpiece, *Liberation*, points out the contradiction into which its Naxalite rivals have become mired: under the pretence of waging war on the state, they actually find themselves compromised in shady transactions with corrupt state officials.[73] Despite its desire to pose as a democratic alternative for Bihar, this group that adopted the difficult path of legality finds itself caught up in a contradictory approach, divided between its quest for respectability and the need to protect its strongholds by maintaining militias there for the sake of its activists' and supporters' basic security. The situation appears all the more delicate since some of its electoral competitors do not hesitate to use the other militias' violence to oust them, as can be seen in RJD's attitude during the 1997 election campaign. In Siwan district, where Liberation has extended its influence in the past ten years, thugs allegedly hired by an incumbent RJD MP murdered Chandra Shekhar, leader of the party's student union, who had come to campaign. A native of this district who had been elected president of the Jawaharlal Nehru University students in New Delhi, this young activist who had decided to devote himself to a political career was seen as a potential national leader for the party. His murder on 31 March 1997 continues to fuel a thirst for revenge, as was clear in discussions I had with party cadres. Along with the repeated Ranvir Sena attacks, his murder highlighted the difficulties for the legal Naxalites to assert themselves democratically without maintaining a self-defence force. CPI (ML) Liberation thus provides an interesting example of how to deal with violence for a democratic struggle operating in a non-democratic atmosphere without falling into the trap of an undemocratic spiral of mere violence. An internal party document published in 2004 states that "The challenge of resisting the enemy's attacks often has its own compelling logic, but we must keep it subordinated to the needs and level of the movement and ensure the greatest possible involvement and initiative of the concerned masses".[74] This formula, called "organized mass resistance",[75] recommends that "instead of treating our armed contenders as isolated military threats, we must master the strategy of overcoming them in the course of a protracted political struggle by placing still greater reliance on unleashing all-out mass initiatives".[76]

The party in fact believes that its main strength lies in the mass support that the dynamism of its various trade union, agrarian, cultural, feminist, student, and other mass organisations can generate. Its strategy thus involves maintaining constant presence in the public space through which to denounce the rotten political system in Bihar and its main contenders for power, as well as to make constant public shows of its popularity through elections and mass events. In its December 2004 issue, the party's nationally circulated magazine *Liberation* sought to prove the wisdom of this strategy by giving examples of effective popular resistance to oppression, whether spontaneous or instigated by local party sections.[77] Peaceful mass demonstrations and *dharna*s (sit-ins) were systematically held at district and state level to denounce continuing oppression of Dalits, the deplorable living standards of the underprivileged, the deterioration of infrastructure and official corruption. The party thus tried to channel popular discontent by maximising the primary asset of its legality: access to the public space. Relying on coverage of its public demonstrations by the media—including its own, the most widely circulated being *Samkalin Lokyuddh*, "Contemporary People's War", a weekly in Hindi whose title indicates a desire to maintain a Naxalite identity despite its move towards legality—the party thus creates a popular wave of protest of which it is both the instigator and the spokesman.

Conclusion

Naxalite trajectories in Bihar show that the entrenched violence of the social conflict has led to complications. Armed Naxalite groups end up asserting a form of parallel authority in their areas of influence, which they sometime share with local elected officials. Such collusion reveals the capacity of the ruling classes to tap into Naxalite power. These armed groups have enabled the poor peasantry to assert its dignity and obtain certain improvements in production relations as long as they settle for playing a self-defensive role, especially in poor peasants' struggles over farm incomes and other agrarian issues. But they seem less and less able to ensure such progress when they revert to the Maoist strategy of seizing state power through armed struggle, as the CPI (Maoist) currently understands it. A recent report on the agrarian situation in Bihar in fact discusses the idea of abandoning class struggles in favour of armed operations against state symbols (such as the spectacular Jehanabad prison break), which means that the Maoists will have to strengthen their authority in the villages they control and therefore give up certain demands that are potential sources of local conflict.[78] Thus they tend to prefer compromises between landholders and tenant farmers, though the rents paid—nearly half the proceeds of the harvest (i.e. twice as much as that recommended by the first Indian five-year plan)—are among the highest in India.

While the poor peasantry in Bihar adopted Naxalism because it adapted to its struggles at the expense of its political aims, this "marriage of convenience"[79] could end up producing tensions at the grassroots level, since the implicit terms of the contract seem to have changed. There is also the risk that this underground authority will eventually come to rely increasingly on the armed coercion of the underprivileged, thus paradoxically reproducing the Indian state's repressive stance towards them.

The CPI (ML) (Liberation) group, which chose to take the petty peasantry's struggle into the electoral field and endow it with political capital, has today confirmed the ability of its candidates to retain its strongholds. However, the murder of one of its MPs in the neighbouring state of Jharkhand on 16 January 2005, by a police officer seeking revenge for denunciation of his ties with the Dhanbad coal "mafia" before the state assembly,[80] confirms the party's vulnerability. This murder dealt it yet another blow, while its sustained popularity among the poor peasantry speaks for the hope that the most destitute continue to place in the possibility of obtaining recognition for their demands, rights and dignity by democratic means.

So, while harming an authentic democratic movement of the unprivileged in the name of curbing Naxalism, the Indian state (or those local powers that have captured it) also finds itself reaching compromises with real armed rebellions in areas where the two authorities overlap. But it is likely that by impairing the democratic assertion of the underprivileged the democratic state also jeopardises, by a ricochet effect, its own legitimacy among the very people that still expect the most from it.

BIBLIOGRAPHY

Books

Banerjee, Sumanta, *India's Simmering Revolution. The Naxalite Uprising*, London, Zed Books, 1984.

Das, Arvind N., *Agrarian Unrest and Socio-Economic Change, 1900–1980*, Delhi, Manohar, 1983.

Graff, Violette, *Les Partis communistes indiens*, Paris, Presses de Sciences Po, 1974.

Jaffrelot, Christophe, *Inde. La démocratie par la caste: histoire d'une mutation sociopolitique (1885–2005)*, Paris, Fayard, 2005.

Louis Prakash, *People Power. The Naxalite Movement in Central Bihar*, Delhi, Wordsmiths, 2002.

Mukherjee, Kalyan and Rajendra Singh Yadav, *Bhojpur. Naxalism in the Plains of Bihar*, Delhi, Radhakrishna Prakashan, 1980.

Singh, Prakash, *The Naxalite Movement in India*, New Delhi, Rupa & Co., 2006.

Articles and chapters in edited volumes

Bandopadhyay, D., "A Visit to Two 'Flaming Fields' of Bihar," *Economic and Political Weekly*, 30 December 2006: 5302–4.

Bhatia, Bela, "The Naxalite Movement in Central Bihar," *Economic and Political Weekly*, 9 April 2005: 1536–49.

Brass, Paul R., "Horror Stories," in *The Theft of an Idol*, Princeton University Press, 1997: 129–76.

Kunnath, George J., "Becoming a Naxalite in Rural Bihar: Class Struggle and its Contradictions," *The Journal of Peasant Studies*, vol. 33, n° 1, 2006: 89–123.

Mendelsohn, Oliver and Marika Vicziany, "Public Policy II: the Anti-Poverty Programs," in *The Untouchables. Subordination, Poverty and the State in Modern India*, Cambridge University Press, 1998: 147–75.

Shah, Alpa, "Markets of Protection: The 'Terrorist' Maoist Movement and the State in Jharkhand, India," *Critique of Anthropology*, vol. 26, n° 3, 2006: 297–314.

Zins, Max-Jean, "Le puzzle identitaire communiste: le cas du parti communiste indien (PCI) et du parti communiste indien-marxiste (PCI-M)," in Jean-Luc Racine (ed.), *La Question identitaire en Asie du Sud*, Paris, EHESS, "Purushartha," 22, 2001: 303–35.

Official documents

Election Commission of India, New Delhi, *Statistical Report on General Elections, 2004 to the 14th Lok Sabha*, vol. 1.

Maoist publications

"A Declaration to Stop Mutual Clashes and to Fight Unitedly Against the Enemy: A Joint Call from the CPI (ML) People's War and the MCC," *People's March*, October 2001.

"Amir Das Commission Disbanded: Nitish's Desperate Attempt to Shield Political Patrons of Ranvir Sena," *Liberation*, May 2006.

"Com. Mahendra Singh's Murder: State Sponsored Political Killing," *ML Update*, 18 January 2005.

CPI (ML) Central Committee (2004). "Thirtieth Anniversary of CPI (ML)'s Reorganisation: The New Situation and our Urgent Tasks." A CPI (ML) Publication. Delhi.

"CPI (ML) Demands Extension for Amir Das Commission," *ML Update*, 9 (15), 11–17 April 2006.

"Editorial: PWG's War against People's Leaders," *Liberation*, September 2004.

"Joint Self-Criticism and Call by CPI (ML) PW and MCCI in Front of Revolutionary Ranks and People," *People's March*, April-May 2003.

"30 November rally ko tarikhi rally bana dein" (Hindi) ("Let's make the November 30 rally a historic event"), *Samkalin Lokyuddh* (Patna), 5 November 2004.

"Obituary: Long Live the Memory of Comrade Yogendra!" *Liberation*, October 2004.

"Paliganj Jan Pratirodh Rally: Call for Intensification of People's Movement against the Laloo-Rabri Regime; Resolve to Expose, Isolate and Disarm the Killer Squads of RJD-PWG Nexus," *ML Update*, 28 September 2004.

"Self-Criticism, PWG Style: Kill Now and Repent Later," *Liberation*, December 2004.

"Successful Bihar Bandh on 23 August: Paliganj RJD MLA's PWG Links Revealed," *Liberation*, September 2004.

"Struggles in Rural Bihar," *Liberation*, December 2004.

"The Emerging Politics of the People's War Group: Negotiating with the State and Waging War on Revolution," *Liberation*, September 2004.

NOTES

1. The Dalits ("Untouchables") are a group of castes subject to discrimination by virtue of ritual pollution taboos. They make up 16.5% of the Indian population. They represent 15.7% in Bihar (18.2% in Central Bihar), where 77.6% of them are farm workers, and where their literacy rate is only 28.5% (source: 2001 census).
2. Christophe Jaffrelot (2005).
3. $94 compared to the national average of $255.
4. 47.5% compared to the national average of 65.4%.
5. This leader, who became Chief Minister of Bihar in 1990 on the strength of votes from his caste of cowherds and the Muslim vote, personifies the rise of lower castes. His exuberance, the alleged corruption scandals tied in with his party's management of Bihar, and his reliance on caste identities and networks have made him the nemesis of the traditional elites who perceive him as a symbol of the county's decline following Bihar's example. He is currently head of the Rashtriya Janata Dal (RJD), the party founded in 1997 after a split from the Janata Dal.
6. The new criteria the NSSO used to measure poverty in this survey are disputed because they are said to lower the rates artificially.
7. Considering the state of underdevelopment and misrule, capital from Bihar tends to be invested in other states, which aggravates the low rate of Bihar's tax contributions to the central government, on which the latter's aid is paradoxically based. This situation has been compared to the economic plundering of India by the colonial powers under British rule. Mohan Guruswamy and Abhishek Kaul, "The Economic Strangulation of Bihar," *The Hindu*, "Business Line" supplement, 7 February 2004.
8. Max-Jean Zins (2001), pp. 303–35. See also Violette Graff (1974).
9. Sumanta Banerjee (1984), p. 198.
10. Prakash Singh (2006).
11. Ibid., p. 28.
12. Ibid.
13. Ibid.
14. The Maoist Communist Centre, which only took this name in October 1969, went underground as soon as the CPI (M) was formed. It refused to join the CPI (ML), considering its ultra-left positions as a deviation from the Maoist doctrine.
15. Prakash Louis (2002).
16. Arvind N. Das (1983).
17. Zamindars were in charge of collecting taxes for the British and were often large landholders.
18. Mahto is a Koeri and Ahir a Yadav. They thus both belong to the Other Backward Classes (OBC). This category was defined by the first Commission on Backward Classes (1953). The OBCs include the shudra castes (lower class "servants," but not "Untouchables") considered as "backward" from an educational standpoint and their low level of representation in the administration. In 1990, V.P. Singh's government granted them 27% of reserved civil service positions.
19. The former was beaten up by Bhumihars—the upper caste that dominates the village—for having attempted to prevent the stuffing of ballot boxes in the 1967 elections; Kalyan Mukherjee and Rajendra Singh Yadav (1980).
20. Prakash Singh (2006).

21. Interview with K.D.Yadav, November 2004, Patna.
22. Actually there are more Naxalite groups active in Central Bihar. B. Bhatia counted 17 in 1996, whereas in the early 2000s Prakash Louis found 12 of them.
23. The MKSS was banned in 1986 and reappeared under the name Mazdur Kisan Sangham Parishad in 1994.
24. Bela Bhatia (2005), pp. 1536–49.
25. Ibid.
26. Prakash Louis (2002).
27. Ibid.
28. Bela Bhatia (2005).
29. Ibid., p. 1540.
30. This geographic denomination dates from the former map of Bihar, which also included Jharkhand. Today the old name remains in use although it corresponds to South Bihar.
31. Prakash Louis (2002).
32. Ibid.
33. Ibid.
34. Ibid.
35. The Bihar Land Reforms Fixation of Ceiling Area and Acquisition of Surplus Land Act, 1961.
36. Oliver Mendelsohn and Marika Vicziany (1998), pp. 147–75.
37. This organisation took the name of the former landholders' organisation formed in 1929, first linked to the Congress Socialist Party, then to the Communist Party in the 1940s. Liberation thereby attempted to tie its movement in with the local history of peasant protest.
38. Bela Bhatia (2005).
39. In the 1995 statewide elections, the party garnered an average 8.8% of the vote in the 89 constituencies where it fielded candidates and 2.36% overall in Bihar; in 2000, it won an average of 7.34% of the vote in the 107 constituencies where it fielded candidates and 2.5 % overall in Bihar.
40. "Verdict 2004: A Caste Formula that Clicks," *Frontline*, 22 May 2004.
41. In UP, the BSP became the second largest provincial party in 2002. Thanks to a policy of alliances with the Hindu nationalists between 1995 and 2002, it participated in this state's government three times and conducted a pro-Dalit policy without, however, taking significant agrarian measures. The BSP emerged victorious in the 2007 state elections after forming an alliance with the Brahmins.
42. Election Commission of India, New Delhi (2004).
43. Prakash Louis (2002), p. 208.
44. Ibid.
45. These figures were calculated on the basis of the summary chart of the massacres, ibid., pp. 242–6.
46. Paul R. Brass (1998), pp. 129–76.
47. Prakash Louis (2002).
48. Ibid.
49. During the colonial period, the Bhumihars came under the zamindars, and they were involved in the Kisan Sabha peasant protest movement starting in the 1930s. Upon independence, abolition of the zamindari system enabled them to expand their property or simply acquire land.
50. "End of a Terror Trail," *Frontline*, 19 (19), 14–27 September 2002.
51. Prakash Louis (2002).

52. CPI (ML) (Liberation) did not, however, totally demilitarise, as was shown by two retaliatory massacres committed by its militants in 1997 (Chauram, nine dead) and in 1999 (Usri Bazar, seven dead) in Jehanabad district.

53. Ibid.

54. Prakash Louis (2002).

55. The PWG grew out of a pro-armed struggle faction that disagreed with Liberation's turn to legality in April 1980.

56. "Amir Das Commission Disbanded: Nitish's Desperate Attempt to Shield Political Patrons of Ranvir Sena" (2006).

57. Interview with Ram Jatan Sharma, Liberation state secretary, Patna, November 2004.

58. "CPI (ML) Demands Extension for Amir Das Commission" (2006).

59. Discussion with peasants in the village of Isse Bigha, Jehanabad district, November 2004.

60. "A Declaration To Stop Mutual Clashes And To Fight Unitedly Against The Enemy: A Joint Call from the CPI (ML) People's War and the MCC" (2001); "Joint Self-Criticism and Call by CPI (ML) PW and MCC in Front of Revolutionary Ranks and People" (2003).

61. Prakash Louis (2002).

62. "Self-Criticism, PWG Style: Kill Now and Repent Later" (2004).

63. "Editorial: PWG's War against People's Leaders" (2004); "Obituary: Long Live the Memory of Comrade Yogendra!," (2004).

64. "Editorial: PWG's War against People's Leaders" (2004).

65. "Paliganj Jan Pratirodh Rally: Call for Intensification of People's Movement against the Laloo-Rabri Regime; Resolve to Expose, Isolate and Disarm the Killer Squads of RJD-PWG Nexus" (2004); "Successful Bihar Bandh on 23rd August: Paliganj RJD MLA's PWG Links Revealed" (2004).

66. Prakash Singh (2006).

67. Whereas the CPI (ML) Liberation provincial committee is dominated by upper castes (45%), half of the MCC provincial committee is made up of Yadavs (over one-quarter Dalits, 11% upper castes and 8% Bengalis), while the CPI (ML) Party Unity (future PWG) is headed by a Kurmi without any particular group being dominant (Kurmis are apparently 25 %, most Backward Castes 25%, and Rajputs 25%). I am grateful to ADRI director Shaibal Gupta for having shared this study with me.

68. George J. Kunnath (2006), pp. 89–123.

69. Prakash Louis (2002).

70. In the neighbouring state of Jharkhand, Alpa Shah well demonstrated these ties between the MCC and local institutions in her research, which emphasises the MCC's intervention in the awarding of procurement contracts as well as the links between a rural elite of entrepreneurs in search of such contracts and the MCC. According to that author, the dividing line between the underground Naxalite power and the Jharkhand state authorities is extremely porous; Alpa Shah (2006), pp. 297–314.

71. Bela Bhatia (2005), p. 1541.

72. Other authors have already pointed out the importance of weapons in the eyes of Liberation supporters; see ibid. and Prakash Louis (2002).

73. "The Emerging Politics of the People's War Group: Negotiating with the State and Waging War on Revolution" (2004).

74. CPI (ML) Central Committee (2004). "Thirtieth Anniversary of CPI (ML)'s Reorganisation: The New Situation and our Urgent Tasks," Delhi, p. 29.
75. Ibid.
76. Ibid.
77. "Struggles in Rural Bihar" (2004).
78. D. Bandopadhyay (2006), pp. 5302–4.
79. B. Bhatia describes this political alliance as a "marriage of convenience between the leaders who dream of a Maoist revolution and people who aspire for practical change," Bela Bhatia, (2005), p. 1547.
80. "Com. Mahendra Singh 's Murder: State Sponsored Political Killing" (2005).

Map 4: Nepal

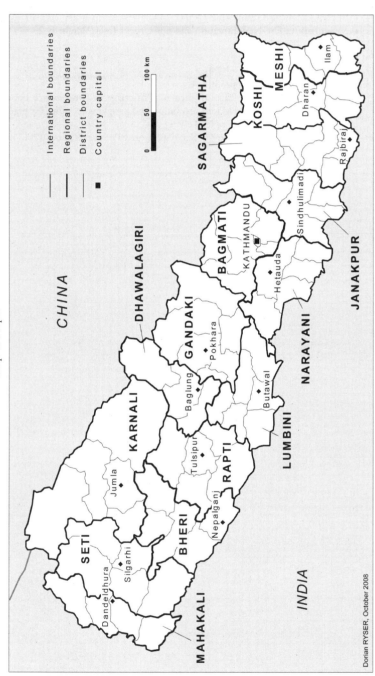

Dorian RYSER, October 2008

2

MAOISM AND THE ETHNIC FACTOR IN THE NEPALESE PEOPLE'S WAR

Gilles Boquérat

On 15 August 2008, Pushpa Kamal Dahal was elected as the new Nepalese Prime Minister. Better known by his *nom de guerre*, Prachanda, the Maoist leader became the head of government not because of a "strategic retaliation" marking the final stage of the protracted people's war, but as a result of more peaceful elections for a constituent assembly held the previous April. It was a victory by a large margin—the Communist Party of Nepal (Maoist) received 30% of the total votes. It garnered almost 1 million votes more than the Nepali Congress and the "rightist" Communist Party of Nepal-Unified Marxist-Leninist (CPN (UML)) and won twice their number of seats in the 601–member constituent assembly. The Maoists in Nepal had in fact formally abandoned armed struggle when they first returned on 15 January 2007 to the Singha Durbar, the seat of Parliament that they had left in 1994.[1] Denouncing as un-representative the political institution in the hands of feudal or bourgeois interests and revisionist parties, they had, in 1996, undertaken a "new democratic revolution". This "people's war" *(jana yuddha)* officially claimed over 13,000 lives between February 1996 and December 2006 (8,377 people killed by the police forces, 4,970 by the Maoists) and spared none of the country's 75 districts.[2] Yet, to the surprise of many observers, the Maoists have not really been affected at the polls either by acts of violence committed during the decade-long conflict or by harassment even in peacetime: a sign that they, more than other parties, managed to capture the pent-up discontent.

The process of rapprochement between the Maoists and the mainstream political parties to undermine the monarchy had in fact picked up steam in November 2005 with the signing of a twelve-point agreement with the

45

seven-party alliance leading to a comprehensive peace accord signed by Prime Minister Girija Prasad Koirala and Prachanda a year later. This was followed by the convening of an interim parliament with Maoist representatives, the adoption of an interim constitution (January 2007) and the formation of an interim coalition government with Maoist ministers (April 2007). Although the Maoists finally had to make a deal with the mainstream polity to extract themselves from an entrenched conflict and venture into a parliamentary system, the "people's war" contributed to a dramatic change in the political balance.[3] It sounded the death knell of the Hindu kingdom and led to the birth of a new secular republic. The mark that it left on society is no less significant, given the extent to which it challenged traditional social relations.

The methods behind the Maoist advance were civilian intimidation when needed and a test of strength with the authorities. No fewer than 1,271 out of the 1,979 police stations throughout the country were evacuated during the war, mainly outside district headquarters.[4] The movement nevertheless had to win support and recruit combatants. To enlist such support, the CPN (M) was able to exploit the social rifts that the return to democracy in 1990 had not really healed, and rally the economically underprivileged, politically marginalised and culturally ostracised segments to its cause. For ten years, the Maoists trained militants to launch head-on attacks against the state and, more generally, all those accused of helping to oppress them. Ethnic minorities thus found in the Maoists a political movement to express their frustrations, for they had been deeply disappointed by the lack of action from mainstream political parties against the monarchical paradigm: "one nation, one language, one religion, one culture"—a disappointment all the more bitterly felt since the popular movement (jan andolan) of the spring of 1990 had resulted in freer speech and opened up a space for the country's various communities to assert their identity.

Cross-border ramifications and analogies

The incongruity at the start of the 21st century of a movement extolling the "Great Cultural Revolution" and castigating the ideological betrayals of the "Great Helmsman's" achievements has often been pointed out. It should not be forgotten, however, that Maoist ideology had never entirely vanished from the Indian subcontinent, and the Nepalese party leaders often received their training from their southern neighbours. Like the Nepali Congress, the Communist Party of Nepal was founded in India, in Calcutta, in September 1949. Manmohan Adhikari (1920–99), the only Communist prime minister to date—in 1994–95—had been a member of the Communist Party of India (CPI) before joining the CPN on its founding by Pushpa Lal Shrestha. It was at the behest of the Indian Communist leader Ajoy Ghosh that the latter had decided to leave the Nepal Rastriya Congress (NRC) headed by Bimal Prasad Koirala.[5] India later played a key role in challenging the undivided power of Nepal's Rana dynasty (1846–1951).[6] Nepalese political leaders would have several opportunities to return to India, especially to go into exile there during the dark years of absolute monarchy (1961–90). Like Mao Zedong, whose only experience abroad was the USSR, the Maoist leader Pushpa Kamal Dahal, known as Prachanda (born 1954), only went to India to establish political contacts and sometimes take refuge there during the "people's war". Prachanda studied agronomy in the southern district of Chitwan, but it was in India that his second-in-command, Baburam Bhattarai (born in 1954), pursued his higher education, first in Chandigarh, then at the Centre for Study of Regional Development of the School of Social Science at Jawaharlal Nehru University in New Delhi, where he earned a PhD.

Democratic India is the Maoists' political point of reference, even if it is often lambasted. Even though Prachanda, by obligation to internationalism, in his writings inveighed against Khrushchev's and Deng Xiaoping's revisionism, he also believes that corruption of the Nepalese communist movements' revolutionary ideal was partly due to the historic links maintained with Indian leaders: "The parliamentarism dominant in the Indian communist movement after the withdrawal of Telangana armed struggle and the company of the then Nepalese communist movement leaders with the (Indian) parliamentary leaders have created an environment to easily accept parliamentarism in Nepal, too".[7] Conversely, although the Chinese Revolution was a source of inspiration, the Nepalese radical left finds its marks primarily in the history of revolutionary struggle in India. Thus it was by attempting to replicate what was then happening in western Bengal that young Nepalese communists from the district of Jhapa launched a movement to eliminate "class enemies" in May 1971, which was harshly put down by the government. The surviving instigators were nevertheless behind the clandestine creation of the CPN (Marxist-Leninist) in 1978.[8]

The peasant movement initiated in the spring of 1967 in the region of Naxalbari, on the other side of Nepal's western border, by Charu Mazumdar and Kanu Sanyal, radical members of the Communist Party of India (Marxist) (CPI (M)), was the founding act of Maoism as a *modus operandi* of revolutionary action in South Asia.[9] Beijing moreover acknowledged it at the time and hoped it was the kindling of a revolutionary wildfire that would sweep the subcontinent, guided by Mao's thought. This uprising against big landowners was organised without the agreement of the CPI (M), which had become a major player in the United Front government in Calcutta. The revolt had been stifled by the summer of 1967, but the Naxalbari movement led to the founding of the Maoist CPI (Marxist-Leninist) (CPI (ML)) in April 1969. Students from the urban petty bourgeoisie engaging in a campaign of targeted murders of class enemies intended to rekindle the peasant uprising. The Naxalite movement in western Bengal, which in a hopeless headlong flight had turned into urban terror, was finally brought under control in 1972. The armed peasant struggle led by the CPI-ML in several districts of Andhra Pradesh, weakened at one point, recovered vigour in the late 1970s and spread to the tribal areas in central India, especially under the leadership of the People's War Group (PWG) as from 1980. Bihar (a state that shares a 735–km border with Nepal) constitutes another insurrection hotbed where the Maoist Communist Centre (MCC) has been trying since 1975 to maintain a revolutionary dynamic by drawing on the most marginalised groups.

Prachanda admitted that before launching the "people's war", Maobadis (Nepalese Maoists) had visited those two states to try and understand the practical problems involved in armed struggle, as well as to receive training and gather material support. CPN (M) advances probably had an impact on the decision made in September 2004 to merge the PWG and the MCC in order to form the CPI-Maoist.

The idea that the Naxalbari movement showed the revolutionaries of the region the path to follow was immediately acknowledged by the Coordination Committee of Maoist Parties and Organisations of South Asia (CCOM-POSA). Founded in 2001, this body aspired to unite the activities of the Maoist movements in the region so as to form a "compact revolutionary zone" stretching from Nepal to Bihar and the tribal areas of Chhattisgarh, Jharkhand, Orissa, Madhya Pradesh and Andhra Pradesh. It held its fourth conference in Nepal in August 2006, but seems to have lost its revolutionary cohesion. Whereas Naxalite groups in India were getting more and more involved in guerrilla operations, the decision of the Nepalese Maoists to abandon armed struggle and reach a compromise with mainstream political parties was greeted rather icily by the CPI (Maoist) which considered that the CPN (M) had sold out on the revolution. To add insult to injury, Prachanda even encouraged the Indian Maoists to learn a lesson from them. Suspicion set in when the CPN (M) hobnobbed with the mainstream CPI (Marxist) in steering the 12–point understanding of November 2005 signed in New Delhi with G.P. Koirala.

In India as in Nepal, the Maoist circle of influence has largely drawn support from the dispossessed tribal populations by promising land redistribution or by attacking various forms of servitude. Tribal populations (Santhals in Naxalbari, Girijans in Srikakulam) were involved from the start in the struggles of the 1960s. In both cases, the populations involved were heirs to a militant past, even dating back for the Santhals to the major uprising of 1855 against the Dikkus (upper caste Hindus) and the British, keen to evict them from their land or proletarianise them on tea plantations. Over the decades, the Girijans had also been dispossessed of part of their land and forest resources, thus finding themselves reduced to becoming labourers. This was a favourable situation for the communist militants to exploit to mobilise the tribal populations against ill-treatment by large landowners or usurers. In the early 1960s one of them, Satyanarayana, founded a *Girijan Sangham*, an organisation in charge of defending the interests of this community.[10] In north Bengal a tribal leader, Jangal Santhal, ran unsuccessfully as the CPI (M) candidate in the 1967 elections in the district of Darjeeling before taking an active part in the Naxalite movement. Mobilisation of tribal groups thus took the form of armed revolts in the spring of 1967 in Naxalbari and in the autumn of 1968 in Srikakulam. These uprisings, however, fit less within the logic of identity claims than within one of class struggle born of opposition to a land tenure system that weakened them economically. As Marius Damas explains, "the history of the Santhals, like the history of other 'tribal' groups in India is the history of their proletarianisation. They participated in the Naxalite movement not just subjectively as tribals, but objectively as members of a class. In doing so they were joined by people from various cultural backgrounds. What brought them together was a similar history of exploitation and alienation from what is in India the predominant means of production: land".[11] Today, in the natural resources-rich states of Central India, the Maoists moreover find support among the tribal populations that have been displaced to make way for mining.

The rise of the ethnic factor

In the case of the Nepalese Maoist movement, class struggle went hand-in-hand with recognition of tribal population and ethnic group identity claims. Officially there are 44 minority ethnic groups listed in Nepal, which make up over one-third of the total population (36.4% in the 2001 census). But in relations between upper caste Hindus and ethnic groups, "the processes of exclusion, labelling and stigmatisation have often been the norm".[12] Very poorly represented in the state apparatus, elected office or management positions, ethnic groups are also handicapped by the geographic concentration of power in the valley of Kathmandu, whereas they themselves often live in remote regions, far from urban centres that are the first to benefit from development.

In the early 1990s, the return to pluralism at least enabled the various *janajatis* (nationalities) to work more freely for recognition of local cultural, linguistic and religious customs and to raise the issue of their political under-representation. The Constitution of 1990 marked progress, because for the first time it recognised the pluralistic nature of Nepalese society. The apparent desire to promote a "multiethnic" *(bahujati)* and "multilingual" *(bahubhasika)* Nepal departed from the historic model of national integration that sought homogenisation by assimilation. The constitutional commitments to protect cultural diversity and the right to promote the literature, script, arts and culture of the various groups was also a novelty. However, Nepal remained defined as a unified state and Hinduism was still the state religion (article 4). National symbols, mostly associated with the monarchy and the Hindu religion, remained unchanged.[13] Nepali, written using the *devanagari* script, retained the status of official language, but the other languages spoken in Nepal were at least given the status of national languages (article 6.2), even though they could not be the language of instruction beyond primary school (article 18.2).[14] Although the Constitution offered ethnic organisations the opportunity to rise up against the "one nation, one language, one religion" triad, it also set limits by allowing the making of laws aiming to impose "reasonable restrictions" on any act which might jeopardise the "harmonious relations subsisting among the peoples of various castes, tribes or communities" (article 12.2). The laws on divorce, marriage and inheritance remained based on Hindu patriarchal norms. The Constitution of 1990 was in reality a sort of synthesis between recognition of cultural pluralism integrated into the Hindu hierarchal framework developed in the Rana era and the Panchayat regime's determination to dissolve this pluralism in a homogenised culture. It also fitted into a certain continuity with the past by providing no constitutional framework able to offset the marginalisation suffered by ethnic groups or the Madhesis (peoples of Indian stock) living in the southern Terai region.

The Nepal Janajati Mahasangh (Nepal Federation of Nationalities, NEFEN) was founded in 1990 in order to federate the existing ethnic associations and thus form a pressure group. The since then common use of the term *janajati* to define ethnic groups clearly reflected the desire to avoid being locked into an ethnographic definition that emphasised cultural diversity, and express political aspirations by demanding the constitutive attributes of a nation: a specific identity based on language and territory as well as a common history.

The demands submitted by the NEFEN fell into three categories: acknowledgment of cultural pluralism, fair representation in all aspects of the life of the nation, and the sharing of resources. The moment was theoretically favourable to make themselves heard: multiethnic states had broken up or were plagued by separatist movements, and defence of cultural diversity was very much in evidence at the UN with the decade of indigenous people (1995–2004). The NEFEN moreover turned into the NEFIN, the Nepal Federation of Indigenous Nationalities, which today consists of 54 member organisations. Its goal was to highlight ethnic particularisms, while bringing them up to the same level as the dominant groups in terms of development and political participation. To achieve this end, it envisaged six measures: secularisation of the state, to do away with all latent or active discrimination in favor of Hinduism; the principle of linguistic equality, particularly in the educational realm; restructuring of administrative divisions along community lines, granting them considerable autonomy; affirmative action in employment and education; respect for natural resource and land rights; and lastly, the financial means to fulfil these aspirations. The ideas defended openly or implicitly by the state—that identity claims were actually redolent of communitarianism and led to disintegration of the nation—was turned around with the argument that it was the state that had always been guilty of practicing divisive cultural imperialism. The response of the governing elites and the state to all these demands was primarily marked by indifference, if not outright refusal to acknowledge multiple identities, reflecting a reluctance to re-examine the organisation of society so as not to challenge the prerogatives and power of the dominant groups. For Krishna Bhattachan, one of the academics most involved in denouncing what he calls "internal colonialism" initiated by Prithvi Narayan Shah, and an adviser to NEFIN, "the predatory nature of the unitary Hindu state has given birth to the people's war".[15]

To make themselves heard, indigenous organisations in which many intellectuals close to the government and academic and NGO circles were active[16] adopted several strategies: the parliamentary route, work within or in conjunction with political parties as well as local and international NGOs, or, as we shall see, participation in the Maoist movement which offered a space for mobilisation for violent protest against the established order.

Maoist discourse and practice

In March 1995, when the CPN (Unity Centre) took the name CPN (Maoist) and emphasised the need to resort to armed struggle to build a new society, it wanted to generate enough support to provide the "people's war" with combatants.[17] This war effort was determined not to betray Marxism-Leninism and remained basically a class struggle between feudal overlords, the bourgeoisie and the proletariat, even if the latter two could work together against the monarchy. But from Maoism it borrowed the idea that the peasantry was destined to play a key role in the revolutionary struggle. It also adopted the tactic of encircling cities by rural areas. Given the socio-occupational structure of Nepalese society, it was very tempting to include the ethnic dimension in revolutionary discourse, all the more so since criticism of the Nepalese state in many ways overlapped that made by intellectuals and activists defending the ethnic cause. The piecemeal approach of the government left the Maoists free to exploit this source of discontent, but to rally support would not necessarily be simple. The radical movement represented by the United People's Front of Nepal (UPFN) had won less than 5% of the votes cast in the parliamentary elections of 1991, and a study conducted by the Political Science Association of Nepal (POLSAN) on the profile of UPFN sympathisers showed that these came from all socioeconomic strata: they were not primarily recruited among the poor, uneducated milieus. Over one-third of the voters were Chhetris (Kshatriyas), a little over one-fifth Bahuns (Brahmins), and 15% Newars. The original feature, however, was the proportionally significant support of the Magars (8.5%).[18]

In February 1996, from the very start of the "people's war", the Maoists presented themselves as champions of ethnic groups against a monarchical, centralised and feudal regime that had historically unified the country not through fraternal harmony but by way of repression, subjection and discrimination. The Maoist interpretation of the country's history emphasised the dispossession and pauperisation suffered by ethnic groups on the arrival of the Indo-Nepalese invaders. "The oppressed regions within the country are primarily the regions inhabited by the indigenous people since time immemorial", Baburam Bhattarai emphasised. "These indigenous people dominated regions that were independent tribal states prior to the formation of the centralised state in the later half of the eighteenth century, have been reduced to the present most backward and oppressed condition due to the internal feudal exploitation and the external semi-colonial oppression".[19] Before Prithvi

Narayan Shah, Nepal was divided into small kingdoms, principalities and "republican tribal states". According to Prachanda, the existence of a tribal type of democratic system proved that Nepalese society was not monarchical by tradition, but that the centralised feudal state had imposed "Hindu feudal and Brahmanist ethnic chauvinism on lingual, ethnic, religious, cultural and traditional rights of people of various communities, nationalities and religions of Nepal and thereby hindered the natural development of genuine national unity and power". Thus, it was necessary to lay the foundations of a consolidated national unity on the basis of equality and freedom in accordance with the right of nations to self-determination in the context of the new democratic revolution.[20]

The Maoists thoroughly intended to capitalise on this discriminatory social order and the attendant economic distortions that ethnic groups were the first to suffer from. Highlighting the spatial imbalances in development, Baburam Bhattarai, whose PhD thesis was entitled "The Nature of Underdevelopment and Regional Structure of Nepal", believed that regional autonomy would remedy them.

In the old social systems, particularly because of the centralisation of the basic economic, social and physical services and infrastructure only in a few urban centres, an uncontrolled population, concentration in the big cities takes place leading to the "ruralisation of the cities". Against this, in the New Democratic system, economic, social and physical services and infrastructure (e.g. industries, banks, colleges, hospitals, electricity, motorable roads, etc.) would be provided in the rural areas and a policy of "urbanisation of the countryside" would be followed.[21]

In 1994, the resolution regarding issue of nationalities adopted during the first National Conference of what was still called the CPN (Unity Centre) included demands formulated by the NEFIN. The ethnic question was mentioned several times in the 40 demands submitted by the CPN (M) to Sher Bahadur Deuba's government on 4 February 1996. Demand no. 20 called for the end of any racial exploitation and prejudice and, in areas having a majority of one ethnic group, for such a group to be allowed to form its own autonomous government. It was also demanded that regional discrimination between the hills and the Terai plain should be eliminated and that backward areas should be given regional autonomy (demand no. 25). Local bodies should be empowered and have control over resources (demand no. 26). Lastly, all languages and dialects should be given equal opportunities to prosper and the right to education in the mother tongue up to higher levels should be guaranteed (demand no. 22).

The Common Minimum and Policy Programme adopted in September 2001 by the United Revolutionary People's Council (UPRC), the central body headed by Baburam Bhattarai that had grown out of a united front incorporating pro-Maoist ethnic organisations, provided more detail about what the transfer of responsibilities to the planned autonomous regions would imply. It mentioned that the people's committees/governments and local representatives that the various nationalities would elect would be given large autonomy except for an extensive list of matters related to the people's army, foreign relations, currency, communications, large basic industries and large hydroelectric projects. In areas of mixed nationalities, there would be representation of all in the local state powers on a proportional basis. All the nationalities would have the right to join the people's army and they could form people's militias under the central command as a security force at the local level. They would also enjoy the freedom to promote their languages and culture, the central government assisting those nationalities in these endeavours as well in their overall development.[22]

The creation of nine autonomous regions was outlined: six on an ethnic basis (Tharuwan, Magarant, Tamuwan, Tamang, Newar, Kirant) and three on a purely territorial basis where there was no dominant group (Seti-Mahakali, Bheri-Karnali, Madhesh). They were instituted in early 2004 for organisational purposes and expanded to eleven in August 2007 with three subdivisions for the Madhesh region. These regions were necessarily diverse, because actually there were only five districts where a single ethnic group held an absolute majority.[23] In 33 districts one ethnic group had a relative majority, and in 31 districts all of the *janajatis* together accounted for more than 50% of the population. In 22 districts the Chhetris were the dominant group, the Bahuns in ten others. The importance of the two dominant castes in terms of geographic extension was reinforced by the fact that the Chhetris came in second position in 22 districts and the Bahuns in 18 districts.[24] These figures are a good illustration of how complex the search for an administrative and territorial solution to ethnic claims can be.

Although the right to secede was theoretically recognised, such a possibility, it was thought, would become superfluous once nationalities were no longer exploited. Chinese autonomous regions were taken as a reference in this regard. After hostilities resumed following the breakdown of initial peace talks (August/November 2001), the Maoist leadership strengthened the "people's governments" (*jan sarkar*) that were to be elected by representatives of similar units at the village level. They were primarily concentrated in regions where hill-dwelling ethnic groups lived, which explains the lack of them in the far west hill region, populated almost exclusively by people of caste.

The CPN (M) needed to find a way to rectify the image of a party that scarcely differed from others in that it was also dominated by upper castes—five out of the seven members of the politburo standing committee were Bahuns (including Prachanda and Baburam Bhattarai) and Chhetris.[25] To prove their good faith, the Maoist leaders undertook to promote members from ethnic minorities in areas controlled by the CPN (M). Of the 37 founding members of the UPRC provisional central committee, 20 were from ethnic communities and Dalits. Within the *jana sarkar* (dissolved in January 2007) there was a fairly good match between the local dominant ethnic group or caste and the composition of these governments, 16 presidents of these "people's governments" being of ethnic origin.[26] In a similar vein, the five-member Maoist delegation sent to Kathmandu for new negotiations with the government (April–August 2003) included, alongside Baburam Bhattarai and Krishna Bahadur Mahara (a Chhetri, now Minister of Information and Communications), Matrika Prasad Yadav (a Madhesi, now Minister of Land Reform and Management) and two leaders of ethnic origin, Ram Bahadur Thapa (a Magar, who became Minister of Defence in 2008) and Dev Gurung, the latter moreover in charge of ethnic questions at the CPN (M) central committee and who became Minister of Law and Constituent Assembly in 2008. During these negotiations, the Maoists requested that the elections to a constituent assembly, scheduled to follow the formation of an interim government, should guarantee adequate representation of women, the various classes, nationalities, regions and communities. The new Constitution was to contain provisions for a national assembly and government that would be representative of all components of society, and provided that at the local level, regional autonomy with the right to self-determination would be guaranteed for all "oppressed nationalities and regions".

The phasing of two discourses, one turned against the Brahminical norm, the other against the monarchy, was also manifested by action taken against their symbols. In areas under Maoist control, the teaching of Sanskrit and the national anthem extolling the virtue of the King's achievements and well-being as being emblematic of patriotism were banned.[27] In May 2002, Maoist militants attacked the Mahendra Sanskrit University in Dang valley. They slaughtered cows, organised community meals where the dishes were prepared by Untouchables, and encouraged inter-caste marriages and widow remarriage—at the risk perhaps of sometimes going too far for the ethnic populations that had often interiorised the dominant culture and norms, especially when such a process of acculturation was necessary to improve one's social status. But sometimes, the conduct of certain indigenous organisations was similar to that of the Maoists. For instance, calls to boycott Hindu celebrations used the argument that social relations within ethnic groups were supposedly egalitarian in nature before specifically Hindu hierarchal principles were introduced, and the "de-Sanskritisation" of proper names and place names in tribal areas was advocated. The aim was to encourage the reappropriation of cultural heritage cleansed of the stains of Hinduisation.

The government implicitly acknowledged that Maoist propaganda criticising its ineffectiveness in tackling the ethnic issue provided a measure of success among the indigenous people.[28] This even provided it with food for thought. In 2001, Deuba accompanied his offer to open talks with a series of legislative proposals aiming to impose a ceiling on landownership, open places of worship to lower castes, allow girls a share of their parent's inheritance, grant land and housing to indentured farm workers (this especially pertained to Kamaiya Tharus to whom the Maoists redistributed land via the All Nepal Peasants Association); and, more particularly regarding ethnic groups, he offered to establish an academy and initiate a long-term education and employment programme. When talks resumed with the Maoists in 2003, following the establishment the year before of a national foundation for the development of indigenous nationalities, the government announced its intention to introduce reforms regarding ethnic groups by amending the Constitution. On the agenda was proportional representation of ethnic groups in the Upper House of the Parliament, the possibility of using local languages as a second language in local administrations,[29] and the introduction of a quota system in favour of 59 identified ethnic communities according to their demographic weight for a period depending on the evolution of human development indicators. Governmental instability ensured that no decisions were ultimately made in this regard.

The involvement of ethnic organizations

Although organisations of "oppressed nationalities and regions" were to play a historic role in the revolutionary process, it was with uneven success as the CPN (M) often had to create affiliate organisations, a number of ethnic groups being repelled by Maoist ideology and/or violent tactics.[30] The attraction of Maoism for the tribals nevertheless grew in the course of the 1990s. It is from this perspective that Prachanda's remark, made two years after the "people's war" was launched, should be interpreted: "A new consciousness for fighting for their own rights and liberation is spreading amongst many oppressed nationalities of the country such as the Magars, Gurungs, Tamangs, Newars, Tharus, Rais, Limbus and Madhises. People's War has speeded up the process of formation of various national liberation fronts and expansion of nationality organisations".[31] Conflict situations tend to exacerbate prejudices, and ethnic groups were particularly subject to police harassment and abuse. It is therefore not surprising that they were increasingly drawn to a guerrilla resistance that enabled them to hope to punish their upper caste oppressors. Similarly, 70% of the female Maoist fighters were said to belong to *janajatis*.

The "people's war" had been launched from the Kham Magar country, the true epicentre of the rebellion. The region had just endured "operation Romeo", a police operation ordered by the Nepali Congress government to crush radical protest, but mainly producing the reverse effect—it strengthened the Maoist ranks through excessive repression (as moreover did "Operation Kilo Sierra 2" in 1998–99). In Rolpa, the Kham Magars made up 44% of the population, and in Rukum 23%. When asked what had led him to establish the party in these areas, Prachanda mentioned a string of various reasons, including the rugged terrain, the lack of feudal traditions among the indigenous populations—which he believed practiced a primitive form of democracy—social oppression imposed by the upper castes, and the isolation that had led the region to be economically neglected.[32] It is true that the rare interventions of the central government in this region were perceived as being rather negative. For instance, in 1976, a ban on growing hashish led to the impoverishment of the local population. There were few jobs to be had and traditionally a number of young people migrated to other parts of Nepal or to India in search of employment. Livelihood in Rolpa depends mainly on agriculture and stockbreeding, but since 90% of the inhabitants own less than one hectare, there is very little marketable surplus.[33] Anne de Sales, a French anthropologist, remarks that young peasants who have tried unsuccessfully to migrate to urban centres or abroad have joined the guerrilla campaign.[34] Another important explanatory factor was that the Kham Magar country differs from other regions that are equally underdeveloped because of the long-established communist presence there.[35] One of the historic figures of the communist movement in Nepal, Mohan Bikram Singh, was already working in this area in the 1950s. In September 1974, he founded the CPN-Fourth Convention which he left in 1983 to found the CPN (Masal). In 1986, M.B. Singh allowed himself to be outflanked on the left by Mohan Baidya (Comrade Kiran), a future member of the standing committee of the CPN (M) politburo who formed the CPN (Mashal). The "revisionist" faction behind M.B. Singh regrouped in the neighbouring district of Pyuthan, whereas Rolpa came under the influence of the CPN (Mashal) of which Prachanda became secretary-general. Another local figure of the communist movement, Burman Budha, mayor of Thawang (Rolpa), attracted notice during the referendum organised by Birendra in 1980, by calling for a boycott of it and then replacing the portraits of the King and Queen with those of Marx and Lenin.

During the parliamentary elections of May 1991, three out of four contested seats in Rolpa and Rukum districts went to the UPFN (Burman Budha was one of the elected). This performance at the polls was repeated during the local elections that took place the following year. The UPFN won a majority in Rolpa and came in second behind the Nepali Congress in Rukum. In 1994, the Maoists organised an awareness and political mobilisation campaign that was orchestrated by one of their military commandants, Ram Bahadur Thapa, also known as Comrade Badal. The Magar ethnic group offers an interesting case of complementarity/confrontation between identitarian aspirations and the Maoist movement.[36] There was confrontation because although the Maoists sympathised with the Magars' grievances, even joined in with them, some of them also stood apart. Many Magars worked in the police and armed forces and were thus Maoist targets; their families sometimes had to flee to the Terai region.[37] Magars were also the first victims of security forces, highlighting the fact that while an ethnic group may be homogeneous from a cultural standpoint, this is not the case socially and politically. The most sceptical as to the CPN (M)'s real intentions accused the Maoist leadership, dominated by Bahuns, of exploiting the people's legitimate discontent with the authorities to swell the ranks of their own troops, in the same way that Prithvi Narayan Shah had used the Magars to begin unifying the country and conquer the Valley of Kathmandu in 1768–69.

One of the most prominent personalities of the ethnic cause, Gore Bahadur Khapangi, president of the Nepal Magar Sangh, refused to be affiliated with the Maoists. He established the first indigenous political party after the popular movement of the spring of 1990, the Nepal Rastriya Janamukti

Morcha (Nepal National Janajati Liberation Front), none of whose fifty candidates managed to get elected the following year. Having become leader of the Rastriya Janamukti Party, Khapangi was no luckier in the 1999 elections. He was finally appointed Minister for Social Affairs by the King in November 2002. On the other hand, Suresh Ale Magar is a typical example of an ethnic militant who joined the upper echelons of the Maoist apparatus. He was among the founding members of the NEFEN before heading the Akhil Nepal Janajati Sangh (All Nepal Nationalities Association, ANNA) in 1994, a rival organisation close to the Maoists. He was later nominated as a member of the Interim Central Committee of the URPC. He was arrested, then released, several times by the Nepalese authorities before the Indian police finally arrested him in Lucknow in February 2004–along with Matrika Prasad Yadav, a member of the CPN (M) politburo and chief of the Madhesh autonomous government—and extradited him to Nepal. Lok Bahadur Thapa Magar, member of Nepal Magar Sangh, also decided to join the Maoist cause and was made head of the Magarant Rastriya Mukti Morcha (Magarant National Liberation Front). In a book published in the late 1990s, he vehemently criticised the Aryans who had invaded Magarant from India, Sanskritised the Magars, and confiscated the best lands, relegating the Magars to the steep mountain slopes. The author's line of argument spoke of exploitation of an ethnic nature and class exploitation transcending ethnic categories.

The Magarant Rastriya Mukti Morcha is one of those Maoist-induced ethnic organisations created between 1998 and 2000, a common feature being inclusion in their names of the label "national liberation front" (the adjective "national" being added to distinguish themselves from "liberation fronts", a name already used by several ethnic organisations, and also to echo the name taken by many communist anti-colonial movements). Most of these fronts were part of the Ethnic and Regional Fronts Coordination Committee (ERFCC) created in May 2001 to replace the ANNA. They were associated with the UPRC's September 2001 Common Minimum Policy and Programme. These fronts occasionally made headlines by declaring strikes and blockades.

As in the case of the Kham Magar region, Maoist presence in tribal areas was facilitated where there already existed a tradition of communist or ethnic militancy. An example was the Eastern districts of Sankhuwasabha and Terhathum, respectively dominated by the Rai and Limbu ethnic groups, where the CPN (UML) controlled the district development committees when the Maoists set up *jana sarkar*. The establishment of these "people's governments" at the district level often placed them in strong opposition more to the CPN (UML) than to the Nepali Congress.[38] Prachanda admitted that each region and community had its specific features and that one had to study carefully "(what) traditional constraints, what forms of feudal exploitation and feudal oppression are prevailing in that group".[39] Fieldwork in the district of Dolakha, where in July 2001 the formation of a "people's government" was announced, showed that the local population was almost equally divided between the Bahuns/Chhetris on one hand and various ethnic and caste communities on the other hand, not sufficiently organised among themselves to be in a position to oppose the Maoist influence, but yet a potential source of support because of their sheer poverty. The Maoists managed to gather the support of the Thami and Tamang communities, traditionally exploited by upper caste landlords.[40] The power of Maoist influence clearly depended also on existing ethnic structures, some of which had refused to equate empowerment automatically with political struggle. A study underscored for instance the example of the Tharu Workers' Liberation Organisation, which had transformed into a non-political NGO "adjusted to the international features of human rights activism".[41]

The Kirant populations (Limbu and Rai) have a long tradition of independence and opposition to the central power. When the Maoists tried to invest a region that was less familiar to them than their historic stronghold, they had to compromise with the Limbuwan Liberation Front (LLF) and the Khambuwan National Front (KNF), which were fighting for ethnic autonomy and the right to self-determination. In 1997 the KNF had even perpetrated acts of violence, particularly against Sanskrit schools in the districts of Bhojpur and Solukhumbu. The following year the CPN (M) and the KNF, under the leadership of the virulent Gopal Khambu, opened talks. The Maoists later favoured the merger of the KNF and the LLF, giving rise to the Kirant Rastriya Morcha (National Kirant Front). The partnership between Maoists and the Kiranti autonomists first appeared to be *ad hoc* in the context of armed struggle against the regime in Kathmandu, and moreover was not devoid of tensions and renegotiations over the alliance. In 2004, although Gopal Khambu was appointed chief of the Kiranti autonomous region, the fact that in the same year a faction of the Kirant Workers' Party—which he had founded after the KNF was dissolved—had announced that it was withdrawing from the alliance with the Maoists betrayed recurrent divergences and suspicions.[42] Eventually, in August 2008, the CPN (M) nominated the maverick Kiranti leader as Minister of Culture and State Reconstruction.

Joining the Maoists, which posed little problem when ethnic leaders had a past of left-wing activism, was guided by a concern to be better armed to make their demands heard. But it did not necessarily allow the CPN (M) to instrumentalise ethnic groups. The party still inspires a certain wariness as regards its true intentions on the federal issue and power-sharing. In fact, the proliferation and dissemination of organisations linked to the Maoist guerrilla campaign has become a potential factor for insubordination and criminal inclinations. But having the capacity to conduct guerrilla operations in several places throughout the country was valuable, as it obliged Nepalese security forces to deploy over the length and breadth of the territory.

Conclusion

During the "people's war", the Maoists capitalised on the fact that all the mainstream political parties loyal to the 1990 Constitution paid only lip-service, at best, to the rights of ethnic groups. Although the interim Constitution promulgated in January 2007 contained some provisions for the empowerment and advancement of the interests of marginalised communities, and mentioned an inclusive and forward-looking restructuring of the state by eliminating its centralised and unitary model in order to address the problems of deprived groups, these provisions remained too vague and too few to really satisfy those groups' aspirations for a federal framework ensuring fair representation in state mechanisms and bodies. For militants of disadvantaged groups that did not identify or no longer identified with the CPN (M), it was inevitably tempting to draw inspiration from the violent methods used fairly successfully by the Maoists. Soon, in the southern region of Terai where nearly half of the Nepalese population lives, the Madhesis' long-repressed feeling of discrimination at the hands of the Pahadis, the "hill people" (particularly because they are often perceived as not "Nepali" enough, owing to their close links with India), took a violent turn. The Maoists trained many deprived groups to launch a war against the state, and in the process the importance of violence for political power gained currency. As identity politics was not the monopoly of the Maoists, clashes erupted between the MPRF, which spearheaded the movement, and militants of the CPN (M). They differed on the idea of a single Madhesh state covering the Terai region (the Maoists recognise a separate Tharuwan as well) but also because the Maoists were accused of showing the hill people's traditional contempt for the Madeshis and suspecting them of intriguing with some Indian groups and palace supporters distressed by the turn of events. While the MPRF, after protracted negotiations with the government, joined the peaceful political process and took part of the short-lived Maoist-led coalition government[43] to advance the cause of a federal republic, the faction-ridden Janatantrik Tarai Mukti Morcha (Terai Peoples Liberation Front), an underground outfit, has carried on a separatist armed struggle. The JTMM was founded in July 2004 by dissidents of the Terai National Liberation Front, of Maoist allegiance.

Whereas the MPRF demanded fair representation for the Madeshi people in all the organs of a federal state, including security bodies, and an autonomous Madhesh state, the NEFIN joined the calls for an all-out proportional representation system for the constituent assembly elections and assured minimum representation for all the ethnic communities in the parliament. Both held talks with the Koirala government leading to compromise formulas like the agreements signed in August 2007. The elections to the constituent assembly of April 2008 were finally held under a mixed electoral system (240 seats were allocated under the first-past-the-post principle and 361 seats under proportional representation), and article 63.4 of the interim Constitution, stating that the political parties must select their candidates by following the principle of inclusiveness, produced varying effects. In those elections the Maoists opened up, more than the other major parties, to candidacies from members of the deprived communities, and the first government of the Federal Democratic Republic of Nepal (officially declared in May 2008) presented a more inclusive look than any of its predecessors. This might be the easy part. Far more complicated will be to give shape on the ground to the federalist agenda, to implement the demands for equitable participation in the larger state administrative and institutional set-up and for ethnic and regional-based autonomy while ensuring that the political process remains free of violence.

BIBLIOGRAPHY

Documents

Problems and Prospects of Revolution in Nepal. A Collection of Articles by Com. Prachanda and Other Leaders of the CPN (Maoist), Kathmandu, Janadisha Publications, 2004.
Some Important Documents of Communist Party of Nepal (Maoist), Nepal, Janadisha Publications, 2004.

Books

Baral, Lok Raj, Krishna Hachhethu and Hari Sharma, *Leadership in Nepal*, Delhi, Adroit, 2001.
Bhattarai, Baburam, *Monarchy vs. Democracy. The Epic Fight in Nepal*, New Delhi, Samkaleen Teesari Duniya, 2005.
Centre for Investigative Journalism, *People in the "People's War,"* Kathmandu, Himal Books, 2004.
Gellner, David N., *Resistance and the State. Nepalese Experiences*, Delhi, Social Science Press, 2003.
Gurung, Harka, *Social Demography and Expressions*, Kathmandu, New Era, 1998.
——— *Social Demography of Nepal. Census 2001*, Kathmandu, Himal Books, 2003.
Hutt, Michael (ed.), *Himalayan "People's War". Nepal's Maoist Rebellion*, London, Hurst, 2004.
Karki, Arjun and Binod Bhattarai, *Whose War? Economic and Socio-Cultural Impacts of Nepal's Maoist-Government Conflict*, Kathmandu, NGO Federation of Nepal, 2004.
Karki, Arjun and David Seddon (eds), *The People's War in Nepal. Left Perspectives*, Delhi, Adroit Publishers, 2003.
Kumar, Dhruba (ed.), *Domestic Conflict and Crisis of Governability in Nepal*, Kathmandu, CNAS, 2000.
NESAC, *Nepal Human Development Report 1998*, Kathmandu, Nepal South Asia Centre (NESAC), 1999.
POLSAN, *Political Parties and the Parliamentary Process in Nepal*, Kathmandu, Political Science Association of Nepal, 1992.
Serchan, Sanjaya, *Democracy, Pluralism and Change. An Inquiry in the Nepalese Context*, Kathmandu, Chhye Pahuppe, 2001.
Shrestha, Prakash (ed.), *Quest for Peace*, Kathmandu, SAP-Nepal, 2001.
Steinmann, Brigitte (ed.), *Le Maoisme au Nepal. Lectures d'une révolution*, Paris, CNRS Éditions, 2006.
Thapa, Deepak (ed.), *Understanding the Maoist Movement of Nepal*, Kathmandu, Martin Chautari, 2003.
Thapa, Deepak and Bandita Sijapati, *A Kingdom Under Siege. Nepal's Maoist Insurgency, 1996 to 2003*, Kathmandu, The Printhouse, 2003.

Articles and papers

Bhattachan, Krishna B., "Expected Model & Process of Inclusive Democracy in Nepal," paper given at the seminar "The Agenda of Transformation: Inclusion in Nepali Democracy," Kathmandu, 24–26 April 2003.

Bhattarai, Hari Prasad, "Cultural Diversity and Pluralism in Nepal: Emerging Issues and the Search for a New Paradigm," *Contributions to Nepalese Studies* 31 (2), July 2004: 293–340.

Dahal, Dilli R., "Madhese, Regionalism and National Integration: A Case of the Nepal Terai," *Nepali Journal of Contemporary Studies* 2 (1), March 2002: 1–19.

Gurung, Harka, "Nepal: Maoist Insurgency and Indigenous People," *Nepali Journal of Contemporary Studies*, 3 (2), September 2003: 1–18.

Hachhethu, Krishna, "Democracy and Nationalism Interface between State and Ethnicity in Nepal," *Contributions to Nepalese Studies*, 30 (2), July 2003: 217–52.

Kumar, Dhruba, "Consequences of the Militarized Conflict and the Cost of Violence in Nepal," *Contributions to Nepalese Studies*, 30 (2), July 2003: 167–216.

Lawoti, Mahendra, "Defining Minorities in Nepal," *Nepali Journal of Contemporary Studies*, 2 (1), March 2002: 20–52.

Niroula, Badri P., "Caste Ethnic Composition of Population of Nepal," *Contributions to Nepalese Studies*, 25 (1), January 1998: 15–56.

NOTES

1. The Maoists of the United People's Front of Nepal (UPFN) won 9 seats in the House of Representatives in the 1991 legislative elections that marked the end of the authoritarian Panchayat regime. The UPFN, with Baburam Bhattarai as campaign leader, was the electoral incarnation of the CPN (Unity Centre) of which Prachanda was secretary-general and which brought under its label three small Maoist factions: the CPN (Mashal), the CPN-4th Convention and a faction of the CPN (Masal). The UPFN, or Sanyukta Janamorcha Nepal, did not long survive the traditional divisions that rent the far left. The CPN (Unity Centre) split into two groups in May 1994. Only the group led by Nirmal Lama was recognised by the electoral commission during the early elections of 1994 (it won no seats), whereas the group led by Prachanda called for a boycott of the polls.

2. See the website of the Informal Sector Service Centre (INSEC), a human rights organisation based in Kathmandu. www.inseconline.org

3. By the end of 2008, a group within the central committee of CPN (Maoist), led by hardline ideologue Mohan Baidya, was still bent on switching to a "people's republic" in opposition to the accommodative approach defended by the party chairman Pushpa Kamal Dahal.

4. *The Kathmandu Post*, 16 January 2007.

5. The historic figure of the Nepali Congress, B.P. Koirala (1914–82), received his education in Northern India and was active in the Indian National Congress before forming the Akhil Bharatiya Nepal Rastriya Congress on 31 October 1946, along with other Nepalese in exile, in Benares. This organisation held its inaugural congress in January 1947 in Calcutta where, with the contribution of the Nepali Sangh and the Gorkha Congress, it took on the name of Nepali Rastriya Congress to become the Nepali Congress in April 1950, after merging with the Nepali Prajatantrik Congress.

6. To measure India's interference and the frequent interaction with Indian politicians and senior civil servants, see B.P. Koirala's memoirs, *Atmabrittanta. Late Life Recollections*, Kathmandu, Himal Books, 2001.

7. Prachanda, "The Problem of Ideological Deviation in the Nepalese People's Revolution," in *Problems and Prospects of Revolution in Nepal. A Collection of Articles by Com. Prachanda and Other Leaders of the CPN (Maoist)*, (2004), p. 14. Upon India's independence, Telangana, a region in the north of the state of Andhra Pradesh, experienced a peasant revolt overseen by Communists with the creation of village soviets.

8. Chandra Prakash Mainali, who was party secretary-general, later became a tamed minister in Man Mohan Adhikari's communist government before reforming the CPN (ML). His brother, Radha Krishna, after long following a similar itinerary, decided to back the royal coup of 1 February 2005 and became Minister of Education and Sports in the government led by King Gyanendra.

9. In an ironic twist of history, the region of Naxalbari had been annexed by Prithvi Narayan Shah's Gorkhalis shortly before his death and was lost to the British with the Sugauli Treaty of 1815. Certain ethnic groups (Rajbhansi, Meche, Dhimal) are presently found on both sides of the border.

10. Sumanta Banerjee, "Naxalbari and the Left Movement," in Ghanshyam Shah, *Social Movements and the State*, New Delhi, Sage, 2002, pp. 139–41.

11. Marius Damas, *Approaching Naxalbari*, Calcutta, Radical Impression, 1991, p. 144.

12. Sanjaya Serchan, (2001), p. 70.

13. "Traditional practices" in places of worship were not considered discriminatory, including a provision banning Untouchables from temples. Killing a cow was an act punishable by twelve years of imprisonment. Although that never prevented the clandestine slaughter of animals, this provision is experienced by certain ethnic groups as yet another discriminatory measure imposed by Hindu morality. In the current interim Constitution, despite Maoist objections, the cow remains the national animal.

14. The interim Constitution of 2007 does not say anything different on this point, apart from the possibility of using the mother language in local bodies and offices (article 5.3).

15. Krishna Bhattachan, "Possible Ethnic Revolution or Insurgency in a Predatory Unitary Hindu State, Nepal," in Dhruba Kumar, (2000), p. 159. Prithvi Narayan Shah (1744–75) conquered Kathmandu in 1768 and worked to unify the country. Hinduism was to serve as a foundation for the building of a new state. For ethnic militants, Prithvi Narayan Shah was not only the first Shah king to rule the country—Gyanendra being the last—but also the one who initiated the process of cultural and religious unification.

16. Two examples: first, Padma Ratna Tuladhar, a human rights activist on whose initiative the Nepal Bhasa Manka Khala, a Newar ethnic organisation, was created in 1979, then held a ministerial position in Manmohan Adhikari's communist government and acted as mediator for contacts between the government and the Maoists. Second, Parshuram Tamang, professor of economics at Tribhuvan University in Kathmandu, a founding member of the NEFEN, is affiliated with various regional and international organisations dealing with the problems of indigenous peoples.

17. As has often been emphasised, it is important for the Maoists to attract into their ranks a significant number of Magars and Gurungs, which together dominate the Gurkha regiments in the Indian and British armies.

18. Political Science Association of Nepal (1992), p. 35.
19. Baburam Bhattarai, "Politico-Economic Rationale of People's War in Nepal," *Problems and Prospects of Revolution in Nepal* (2004), p. 98.
20. Prachanda, "The Great Leap Forward: An Inevitable Need of History," *Some Important Documents of Communist Party of Nepal (Maoist)* (2004), p. 74.
21. Baburam Bhattarai, op cit., (2004), p. 107.
22. Common Minimum Policy and Programme of United Revolutionary People's Council, *Some Important Documents of Communist Party of Nepal (Maoist)* (2004), p. 172.
23. The districts of Bardya (Tharu majority), Bhaktapur (Newar majority), Manang (Gurung majority), Palpa (Magar majority), Rasuwa (Tamang majority).
24. See the Central Bureau of Statistics, Population Census 2001–Caste/Ethnicity, Mother Tongue & Religion (District Level), Kathmandu, September 2003, p. 248.
25. After the royal family was massacred on 1 June 2001, Baburam Bhattarai praised the patriotism of King Birendra and his ancestor Prithvi Narayan Shah in preserving "Nepali independence and sovereign status from the hands of British imperialism and later from Indian expansionism". "Let's not legitimize the new Kot massacre," *Kantipur*, 6 June 2001, reprinted in: Baburam Bhattarai, (2005), p. 21. That comment was not really appreciated by ethnic leaders.
26. The listing of the Maoist leadership of the *jan sarkar* according to ethnicity and caste is found in Arjun Karki and Binod Bhattarai (eds), (2004), p. 180–181.
27. The new national anthem adopted in August 2007 by the parliament makes reference to the various races, languages, faiths, and cultures.
28. *Report of the High Level Recommendation Committee on Resolution of the Maoist Problem*, 2057 B. S. [2000], p. 31. Quoted by Sudheer Sharma, *The Ethnic Dimension of the Maoist Insurgency*, 2002. Unpublished report. 35 p.
29. The Supreme Court had handed down its decision in June 1999, overturning the city of Kathmandu's decision to authorise use of Newari along with Nepali as language of administrative communication in the constituency. This ban also applied to the town of Rajbiraj and the district development committee of Dhanusha that had allowed the use of Maithili—despite the adoption of the Local Governance Act of 1999 that theoretically allowed the local authorities to take measures to defend local languages and cultures.
30. Thus, to gain a foothold in the Newar community, the Maoists sought in vain to win support from Padma Ratna Tuladhar's Nepal Bhasa Manka Khala and resigned themselves to founding a rival organisation, the Newa Khala, under the leadership of a local CPN (M) chief, Dilip Maharjan (who was arrested in India in 2004).
31. Prachanda, "Two Momentous Years of Revolutionary Transformation," in *Problems & Prospects…*, (2004), p. 158.
32. The first road to serve the district of Rukum and Musikot, its capital, was inaugurated in May 2003. As for Rolpa, the first road to serve the capital, Liwang, was completed in 2002.
33. See Robert Gersony, "Sowing the Wind… History and Dynamics of the Maoist Revolt in Nepal's Rapti Hills," unpublished report for Mercy Corps International, October 2003, p. 10 and 18 maps.
34. Anne de Sales, "The Kham Magar Country: Between Ethnic Claims and Maoism," in David Gellner (ed.) (2003), p. 348.
35. Arjun Karki and David Seddon, "The Revolution in Nepal: An Interview with Comrade Prachanda," in A. Karki and D. Seddon (eds) (2003), pp. 83–4.

36. See especially Marie-Lecomte Tilouine, "Ethnic Demands within Maoism: Questions of Magar Territorial Autonomy, Nationality and Class," in Michael Hutt (ed.) (2004), pp. 112–35.

37. Ram Bahadur Thapa himself was born in the neighbouring district of Gulmi in 1955 into one of those families in which the father had found a job in the Indian army, leading them to live in Meghalaya and Andhra Pradesh. He became commander of the Maoist forces in the eastern zone after Kiran was arrested in June 2004.

38. Krishna Hachhethu, "The Nepali State and the Maoist Insurgency, 1996–2001," in Michael Hutt (ed.) (2004), p. 77.

39. Arjun Karki and David Seddon (2003), p. 109.

40. Sara Shneiderman and Mark Turin, "The Path to Jan Sarkar in Dolakha District," in Michael Hutt (ed.) (2004), p. 102.

41. Gisèle Krauskopff, "An "Indigenous Minority" in a Border Area: Tharu Ethnic Associations, NGOs, and the Nepalese State," in David N. Gellner (ed.) (2003), p. 240.

42. Regarding the ups and downs in relations between the CPN (M) and ethnic militancy in Kirant, see Dambar Krishna Shrestha, "Ethnic Autonomy in the East," in: Centre for Investigative Journalism, *People in the "People's War*, Lalitpur, 2004, pp. 19–40.

43. Prachanda resigned from the position of Prime Minister in May 2009 after having failed to remove the head of the army.

3

FIGHTING WITH IDEAS

MAOIST AND POPULAR CONCEPTIONS OF THE NEPALESE PEOPLE'S WAR

Marie Lecomte-Tilouine

The conception and perception of war are important aspects of revolutionary movements such as the Nepalese People's War. Indeed, this movement reached its remarkable national and worldwide audience and achieved success mainly because of its armed actions and military prowess. War is also the major element defining the Maoist position within the Nepalese political landscape: by launching the People's War in February 1996, the Communist Party of Nepal (Maoist) positioned itself as unique and in opposition to all other parties, be they conservative or not. The very creation of this party was conditioned by war, since its founder, Prachanda, reformed the views of the Marxist leaders Nirmal Lama and M.B. Singh by proposing the army as the principal form of organisation, and war as the principal form of struggle.[1]

The conception of war at a theoretical level is therefore a prerequisite for analysing the Nepalese Maoist revolution. But the CPN (M) would probably not have attracted such a large part of the population without moving into action, and its ideology would have remained a dead letter if it had not been complemented by the People's Liberation Army fighters' perception of it.

My investigations have been based mainly on the reading of Nepalese revolutionary texts and interviews, which have not yet been analysed as such. I consider first Maoist writers' theoretical views of war and the transformative effect they attribute to war; then, the issue of women in war, for they are presented as the main category of oppressed people who benefited from this transformation; finally, the way a villager and a Maoist commander interact verbally around the question of a major attack, in order to show that their respective perceptions of violence and war are not fully delineated.

In Nepal, the People's War gave birth to a spate of narratives and reflections. Until the 2006 peace agreement, these could be found in weekly clandestine Maoist publications posted on the Internet.[2] Since then, the number of Maoist publications has exploded; they now include a dozen journals, compiled works on Maoist theory, novels, diaries and volumes of poetry. Except for a limited number of English translations of the leaders' writings, the language of these publications is Nepali. However, it makes use of a lexicon far removed from spoken Nepali, borrowing many abstract notions from Hindi and Sanskrit—as well as technical military terms from English—which are simply not to be found in a standard Nepali dictionary. The Maoists do not, however, point to the Indian scholarly tradition as being a source of inspiration: that would not support their claim, on the one hand, of being the Nepalese people's mouthpiece, and on the other hand, of being the last inheritors of a Marxist heritage, which has not encountered major theoretical developments in India. In spite of its linguistic detour via India, the Marxist heritage introduced Nepal to a kind of globalisation that includes a new knowledge and conception of world history and politics. A Maoist poet thus claims:

> I have signed a contract with Death
> And dancing in the fire flame
> I cause red flowers to blossom ...
> I teach
> Che Guevara's courage,
> Chiang Ching's boundless boldness,
> And the Vietnamese people's realism,
> To the oppressed hamlets and villages (V.M. 2004)

These teachings reached Nepal's remotest places, where in turn, new historical revolutionary centres emerged, positioning Nepal as the new vanguard of the 21st century for the entire world.[3] Thabang, where the People's War took root and which became the capital of the Magarant Autonomous Region created by the CPN(M), is thus the latest avatar of the revolutionary movement born during the Paris Commune.[4]

> Paris is not dead, it has just been born,
> It developed in the Soviets and in Yenan,
> Thabang is grafted on Paris. (Ksetri 2004)

The historical line lauded by the poet follows the teachings of Marx, Engels, Lenin, Stalin, Mao and Prachanda, portraits of whom form the Nepalese Maoists' emblem. It reflects the theoretical dimension of the People's War, and the fact that African Marxist movements are simply ignored in Nepalese Maoist writings, as is Cambodia, while Peru inspired Prachanda only during the early phase.[5]

Violence and war

Violence is often said to be a relative concept, the definition of which radically varies over time and space, as well as between the various groups or individuals making up society. The way a violent act is described can also differ considerably according to circumstances: a murderer murders, a soldier kills (or even cleanses), and an executioner puts to death. The perception of violence is linked to the nature of power as well: for authoritarian regimes it is a threat to order, while for revolutionaries it stems from domination and exploitation.

The Nepalese Maoists developed this view, and presented their own violence as a sane reaction to injustice, domination and exploitation. Individually, this reaction takes the shape of anger (*ris*) and fury (*akros*), which are diffused among the people, and lead them to take up a rifle, in order to carry out their "revenge" (*badala*).

Violence lies behind this process in reality, but the notion itself is rarely used in Maoist writings. Its internal manifestation, anger or fury, is—like violence—evaluated differently according to circumstances, ideas and political contexts. The Maoist "anger" procures energy both to the individual and to the revolution; it thus contrasts with the perception of anger as a weakness, or even as one among the six "deteriorations of the mind" (*manko bikar*) which kill the self, as stated by the pundit B.M.S. Varma (n.d.). In Varma's pre-revolutionary understanding, three kinds of violence are distinguished: verbal, mental, and actual. Verbal violence, in this view, consists in verbal abuse, yet also, more surprisingly, in gossip (the suggestion being that it is self-centred, as it may denote interaction with no direct, or even necessarily any indirect, relation to the object of violence). The second form of violence is mental, and thus entirely self-centred: it consists in envying others and wishing them hardship. Finally, "actual" (*karmik*) violence is the only one that systematically affects another person in a direct manner: it includes the action of striking, killing or robbing someone or eloping with someone's wife.

In addition to these negative forms of violence, Varma adds that for the Kshatriyas (warriors) there exists a sort of violence which does not constitute a sin, *pap*, and which has "inversed merit" (*ulto punya*)—that is, it is sinful for all, but meritorious for the warriors. This positive violence (called Vedic, *vaidik himsa*) aims at protecting the people against "violent beings" such as tigers or criminals, which "must be killed immediately, without a thought", says the pundit. "Vedic violence is not violence", Varma declared, while he treated it together with other forms of violence. Their common nature appears in their shared denomination, *himsa*, but they stand at two extremes in terms of moral evaluation.[6] This phenomenon is also true of war. Thus, Nepalese Maoists distinguish "just wars", which are beneficial and lead to progress, from "unjust wars", which lead to social regression. For them, "all revolutionary wars are just", a principle by which "the war conducted by the Nepalese People to establish a new republic against the feudal monarchy is a just war" while the war conducted by the Royal Army "against the Nepalese people" is a "terrorist" and "unjust war".[7]

This distinction was already discussed by the Nepalese novelist H.C.S. Pradhan (1915–60), who defined war (*yuddha*) as the greatest form of sacrifice (*yagya*). Yet, "When war does not aim to cultivate peace by clearing the jungle of aggression (*atyacarko jangal phandera shantiko avadi garnu*), this is not war (*yuddha*), but only aggression and cruelty ... this is not a sacrifice, but a massacre (*markat*) and soldiers are butchers (*kasai*)".[8] In this case, the difference is such that the positive and negative forms—defensive war and war of aggression—are not referred to by the same name, with one notable exception: "A war aiming at fighting oppression and exploitation is a war of aggression, but it is excellent (*uttam*), because it is in fact a defensive war, aiming at people's defence".[9] At the other end of the spectrum, the worst forms of war are "those wars of aggression which are only motivated by self-interest".[10]

Maoist violence (or "fury") fits in well with Varma's definition of positive and detached violence for the well-being of the community. It finds its justification and acceptability in being altruistic, in being a reaction against mistreatment of others, especially the weak, the proletariat. But it differs from it in other respects, since the Maoists advocate a generalised and permanent use of violence, in the form of a continuous struggle or revolution, as the only means to maintain an acceptable order for the self, the party, the country and the world. The People's War also corresponds to the only "excellent" form of war of aggression defined by Pradhan, the difference being that rather than merely aiming at people's protection, it seeks "revenge" (*badala*).

War in the Nepalese Maoists' view

During fieldwork in Western Nepal in autumn 2005, the few villagers I asked to define the Prachanda Path had no clear idea of its exact contents, but they qualified it as the "most correct form of Marxism", which has benefited from a historical and theoretical Marxist heritage and has corrected its "mistakes". Publications by Nepalese Maoist theorists show that this popular view is not far wrong, as the main contribution of the Prachanda Path seems to be not innovation, but rather a synthesis of Marxist concepts. A volume by Rajan, published in 2006 by the People's Liberation Army, examines the science of war within Marxism-Leninism-Maoism and the Prachanda Path. Rajan introduces himself as an "ordinary soldier" and presents the book as a simple compilation of the notes he took during his "schooling". His volume is thus a precious testimony to how the Prachanda Path was transmitted and understood by those who fought in its name. As it received the approbation of the commander Vikalpa in a preface, we may assume that it does not introduce major biases.

Rajan was taught historical materialism, and his review of the various forms of war starts at the beginning: life is a struggle since all living beings struggle against other living beings and against nature in order to survive. In this struggle, those who are strong develop whereas the vanquished simply disappear. This is how dinosaurs are thought to have died out, whereas Man multiplied. The origin of violence and war is then suddenly related to social division, suggesting that the social classes have something in common with species.

Rajan explains that men first created weapons, before tools, and that the first social organisations were intended for war, not for peace. In a rather paradoxical demonstration, this would explain why matriarchy has disappeared, because women were excluded from the war field. The winners became governors, while the vanquished groups were ruled over. Rajan distinguishes three periods in this general scheme: first, the ancient period, when man was wild and used to fight for land and food with stone weapons, and the defeated were turned into slaves or killed; then, the medieval period, when lords used to make war amongst themselves to assert their authority, though strategy, tactics and war leadership were still unknown. In the late medieval period, during the monarchical wars, regular armies were created thanks to the accumulation of wealth by kings. Then, strategy, tactics and leadership developed. The petty kings' kingdoms grew in size and war developed. The third, modern period started around 1500, with the first use of powder for military purposes, although it does not apply to Nepal. Destructive weapons were progressively invented, such as missiles, bombs, rockets and tanks. The reactionaries undermined the people and terrorised them, and finally developed weapons of total destruction, as "rather than sinking they prefer the end of the human species".

Peace, on the other hand, is a period of victory of one party over the other, and "those who sing peace are exploiters, capitalists and imperialists who fight against the people by terror, violence, theft and exploitation". Instead of peace, the Maoists seek "the end of war" as their ultimate goal, yet this cannot happen without an end to the classes, which are the source of violence. To end war revolutionaries are ready to make war, or to make a just war to end an unjust war. The Paris Commune, the Chinese Revolution and the Russian October Revolution are cited by Rajan as "the greatest and the most just wars" while the First and Second World Wars are defined as the most unjust wars for the people, a description which breaks radically with the usual perception of the latter war in Nepal.

A more detailed classification of the types of war,[11] based not on the social forces involved but on the types of strategies and weapons used, shows a first broad division between "violent" and "cold" wars.[12] Cold wars are subdivided into economic, psychological and political wars, while violent wars are first divided into conventional and unconventional, conventional wars then being subdivided into total or limited wars, and unconventional ones into guerrilla and atomic wars. Once again the author is not consistent with his own statement, as he then defines the Nepalese People's War both as a guerrilla[13] (or unconventional) war and as total war (a sub-category of conventional war). We are thus led to understand that the People's War is bi-dimensional: it is guerrilla warfare directed against the Nepalese government, but it is opposed by imperialist forces in the form of a total war.[14] In counter-reaction, the CPN (M) engaged in total war. The new imperialist strategy of "liberalization", "globalization" and "world militarization" has "made World War and World Revolution come face to face" (Ananta 2004). Nepal thus faced the imperialist forces of the world directly, and consequently formed the base area for world revolution.

This dimension gave the Prachanda Path some features of an anti-globalisation movement, and of a Third-World movement, since, among the four contradictions in the world identified by Prachanda (2006), the principal one is the "contradiction between imperialism and oppressed nations and people".

By its dual nature, the Nepalese People's War seems to combine the different phases of the Chinese Revolution, which started as guerrilla warfare and evolved into conventional war, in the same way as it is said to combine "destruction" and "construction", which represented two successive phases in China. The CPN (M) carried out an armed revolution (destruction) and a cultural revolution (construction) in a simultaneous manner, while in China the second phase started after completion of the first. The multidimensional or condensed form of the Nepalese People's War is consistent with the fact that one of the main concepts of the Prachanda Path with regard to strategy is "fusion". This "concept" is presented as the Prachanda Path's major contribution to catering to the present context. It refers to fusion of the strategies of armed insurrection and of protracted People's War, and contains ten tactical principles, the most important of which are:

– *Give priority to the work in villages, but don't leave work in cities too.*
– *Give priority to the illegal struggle, but don't leave the legal struggle too.*
– *Give priority to certain strategic areas, but don't leave other areas too.*
– *Give priority to the work of war, but don't leave works of the mass movement too.*[15]

In a word, this fusion of Russian and Chinese types of war puts stress on the latter, or on rural regions and their inhabitants, on illegality and clandestinity, on war and the army, on the nation, but advises against neglecting complementary aspects. As vague as its ten principles may appear, "fusion" is presented as a theory without which no revolution is possible today.[16] Many other precepts advocated by Prachanda, such as the importance of "balance between political and military actions", or of "strategic firmness and tactical flexibility", were undefined and flexible principles linking two realities, which may be qualified as pragmatism. The pragmatic aspect of "tactical flexibility", in particular, was somewhat developed: it not only allowed revolutionaries to sign an alliance with revisionists and conservative parties, but even to enter the parliament they rule. In fact, suppression of the various political parties was not advocated in the future socialist society envisaged by the Prachanda Path, as they allow the revolution to remain "alive", or to maintain a state of "continuous revolution" which prevents counter-revolution. Indeed,

the Party believes that … only through multi Party competition even in a socialist society can counter-revolution be prevented and proletariat's rule be strengthened … Only such a rule … can prepare the necessary infrastructure for the ultimate dissolution of class, Party and the state. … [T]o imagine a classless state is just a bourgeois idealistic hypocrisy. The people's democratic state that we have envisaged is a state under the leadership of the proletariat with collective dictatorship of various classes of anti-feudal and anti-imperialist people. … [T]he political parties that represent various classes and ideological beliefs will not need to set up separate armies because [their] interests will not be antagonistic.

Prachanda thus suggests that the violence inherent in social division may be contained by a common project of opposition to external forces (feudal or imperialist). Dictatorship is not exercised by the proletariat in this model (it has only the leadership), but by a collective of different classes. We still remain in doubt, since neither the proletariat nor the various classes referred to are defined. Not only will political parties have no separate armies, but the CPN (M)'s idea was to create a state with no permanent army, where the people would be trained and provided with weapons "under certain conditions", in order to make them "the master[s] of their own fate". A strong People's Liberation Army is only needed "while fighting a guerrilla [war]", after which its role is to create "an ocean of armed people" and to dissolve itself in it.[17] In the long term, the main question thus revolves around the Cultural Revolution, which is more fundamental than any political transformation.

The Cultural Revolution is a struggle not only against feudal and imperialist culture, but also against the deviation of the party,[18] as well as against self-weaknesses. A purification (*suddhikaran*) of various kinds of dangerous "pollutions"[19] is needed to develop the qualities of a communist.[20] This purification is undertaken "amidst class struggle and inner struggle", along the "path of continued revolution", through collective and mutual education (Kiran 2006). The communist purification is portrayed as an apocalypse, in which no one is spared, as it consists in "igniting one's own body" and fanning "the flame to blaze it" all around (Kiran 2006). This purification is another war, with its victories and defeats, which altogether allows the development of the People's War and prolongs it: "Becoming victorious one after another over different kinds of perversions, ... defeating different shades of opportunists ... we have now arrived here in this great expedition of People's War" (Kiran 2006).

War is thus endless, and must spread to all aspects of life and to every person, who once consciously and physically armed, becomes able to defend the common interests. The transformative and beneficial effect of war allows the reactionary regime to be set in a New Democratic Republic and then enables the revolutionary order to remain intact, while transforming every member of society. Within this scheme, those who participate the most directly in the People's War, the PLA soldiers, first experience its transformative effect.

The transformation of the individual by war is particularly emphasised when it comes to weaker categories of people, such as women. As a matter of fact, the People's War brought a major transformation to Nepalese women, who prior to the creation of the PLA had no possibility of pursuing a military career, while they formed a quarter of its contingent in 2006. Their motivation and their transformation are here presented in a general approach by Hismila Yami, alias Parvati, a CPN (M) central committee member, then through the examination of some PLA female soldiers' interviews published in the Maoist weekly *Janadesh*.

Women and war

Comrade Parvati (2004) offers a general outline of women's participation in the People's Liberation Army (PLA). According to her, the political wing of the CPN (M) attracts women to a much lesser extent than the PLA, even though military service was strictly inaccessible to women until the launching of the People's War. Although they are said to represent one third of the PLA's contingent in 2004, women have never reached the highest ranks within it (that is, division commander). To add to Parvati's observations, in addition to being found mostly in subordinate positions within the PLA, women were said to be present in even greater numbers in the militia[21] where, so villagers say, elders and teenagers enrolled along with women.

Parvati ascertains the existence of an original "matriarchal primitive system". With the end of this utopian Marxist stage, she depicts the rise of another one, in which women ensured the mere role of reproducing the classes and only played a secondary role in war, as morale boosters, nurses or spies. Women are said to have been active in war only when "class wars", such as the Paris Commune, broke out. Finally, protracted war has attracted women the most, because of the protracted nature of the oppression they suffer from.

In Parvati's description, Nepalese women's enrolment in the PLA is not as altruistic as men's since it is supposed to be motivated by revenge against their male oppressors. She mentions polygamy as a frequent motivation, with women taking "revenge" by sending their daughters to the PLA. The author then distinguishes three types of motivation, according to social origin: among the "Indo-Aryan", it is to escape early arranged marriage; for the "Tibeto-Burman", to experiment new forms of freedom; while Dalit women's enrolment in the army would offer them "teeth to bite" the rigid caste system. Waging war would thus reflect each group's specific form of oppression, and interestingly the groups that stand out are far from being Marxist classes, though in theory the People's War was a class war.[22]

War has transformed Nepalese women not only "in essence, but also in form", says Parvati. Their new essence consists in a new meaning and value added "to their lives and to their death as well" and the new form refers to their appearance, as the PLA has "totally undressed them from their feudal frills to functional unisex dress". The PLA has helped the Nepalese woman to break the four walls of her house, and has transformed her "from an anonymous domestic slave to a very visible rebellious professional fighter". It has helped her to evolve from a savage stage to become a highly skilled technician: "Earlier she had no idea of time … today she is recording time while planting time bombs". "Previously she could only pull other's hair, today the PLA is teaching her to pull 3–0–3 [rifle]". "Whereas she used to pay attention to gossip only, now she is listening to local, national and international news on the radio". She has become literate and has "enriched (her) vocabulary with ideological and military terminologies". In a word, the PLA "has expanded her sphere of activity from uterus to universality".

The uterus forms a quite crucial paradigm in how a woman is transformed by war. She has henceforth found a new form of bleeding, which is extolled: "earlier, she only bled to throw away her menstrual blood; today she is bleeding to throw away American imperialist backed monarchy system". This idea that menstrual bleeding purifies, which is strongly anchored in Hinduism, finds a new extended meaning in Maoist ideology, and in this respect, the nation is assimilated to a woman: its bleeding plays a similar role of purification. In a reciprocal movement, women are said to have transformed the nature of the PLA:[23] they have brought "gentleness, compassionate feelings in rigorous combatant life",[24] as if this image of "fierce rebellious fighters" which was first ascertained by the author did not fully correspond to the image she had in mind. Similarly, women are assigned the same role of controlling male excesses in the PLA as in village life, but this control is presented as a form of purification in the military context: "their involvement has a self-cleansing effect on the PLA as drinking, gambling, cheap entertainment and womanizing cannot go hand in hand with their participation in war". Their role is said to be central in "hostile areas", for they are "readily accepted and believed".[25] More gentle and compassionate, female fighters are also said to be more tenacious and disciplined, as well as more resistant to torture than their male counterparts. Clearly these stereotypes of the female attitude show the persistence of their dominated features within the revolutionary universe.

For Parvati, women encounter specific problems within the PLA, which are related to their nature and sexuality: they "lack initiative", "have problem synthesizing their work", suffer from "inner conflict" which results in "hysteria", show "jealousy amongst themselves", "doubt women's leadership", and are "victims of circumstances" (especially unplanned pregnancy). Their military career is therefore very short: "men well above 40 are fighting whereas one hardly finds women above 25 fighting in the field". The author deplores that the Party did not fix a minimum age for pregnancy, in the same way as for marriage (i.e. 20 years old).[26] Interestingly, Parvati claims that "it is the men who insist on early pregnancy" as "the rate of casualty and uncertainty of death seem to make them keen to leave behind their physical mark".[27]

Women are also said to suffer more often from health problems than male combatants, especially "during menstrual period, when additional nutrition is most required". While she considers that women have periods of weakness, Parvati also stresses that "the self-cleansing system of menstrual period and the biological protection that the womb gives to women … makes them biologically stronger than men" and criticises the PLA for underestimating the fighting power of women. Thus, she recommends keeping the PLA in control, by "militarizing the masses",[28] as if what was not achievable within the armed organisation would become possible once everyone has become part of it.

Although Parvati does not develop her last idea, we are led to understand that women's liberation will finally be obtained through generalised militarisation, or equal empowerment of all individuals. As a matter of fact, several female PLA fighters express the idea that with rifle in hand, there is no longer any distinction between men and women. However, in other respects, their life stories and interviews portray a different picture from the one described by Parvati.

First, contrary to Parvati's depiction of uneducated housewives who leave the saucepan for the rifle, many women PLA soldiers are former students, or teenagers who have not yet started taking charge of a household. In addition, several of them have received a Marxist political education from a very early age. Comrade Usha (Onasari Gharti) recounts:

> I was born in 1974 in Rolpa. Around 1979/1980 a Youth Club named Jaljala Club opened in our village. I became a member. It was a communist club. This is where I received my first political instruction. I borrowed a novel entitled *The Bright Star*. Things were like those in my life. At that time, I also had the chance to listen Krishna Bahadur Mahara telling the story of one martyred Comrade and it touched me a lot. The reason for my enrolment was justice, autonomy and equality. My main goal was to change society.[29]

Usha took part in the first armed raid on Holeri after the launching of the People's War in 1996. She then underwent a rapid rise in the party and was chosen as a CA member on the proportional list of the CPN (M) in 2008.

Like many other women combatants, Usha was not motivated to enlist by any personal revenge or event, or even by women's condition. Born in the region where the CPN (M) was formed, and where the Maoist ideologue Mohan Bikram Singh had been active for a few decades,[30] she benefited from a Maoist education as soon as she reached school age and was moved by its literature: she thus decided to "change society".

The three PLA women interviewed by P.J. Quiers[31] give similar universal political ideals as their motivation to enter the party: to liberate the proletariat, to put an end to domination and exploitation. Several other women soldiers, such as comrade Sanjaya or comrade Dipa, relate their early Marxist education and their first experience with the Communist Party of Nepal (United Marxist Leninist) party (or UML), which did not however live up to their expectations, whereas they found what they were looking for in the Maoist CPN (M).

The fact that many women apparently joined People's War because it corresponded to their political ideas thus needs to be stated in a first stance. It is true that practical goals also played an important role, as it clearly emerges from interviews that the Maoist party offered women an opportunity to take "their revenge". But contrary to the impression given by Parvati, there are very few examples in all the material published in the Maoist weekly *Janadesh* of revenge for the social conditions inflicted on women, such as forced marriage or polygamy. Instead, in most cases, women's desire for revenge, and sometimes their enrolment, responded to different forms of political violence, whether directed against their close relations or, to a lesser extent, against themselves.

Comrade Sanjaya, a Company Vice-Commander in the 16th battalion of the PLA, tells how, when she was a child in 1983, the police killed her father and some other villagers at a fair where people were singing anti-*panchayat* songs. She explains, "UML wanted to utilise the massacre. But UML did not understand the Piskar massacre. They said that they were revolutionaries, but they were nothing of the sort. They couldn't understand the spilled blood. After the launching of the People's War, I found the right party. They understood the hidden meaning of the martyrs and of their great death. They said: blood flows and its price is obtained by revenge".[32] Sanjaya thus shows that she found revelation in the Maoist party: it brought a meaningful dimension to the violence she had witnessed, and offered her the means to respond to it.

The life story of the two sisters Adhar and Ilaka (meaning "Base" and "Region"), who enrolled during their 16th and 14th year respectively, also suggests that they primarily see the party as an instrument for revenge, their revenge for the killing of their paternal uncle and their father by the police in 1999.[33] Ilaka says: "If there were no Maoists, the enemy would kill innocent people. In order for them to be able to take their revenge, the Maoists must exist: this seemed right to us and we started to walk in alongside the party". The sisters add: "We have also acquired the same rights as men and we have challenged the macho ideas that women can't do anything".[34] Comrade Anupam was born in 1981. In 1997, her maternal uncle's son, a PLA soldier, became a martyr. At that time she was an activist in the All Nepal Women's Organisation (Revolutionary), the women's organisation in the CPN (M). "I told to myself: I shall avenge my beloved cousin killed like that. I understood that to avenge him, I needed to join the organisation, so I joined it". She then participated in many attacks, and "cleansed" seven RNA soldiers with her SLR, and fourteen others with her grenades. "When the enemy learns that women are coming to fight, what is their behaviour?", asks the journalist. "They underestimate us. They abuse us verbally. They fire a lot in our direction, thinking that we are weak. But we don't think that we are weak". (Anupam, 2003)

Several PLA fighters were victims of political rape. Interviewed by a Maoist journalist, Sangrami says: "In 1990 [she was 9 at the time], I was at school and I was active in a United-Marxist-Leninist organisation for some years. In 1996, I passed my School Leaving Certificate. The UML party's line didn't seem right to me at the time so I told to myself that I should join the People's War. In 1999, some Maoist friends came to me and I decided to join them". She then retells how she was raped by policemen some months later and finally enrolled in the PLA afterwards. Yet she does not portray her enrolment as a mere consequence of the violence she suffered, but summarises her life as follows: "Since my childhood, Communism has influenced me. I was suffering from injustice and exploitation. I wanted a government run by the proletariat and I had to take a stance to establish it. Being raped also decided me to join the People's War". In contrast with her own statement, the journalist interviewing her chose to emphasise violence and to present her enrolment as a form of "revenge" by entitling the article: "Revenge for my rape ..."[35] Similarly, an interview with another PLA soldier introduces her as "Comrade Asmita, a woman soldier raped by policemen", as if it was the main determinant of her identity. Like Sangrami, however, Asmita puts forward her ideals and states: "I had always wanted to fight for the liberation of the oppressed classes". She thus became a whole-time Maoist activist. Later, she was caught and raped by policemen and comments: "this event just increased my hate of the government and my anger towards it". (Asmita 2005)

Dipa was a student and had passed her school leaving certificate. Then, as she says, "seeing oppression, injustice and atrocities in society, I joined the People's War". She, too, was captured by the army and raped, but this event was clearly not her motivation to join the revolution, as she was already a PLA soldier at the time. Yet this interview is entitled "One can take ultimate revenge only in the People's War". (Dipa, 2004)

Clearly in these cases, physical violence is secondary, both in time and importance, to a long history of political activity initiated during childhood, yet it is obviously emphasised in the way women soldiers are presented to readers. However, this observation should be qualified in that, apart from the initial stress portrayed in the title, which systematically reflects women's mistreatment and/or desire for revenge rather than their political ideas, a balance is maintained, with the presentation of elements not exactly in keeping with the title.

Whatever the role assigned to physical violence by the different actors in the People's War, its presence is felt at some point in most women soldiers' life stories, whether as a starting point in their career, which is often determined or preceded by a father's, brother's or life companion's death, or as part of their experience as women activists or PLA fighters, in which case it is usually they who are the object of violence, and are raped. On the other hand, I have not yet encountered any male soldier or activist claiming that violence inflicted on their female kin led them to join the revolution, though it is said that rape was a regular occurrence even during the police "Romeo operation" which took place before the launching of the People's War in Western Nepal. Thus, avenging women's honour was not a motivation for male revolutionaries. Instead, they encouraged women to take revenge themselves, as clearly appears in the case of Bharatkumari (Regmi 2003). This woman was victim of gang rape by RNA soldiers, apparently because of her husband's political activities, since she retells how these soldiers burned her husband's photograph before raping her. "Fearing disrespect from society and from her husband", she did not tell the latter anything for three months. Yet he was eventually informed by some other means and instead of disrespect, "showed her more love": "Seeing this, she went to work in the organisation". Bharatkumari reports her husband's words then: "He told me: 'You should take your revenge. You too should join the organisation. If you can't, I'll take revenge for this'".

In addition to the desire for revenge which seems to be gender-oriented (as well as being instrumentalised by Maoist journalists), Maoist reports and homage to martyrs reinforce the feeling that political engagement is different in the case of men and women: male enrolment is presented as self-determined while women are "alter-determined", i.e. often quite simply determined by the menfolk. While male martyrs are presented as in revolt by nature, and as fighting injustice since their childhood, female ones are usually said to have "received" (*paunu*) their political ideas from their "life companions" or some other male figure. Take, for example, the case of a female member of the Sindhuli District Committee, as presented by Naresh Shrestha (2005). Shrestha does not mention the name of this woman but simply introduces her as "the life companion of Kamal Devkota (Comrade P.K.)", from whom, he says, "she has received her political ideas" and "with the help of whom and on the advice of whom, she engaged as a whole timer". The typical scheme of domination found in the Maoist depiction of women's revolutionary engagement is also largely interiorised by these women who often formulate this perspective themselves.[36] Thus, Comrade Vina declares: "my life companion modelled (*rupantaran*) me", he who "hesitated in leading me to the revolutionary side". (Vina 2005) Even Sanjaya, who had professed her choices, stating that UML did not understand the martyrs' blood whereas she had finally found the right party in the CPN (M), presents her enrolment as mediated by a male instigator and intermediary: "The person who instigated my entry in the People's War is comrade Akhand", she says.

A clear picture of how men are active and women activated by them within the People's War, is portrayed by this revolutionary song from Western Nepal,

The brothers: Stand up sisters! All together in order to create opposition, To fight the last war which will destroy the empire's palace.

The sisters: Why O brothers? What is happening? Are there some people dying in the country? What is the government doing? Explain it all to us!

The brothers: O sisters! While the sound of liberation is being heard, they kill, they steal. ...

The sisters: We have understood; if it is thus, we are going to revolt ... holding sickles and hoes and all the household tools.

The brothers: Come on, come on, sisters, you should stand up, ... and with the household tools, break the emperor's head.

In this respect, we are far from the Nepalese Maoist images, showing a woman brandishing a red flag in front of the People's Liberation Army, but rather presented with ignorant and passive persons, suddenly activated by males, so that they defend themselves while fighting alongside them.

In the same manner that women's enrolment is motivated by some male intermediary, not by their own ideas in the usual way presented in Maoist publications, revolutionary women are unanimous in explaining that their own "liberation" is a second step, and thus subordinate. This will only come about after "class liberation", which is the immediate goal they were assigned to.[37] Meanwhile, war constitutes an essential period, the only one during which they can show that "women can do everything".

Subjective accounts of war

Although subjectivity is often described as a weakness by the Maoists, it is far from being absent from their writings. It was first expressed in poems, letters, diaries and interviews, while it more recently found a more developed form in whole volumes of accounts or novels depicting the revolution.

In this literature, the revolutionaries' engagement in war is depicted as a self-sacrifice (bali dan) of the material body (bhautik sarir), or expressed as a Brahmanical offering to the sacrificial fire (hominu), as an ascetic renouncement (tyag garnu), which strengthens the mind and transforms the body into an indestructible weapon that nothing can affect. The warrior's initial sacrifice renders him insensitive to violence. His enlistment is a symbolic death and his values are thus inversed; in particular, death becomes the greatest possible achievement, beautiful and desirable in the form of a glorious death, which brings a form of eternity: the martyrs inscribe their names in the pages of history, they become bright stars in the dark night. Peace is synonymous with violence (i.e. domination and exploitation), whereas war is not only necessary and just but even joyful.

> When war becomes synonymous with life
> Let us enjoy it and rejoice. (Giri 2005)

Although they are not part of the acknowledged values, festive and joyful aspects of the People's War are expressed in feelings of excitement and exultation, as related by Maoist soldiers. Even the Supreme Leader of the Party is no exception, when recalling the 1990–95 period: "*I still feel very excited to recall the incident* when I and Comrade Badal were going to Gorkha with army documents, a pistol that Comrade Lekhnath Bhatta had made available to the Party and ten pieces of gelatine, and narrowly escaped a search carried out by Tanabu district's DSP and CDO just across the Muglin bridge".

In contrast to this excitement, fear and terror are attributed to those who remain outside the revolutionary movement: the enemy, of course, but also non-revolutionary Marxists,[38] and the people (until they in turn understand and become enthusiastic). Interestingly, PLA soldiers also recall the feeling of fear, but with the difference that it is not in the face of death that they claim to experience it, during major attacks, but rather when isolated from the group, during missions, or when not yet fully integrated in the group, as new recruits.

More than merely reversing values, a striking feature of the Maoist thought process is how it combines revolutionary values with conventional ones, in such a manner that it becomes all-inclusive. As far as war is concerned, the common glorification of victory and superiority coexists with the idea that defeat and inferiority are of equal worth, in such a manner that the Maoists are some-how always at their advantage, whether they win or lose. They learn from their mistakes and from their defeats; each of their fallen not only becomes immortal but also gives birth to a multitude of new revolutionaries.

The fact that they are winners as well as victims recurs in Maoist literature, as in this poem which lauds the victim's victory:

> By the supremacy of self-sacrifice
> They were vanquished, you were victorious
> By the drops of your blood which flowed
> By your convictions, your ideals
> By the lacerations of your wounds. (Shashikiran, 2005)[39]

The Nepalese Maoist publications present military actions as writing history in real time, and each military victory is said to open a door to another more important one in such a way that all attacks are linked, often two by two. They upset the established order and make the sky and the earth tremble. They plunge the country into uncertainty, showing that no place and no time are safe.

During attacks, the Maobadis feel invincible thanks to the Thought that they interiorise, which they present as their most terrible weapon (*hatiyar*), sharp (*dharilo*), all-powerful (*sarvashaktiman*), and invincible (*ajeya*). Thus, just after the Pili attack, when answering the question: How was this historical victory achieved? the Western division Commander said, "There are many aspects to this victory. In the first place, we have an all-powerful thought: Marxism-Leninism-Maoism and the Prachanda Path, which are are our intel-lectual weapons". (Prabhakar 2005) Ordinary PLA soldiers express the same idea and explain that the thought, *bicar*, confers on them military superiority though they are poorly armed, as it empowers women, raising them to equal status with men.

The Nepalese Maoists thus emphasise the specificity of their conceptions, portraying themselves, on this basis, as a distinct category of beings: the red men. But more than their social ideology (advocating equality, collective work, non-profit, etc.), it is their warlike and violent culture that marked them out from ordinary villagers: their bloody universe inspired awe in the population (even if it was mixed with admiration for their power and effi-ciency). People had very few contacts with the People's Liberation Army. Most of them had just crossed a group of PLA soldiers on their path, or housed some of them for a night, without any exchange. Communication regarding their actions was ensured through printed media and radio, as well as during meetings, with the population in whose name the war was launched being a mere receptor. Villagers had closer contact with political activists only, who ruled their locality. Yet their bilateral communication was limited to a strict minimum, as Mahabir Pun expressed in 2004:

The only way one can survive in the moutain villages is that one should not speak and act anything against them. Even if people don't agree with or support the Maoists, they have to shut their mouth up … The reason I am alive in the mountain and the Maoists have let me stay there is because I have shut my mouth up. Keeping my mouth shut has been the hardest thing for me to do.[40]

The following recorded conversation between a villager and a Maoist commander who took part in the attack on p. is thus a unique testimony. In particular, it offers interesting insight for investigating the revolutionary and "ordinary" perception of war and violence, and their interplay. Their conversation started with the villager accusing the commander:

The Villager: Many people were killed at p. Some were not trained. Is it true?

The Maoist: Well, there were some who were trained and some who were not. They were mixed together there.

V: People say that they were not trained.

M: Those who were not trained, we took them with us. We placed 30 persons in a line, and we killed them. Those to whom we did that, had received training.

The villager received assurance that there were no innocent victims in the attack. Still, he sought justification for the attack itself and continued his investigation:

V: Did they attack you first or did you attack them?

M: First they bothered many people; they bothered many village activists.

V: Maoist activists?

M: Yes, and then more soldiers arrived and they started to say to the village people: "Maoists come here and you feed them" and they caused the people a lot of trouble. They were doing that and finally they said that we were begging. … They caught one village activist. He was beaten, and the people too, so the people called us.

V: Why did they call you? Did they say: "fight!"?

M: Yes, they did.

The commander went on to explain that they received a letter from "the people", and the Villager again asked:

V: So it is the people who called you?

M: It is the people who called us, it is after this call that we drew up our plan and that we went in. Otherwise, why would we have gone?

This verbal exchange is interesting in that the villager situated the attack in its local setting and brought the commander round to this topic. He obviously did not consider the raid as "a turning point in the revolution", as usually presented in Maoist publications, but rather as an upsetting event, which called for an explanation and justification: not to attack first or without definite reason, not to kill young and inexperienced people, and not to execute people (though the status of the victims, trained or untrained soldiers, seems more important than the method of killing, with the commander not finding it necessary to deny the line execution). He finally verified that the Maoists were indeed fighting a People's War, or, in his understanding, avenging them on their explicit demand.

The villager seemed eager to check the morality of the Maoist troops regarding every aspect. He thus inquired about stolen goods, but rather than referring to the weapons which make up the Maoists' valued booty, he was concerned about food, clothes and money. Now that he had been given reassuring answers showing that the Maoist did not attack but responded to an initial aggression, he apparently wanted to check if they were not simply looters:

V: There was probably some rice and clothes?

M: All the rice was given to the people, as well as the very big pots of ghee, you know the yellow and green ones; we also gave them the petrol jerrycans. We only took the lentils.

V: Perhaps there was also money?

M: We haven't found any. Maybe the soldiers shared it beforehand. They found it and shared it, or those who were in charge of it took it away, since there was no money.

The commander showed how truthful and generous they were in this matter too, and rather suggested that the soldiers seized the occasion to swindle. Despite his efforts to try and convince the villager of his honesty and morality, the latter was still not entirely satisfied, and then hinted at their lack of humanity:

V: Don't you suffer when you kill someone?

M: In p. we were kind: after having killed one or two, we felt some compassion (*dayâ*).

V: Then how could you kill them one after another! People say that you lined them up.

The commander once again gave his first answer in keeping with the question, referring to their kindness and compassion, but on the villager's insistence, he evaded the last reproach, and instead offered a detailed description of the RNA soldiers' state of panic: running on all sides, some shredded by the barbed wire, others preferring to jump from the cliff and die, few were able to escape. He had now taken control of the conversation and pursued with an account of the battle itself, saying that they could not have done anything without their "*ettivan*" ("81"). With it they exploded the well-guarded LMG, which protected the camp. As the villager had no idea of what an "*ettivan*" was, he explains:

M: It is made of two parts. It is at least 15–20 cubits long (4,50–6 meters), made of iron and ten to twelve persons are needed to carry it. One alone is not enough. The pieces are taken separately and re-assembled later. … we have an old man with us, who taught us about the "*ettivan*"; he was riding a horse along with Prabhakar, and he trained us, explaining the distance and range to kill.

The villager also showed great curiosity about the women soldiers, asking various questions about them and alluding to their possible fear:

V: Don't they say that they are scared?

M: And what would it matter if they said so? We too were scared at the beginning and now no longer; we rather enjoy fighting.

V: You are not bothered about shooting someone? (It is the second time he asks this question)

M: No, when two friends have fallen before you, one does not see the enemy any more, nor does one see the bullets coming either. Man wears another disguise (*bhesh*) then, and even if wounded by a bullet, one does not realise it. Because of one's anger (*ris*), it does not hurt, one does not bother about one's body, we are not concerned about our body.

Fury depersonalises the warrior, who loses any consciousness of his own body when inhabited by it. In a reverse movement, fury is often portrayed as a personalised force, and external to those who experience it, which catches you and leads you into the realm of death. Later in the description, when the commander reached the point when they were attacked by a helicopter on their way back, the villager remembered their powerful weapon and asked:

V: Did you shoot the helicopter with your 81?

M: No, they don't go under 1,500.

V: 1,500 kilometres?

M: No, metres. The 81 can't, but there is another one that can, the *"Rejar lenge"*. They first made them of 1,000, but now there are some 1,500.

Weapons play a major role in armed action and the commander kept an exact count of those they had seized: 20 LMGs, 30 INSAS, 40 SLRs, etc. In an attempt to bring the conversation back to a more familiar register, the villager then inquired:

V: Do you only fight with SMGs, LMGs and rifles or do you also fight with *khukuris* [knives]?

M: We don't even have *khukuris*. But at P., I didn't have an SLR, I had a discharge.

V: What is it?

M: It is the upper part of a rifle.

As when he heard of the *"etivan"* or of the *"discharj"*, the villager is confused, confessing that he had never set eyes on the equipment his younger kinsman was referring to. He is also often baffled by the latter's language, which is composite, using both their common dialectal form of Nepali (Kalikote Bhasha), and numerous technical terms from English used for military matters, such as *"ofens"*, *"difens"*, *"ranj"*, *"pojision"*, or *"pasport"* (a word which means password in the commander's understanding), etc. The commander then described in detail how he used the "discharge", sometimes even without any ammunition, to "terrorise".

M: It is like that: the iron gun is cut and it has to be well adjusted. It is a bomb, like a grenade: it is big like that and placed in it. When it is inserted one needs a backrest. It doesn't go like that. One has to fix its range and assemble it from the bottom and try again. It has to be held in position ... It is possible to put something in it or to use powder only. If there is no bullet, but only powder, the blow from the powder, if well fixed, can hit that house from here. It has to be well held, with the feet also, and then it goes… fast. For example, here there is an enemy, this is a tree, and this is a stone. It makes a lot of black smoke in front of him and the stone reaches him and this enemy is terrorised. We make it ourselves, I did it myself.

V: Who taught you how to make it?

M: Someone who had come from outside to teach. Today we don't use much rifle, rather discharge.

V: You made it yourself, you learned everything, and now fighting is easy for you, isn't it?

M: We make everything: look I made this grenade, I made this myself, I did it with my hands. If my weapon is damaged, I clean it myself.

V: There are no boys to clean it?

C: There are some in D., above T.: there is a training centre.

V: A centre for repairing weapons: no one knows, only me, others do not know.

These snippets of conversation have to be placed in their context for us to appreciate their real dimension: the two persons belong to the same clan, but the villager is the elder. Whether it is because of the latter's traditional authority over the former or because the revolutionaries are bi-cultural, one can see that the commander not only answers the villager's reproving questions willingly, but is somehow caught in the villager's subjective perspective where revolutionary ideals have no place. From this perspective, he is forced to reduce the raid to a punitive expedition, to deny its cruelty and to endorse a morality acceptable to his questioner. In a reciprocal move, the latter is then drawn into the revolutionary universe, and gradually abandons his apparent condemnation of violence through his fascination with the power of modern weapons, to finally express his admiration for their technical skills and even some connivance with the commander about the "secret training centre". Such a verbal exchange shows that violence is not wholly relative, even in a revolutionary context. Each side in turn adopts the values of the other, these apparently diverging values actually coexisting in the same time and place, and being expressed in a common language, though interspersed with new words in the case of the progressive side. Here the evocation of the battle, the description of weapons leads obviously to a transformation of the villager's appreciation of war. We would suggest that what is clearly apparent in the conversation is probably true on a larger scale.

Conclusion

Revolutionary Marxist ideology played a fundamental role in the transformation of Nepalese society, as the basis on which opposition to the government developed during the no-party Panchayat regime (1961–90). This happened within a context of contradiction between the Panchayat official ideology, which advocated equality, and the *laissez-faire* regarding caste organisation, rules of which were maintained *de facto* and enforced by villagers themselves, following the 1963 code which prohibited any legal ruling on affairs related to caste. This hypocritical or schizophrenic system[41] had thus a legal democratic façade (despite the fact that political parties were forbidden) and a completely different social reality, entrusted to the local "big men". This recalls David Nugent's observations on the period 1885–1935 in Peru, when the ruling aristocracy, in official discourse and political rituals, presented itself as being inspired by the principles of the people's sovereignty, and developed a mythical social order antithetic to its real functioning. He notes: "The elite's active celebration of the principles of equality, citizenship, and individual rights in all political ritual and discourse, even as it ridiculed and violated these principles in everyday life, was ultimately its undoing … it proved very powerful for people of all social classes".

When party politics were restored in Nepal in November 1990, the past repression benefited the small Maoist party, especially in the region of Rolpa where Mohan Bikram Singh spread Maoism in the 1970s. The Maoists had already forged a pantheon of great men and a history of rebellion. They then started to seduce (and frighten) the rural population on a wider scale when their activities became legal in the early 1990s, using cultural programmes and violent attacks on their opponents.[42] They offered a framework which attracted many young people and which formed the basis on which the People's War was launched in 1996. In spite of its rhetoric, the Nepalese People's War was not a class war, and contrary to the Mozambican case, it did not polarise the population on the basis of ancient, ethnic differences.[43] It rather mobilised young people individually, offering them a career, which in many aspects appeared as a (noble) alternative to migration.[44] The Nepalese People's War then fed on itself, growing with its repression, as it appeared legitimate and necessary by responding to government violence. Its rhetoric, frightening at first sight,[45] drew more and more individuals, often seeking to take personal revenge within this framework. But the organisation was strong enough to enrol all the angry people in a common project, which partially took their life histories and personal sufferings into account, while interpreting them as manifold manifestations of the evil reactionary government to be overthrown. It brought a simple diagnostic to social suffering and a practical method to end it. Maoist publications reflect this process well, with a large number of personal interviews and life histories, alongside synopses of various issues, which capture them in a formatted framework. People's War's growing military capacity also contributed to its legitimacy, showing a concrete image of people's empowerment. During the simple conversation reported in these pages, the same process is perceivable, whereby an attack becomes defensive and thus "excellent", and the evocation of weapons' power progressively exerts its power of fascination on ordinary people.

The final resolution of the conflict, following the political alliance signed by the CPN (M) and the seven main political parties, which led to the April 2006 mass movement and the 21 November 2006 peace agreement, disappointed many among those who were taught that "Political power grows out of the barrel of a gun". As a PLA brigade commissar says: "This is not our full success".[46]

BIBLIOGRAPHY

Ananta, "People's War in the 21st Century and Prachanda Path", in *Problems and Prospects of Revolution in Nepal*, Nepal, Janadisha Publications, 2004: 214–25.

Anupam (Interview with Comrade), "Asaltko pani phast asaltma nai rahera ladiraheki chu" [I am fighting in the first assault group during the assault], interview with *Janaawaj* 1(46), 31 January 2003.

Asmita (Interview with Comrade), "Dusmanpratiko ghrina ra akros morcama gaeara visphot hune garcha" [Hatred and fury against the enemy will explode on the battlefield], *Janadesh* 14 (44), 25 October 2005.

"Bhramapurna samacarko khandan" [News section], *Janadesh* 13(17), 23 March 2004.

Bodewitz, H.W., "Hindu ahimsa and its roots", in J.E.M. Houben and K.R. Van Kooij (eds), *Violence Denied*, Brill: Leiden, 1999: 17–44.

Bourdieu, Pierre, *La domination masculine*, Paris, Seuil, 1998.

Geffray, Christian, *La cause des armes au Mozambique. Anthropologie d'une guerre civile*, Paris, Karthala, 1990.

Giri, Kulananda, "Vivasatale bandu uthaunu parcha" [Compelled to raise the rifle], *Janadesh* 14(19), 19 April 2005.

Hall, Andrew, "Himalayan Exodus: Nepalese Migrant Groups," *Asian Affairs* 27 (2), 1996: 131–42.

Dipa (Interview with Comrade), "Janayuddhako morcabat matrai ucit badala lina sakcha" [One can take ultimate revenge only in the People's War], *Janadesh*, 13(19), 6 April 2004.

Kiran, "Problems of Cultural transformation," *The Worker*, 10 May 2006. Online edition: www.cpnm.org

Ksetri, Puran, "Thabang Perisma kalami bhaeko cha" [Thabang is grafted on Paris], *Janadesh* 14(2), 30 November 2004.

Nugent, David, "Modernity at the Edge of Empire," in J. Vincent (ed.), *The Anthropology of Politics*, Oxford, Blackwell, 2002 [1997]: 313–24.

Parvati, "The Question of Women's Leadership in People's War in Nepal," *The Worker* 8, January 2003: 37–44. Online edition: www.cpnm.org

Parvati, "Women's Participation in People's Army," *The Worker* 9, 2004. Online edition: www.cpnm.org

Prabhakar, "Vaigyanik drishtikon ra yojana nai vijayako adhar ho" [Scientific view and plan are the base of victory]", *Janadesh* 14(35), 9 August 2005.

Prachanda (interview with): "Hoist the Revolutionary Flag on Mount Everest in the 21st Century," *The Worker* 10, May 2006. Online edition: www.cpnm.org

Pradhan, Hridaya Chandra Singh, "Yuddha ra yoddha" [War and warrior], in *Aphasos* [Sorrow], Lalitpur, Sajha Prakashan, 1970 (2027 VS); 33–51.

Rajan, *Malemavad ra prachandapathma sainyavigyan* [Military science in Marxism-Leninism-Maoism and the Prachanda path], Nepal, Jana Mukti Sena, 2006 (2063 VS).

Regmi, Bharatkumari, "Aphno sthanbat ma badala lierai chadnechu" [I will liberate myself by taking my revenge], *Janaawaj* 1(51), 6 March 2003.

Sangrami (interview with Comrade) "Ma mathiko balatkar ra bubako hatyako badala purano sattako antyapachi pura hunecha" [Revenge for my rape and my father's murder will be achieved after the end of the old power], *Janadesh* 13(26), 25 May 2004.

Sanjaya (Interview with Comrade), "Janayuddhako antyasamma ladnu ra tyaslai viyayi banaunu nai ragatko badala linu ho" [Taking revenge for the blood by fighting until the end of the People's War and making it victorious], *Janadesh* 14(11), 22 February 2005.

Shashikiran, "Abhimanyulai salam" [Salute to Abhimanyu], *Janadesh*, 14(14), 15 March 2005.

Shrestha, Naresh, "Janayuddhama jivansathi ra chori gumaeki amako pratibaddhata" [The affection of a mother who lost her daughter and her life companion], *Janadesh* 14(41), 20 September 2005.

"Strategy and Tactics of Armed Struggle in Nepal (Document adopted by the Third Plenum of the CC of CPN (Maoist) in March 1995)," *The Worker* 3, February 1997. Online edition: www.cpnm.org.

Thapa, Shila, "Timro samjhanama" [In your memory], *Janadesh* 14 (2), 30 November 2004.

V.M., Kopila, "Ama malai phursad chaina" [Mother I have no time], *Janadesh* 14(4), 14 December 2004.

Vina, "Manaspatalma sajieko euta tasbir, ka. Ujjval" [A portrait which decorates my memory: Comrade Ujjval], *Janadesh* 15(1), 22 November 2005.

NOTES

1. These new principles were exposed in his speech at the Party's 3rd meeting, in March 1995. All of them state, in a different manner, that the Nepalese are a violent people and that they have always fought for their rights and against their enemies; their image as a peaceful population is a reactionary lie. See "Strategy ...".
2. Mainly in two weeklies: *Janaawaj* (period 2001–03), and *Janadesh* (1991 to date, but posting on internet only started in 2003).
3. As expressed by S. Thapa (2004): "You, a son of the proletariat/Real patriot, faithful red soldier/You have taken command/Not only of millions of Nepalese/But of the entire world's proletariat".
4. Kancha (2005) refers to the Communards as "our ancestors", stressing the genealogical nature of this descent.
5. As Prachanda (2006) claims.
6. Bodewitz (1999) has shown that in medieval India, *ahimsa* or non-violence never applied to the political realm or to war in particular.
7. Rajan, (2006), p. 10.
8. Pradhan (1970), p. 3 and 50. Interestingly, Pradhan (pp. 34–5) uses images which became leitmotifs within the People's War, such as: "The warriors impregnate the country with their blood for its wellness. Those who laugh while dying manure (*mal garchan*) the country to make it fructify... All the stars in the sky are ascetic warrior-seers (*yoddha-rishi*)."
9. Pradhan (1970), p. 47.
10. Ibid.

11. For the Maoists, war is more an art form than a science, as men constitute a more important factor than weapons.
12. Rajan (2006), pp. 12–14.
13. *Chapamar* types of war (etymologically "quick killing") are defined by asymmetry or "when one party is stronger than the other". Within this category, the *bidroha*, or rebellion, is a rising in opposition to state government; an *am sasastra bidroha* or revolt is characterised by its immediate result. Guerrilla warfare (*gurilla*) is an armed battle between small armed groups and an army. Revolutionary guerrilla warfare is defined as maintaining a relationship with the people like that of fish with water. See Rajan (2006).
14. In total war, each nation or class, using all its power (*sakti*), tries to annihilate the enemy class or nation. "The present struggle of the Imperialists against the Maoist People's War, which is global, is an example of total war". This war has a psychological form: the enemy uses "false notions" of "terrorism", of "the fall of socialism" and of the excellence of capitalism to influence the people.
15. The remaining six principles "give priority" to: clandestine work, "the rural class struggle", "the guerilla actions", "the work inside the country", "the work of military organization", and "to depending upon own organizations and strength," Ananta (2004).
16. Ananta (2004): "Revolution in any country is almost impossible in today's world without this theory".
17. Prachanda (2006) holds that this situation "will truly reflect the balance between people's democracy and dictatorship and dissolution of the state". This project is however purely utopian, as the chairman guarantees that: "After the 12–point agreement with the seven parliamentary parties, … we are ready to restructure the military organization according to the decision of a free and fair constituent assembly election".
18. The revolution within the party addresses the problem of leadership as "the suppressed class cannot achieve success without giving birth to a leadership from within itself". Nevertheless, Prachanda (2006) does not imagine succession before the chief leader's (i.e. his) death: "[T]his process of producing successors ensures continuous revolution by preventing the danger of counter-revolution that is likely to take place following the death of the chief leader".
19. These pollutions are determinism, romanticism, religious superstition, casteism and untouchability. See Kiran (2006). He also mentions "post-modernism", a "regressive cultural thinking", "pretending to attack an exploitative system and state power" while being servile to imperialism.
20. Kiran (2006): "Firm belief in country, people, principle and revolution, proletarian internationalist outlook, class conscious discipline, deep sense of responsibility towards Party decisions, uniformity in saying and doing, high sense of devotion, sacrifice and people's service, emotional relation among people, cadres and leaders, revolutionary acumen, politeness, farsightedness and high morale, good qualities like high ability to go ahead by acquiring victory upon hardships to understand and change the world are necessary qualities for a genuine communist".
21. The People's Militia is distinct from the People's Liberation Army: the militia were usually recruited among villagers and posted to their own locality; their task was to collect information, to protect the people and to attract new recruits to the PLA.
22. Another passage from Parvati suggests that women are instrumentalised by the Party: they are not said to enrol themselves, but to be "infused": "By infusing

women in PLA it has catalysed the process of integration between different castes, races, ethnic groups, regional groups through inter-marriages between these communities within the PLA".

23. Again a rather strange assertion, if we consider that its very creation involved women's participation.

24. Medical care is also said to have improved thanks to the presence of women.

25. "Due to the presence of women combatants, people find PLA more approachable as it is much easier for them to communicate their problems through women combatants in PLA than men".

26. Parvati does not advocate the use of contraceptive methods, which represent an easier solution to this problem.

27. She says: "there is no dearth of courage to sacrifice one's life for the sake of revolution, but there is still hesitation to sacrifice motherhood or fatherhood". As for women, many "are found to complain that having babies is like undergoing disciplinary action, because they are cut off from the party's activities for a long period". See Parvati (2003).

28. In this process, women should pursue a "continuous revolution" until they achieve their own liberation.

29. Personal communication, 2006.

30. Born in 1935 in Pyuthan (near Rolpa), M.B. Singh joined the united Communist Party of Nepal in 1953. In 1961, he joined the leftist sections. When jailed for his political activities, he met Thabang village leaders and settled in their village to spread his ideas when he was released in 1971. In 1974, he and Nirmal Lama constituted a separate Communist Party; the two leaders split in 1983 and M.B. Singh created the Communist Party of Nepal (Masal). On the role of M.B. Singh, see B. Cailmail's forthcoming PhD thesis.

31. Taken from his film *Between Two Stones*, IRIN Films.

32. Sanjaya (2005).

33. In this case, it is not clear why these two men were killed. Their daughters present them as innocent, yet say they used to take the whole family to spend each night in the forest for its protection from the police, suggesting that they were political opponents. They then took refuge in India, and the killing happened a few days after they came back to the village but had not yet returned to the previous habit of sleeping in the forest.

34. "Bhramapurna samacarko khandan" (2004).

35. Sangrami (2004).

36. This phenomenon recalls Bourdieu (1998)'s observation that many Kabyle women in Algeria became agoraphobic after being allowed to go out freely.

37. As Chairman Mao said: "Genuine equality between the sexes can only be realized in the process of the socialist transformation of society as a whole".

38. Prachanda (2006): "Seeing our preparations, the representatives of reformists in the Party chiefly Nirmal Lama, Ruplal Bishwakarma etc. were terrified". There was some doubt about B. Bhattarai joining the People's War, "because he was still seen as an intellectual".

39. This poem is addressed to Abhimanyu, the tragic hero of the Mahabharata, who broke into the Kauravas' circle and was killed by them in an unfair way. His death is said to mark the end of the rules of war.

40. Interview posted on 07/05/2004, http://since 1968.com/article/50/

41. One of my experiences of this strange organisation took place in 1986. After a long stay in a village in Western Nepal, I went to the district headquarters, accom-

panied by a "big man" of the locality, who had always been careful to ensure that I did not interact with low-caste people in any manner which could upset the social order. He hired a low-caste neighbour to carry our luggage. During the walk, our porter never entered any of the houses where we stopped, sleeping outside in spite of the cold, drinking his tea in the rain, and cleaning his glass himself before giving it back. Yet once in the bazaar, the porter was put in my room and sat around the fire in the kitchen. Detecting my surprise, the "big man" took me to one side and told me: "We are in a communist hotel".

42. The awe and fascination exerted by the Maoists was expressed by a villager who, in 1990, suggested I should go and attend a cultural programme organised by various political parties in Kharra, Baglung. She warned me thus: "It will end with a fight: the Masal will participate, and they always bring their *khukuri* knives. But it is they who sing and dance the best". CPN (Masal), led by M.B. Singh, was formed in 1983, following a split in the Communist Party of Nepal (4th congress).

43. Geffray (1990), p. 40.

44. Economic migration, which A. Hall labelled a "Himalayan exodus" in 1996, directly concerns 10% of the population, with the number of migrants estimated at 2 to 3 million of a total population of 28 million.

45. Even the determined soldier Anupam (2003) recounts this fear: "Before there were no Maobadis. They were using the name Janamorcha. When we were young, we were frightened on merely hearing the name Janamorcha". When CPN (Unity Centre) merged with CPN (Masal) in 2002, their mass fronts merged and formed the Janamorcha or People's Front. The CPN (Maoist) was formed in 1995, following a split in the CPN (Unity Centre).

46. Taken from "Maoist Army in Writing: Interview with Comrade Commissar", by Neil Horning. posted on 4 July 2006. http://blog.com.np/united-we-blog.

Map 5: Sri Lanka: main ethnic groups by province

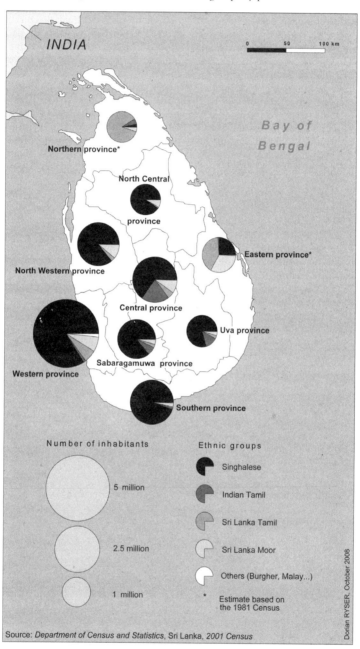

INDIA

0   50   100 km

Bay of
Bengal

Northern province*

North Central
province

Eastern province*

North Western province

Central province

Western province

Sabaragamuwa province

Uva province

Southern province

Number of inhabitants

5 million

2.5 million

1 million

Ethnic groups

Singhalese

Indian Tamil

Sri Lanka Tamil

Sri Lanka Moor

Others (Burgher, Malay...)

*   Estimate based on
     the 1981 Census

Dorian RYSER, October 2008

Source: Department of Census and Statistics, Sri Lanka, 2001 Census

4

THE LTTE

A NATIONAL LIBERATION
AND OPPRESSION MOVEMENT

Chris Smith

The Liberation Tamil Tigers of Eelam (LTTE)[1] have occupied a place of their own on the international stage since 1983 and until their recent military defeat. Their military operations rarely extended beyond Sri Lanka—the assassination of Rajiv Gandhi being an important exception that proves the rule. Within Sri Lanka, however, the LTTE has conducted a ruthless and effective campaign that at one point brought it to the brink of success, although its balance of power with the Sri Lankan authorities started shifting after the election of President Mahinda Rajapakse in 2005. Linking the national and the international was an extremely effective and resourceful procurement network—a "globalised Ho Chi Minh trail"—that permitted the LTTE to wage war against the Government of Sri Lanka (GoSL) using technologies and weaponry that facilitated both firepower and mobility.

Action-reaction: post-independence government and the Tamil reaction

The impetus for the emergence of many anti-state Tamil political organisations was, and still is, firmly rooted in Sri Lankan state policies towards the Tamil communities, in the north especially but also the east. The Tamils had traditionally achieved success as administrators, professionals and civil servants under the conditions offered by the British Empire, across Sri Lanka and in Malaya where, for example, the peninsular railway system was almost entirely run by (high caste) Sri Lankan Tamils. After independence in Ceylon, however, Tamils found themselves systematically and insidiously marginalised from education and the public sector. The Jaffna peninsula, where most of the Tamil population on the island lives, especially offered little opportunity for local concentration and regional development. Marginalisation nourished feelings of profound resentment among the Tamils, contributing to the emergence of nationalist organisations with a separatist agenda. This was followed by a gradual erosion of civil liberties as kneejerk prevention of terrorism and state emergency legislation constructed a legal security blanket for the Sinhalese élite which endangered not only what little post-independence solidarity existed but also the civil liberties and, increasingly, the human rights of ordinary Tamils.

The Tamil response was initially disparate, organisationally and politically inept overall, but indicative of the real concerns affecting the Tamil people. Political organisations were constructed along class and caste lines, which hindered virtually any possibility of a common front. The need for finance encouraged extortion and crime. By the early 1980s Tamil opposition was in place, but it was disorganised, prone to intense dispute, under-resourced and ideologically dishevelled. The Sri Lankan state was better organised and prone to exercise its monopoly of violence with little caution or concern. In 1981, local elections in Jaffna were disrupted by Tamil groups prepared to use violence and assassination to prevent the United National Party (UNP)[2] from establishing a political foothold in the Jaffna peninsula. Although that plan was unsuccessful, once the ruling UNP had made common cause with the Tamil United Liberation Front (TULF)[3] the Jaffna peninsula dissolved into an anarchic cycle of state repression and fratricidal conflict amongst fragmented Tamil separatist groups.[4]

The 1983 ethnic riots were a turning point in Sri Lankan history and the point at which the LTTE, founded in 1976, came of age. On 23 July 1983, thirteen soldiers were killed in Jaffna in a Tamil insurgent attack. The attack first stemmed from internal Tamil nationalist movement disputes, in that it aimed to upstage a TULF convention designed to calibrate the movement's growing communal support in relation to its increasingly hard line towards the Sri Lankan state. It was met by violent reprisals from the Sinhalese majority against the Tamil population, which spread to other urban areas, including Colombo, and the ensuing riots led to serious loss of life and destruction of property.

Against this backdrop of political polarisation between the state and the Tamil community, chronic discord amongst rival Tamil groups and growing levels of violence and repression, the rival Tamil organisations engaged in internecine struggles. The LTTE moved to eliminate systematically all forms of meaningful Tamil resistance other than themselves, not least those who favoured an alliance with New Delhi, such as the Tamil Eelam Liberation Organisation (TELO). By the late 1980s the LTTE thus managed to deprive India of one of its principal links to the complicated political situation in Sri Lanka and became in addition the sole representative of Eelam, the separate Tamil homeland defined by ambiguous geographical contours and uncertain ideology.

The LTTE were formed and were led by Vilupillai Prabhakaran until his death in combat in May 2009.[5] The roots of the LTTE are to be found in Velvetithurai (VVT), a small fishing village located towards the very north of the Jaffna peninsula. VVT was an important centre of gravity for several reasons. The LTTE drew its cadres at that time primarily from those perceived as middle and low caste fisherman and coastal traders, some of them Hindu, but many of them Christian. These distinctions brought internal problems of their own to the LTTE when they began to fracture along caste lines. In 1981 Uma Maheswaran, the former Chairman of the LTTE Central Committee, split from the LTTE over ideological, caste and strategic visions, to form the People's Liberation Organisation of Tamil Eelam (PLOTE) which attracted the sympathies of upper caste Tamils, especially landowning Vellalars. In turn, this opened the way for Prabhakaran, a member of the second major but lower-ranking Tamil caste, the Karaiyar (or Karava), to take control and find a political home for non-high-caste Tamils.[6] The inner leadership of the LTTE continued to be dominated by Karaiyar caste members, which may explain its relative cohesion and functionality over the years. Skills, contacts and networks developed by fishing and trading castes were to prove extremely valuable as the civil war developed and the need for weapons and matériel increased.

The internecine conflict between the rival Tamil groups created anarchy across the Jaffna peninsula. As the LTTE consolidated their political hegemony and territorial presence in the peninsula, rival Tamil groups moved to side with the government and attempted to enter mainstream politics. General degeneration by these anti-LTTE groups into political and social gangsterism diminished their appeal to the wider Tamil community. In any case, Tamils began to leave the Jaffna peninsula and to a lesser extent the East in their droves, for Colombo, India and further afield (Canada, Western Europe, Australia and New Zealand in particular). This diaspora mostly came from the Jaffna peninsula (east coast Tamils were generally poorer and less well qualified professionally). The post-1983 diaspora quickly and successfully established professional and commercial careers across the world, which would in turn become a significant part of the life support network upon which the LTTE depended to prosecute successive phases of the war for Eelam.[7] By and large, however, the pre-1983 Tamil diaspora forms a peaceable and conservative ethnic group more interested in grooming its image in the host societies than in actively supporting the LTTE. Its contributions tend not to be much more than financial and then, for the most part, directed towards humanitarian projects, even though there have been suspicions that not all contributions are for non-military, development purposes.

Over the past decade, a new wave of Tamil diaspora has emerged. The main body of the Tamil diaspora both before and after the war was from the Jaffna peninsula and high caste (either Brahmin or Vellalar), but the most recent diaspora appears to have been from the Karaiyar caste and below, identical to the LTTE caste make-up. Minority groups amongst the recent waves of migration from the north and east of Sri Lanka have emerged as members of street crime gangs, especially in Canada and the UK. The LTTE do not appear to "line manage" these groups but they may profit substantially from large donations from individuals in search of legitimacy and social standing. In France, the LTTE are thought to have gone so far as to outsource their fundraising activities to these gangs, giving them a 20% cut of the "donations".[8]

Military escalation and the internationalisation of the conflict

The growing maturity of the LTTE and their ambivalence towards New Delhi in contrast to their support base in Tamil Nadu concerned India, the rising regional superpower that was at that time beset with communal strife itself.

India's response to the rise of the LTTE was a mediation offer in the form of the Indian Peace Keeping Force (IPKF), designed to disarm the LTTE of weapons many of which had been acquired from Indian intelligence sources. Bitterly resented by all the parties in conflict in Sri Lanka, the IPKF failed to disarm or quell the LTTE, to the quiet delight of even the government in Colombo. The IPKF remained in Sri Lanka for 32 months, losing men, money and reputation in copious amounts before an ignominious withdrawal in early 1990.

The political and security vacuum left by the departing IPKF was swiftly and ruthlessly exploited by the LTTE. At the same time, the Sri Lankan government was seriously distracted by the far-left Janatha Vimukhti Peramuna (Popular Liberation Front, JVP)[9] uprising in the south. The LTTE, however, were evolving rapidly to become a mature insurgency group capable of challenging and eroding the state monopoly of force. The LTTE owed this military power primarily to their very elaborate system of arms procurement developed over time (see below), but they also drew their strength from extremely strict martial and political discipline. LTTE insurgents were indoctrinated and put through gruelling physical training. The use of alcohol or tobacco is banned and extramarital relations were severely punished in the movement. On the other hand, marriages between combatants were encouraged and were performed according to simple rites attesting to a reinterpretation of the Hindu tradition in a secular nationalist framework.[10]

The LTTE were followers of "martial feminism"[11] and since 1985 have formed a Women's Military Unit, the Suthanthirap Paravaikal ("Birds of Freedom"), whose first female combatants were trained by the Indian secret services; however, it was under fire from the IPKF that the first of these "Tigresses", Malathi, fell on 10 October 1987.[12] But even more than this strong feminine presence in the insurgent ranks, which also exists among Nepalese Maoists and to a lesser extent the Indian Naxalites, it is the recruitment of children—especially teenagers between the ages of 12 and 15–that made LTTE stand out in the South Asia militia landscape. And despite protests from human rights organisations, recruitment of child soldiers has been on the rise in recent years, chiefly in the east of the country.[13] The breakaway

Karuna group has recently agreed to demobilise child soldiers in the east; it is unclear whether the mainstream LTTE have resumed child conscription to assist the final phase of the civil war, between 2005 and 2009. During the second phase in the separatist struggle known as Eelam II, the LTTE made their mark in several ways. Apart from displaying advanced resourcefulness and organisation, the LTTE also stood out by the extreme brutality of their methods both within the organisation and towards the civilian population. Internally, the use of physical violence was intended to discourage defection and dissent. Among the population, coercion was used to fund the movement, gain territory and exercise political control.

The most significant and intense fighting of this phase was the battle for Elephant Pass, the strategic bottleneck that provides the only land-based access between the south of the island and the Jaffna peninsula and the location of a major Sri Lankan Army base. However, the battle for Elephant Pass was a turning point insofar as it defined the LTTE as a militia capable of deploying as a conventional military force, which substantially raised the stakes in the war. Eelam II also marked the start of suicide attacks. The LTTE first used a "Black Tiger" suicide bomber in 1987 against a fortified army post. Over the following years, these Black Tiger operations multiplied (240 were listed between 1987 and 2006), reaching their height in 1993 with the assassination of President Ranasinghe Premadasa.[14]

The LTTE emerged from Eelam II with substantial gains. They gained territory in the north and east and the GoSL could no longer claim the monopoly of force across the island. The LTTE also honed the use of Black Tiger suicide bombers as a highly targeted "weapon" capable of inflicting severe damage at minimal cost. Black Tiger operations have grown significantly in sophistication, on both land and sea. The LTTE appear to have analysed well how and when to use this capability and there appears to have been no shortage of young Tamil men and women willing to become martyrs.

The 1994 election of the People's Alliance also brought Chandrika Kumaratunga to power; during the campaign the LTTE assassinated Gamini Dissanayake, the UNP candidate. The new President engineered a ceasefire in January 1995, which was ended abruptly by the LTTE on 19 April 1995 with the start of Eelam III.

The government responded with its own "war for peace" with the primary aim of recapturing Jaffna. Laws of war frequently went by the board as government forces pounded the peninsula and entered the abandoned city in December 1995 after seven weeks of fighting. As the fighting raged in the north LTTE Black Tiger suicide operations in the south forced the government to withdraw troops from the frontline. In January 1996 a Black Tiger bomber attacked the Central Bank in Colombo, killing 90 and injuring 1,400. In October 1997 the LTTE bombed the twin towered World Trade Centre in Colombo, and in January 1998 they damaged the Buddhist Temple of the Tooth in Kandy shortly before a planned visit by Prince Charles to commemorate fifty years of independence. Following the Kandy bombing the government was forced to offer the LTTE a degree of back-handed recognition through proscription, whereas the preferred position was to ignore the movement's growing military power and importance. Proscription by the government also kick-started a diplomatic effort to encourage international proscription to stem the flow of arms and money.

In March 1999 the government attempted to invade the Vanni, the area controlled by the LTTE and the location of their headquarters, from the south (operation Rana Gosa). This attempt failed, and the LTTE responded with Operation Unceasing Waves in November 1999, which established control over the whole of the Vanni and allowed the LTTE to advance towards Elephant Pass and Jaffna. In December 1999 President Kumaratunga was badly injured, narrowly escaping death at the hands of yet another Black Tiger. However, this did not prevent her from making a successful bid to serve a second term in office.

Eelam III was devastating in terms of human security. By mid-2000, one million civilians were internally displaced. The Tamil diaspora grew in size—Canada, Australia and Western Europe for the lucky ones, the refugee camps of Tamil Nadu for the less fortunate. Inside the IDP (internally displaced persons) camps, social problems grew as many began to give up hope of returning to their homes and villages.[15] Development in the north ground to a halt. Anti-personnel landmines became a major concern. The north and the east became war-torn and seriously impoverished. Having no geopolitical importance, the plight of the civilian population in the north was largely overlooked by an international community consumed by and committed to Africa, the Middle East, Afghanistan and, in due course, the attacks of September 11, 2001.

After a brief unilateral ceasefire, announced in 2001 and abandoned in April 2001, the LTTE attacked from the south and took control of the Elephant Pass army base and with it significant stocks of arms and ammunition. Encouraged by the Sri Lankan Army's poor performance, the LTTE fought on towards Jaffna and nearly reached it.

The ceasefire agreement

With the GoSL's "war for peace" strategy in disarray, and with mounting public criticism mounting and, not least, the impact upon tourism following the LTTE attack on Colombo's Bandaranaike Airport, the group appeared to be in an advantageous position in 2001. Nevertheless, the LTTE leadership decided against pressing home its advantage and opted to sue for peace instead.

The reasons for this decision that, ultimately, could only have been made by Prabhakaran alone are unclear. The first meeting between Prabhakaran and the Norwegian delegation that was to go on to broker the peace process took place on 31 October 2000, which means that a decision in principle must have been made well before that. The fact that Prabhakaran stressed above all that peace talks could only take place against a backdrop of discernible de-escalation and a cessation of conflict possibly provides a significant clue.[16] Prabhakaran's decision may have been motivated by a resource crunch in either money or matériel.

The prospects for peace were greatly enhanced by the 5 December 2001 election of the United National Front coalition government. The electorate had developed an appetite for peace and the newly elected government led by Ranil Wickremasinghe offered a plausible and peace-oriented alternative to the discredited and failed "war for peace". On 19 December 2001, nudged gently forward by the Norwegian delegation, the LTTE announced a unilateral ceasefire, which was quickly reciprocated by the GoSL. A Memorandum of Understanding (MoU) was signed on 22 February 2002 and brought into effect a permanent ceasefire agreement (CFA).

In the immediate aftermath of the MoU, all the signs pointed towards a permanent peace. The Wickremasinghe government struck every positive note possible and the LTTE did much to reciprocate. Indeed, throughout 2002 both sides, the LTTE especially, seemed to be gaining disproportionately from the peace process so as to make a return to hostilities counter-productive. The LTTE were given *carte blanche* to open political offices in the "cleared" areas under the control of the government, the east and Colombo especially. The donor community committed generously to the peacebuilding process. Tourists began to arrive once more; inward investment increased; with the A9 arterial road opened, the local economy in the north boomed as pent-up savings were released.

Yet, not far below the surface, the situation was less positive. In Colombo, Prime Minister Wickremasinghe and President Kumaratunga failed to contain their deep and personal enmity towards each other. Despite pledges and commitments, neither could deliver on the need for cohabitation and political gridlock at the highest level soon became evident. Equally important, the mood in the south towards the peace process was informed at the most fundamental level by a false analysis and expectation of the dynamics at work. In the south, Colombo especially, the basic expectation was that the peace process would project Sri Lanka back to the pre-war situation, with perhaps a conciliatory measure of federalism. Thus, the LTTE would demobilise and disarm and join the political mainstream; Sri Lanka would remain unified even if federalised, no constitutional change would be necessary—the LTTE had thrown in the towel. However, nothing could have been further from the LTTE's ideas. The LTTE and Prabhakaran in particular had not given up on Eelam, which had defined the Tamil struggle for two decades. For the LTTE, the Sri Lankan Tamil population and the disapora, the CFA was not a capitulation but a fundamental change of strategy, based perhaps upon declining support from the diaspora and bolstered by events that followed 9/11. The intention was to achieve Eelam by other, more peaceful and political means.

A new series of peace talks between the government and the LTTE yielded little, and they were largely talks about talks. However, the peace talks did throw into sharp focus the gulf between the two sides. Although goodwill and commitment towards the LTTE from the international community remained both considerable and genuine, it also became clear that the international consensus was for Sri Lanka to remain a unified state and that territorial integrity was paramount. Put another way, the international community was positioned to come down on the side of the GoSL over the long term.

Tensions came to a head in April 2003 when the LTTE were excluded from attending talks in Washington on account of their perceived status as terrorists and the LTTE leadership was, because of proscription in the US, not allowed to attend talks covering reconstruction, with all the attendant resource and political implications. On 21 April 2003, one week after the Washington talks from which it was excluded, the LTTE withdrew from the peace talks. On 31 October the LTTE raised the stakes to a level that it knew would never be acceptable to the GoSL and presented to the government its plans for an Interim Self-Governing Authority (ISGA). Effectively, the LTTE were attempting to force a discussion over the meaning of (con)federalism. If the peace process was to mean anything more than a ceasefire, both sides had to begin to plan for a new political configuration and, not least, one that the LTTE could be seen to be delivering to the Tamil people.

Although the outright rejection by the government was predictable enough, the political backlash in Colombo was disproportionate. For Chandrika Kumaratunga this was a step too far, as it was for the nationalist parties such as the JVP (Marxist/nationalist) and the Jathika Hela Urumaya (JHU, the Buddhist National Heritage Party close to the clergy). One of the main impediments to harmonious cohabitation in the executive was the feeling amongst Wickremasinghe's detractors that too many concessions had been afforded to the LTTE, and the ISGA proposal was seen as tangible evidence. This in turn fuelled tensions between the two leaders, making progress on most fronts all but impossible.

Exercising to the full her powers as President, Kumaratunga declared a state of emergency. She suspended parliament, assumed control of the mass media and the Interior and Defence portfolios and called for fresh elections that in April 2004 were duly won by the People's Freedom Alliance, spearheaded by her own party and with the JVP as a crucial coalition member. Mahinda Rajapakse replaced Wickremasinghe as Prime Minister. Although hostilities did not resume immediately and both sides made the appropriate genuflections to the CFA, it was clear that the peace process was in deep trouble.

The peace process was dealt a further blow in March 2004 when the LTTE commander in the east, Colonel Karuna, defected from the LTTE taking with him an estimated 2,000 cadres. The LTTE moved immediately against the renegade group, which was quickly disbanded by Karuna when he realised the scale of carnage that would result if the two sides continued their confrontation. Many of the defectors worked through employment agents to find jobs abroad, notably Qatar, while some returned to the LTTE in the Vanni. Only a small number stayed with Karuna, and thereafter they played a valuable role as government hit-men against LTTE targets.[17] Also, Karuna must surely have parted with significant amounts of intelligence on all aspects of the LTTE. It is rumoured, for example, that Prabhakaran temporarily closed down all fundraising and arms procurement operations in the wake of the Karuna defection, such was the quality of intelligence information at Karuna's disposal.[18]

During 2004, fears mounted that the LTTE were on the verge of returning to war. Violations of the CFA increased dramatically. Under the terms and conditions of the CFA, each side promised to serve two weeks' notice in the event of a return to hostilities. The LTTE were widely thought to have considered serving notice in or around January 2005. However, all plans were shelved as a direct result of the tsunami.

The December 2004 tsunami devastated the northeast coastline of Sri Lanka and LTTE-held, "uncleared" areas were amongst the worst hit, especially the Mullaitivu district. The priority for the LTTE in the immediate aftermath was relief for civilians, which they are thought to have provided with considerable energy. The extent to which the LTTE, the Sea Tigers in particular, were affected directly by the tsunami is unknown; it is believed they lost between 1,000 and 1,500 cadres, but that is not certain. The Sea Tigers, for example, usually hid their boats well inland and fewer may have been operational on Boxing Day (many of the Sea Tigers were Christians). LTTE communications are thought to have been affected but given their low tech character and resilience, the damage may have been both minor and temporary.

The drift back to war

By the end of 2005, it was clear that the LTTE had restored their military strength, although the entry of the Karuna faction into the political equation complicated matters for them. Effectively assisted by Indian intelligence (RAW) and the GoSL, Karuna was able to mount a campaign against the LTTE using essentially the insurgency tactics that the LTTE had traditionally used against the GoSL.[19]

In November 2005 Mahinda Rajapakse was elected President, on a clear mandate to rewrite the terms and conditions of the peace process. Unwittingly, the LTTE were responsible for Rajapakse's election in so far as Tamils in the North were "dissuaded" from voting; but for that most would have voted for Rajapakse's opponent, the former Prime Minister Ranil Wickremasinghe, a key architect of the original peace process, and he would have been elected. Amidst allegations of vote rigging in Colombo and elsewhere, and because of lost Tamil votes, Wickremasinghe could only muster 49% of the votes, against Rajapakse's 51%. Quite why the LTTE "dissuaded" Tamils in the north from casting their votes is unclear. It may have surmised that the election of Wickremasinghe would bring with it some very awkward problems and choices. As president, Wickremasinghe would have been in a position to offer the LTTE a new peace agreement and he would have easily gained the enthusiastic support of the international community. However, over the course of the peace process it became abundantly obvious that the GoSL and the international community were in broad general agreement with regard to Sri Lanka's "territorial integrity". That meant that the LTTE were unlikely to be offered anything like the type of settlement that would have been acceptable to the LTTE leadership and influential elements of the diaspora—although, tellingly, the Tamils still living in the north appear to have wanted Wickremasinghe and all that he represented. The LTTE preferred the hard line of Rajapakse and the inevitable polarisation of positions rather than the alternative. Understandably, the international community despaired.

By the end of 2005, the LTTE strategy for "Eelam IV" began to unfold. Although both the GoSL and the LTTE paid lip service to the peace process, statements of commitment from both sides became increasingly disingenuous. In the east, internecine fighting between the Karuna faction and the LTTE proceeded apace, throwing the region into anarchy, which masked the LTTE's declining grip upon the east. In Jaffna and Trincomalee, the security situation began to implode. Across both districts, the LTTE coordinated and sanctioned attacks against security checkpoints in order to raise the temperature and place certain areas on a war footing once more. This was followed by a number of Claymore landmine attacks on military targets, suicide bomb attacks in and around the capital targeting senior members of the security forces, and attacks against civilian targets in the grey areas between "cleared" and "uncleared" areas.

The LTTE also increased their operations at sea. Through 2006 the Sea Tigers mounted operations off both the east and west coasts. The main strategic aim was to deny the Sri Lankan Navy sea lines of communication to the High Security Zone (HSZ) in the far north of the Jaffna peninsula, which was a strategically important staging post. Without constant logistical replenishment of the HSZ, the security forces would be unable to mount operations in the Jaffna peninsula. Also, by threatening on one occasion an unarmed troop carrier, the Sea Tigers may well have expected to maintain high levels of desertion amongst the Sri Lankan armed forces. Politically, the LTTE added value to their naval strategy with a series of press statements condemning the government for straying into LTTE territorial waters. This was subtler than it seemed—it added another avenue through which to remind the international community that the GoSL no longer commanded a monopoly of force on land and sea, and soon enough even in the air.

In November 2006, the LTTE leader stated in his Fallen Heroes address that the CFA and the peace process were no longer an option. The civil war had indeed restarted and by the year's end it was also clear that honours were far from even. The government had effectively won the campaign to retake control over the east, albeit at huge civilian cost in terms of death, injury and displacement. On closer inspection, however, the situation was more complicated. Certainly, the LTTE no longer controlled parts of the east where, in any case, the areas it controlled were always more diffused than the "uncleared" areas of the north, where boundaries and checkpoints separate the territory controlled by either side.

It would seem that the LTTE fought a somewhat lacklustre campaign to retain what control they still had in the east. The battles that saw the loss of Sampur and then Vakarai amounted to a loss of the east for the LTTE. At the same time, however, the LTTE appeared to do little more than deploy the Makkal Padia, the equivalent of a home guard, conscripted hastily after the Karuna defection to provide a semblance of presence and control in the east. Given the strategic importance of Vakarai in particular, especially with regard to Sea Tiger operations against the Sri Lankan Navy operating out of Trincomalee harbour, defending territory with under-trained conscripts of dubious worth and loyalty raises questions about Prabhakaran's legendary strategic acumen.

LTTE strategy

By early 2007, it remained unclear how the LTTE planned to fight and prevail over the course of Eelam IV. The east was important within the concept of Eelam and for deeper political and sociological reasons. Therefore, to prompt Eelam IV and then surrender the east by not deploying trained and committed cadres seemed like strategic misjudgment. However, perhaps the LTTE leadership had recognised the futility of holding on to the east without Karuna and his supporters. The resulting situation at least permitted a concentration of resources and effort in the Vanni and the Jaffna peninsula, and the defeat of the LTTE was contemplated by the security forces, which were operating with newfound confidence as a result of the success in the east and more recently the north.

More than ever, Prabhakaran remained an enigma. During previous campaigns for Eelam strategy was discernible, despite the lack of communications and policy statements from the Vanni headquarters. LTTE strategy was clearly geared to denying the GoSL the monopoly of force, to take areas of territory that could, at least until the Karuna defection in the east, be safely defended and over time patched and knitted together until Eelam could be said to exist.

Little is known about Prabhakaran as an individual, beyond his rise to power within the LTTE when he established a reputation for ruthlessness and unstinting commitment to the Eelam cause. By and large Prabhakaran has managed to maintain order and discipline throughout the movement—even overseas—through a mix of ideological commitment, a cult of personality and a predisposition towards authoritarianism. Until his brutal death in 2009, he had kept the LTTE on track. Until the last offensive of the Sri Lankan army in 2006-2009 the LTTE, clearly dominated by Prabhakaran, continued to be seen by Sri Lankan Tamils as the sole "bodyguard" of Tamil nationalism.

The proto-state within a state

Meanwhile, in order to establish credentials both at home and abroad, the LTTE attempted to build a state within a state and the proto-state of Eelam emerged in Kilinochchi, in the hinterland of the Vanni. In part, the aim was to consolidate control and exercise power, to raise taxes and instill order and discipline, even down to the policing of traffic—LTTE traffic police became a popular news story that epitomised the seriousness and breadth of the LTTE programme.[20] Civil servants and teachers were trained and parallel courts established.

The importance of the LTTE programme in the Vanni cannot be underestimated. If the LTTE could have put in place enough of the relevant building blocks, such as police and judiciary, given the governance and democracy deficits that prevail in Colombo a more robust case for confederal status could have increasingly been made by default. Moreover, it was speculated by the LTTE leaders that during the next peace process, if the state building programme was well advanced, the negotiation goalposts would move closer to Eelam than to anything else that the state was prepared to concede. However, this project is clearly now in ruins given the outcome of Eelam IV, and the LTTE eventually had to abandon Kilinochchi and all it represents.

Equally important is, and will continue to be, the role of the diaspora. With the failure of the peace process, the donor community became reluctant to fund any project that might have contributed to separate state creation by default. The diaspora, however, had no such qualms and, in all probability, the centre of gravity of Tamil nationalism would shift to these expatriate communities. Such a process has no real precedent: diasporas have contributed significantly to state creation, as in the case of Israel, but only as a part of an overall effort by the international community. However, given the dramatic outcome of the recent battles in the north, any such strategy looks now to be off the agenda—for a generation at least.

The LTTE's transnational arms supply network

The illegal weapons procurement system developed by the LTTE over the course of the conflict is perhaps the most innovative and comprehensive ever constructed by a non-state organisation. Backed by expatriate Tamils willing to provide expertise, organisation, money and contacts, the LTTE were able to trawl many countries in Asia—Singapore, Bangladesh, Hong Kong, Burma and India, for example—for the weapons and non-military equipment they required to sustain the civil war. The end of the Cold War brought fresh opportunities as new, illegal markets developed in the former states of the Soviet Union and Eastern Europe, such as the supply of explosives from the Ukraine.

Entry points for LTTE weapons into the north and the east have varied according to the balance of power and territory. Control of Jaffna meant, by and large, control by the LTTE of the entry points across the Jaffna peninsula.

The LTTE are also thought to have developed entry points across Palk Bay and, especially, the lagoon to the south of the peninsula. By 2007, the entry points along the west coast had been lost and the Sea Tigers could no longer operate out of Sampur, which is the southern quadrant of Trincomalee harbour. On the eastern side of the island, weapons were entering via the Mannar peninsula but this access point has also been lost in the course of Eelam IV.[21]

The VVT factor and the Indian connection. Many of the most prominent LTTE leaders originate from the small fishing port of Velvetithurai (VVT), which is the base for a distinct Tamil caste of seafarers, traditionally adept at smuggling goods across the Palk Strait, the narrow stretch of water that separates India from Sri Lanka. They are also known to have operated across the Bay of Bengal and are capable of reaching as far as Java, Sumatra and the South China Sea.[22] After independence in 1948, many turned naturally to smuggling goods across the Palk Strait, mainly goods that commanded a high duty if imported legally. This strained relations between the local police and the VVT residents, which had a significant and positive impact upon the ability of the LTTE founders to recruit members locally, and over time the VVT factor helped the LTTE considerably to gain a decisive edge over other Tamil political groups.[23]

The earliest LTTE weapons procurement network was run by a VVT smuggler, Sothilingam, initially with the assistance of the Indian external intelligence service, the Research and Analysis Wing (RAW), and the Tamil Nadu state authorities. The operation expanded dramatically after the Tamil crisis deepened in July 1983. By the mid-1980s the LTTE had established an independent arms procurement programme, which even included the production of basic landmines, grenades and mortars. This was followed by the development of a clandestine international procurement network, which gave the LTTE leadership some independence from the RAW and the political leadership in Tamil Nadu. Conversely, one of the LTTE main rivals, the People's Liberation Organisation of Tamil Eelam (PLOTE), was virtually crippled when Indian customs officers in Chennai intercepted a container-load of weapons and, shortly afterwards, PLOTE agents lost a down-payment of $USD 300,000 for a consignment of weapons from Yasser Arafat's al-Fatah group. A similar incident a year later involved a Tamil businessman from Singapore.[24]

The Southeast Asia connection. In the mid-1980s the LTTE abandoned its practice of chartering vessels to ship arms into India and Sri Lanka in favour of direct purchase and development of their own fleet of ocean-going ships. Until the final phase of the war, which saw its complete destruction, this fleet comprised at least five or six small freighters, registered under flags of convenience, owned by LTTE front companies and crewed by VVT Tamils.[25] This move alone has made the LTTE procurement network unique amongst insurgent groups across the world. These ships were only used for transporting arms when needed; most of the time they were involved in perfectly legal commerce, but they became available when required to collect and deliver illegal weapons to the LTTE.

Singapore emerged as the major centre for the organisation of LTTE arms procurement from the mid-1980s, in part owing to the substantial expatriate Tamil community but also because the port city acts as a trading hub for South East Asia. The LTTE were able to organise the procurement of weapons from other parts of the region and dual-use items were available within Singapore, the procurement and movement of which appeared to present few problems for the Singaporean authorities.[26] For example, the LTTE were able to set up a viable communications network on the strength of radios purchased from Singapore, and subsequent shopping lists included computers, electronics, night-vision binoculars, powerful outboard motors and diving equipment.

Also during the mid-1980s, the LTTE established front companies in Dhaka, Chittagong, Rangoon and Kuala Lumpur, primarily to procure equipment with no obvious dual-use capability. Many of the LTTE weapons were purchased from Khmers Rouges members selling equipment across the border into Thailand. The Andaman sea coast belonging to Thailand provided points from which consignments could be shipped back across the Bay of Bengal to Sri Lanka, and the Thai town of Trang also became an important staging post.[27] A textile business, STS Import Export Co. Ltd, was allegedly a front organisation used by two key members of the KP Department[28]—One of them was the head of LTTE financial operations in the region and allegedly carried an ATM card that allowed him to draw 1 million baht on a daily basis (over US$30,000). A number of other prominent LTTE network members have been living and working from Bangkok, and the burgeoning number of tourists visiting Thailand has provided cover—Sri Lankan Tamils no longer stand out. However, in early 1999, as relations between Sri Lanka and Thailand improved,[29] the Thai authorities began to close down the LTTE, shutting down known operations, closing bank accounts and cutting off indigenous sources of logistical support. The Thai authorities were embarrassed in 2000 when an LTTE submarine building project was discovered in Phuket. Thereafter, the Thai authorities became more focused. In November 2003 they intercepted an LTTE weapons consignment being moved from a resort island in the southern Trang province. Some weapons supplies were thought to have been sourced directly from the Thai police.[30] However, the networks in Thailand proved difficult to unearth and close down. As one Bangkok intelligence official complained, "It all moves through here. There may occasionally be disruptions to the system but it's only a matter of time before they're able to establish new networks".[31]

The nodal points of the LTTE networks were the Thai ports of Sattahip and Rayong. Alternative routes were across the Gulf of Thailand to the southern Thai provinces of Chumporn and Songkhla, after which weapons would be moved by land across the Kra Ithmus to the Andaman Sea coast and then across the Bay of Bengal, using either the Sea Tigers or the Arakanese maritime mafia operating out of Ranong.

In the mid-1990s the coordination of this procurement network shifted to Cambodia. "KP Department" head Kumaran Pathmanathan was sighted several times in Phnom Penh. In particular, it was thought that the LTTE was looking for ex-Soviet SAMs from Cambodia. As the Khmers Rouges were thought not to possess Soviet SAMs whereas the Royal Cambodian Armed Forces had such a weapon, this raised speculation that the Khmers Rouges had captured stocks of SAMs from the RCAF, or else that illegal sales were being made directly from government stockpiles. These were the SAMs that were thought to have been used to shoot down two transport aircraft over Jaffna shortly afterwards, on 29 April 1995 (although they were rumoured at the time to be Stinger surface-to-air missiles). As the LTTE operation took root, it was also thought that Cambodia had become an important transit point for people trafficking and drug running. The operation in Cambodia mirrored the operation set up in Bangkok in the early 1990s.[32] The main shipment points in Cambodia have been Sihanoukville and Koh Kong. The completion of a new road linking Koh Kong and Srei Ambel to Cambodia's road network is thought to have given the LTTE additional options for moving weapons, as did a new bridge that links Koh Kong province with the Thai border province of Trat.

Burma provided the LTTE with an even more entrenched enclave (Prabhakarans's grandfather had owned property there).[33] LTTE vessels were contracted to ship timber from Burma south to Thailand and these contracts allowed links to be made between the LTTE leadership and the Burmese military. By 1992 a semi-permanent LTTE establishment existed near Twantay, a small riverine town in the Irrawaddy delta south of Rangoon. This base was used as a transshipment point and a communications facility, but was closed down in 1995.[34] The LTTE also made common cause with the Arakan Army, hostile to the Burmese regime, which led to a clampdown in mid-2000 by the Burmese authorities, who then broke off ties with the Tamil Tigers.[35] The head of the Arakan Army, Colonel Khaing Zaw, is thought to have surrendered to the Burmese authorities in November 2005.[36]

In Laos the LTTE are known to have approached Rosboronoexport, the Russian state owned defence export company, requesting to purchase SALW, SAMs, and IGLA communications equipment, but there is no evidence of an attempt to establish a permanent presence there. Vietnam had relatively little appeal as a source, since the supplies that existed after the end of the Vietnam War have been largely exhausted, ammunition in particular. Attempts to establish new networks using the Indonesian archipelago appear to have been thwarted by some sustained diplomatic activity on the part of Sri Lanka. The attempt to move to Indonesia was a result of a more difficult operating environment in Thailand. The LTTE were able to infiltrate the established Indian Tamil community in Medan in Sumatra. In Jakarta, the LTTE established legitimate business opportunities such as petrol stations and minimarts. In 2007 the Indonesian authorities arrested an alleged key player in the KP Department, who was then extradited to the United States on charges of attempting to smuggle surface-to-air missiles out of the US. The Indonesian government has yet to proscribe the LTTE, but since the Bali bomb attacks there is real concern over terrorist operations, and in addition there is no tradition of sympathy for the LTTE in the Indonesian government.[37] The LTTE have since attempted to establish themselves in the Philippines, where links with the Moro Islamic Liberation Front (MILF) are thought by some to be longstanding.

It would seem that the LTTE have relied significantly upon their South East Asian networks. These in turn have relied, fundamentally, upon weak states and regimes that are largely diplomatically indifferent towards Sri Lanka. There is a sense that South East Asian governments, such as Singapore, are indifferent to Sri Lanka owing to the inability of the state to govern responsibly and curb discrimination against Tamils, who have been generally well received in South East Asia and admired for their professionalism, leading the local authorities to turn a blind eye to LTTE activities in the port city. At the same time, however, Singapore was not prepared to allow an LTTE arms bazaar to function within its jurisdiction. The LTTE's operations in Malaysia and Singapore have been curtailed since the late-1990s owing to the efficiency of the Malaysian Special Branch and the Singaporean Intelligence Services Division.[38]

When hostilities resumed between the LTTE and the Sri Lankan government, in 2005–2006, the overall picture in South East Asia appeared to be one of declining opportunities for the LTTE. Gradually, governments across the region were responding to the Sri Lankan government's diplomatic overtures for greater vigilance against LTTE operations. Moreover, it would seem that the stocks that have provided so much matériel for the LTTE were then on the verge of depletion and, in the absence of major wars in the region, may remain unreplenished into the future. Ammunition is especially hard to procure, which may have significantly affected LTTE strategy and, in addition, may explain the increasing use of explosives.

Other illegal arms markets. Since the end of the Cold War the LTTE have capitalised upon weapons that have become available on illegal arms markets of former communist countries (Ukraine, Bulgaria, Slovakia and Kazakhstan) while continuing to use traditional networks in Hong Kong, Singapore, Lebanon and Cyprus. There are also allegations that the LTTE had links with organised crime groups in Russia, Lithuania and Bulgaria. Former war zones, such as the former Yugoslavia, Afghanistan and Mozambique, provided another source.

In recent years Ukraine would seem to be where the LTTE obtained most of their arsenal, particularly explosives. The recent Tamil Eelam Air Force attacks on targets close to Colombo are thought to have been made using ZLIN-143 light aircraft produced by Morovan Aeroplanes of the Czech Republic.[39] However, it is not known whether the aircrafts were purchased directly from the Czech Republic or from elsewhere, though they are thought to have been built there.[40]

In the final stage of the war, the drying up of the LTTE's main procurement sources made former routes and networks in India of greater value. In the late 1990s the Tamil Nadu connection increased in importance for non-lethal supplies, such as fuel and medical supplies. Moving these supplies across the Palk Strait was relatively easy for the LTTE. The support extended to the LTTE by the return to power of LTTE sympathisers in Chennai, made the re-creation of an arms supply network in India a tempting option, though the Indian security forces, directed by the centre, managed to disrupt such networks.

Domestic LTTE procurement. Another surprising source of weapons for the LTTE has been the Sri Lankan government itself. Throughout the late 1980s, the Indian government became increasingly concerned about and involved in the Sri Lankan conflict.[41] Understanding the risks involved in direct intervention, the Indian Ministry of External Affairs instructed its High Commissioner in Colombo, Mani Dixit, to persuade the Sri Lankan government to "invite" the Indian government to oversee the surrender of the LTTE through the introduction of a "peacekeeping" force. Sri Lanka's President Jayewardene signed the relevant accord on 29 July 1987 and opened the way for the deployment of Indian troops in Sri Lanka. The Indian government also agreed to stop Tamil Nadu being used as a base for the LTTE. However, the Indo-Sri Lankan Accord, upon which the introduction of the IPKF was based, was deeply disadvantageous to the government in Colombo and was as much intervention as co-operation. This aspect, combined with a high level of perceived haughtiness on the part of New Delhi, only served to increase resentment on the part of Sri Lanka. Such was the level of resentment on the part of the government towards the IPKF and the coercive diplomacy conducted by the Indian government that a decision was taken for the Sri Lankan government to provide the LTTE with weapons to combat the Indian troops.[42]

The IPKF pledged to disarm the LTTE, but in the event it was not a success. Despite claims at the time by the Indian High Commission in Colombo that over a thousand weapons had been collected from the LTTE, eyewitness reports suggested differently. Although the LTTE did collect a large number of weapons, they appear to have been cleaned, greased, packed and buried rather than decommissioned.[43]

The IPKF developed and armed the Tamil National Army (TNA) to act as a puppet force in the north-east. When the IPKF left the region, the LTTE attacked the TNA and captured significant amounts of light weapons including GPMGs, LMGs, handguns, Indian assault rifles, 81mm and 60mm mortars and ammunition. In the final stage of the war, the LTTE have been able to rely much less upon international networks owing to the capture of significant stocks of weapons from the Sri Lankan Army. "Domestic procurement" by the LTTE is thought to have amounted to around 10,000 automatic weapons captured, primarily from the Sri Lankan Army but also from the former IPKF and rival Tamil groups that the LTTE have all but eliminated.[44] The current strength of the armed forces is about 115,000, which suggests that the loss of 10,000 to the LTTE is a very significant amount. Moreover, until their defeat, the LTTE were thought to be in possession of at least two assault rifles per member.[45] The CFA obviously failed to put an end to the LTTE procurement activities.

Although procurement and fundraising networks were thought to have been shut down following the Karuna defection, such was the amount and quality of the intelligence that he took with him, and probably handed over to the Sri Lankan security forces and Interpol, that no measures to build confidence or otherwise appear to have been taken in the aftermath of the MoU that brought the CFA into being. The LTTE continue to raise money amongst the diaspora, even if the authorities in countried that host this emigration have started cracking down on these activities,[46] and the weapons procurement networks seem to have remained as active as ever. However, this proved insufficient to alter the balance of power between the LTTE and the Sri Lanka military, and by mid-May 2009, the army could boast of a complete victory over Tamil rebels.

BIBLIOGRAPHY

Books

Balasingham, Anton, *War and Peace. Armed Struggle and Peace Efforts of Liberation Tigers*, Mitcham, Fairmax, 2004.
De Silva, Kingsley M., *Reaping the Whirlwind. Ethnic Conflict, Ethnic Politics in Sri Lanka*, New Delhi, Penguin, 1998.
Gunaratna, Rohan, *Indian Intervention in Sri Lanka*, Colombo, South Asian Network on Conflict Research, 1993.
McDowell, Christopher, *A Tamil Asylum Diaspora. Sri Lankan Migration, Settlement and Politics in Switzerland*, Oxford, Berghahn Books, 1996.

Articles and chapters in edited volumes

Davis, Anthony, "Tiger International," *Asia Week*, Hong Kong, 27 July 1996.
——— "Tamil Tiger International," *Jane's Intelligence Review*, October 1996: 470–2.
Gunaratna, Rohan, "Illicit Transfer of Conventional Weapons: The Role of State and Non-State Actors in South Asia," in Jayantha Dhanapala *et al.* (eds), *Small Arms Control. Old Weapons, New Issues*, Aldershot, Ashgate, 1999: 251–77.
Jayamaha, Dilshika, "Partners in Arms: LTTE Women Fighters and the Changing Face of the Sri Lankan Civil War," working paper, www.jjay.cuny.edu/terrorism/womencombatants.pdf
Jeyaraj, David B.S., "Humpty-Dumpty Had A Great Fall," *The Lanka Academic*, 6 (114), 29 July 2005.
Rajagopalan, R., "Vellupilai Prabhakaran: LTTE," in Harinder Baweja (ed.), *Most Wanted. Profiles of Terror*, Delhi, Roli, 2002: 95–113.
Schalk, Peter, "Resistance and Martyrdom in the Process of State Formation in Tamililam," in Joyce Pettigrew (ed.), *Martyrdom and Political Resistance. Essays from Asia and Europe*, Amsterdam University Press, 1997: 61–83.

Schalk, Peter, "Tigers Evolve—The Liberation Tigers of Tamil Eelam's Developing
Suicide Attack Methods," *Jane's Intelligence Review*, 1 March 2007: 14–19.

Smith, Chris, "South Asia's Enduring War," in Robert I. Rotberg (ed.), *Creating Peace in Sri Lanka. Civil War and Reconciliation*, Cambridge (Mass.), The World Peace Foundation and the Belfer Center for Science and International Affairs, 1999: 17–40.

Smith, Chris, "In the Shadow of a Ceasefire: The Impacts of Small Arms Availability and Misuse in Sri Lanka," occasional paper, "Small Arms Survey," 11, Geneva, October 2003.

NOTES

1. The tiger figure refers to the Tamil Chola Dynasty that ruled over southern India in the 11th century. As a symbol of the Tamil people's rebirth and armed struggle, the tiger also stands in opposition to the Sinhalese lion figure.

2. Founded in 1946, this centre-left, primarily Sinhalese party has been one of the main actors on the Sri Lankan political scene since independence.

3. The TULF, founded in 1976, belongs to the first generation of Tamil separatist organisations that believed Eelam could be achieved by peaceful means.

4. For a detailed and unbiased history and analysis see Kingsley M. De Silva (1998), pp. 161–92.

5. Prabhakaran, born in 1954, joined the Tamil resistance movement as an adolescent. At the age of 18 he founded the Tamil New Tigers (TNT), before committing his first murder three years later in 1975, by shooting down the Mayor of Jaffna in cold blood. The following year, the TNT were rechristened the LTTE. Married since 1972, he is the father of three children. Although the LTTE are a profoundly secular organisation, their leader allegedly worships the Hindu goddess Kali; cf. R. Rajagopalan, "Vellupilai Prabhakaran: LTTE," in Harinder Baweja (2002), pp. 95–113.

6. Christopher McDowell (1996), p. 88.

7. In 2000, the Tamil diaspora was estimated at about one million individuals, with remittances of over one billion euros.

8. D.B.S. Jeyaraj, "French Crackdown," *Frontline* (Chennai), 24 (8), 21 April-4 May 2007.

9. This Marxist and nationalist revolutionary party was founded in the 1960s by young middle-class Sinhalese. The JVP was behind two insurrections (in 1971 and then from 1987 to 1990) before entering the legal political scene in the late 1990s.

10. LTTE women fighters thus continued to wear the traditional *thali* necklace after marriage, but the pendant was in the shape of a gold rectangle decorated with a sword, a sun and two tiger teeth strung on a simple yellow cord instead of the traditional gold chain; cf. Dilshika Jayamaha, p. 8, *http://www.jjay.cuny.edu/terrorism/womencombatants.pdf*.

11. Peter Schalk (1997), p. 69.

12. On the role of women in the LTTE, ibid.

13. Pierre Prakash, "J'ai vu le van qui repartait avec mon fils," *Libération*, 6 February 2007.

14. For an up-to-date analysis of LTTE Black Tiger strategy and tactics see Peter Chalk (2007).

15. Chris Smith (2003).
16. Anton Balasingham (2004), p. 341.
17. D.B.S. Jeyaraj (2005).
18. Confidential interview with the author, April 2007.
19. D.B.S. Jeyaraj (2005).
20. Nick Bryant, "The Tamil state within a state," *BBC News*, 21 November 2005, http://news.bbc.co.uk/
21. Information made available to the author, Trincomalee, January 2002.
22. The following section on Tamil Tiger arms procurement relies heavily on information taken from Anthony Davis, "Tamil Tiger International" (October 1996), pp. 470–2, which is by far the most authoritative account on this subject to be published so far. The information contained in this article has been corroborated in interviews conducted by the author in Sri Lanka over the past two years.
23. Ibid.
24. Ibid.
25. Ibid.
26. Information made available to the author, Singapore, March 2007.
27. Anthony Davis (October 1996).
28. The KP department, called after its head, Kumaran Pathmanathan, was responsible for LTTE procurement.
29. This warming was confirmed by the March 2007 visit of the Sri Lankan Prime Minister Wickremanayake, the first head of government to visit Thailand since the military coup. Cf. Kavi Chongkittovorn, "Relations Becoming Cosier between Colombo and Bangkok," *The Nation*, Bangkok, 2 April 2007.
30. M. Thip-osod, "Arms were heading for Sri Lanka rebels: Arms seized in Silom Road, belonged to police," *The Nation*, Bangkok, 6 March 2004.
31. Interview, Bangkok, April 2007.
32. I. Vittachi, "Tamil Tigers shopping for arms in Cambodia," *Phnom Penh Post*, 5 (9), 20 September-3 October 1996.
33. Anthony Davis, "Tiger International," *Asia Week* (Hong Kong), 27 July 1996.
34. Anthony Davis, "Tamil Tiger International".
35. Information made available to the author, Bangkok, April 2007.
36. "Arakan army chief surrenders to the Burmese Army," *On the Border/BurmaNet*, 21 November 2005, http://www.burmanet.org/
37. Interview with General Perera, Sri Lankan Ambassador to Indonesia, Jakarta, 29 March 2007.
38. Rohan Gunaratna, "Illicit Transfer of Conventional Weapons: The Role of State and Non-State Actors in South Asia," in J. Dhanapala *et al.* (eds), (1999), p. 264.
39. Roland Buerk, "Tamil Tigers Unveil Latest Tactic," *BBC News*, 26 March 2007, http://news.bbc.co.uk/
40. Iqbal Athas, "Govt. takes off for sky war," *Sunday Times Online*, 41 (49), 6 May 2007, http://www.sundaytimes.lk/
41. On this issue, see Chris Smith "South Asia's Enduring War" in Robert I. Rotberg (ed.), (1999), pp. 17–40.
42. Information made available to the author, Colombo, May 2001.
43. Rohan Gunaratna (1993), pp. 219–20.
44. Interview, Sri Lankan Chief of Defence Staff, Colombo, February 2002.
45. I am grateful to Rohan Gunaratna for this information.
46. The LTTE were officially banned in Great Britain in 2001 under the Terrorism Act 2000. In April 2007, France undertook a spectacular series of crackdowns

against the LTTE as well as their front companies and NGOs in Paris and its suburbs, where the organisation had acquired property with the purpose of confining and torturing its opponents; 19 people were arrested for "extortion, physical violence and illegal confinement against Tamils settled in France". For greater detail about the investigation and the LTTE fundraising system in France, cf. D. B. S. Jeyaraj, "French Crackdown". According to its author, every Tamil family from Sri Lanka was obliged to pay the LTTE 2,000 euros annually, and businesses 6,000 euros. These amounts did not include special fundraising "drives", which raked in even greater sums. In all, the LTTE are thought to have collected 26 million euros annually in France, although the Tamil population is fairly small (70,000 people, 60,000 living in Paris and its suburbs).

Map 6: Burma: main ethnic groups by province

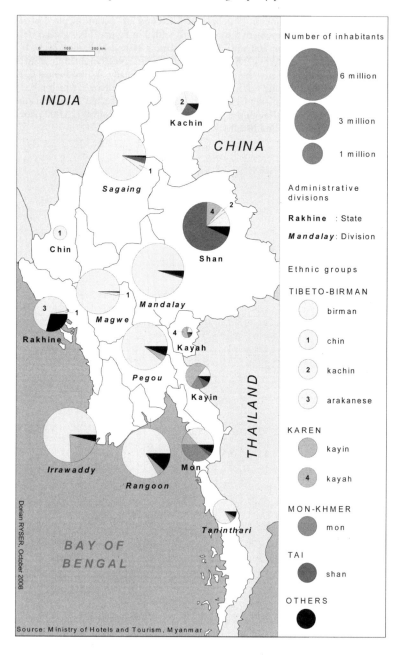

Number of inhabitants

6 million

3 million

1 million

Administrative divisions

Rakhine : State

Mandalay : Division

Ethnic groups

TIBETO-BIRMAN

birman

1 chin

2 kachin

3 arakanese

KAREN

kayin

4 kayah

MON-KHMER

mon

TAI

shan

OTHERS

Source: Ministry of Hotels and Tourism, Myanmar

Dorian RYSER, October 2008

5

BURMA'S MILITIAS

BETWEEN INSURGENCY AND MAINTAINING ORDER

Renaud Egreteau

Burma,[1] a bridge linking the Indian subcontinent and Southeast Asia, is home to a wide variety of ethnically and religiously diverse populations. In 2008, the country had a population of 54 million inhabitants, twice as many as when it gained independence in 1948. Two-thirds of the population belong to the Burman *(Bamar)* ethnic group, or slightly over 35 million individuals, residing primarily in the central part of the country (the Irrawaddy river valley and delta). The remaining third is made up of ethnic minorities (some 18 to 19 million individuals) scattered along the fringes of Burma's territory. Eight major ethnic groups can be distinguished: the Shans, the Karennis, the Karens, the Mons, the Arakanese (with whom the Rohingyas will be included in this analysis), the Chins, the Kachins and the Burmans *(Bamar)*.[2]

Renamed Myanmar by the new military regime in 1989, the country has never managed to achieve unity around the Burman majority. Identity conflicts undermined the policies of U Nu's democratic and parliamentary governments (1948–58 and 1960–62) and those of the military regimes that have succeeded it since 1962 (the General Ne Win era, 1958–60 and 1962–88, and then the SLORC-SPDC since 1988).[3] Successive insurrections and waves of repression[4] have taken a considerable human toll: in six decades, they have claimed between 100,000 and 300,000 victims.[5]

Some ethnic minorities have been fighting the central government since 1948, others rose up against it in the 1960s after the military takeover, still others have negotiated fragile ceasefire agreements with the current military government, and yet others have recently spawned autonomous criminal networks that have taken advantage of the opening of the country's borders after the autarkic Ne Win period. In 2008, Burma's border regions still

113

remained plagued by several separatist conflicts, particularly in the east (Karens, Shans and Karennis along the border with Thailand) and in the west (Chins, Nagas and Arakanese near the Indian and Bangladeshi borders). This chapter will provide an overview of the various insurgent movements and Burman or minority groups that can be termed "militias" in Burma, whether they are militarily active in the country and its border zones or have opted for a truce with the Burmese junta. I will argue hereafter that three types of groups can be qualified as "militias" in Burma: guerrilla organisations leading insurgent ethnic minorities, private armies formed by ethnic groups that have entered into ceasefire agreements with the Burmese regime since 1989, and paramilitary groups that back the junta.

These armed groups maintain different types of relations with the central Burmese state, ranging from open hostility, in the case of insurgent groups, to collusion in the case of pro-junta paramilitary groups. The insurgent movements that have negotiated a ceasefire deal with the military regime occupy an intermediary position on this conflict/collusion continuum with the central authorities, and some of them have literally formed independent "states within the state"; the junta's tolerance of these indicates the extent of the process of privatisation of the state in Burma, particularly in the country's border zones.

This chapter lays no claim to exhaustiveness. It will concentrate on the most representative examples as well as the most significant ones in terms of military capacity, in each of the categories of active militias in Burma, to bring out points to ponder on the process of state formation and privatisation in this socially and politically fragmented country.

Rebel ethnic groups, the last armed opposition to the Burmese junta

Many ethnic minority groups openly rebelling against the central Burmese authorities (whether they are democratic or military) since independence have conducted large-scale guerrilla warfare on their territories at the country's periphery, sinking it into civil war.[6] The regime change that occurred in 1988 revived some of these peripheral insurgent movements, convinced that armed struggle was the only means to achieve their separatist ends. These movements, which perpetuate the traditional opposition of Burma's ethnic minorities to the central Burman power, are currently on the wane, even if they still control large, isolated areas in which they have often established parallel political institutions and a parallel economy.

The Karens (Kayin). The Karens are the longest-standing opponents of the central Burmese regime, both democratic and military. The Karen National Union (KNU), founded in 1947, is this community's main representative body. In 1948, the KNU established a powerful military branch, the Karen National Liberation Army (KNLA), which had as many as 10,000 combatants in the early 1950s. At first trained by the British, on whose side the Karens fought during the colonial era and the Second World War, KNLA combatants were also trained by French mercenaries and later by the CIA. The KNU positioned itself ideologically (and tactically) as an opponent of General Ne Win's "socialist" regime, but also of the rebels of the Communist Party of Burma (CPB) scattered throughout the country. Over time, the Karens have managed to set up a state within a state ("Kawthoolei" or "Land without evil" in the Karen language) in the territories it has controlled for nearly six decades, the borders of which fluctuate depending on the success of the Burmese armed forces (*Tatmadaw*) offensives. This state-within-the-state has formed not only its own "army" but also its own government, civilian administration and educational system.[7] This parallel political structure is managed from a distance, since most of the KNU political leaders live in Thailand, in the vicinity of Mae Sot. The insurgent leaders enjoy the tacit protection of the Thai authorities, and this patronage benefits not only the Karen militia but also the Thai army and intelligence services, which have long viewed this insurgent movement as an instrument of pressure against Thailand's Burmese neighbour, its historic rival. Most of all, this "strategic partnership" between Bangkok and the Karen insurgents has opened up these regions, with bountiful natural resources that escape control of the SPDC, to Thai entrepreneurs (particularly in the logging industry).

Strengthened by the ties they have formed with Burmese students and dissidents behind the popular uprising of 1988,[8] the Karens took the lead in attracting media coverage of the Burmese civil war, reignited by the coup d'état in September 1988, and the SLORC's refusal to recognise the outcome of the democratic elections of 27 May 1990. Thus the All Burma Student Democratic Front (ABSDF, founded in November 1988) and the National Coalition Government of the Union of Burma (NCGUB, founded in December 1990), two of the main Burmese dissident groups, were founded in Karen country, and most of the foreign journalists following the events at the time transited through these regions secretly, thereby benefiting the KNU and KNLA financially and in terms of media coverage. In recent years, the Karen guerrilla war effort has been considerably weakened, owing to a decline in media interest, the exhaustion of its troops (whatever the KNU and KNLA cadres might claim),[9] and especially dissension within the Karen population. In 1994, the first split occurred between Christian and Buddhist Karen leaders; the majority of the urban Karen elite as well as the KNU leaders and officers of the KNLA are Christians—Baptists, Methodists and Seventh-Day Adventists, like General Bo Mya, the historic leader who died in December 2006—whereas a large segment of Burma's Karen population remains Buddhist. Backed by the SLORC military intelligence services, a few Buddhist Karen officers and combatants thus formed the Democratic Karen Buddhist Army (DKBA), which has been fighting fiercely alongside the Burmese army (also predominantly Buddhist) against the KNLA since then.[10]

More *Tatmadaw* offensives, and the capture of Manerplaw (KNLA troop headquarters in the Karen State) in January 1995 thanks to intelligence collected by former KNU activists who had gone over to the DKBA, dealt a severe blow to the Karen rebels' military capabilities, forcing them since then to restrict their action to defensive guerrilla actions in the mountains and jungles along the Thai border. In January 2007, another split occurred when the 7th Brigade of the KNLA (made up of about 300 men) chose to negotiate a separate peace agreement with the SPDC because of divergences between its officers and other KNU leaders following General Bo Mya's death.[11] The assassination of the KNU's revered general secretary, Padoh Mahn Shah, in February 2008 further illustrated the difficulties of an insurgent group that has constantly faced internecine rivalries.[12] Yet the KNU still boasts anywhere from 4,000 to 5,000 trained and equipped combatants, and does not yet seem prepared to give up armed struggle despite attempted negotiations begun with the SPDC in 2003–4 (brought to a halt in October 2004 because of the eviction of General Khin Nyunt, the main architect of the junta's ceasefire policy of the early 1990s). Confronted each year with counterinsurgency operations led by the Tatmadaw, the Karens are one of the minorities that have suffered most from Burma's internal conflicts.[13] However, thanks to financial support from a large Karen community in exile in the West, ties established with Christian militant networks in the United States, Britain and Australia, and especially proximity with Thailand and the cordial and business relations established with the Thai army (as well as the banks and companies that it controls), the Karens have the means to subsist on their lands today. Forest concessions granted to rich Thai entrepreneurs and taxes on trade (in licit and illicit goods) through Karen territory ensure minimal revenues for the guerrilla operations. It should be pointed out that the KNU has always claimed that it has never been involved in drug trafficking,[14] even though poppies are cultivated and processed into opium in the region.[15]

The Karennis (Kayah). The Karennis (Kayah), having been relatively independent during the colonial period under an agreement with the British in 1875 that granted them similar status to the princely states in British India, were incorporated by force into the Union of Burma by the U Nu government in 1948. In the first year of independence their opposition took the form of armed resistance, waged in close political collaboration with the Karens, to whom they are ethnically akin. The Karenni insurgency was nevertheless much weaker in intensity than the Karens', and the Karenni National Organisation (KNO) and then the Karenni National Progressive Party (KNPP, founded in 1957) were unable to gain a strong foothold before the 1970s, their leaders being systematically victims of betrayal and/or arrest. The armed branch of the KNPP (the Karenni Army or KA) expanded considerably in 1974, following the promulgation of the new centralising Constitution crafted by Ne Win.[16] The KA survives today with about 1,000 fairly well-equipped combatants. Over the years, the KNPP and the KA have followed the model offered by the Karens, setting up parallel institutions (with posts of prime minister, foreign minister, etc.) on their territory, which borders the Thai region of Mae Hong Son. Exhausted by successive Tatmadaw campaigns, the Karenni leaders finally broke down and negotiated with the intelligence services of General Khin Nyunt during the years 1994–95. A ceasefire was signed by the KNPP in March 1995. It was nevertheless violated in July 1995, three months after it was adopted. This is the only example of a broken ceasefire in Burma. Since then, the KNPP and the KA have endured brutal *Tatmadaw* offensives despite a brief military truce in early 2004, after Khin Nyunt invited KNPP leaders to the negotiating table.[17] The guerrilla resistance is nevertheless sustained financially by Christian networks abroad (US, British, etc.), various forms of cross-border trafficking (with Thailand), and all manner of taxes.[18]

The Shans (T'ai). Residing in the country's northeast, the Shans represent around 9% of the Burmese population (about 5 million inhabitants). The main Shan resistance movements were formed in the late 1950s in response to the authoritarian positions taken by the interim military government led by Ne Win (1958–60) and the refusal to grant any secession rights to the ethnic groups ten years after independence. It then developed in reaction to repression campaigns targeting Shan princes (and their noble status), after the 1962 coup. Various armed groups have thus been formed in the northeast of Burma: the Shan State Independence Army (SSIA, founded in 1960), the Shan National United Front (SNUF, founded as the SSIA political arm in 1961), the Shan National Army (SNA, founded in 1961 near Kengtung) and especially the Shan State Army (SSA, founded in 1964 and actually joining forces of the SSIA, the SNUF and Kokang and Akha factions), which in the 1960s became one of the main armed opposition groups to the Ne Win government (with the CPB, the KNU and the KIO/A Kachins). A major armed force deriving its livelihood primarily from opium cultivation and the heroin trade,[19] the Shan rebels have counted as many as 10,000 combatants, and recovered some of the Kuomintang underground infrastructure (men, bases, roads) of the 1950s. In 1971, the SSA established a political branch (the Shan State Progressive Party).[20] The opening of negotiations between ethnic minorities and the SLORC in 1989 caused it to implode, given that most of its cadres living along the Chinese border opted to sign a ceasefire agreement with the Burmese military regime in September 1989, thus giving birth to the SSA-North (see below). A small portion of its activists nevertheless decided to pursue the fight (SSA-South) or join the militia of the drug lord Khun Sa (Mong Taï Army, or MTA), then in full economic expansion and in the process of controlling all of the region's drug traffic, as will be seen further on. Since Khun Sa's surrender to the junta in 1996, only the SSA-South (two or three thousand men) and the Shan United Revolutionary Army (SURA, between one and two thousand men, often veterans of Khun Sa's private army who converted after this militia was dissolved in 1996) are still fighting against the central Burmese regime.[21] Many Shan leaders live in exile today in Thailand or North America, and are still demanding independence for the Shan states of Burma, at odds with the democratic ambitions of the Burman civilian opposition led by Aung San Suu Kyi and the federal aspirations proposed by other minorities (Karens, Chins).

The Nagas. The Nagas are spread over India and Burma (about 150,000 to 200,000 on Burmese territory, as opposed to 250,000 to 300,000 on the Indian side), where they occupy one of the most inaccessible regions, the Naga Hills. Most of them were converted to Christianity under the British in the 19th and 20th centuries. Insurgents since 1947, revolting against both the Indian and Burmese governments, they formed a powerful armed force in the 1950s and 60s, benefiting from logistic and financial support from Mao's China. Despite the creation of the federal state of Nagaland in India (1963), the Naga struggle continues, particularly via the National Socialist Council of Nagaland (NSCN), formed in 1980. A split nevertheless occurred in 1988 following the demarcation of the Indian-Burmese border, leaving one group dominant in Burmese territory (NSCN-K or Khaplang faction) and the other a majority on Indian soil (NSCN-IM, or Isaak-Muivah faction).[22] The NSCN-K (which is reported to have about seven to eight hundred highly-armed men and some four to five thousand sympathisers) is mainly present in the Sagaing Division and the west of the Kachin state, where it shares many training camps with the United Liberation Front of Asom (ULFA), the main anti-India separatist group in Assam. Even though its popular base is located in Indian Nagaland and Manipur, the NSCN-IM remains present in Burma also, with some 500 men in isolated camps in the Sagaing Division. Since General Than Shwe's official visit to India in October 2004, India and Burma have been attempting to further their cooperation in counterinsurgency operations. The NSCN-K is one of the privileged targets of this new military partnership, but despite efforts made by India (supply of arms to the *Tatmadaw*, intelligence-sharing)[23] the Naga rebels continue to disrupt the internal policies of these two countries.[24]

The Chins. Ethnically related to the Mizos in India, Christianised in the 19th and 20th centuries, the Chins are also long-standing opponents of the country's massive "Burmanisation" programmes. Chin insurrections however did not begin until the 1960s with the creation of the Chin Independence Army (CIA) in 1961. Formed in opposition to U Nu's democratic government that attempted to impose Buddhism as the state religion in 1961, this army lasted under Ne Win's military regime, which confined it to the northern mountains of Arakan. The movement reawakened in the 1980s with the formation in 1985 of the Chin National Front (CNF) and its armed branch (Chin National Army, CNA), which was trained by Kachin rebels. Still in open conflict with the Burmese military regime,[25] but enjoying very little outside support except from Western Christian militant networks or the Chin diaspora, the CNA is reported only to have 2–300 men-in-arms today among a Chin population of over one million individuals (3% of the population), forty or fifty thousand of whom are still refugees in India.[26]

The Arakanese (Rakhine). Arakan State is located at the border with Bangladesh, which has had a strong cultural influence on it. The Arakanese (Rakhine) are reported to number some 1.5 million (or 3 to 4% of the Burmese population). Arakanese insurgency in opposition to the central Burmese authorities dates back many years: a rebellious monk (U Sein Da) initiated a vast popular anti-Burman movement following the Second World War (1945–46). Two types of separatist movements can be clearly distinguished in Arakan: anti-junta Arakanese Buddhist movements and Islamist-leaning Muslim movements. The main regional opposition front against the central Burmese government is the National United Front of Arakan (NUFA, founded in 1988), which ten years later became the National United Party of Arakan (NUPA). A primarily Buddhist movement (although not bent on fighting Muslims), bringing together more or less violent organisations created in Arakan since independence (the Arakan National Liberation Party in 1960, the Arakan Independence Party/Organisation in 1970, the Arakan Liberation Party/Army in 1972, all of which were trained by the Kachins or the Karens), the NUPA today is more inclined to take part in political rather than armed combat, for lack of both combatants and funds, even if there still are armed fringes confined to the swamps along the border with Bangladesh.[27] The Arakan Liberation Army (ALA), the only armed force of any consequence, reportedly has only about one hundred active men.[28] Alongside the separatist parties, there has been an emergence of Muslim organisations that primarily defend the interests of the non-Rakhine Rohingya minority.[29]

The Rohingyas. The first uprising of this Muslim minority of Bengali origin (Chittagong region) occurred in the 1950s, tacitly backed by East Pakistan (Bangladesh from 1971). The 1960s were marked by a new wave of revolts, organised particularly by the Rohingya Independent Force (RIF) founded in 1963. Shortly after his coup d'état, Ne Win banned Rohingya organisations which until then had remained legal (such as the Rohingya Students Union and the Rohingya Youth League), and launched a first massive military offensive in Arakan, prompting tens of thousands of Rohingyas to flee to East Pakistan. Weakened despite its (rather ambiguous) relations with Pakistan, the RIF became the Rohingya Patriotic Front (RPF) in 1974, which in turn succumbed to internal dissensions in 1985. From the late 1970s, Rohingya movements gained strength after the second wave of offensives by the Tatmadaw in 1978. Over the 1980s, the insurgent movement underwent both a quantitative and a qualitative change. The arrival of funding from the Gulf gave rise to new armed groups, such as the Rohingya Solidarity Organisation (RSO, founded in 1982) and the Arakan Rohingya Islamic Front (ARIF, a splinter group of the RSO formed in 1986), better equipped and more religious than their predecessors. The new Burmese junta (SLORC) in turn organised a third wave of repression against the Rohingyas in late 1991, causing some 250,000 refugees to flee to Bangladesh and reviving territorial aspirations paired with religious demands, such as the application of *Sharia* law, from Rohingya militants.

119

Several movements made a political (but not military) merger in 1998 under the name of Arakan Rohingya National Organisation (ARNO), though an RSO subgroup hostile to the ARNO still remains active with about 300 men (whereas the ARIF reportedly only has about 200 combatants). Rohingya movements form a very loose conglomeration that is difficult to grasp. However, fallacies about their alleged connections to international jihadist groups—such as al-Qaeda's outfits—have stigmatised a community that is no longer welcomed in either Burma or Bangladesh (a number of Rohingyas took part in the Afghan jihad in the 1980s, usually as porters or cooks rather than active combatants).[30]

In addition, Burma harbours a few small non-Rohingya groups such as the Muslim Liberation Organisation, MLO, founded in 1988. These marginal militias (they only have a few dozen combatants) have established financial and ideological links with the Bangladeshi branch of the Jama'at-e Islami, but it would appear that they are no longer active in the 2000s. Chinese and Indian Muslims in northern Burma bordering China's Yunnan province have never formed a political or military organisation.

Many ethnic groups in Burma thus have a long history of armed struggle against the central Burman authorities. Usually organised as militias, sometimes as veritable parallel armies (like the Karens or the Shans), most of these insurgents have maintained underground political and trade relations between them and/or with the outside world. The largest and most coherent "common front" was the National Democratic Front (NDF). In 1976, it brought together the KNU, the KNPP and the ALP, onto which a few Lahu and Shan movements fastened themselves during the 1970s. They were joined later by the Pa' O militias (1980), the Mons (1982), the KIO (1983) and the Chins (1989), but this front gradually fell apart following the ceasefire that the SLORC negotiated with some of its most influential members between 1989 and 1993. The ABSDF and some dozen tiny Burman and Muslim groups were incorporated into the NDF in 1988, giving rise to the Democratic Alliance of Burma (DAB), of which the Karen General Bo Mya was president. This alliance was also shattered when the Kachins signed a preliminary agreement with the military regime in Rangoon in October 1993. The remaining military alliance between the ALP, the CNF, the KNPP, the KNU and the SSA-S is a mere façade, the links among them having slackened owing to the extension of Burmese army control to more territory.[31]

This overview of insurgent movements involved in frontal opposition to the junta suggests that despite their still large numbers, these movements today are in full political and military decline. They no longer represent a significant military threat to the junta, although the Burmese government obstinately continues to assert the contrary and every year launches widespread anti-insurgency campaigns. Most of these armed militias are barely surviving on the fringes of the country. They usually rely on various forms of trafficking to make up for their lack of outside "patrons" (except for the Karens). In fact, except in Thailand and North America as regards the Karens, in India for the Chins and the Nagas, in the Gulf countries and Malaysia for the Rohingyas, the Burmese diaspora is rather small. The platforms that for a time brought these insurrections together against the Burmese junta are now moribund, from a political standpoint among others, in that the ethnic minorities are far from being in agreement about their demands. It would thus appear that the main beneficiaries of the new political configuration in Burma are the ethnic militias that have signed ceasefires with the junta since the early 1990s.

Ceasefire groups: vassalisation or formation of ethnic counter-states?

Ceasefire groups are those ethnic militias whose leaders since 1989 have opted for a tactical arrangement with the Burmese junta (SLORC/SPDC). By virtue of these "gentlemen's agreements", tribal groups, warlords and local community leaders enjoy a more or less extensive degree of autonomy on their territories in exchange for giving up active armed opposition to the Burmese central regime. These ethnic minorities have thus preferred economic pragmatism to nationalist idealism, at least at first, until a new federal constitution is adopted and fully implemented by the central government.[32] Several waves of ceasefires took place between 1989 and 1995, particularly following the more efficient counterinsurgency offensives led by a modernised and newly Chinese-equipped *Tatmadaw*, and the peace talks offered by Khin Nyunt's military intelligence services.[33]

Signatories of the first wave of ceasefires (1989)

The Was. One of the most isolated ethnic groups in Burma, the Was live in the outermost reaches of Yunnan. During the colonial period, the British hardly ventured into these mountainous areas, considering Wa areas as a perfect buffer zone. Throughout the 1950s and 60s, Was struggled to preserve the natural autonomy bestowed by their geographic isolation. Some joined the Chinese Kuomintang forces (withdrawn into the Golden Triangle after 1949), whereas others, in greater numbers, turned toward the CPB of which many Wa leaders were members, more or less sharing the movement's Maoist ideology. Following the collapse of the CPB in March 1989, young Wa nationalist leaders (as well as certain Kokaungs, Kachins and Sino-Shans) parted ways with the former Communist Party bosses and founded one of the richest and most powerful militias in the Sino-Burmese frontier region, the United Wa State Army (UWSA). This militia was the first to negotiate with the new junta that had arrived in power in Rangoon a year earlier, and it concluded the first ceasefire agreement between the SLORC and these ethnic militias that grew out of the collapse of the CPB. Since then, the UWSA has become the largest private army in all of northern Burma. With nearly 20,000 very well equipped men at its disposal, compared with 8–10,000 at the time of the 1989 mutiny (it has benefited since 1996 from

Khun Sa's MTA surrender), it has organised itself around two very lucrative activities: drug trafficking (opium, heroin and since the late 1990s, methamphetamines, called *yaa baa* in Thailand)[34] and smuggling of legal goods over the borders with neighbouring China and Thailand. The Wa border zones (Chinese Yunnan also has several Wa administrative zones) have become some of the most prosperous regions along the Sino-Burmese border.[35] These production, trafficking and cross-border trade activities escape the Burmese central government almost entirely, as it has no official representative in Wa territory (except for delegates from the Immigration Office and the Ministry of Agriculture in charge of monitoring the development of poppy substitute crops), demonstrating the degree of freedom that the Wa militia has enjoyed on its soil since the end of the 1980s. The SLORC-SPDC, tolerating this state of affairs, has almost no means of pressure over the UWSA.

While this freedom of action has come at a price (participation in official government dealings and possibly the payment of unofficial taxes), the UWSA still has considerable room for manoeuvre. Certainly, cordial relations have been established between the Was and the Burmese regime, the UWSA for instance having accepted to take part in the political transition process offered by the military regime in 2003 to lead Burma towards a "disciplined democracy".[36] Not only did the UWSA participate in the regime-controlled National Convention reconvened in 2004, but it seems to be ready to contest the 2010 parliamentary elections also proposed by the Burmese junta. But in October 2004 the fall of General Khin Nyunt, the Was' principal ally in the Burmese junta, largely loosened these pragmatic—because potentially very lucrative—ties. Bao Yuxiang (or "Chairman Bao"), the undisputed UWSA leader still wanted by international anti-narcotics agencies, remains one of the richest—and most ill-famed—figures in the region. Beside, the strategic resettlements of dozens of Wa families near the Thai borders that began in the late 1990s created new socio-political dividing lines in the southern Shan State, with drug production and trafficking increasing and local Wa militias rising independently from the northern UWSA headquarters.[37]

The Kokangs. The Kokangs, neighbours and cousins of the Was, also migrated from China (Yunnan), and live in a high-altitude region where rice cannot be grown and the only truly lucrative crop remains opium. Like the Was, they for the most part supported the CPB troops until their breakup in 1989. A few Kokang leaders later founded their own militant group, the Myanmar National Democratic Alliance Party (MNDAP), which quickly established an armed branch of about 1,500 to 2,000 men (the MNDA Army, MNDAA). Following the UWSA's example, this Kokang militia signed a ceasefire with the SLORC as early as 1989, which as a result earned them autonomy similar to that of the UWSA, even though the MNDAA has less impressive military capacities. Many leaders (who do not belong to the MNDAA) are regional drug barons, virtually independently controlling their territory. The best known of them is Lo Hsing-Han, who began his career back in the 1960s in a pro-government ethnic militia established by Ne Win in order to combat the CPB and Shan rebels (*Ka Kwe Ye*, see *infra)*, but later founded his own militia. Benefiting from the support of SLORC leaders since 1988, he today heads a vast financial and trade empire whose main Burmese company is Asia World Co.[38]

Two other Sino-Burmese ethnic militias were created after the implosion of the CPB and quickly signed ceasefire agreements with the SLORC. The National Democratic Alliance Army (NDAA-Eastern, founded in June 1989), based in the region north of Kengtung and reputed to be close to Yunnanese organised crime circles established around the bustling border town of Mong La,[39] counted some 4–5,000 men in arms at the time (far fewer today). The New Democratic Army (NDA, founded in December 1989), having fewer soldiers (5–600), recruited primarily in the Sinicised Jingphow and Kachin communities north of the Burmese city of Myiktyina.

The ethnic militias that grew out of the CPB breakup were the first to suspend their armed struggle at Rangoon's request, and negotiated lucrative deals with the new junta. While moving closer to the central state, or at least the military junta that took control of it, these militias for the most part have not renounced their parallel states (in particular the Was). Despite deadlines imposed by the Burmese junta (the latest being 2009), they have not been disarmed, with the exception of the NDA which could easily reconstitute its arsenal, and enforce their own laws on their territory where the Burmese Army itself dares not send its representatives. Furthermore, by injecting large sums of money into the official Burmese economy (mainly by money-laundering), these ethnic militias and drug barons have helped to enrich the leaders of the central military regime but also to sustain the informal economy since the early 1990s.[40]

The Shans. The Shans are the last group to have decided to sign a ceasefire with the Burmese junta in 1989. The Shan State Army (SSA), flagship of the Shan resistance since 1964, split into two rival groups in June 1989 for strategic but also and especially financial reasons. A minority faction (SSA-South), recruiting among the Shan populations of the south near the Thai border, wanted to reactivate its armed struggle against the *Tatmadaw* following the SLORC coup d'état, whereas a second group (SSA-North) preferred to engage in talks with Khin Nyunt's intelligence service. This latter group contracted a ceasefire agreement with Rangoon, which left it with considerable margin for manoeuvre in the north of Shan State (Lashio) near the Chinese border. Since then, it has managed to reap profits from its trade networks in licit and illicit goods in an area that ranges from Ruili to the Golden Triangle.[41]

Signatories of the Second Wave of Ceasefires (1990–1991)

The SLORC's refusal to recognise the outcome of the 27 May 1990 election (which it had nevertheless decided to organise) triggered a new political crisis in the country and rekindled various insurrections. But the revolt fizzled out,

123

owing particularly to the modernisation of the Burmese army thanks to Chinese support,[42] and started in 1991 a second wave of ceasefire accords with ethnic militias that were often out of steam and rarely in a position to bargain. Many of them thus had to accept much less advantageous conditions than those the first ceasefire groups such as the UWSA had managed to negotiate.

The Padaungs (Kayans). In the 1960s the Kayans of the south of Shan State, related to the Karens, formed a small militia made up of about 200 men armed and trained by CPB rebels as well as Karennis from the KNPP. In 1989, with the breakup of the CPB, the Padaungs lost their main source of funding, and a few Padaung leaders (the Kayan National Guard) signed the first ceasefire in February 1992. A second ceasefire followed in July 1994 with the Kayan Newland Party, the remaining Padaung combatants who wanted to pursue their struggle having joined the KNPP.

The Palaungs. These are mainly tribal peasants in the south of the Kachin and Wa regions north of the cities of Mandalay and Lashio (they number about one million). They organised into armed groups in the 1960s in alliance with the Kachins and the Shans, but it was especially from 1976 onwards that they developed their militia structure with the creation of the Palaung State Liberation Organisation and its armed branch, the Palaung State Liberation Army (PSLO/A), the latter having been trained in guerrilla warfare by the Kachin Independence Army (KIA) and numbering as many as a thousand men in the early 1990s. Out of steam after the massive *Tatmadaw* offensives during the winter of 1990–91, this militia signed a ceasefire in April 1991 and agreed to disarmament. Only the PSLO remains authorised, although it is subject to pressure from the Burmese intelligence services (which coaxed it into participating in the National Convention and monitored its complete disarmament in 2005) and the Chinese secret services.[43]

Signatories of the Third Wave of Ceasefires (1993–96)

The Kachins. The Kachins, representing 3–4% of the population (i.e. over one million people), have a long tradition of revolt. Kachin insurgents, who took up arms just after independence,[44] first moved in the CPB sphere of influence in the areas bordering China. The Kachin insurgency, with nationalist and Christian rather than socialist components, did not really break out until 1961, after U Nu attempted to impose Buddhism as the state religion. The Kachin Independence Organisation (KIO) was formed at this time and in 1961 established an armed branch, the Kachin Independence Army (KIA). The latter, 8,000 men strong at the height of its power in the 1970s and 80s, for a time enjoyed both CIA and Indian government support. The Kachins constituted the second opposition force against Ne Win's regime after the Karens. Equipped with an extensive underground network, they owe their wealth to arms smuggling (they controlled the strategic areas between the CPB and numerous revolts in northeastern India) and especially timber and precious stones (Kachin State is one of the largest producers of jade and teak-wood in the world). Their seasoned troops have trained a number of rebel groups in Burma and India (the Chins, but also the Kukis in the early 1990s, the Indian intelligence services having sought to use them in their own counterinsurgency operations in the northeast).[45]

However, in the early 1990s, as the SLORC ceasefire policies were proving their effectiveness, the Kachin insurgency movement went through a number of splits. One faction (Kachin National Defence) negotiated a separate agreement with the SLORC in October 1991. Then came the turn of the KIO itself to negotiate a ceasefire at the end of 1993, finalised in February 1994. The KIO has been increasingly subjected to pressure from China since 1989 (Yunnan business circles openly covet the vast resources in Kachin State), and no longer enjoys the lucrative underground contacts established with the CPB traffickers and other ceasefire groups (the main suppliers of and outlets for arms smuggling and opium traffic, especially into Thailand). Kachin rebels thus initiated negotiations with the Burmese junta to be allowed to pursue their various smuggling activities but this time with the blessing of the central authorities, who equally benefit from such trade. It was certainly one of the SLORC's best political "stunts", the Kachins having always constituted a strong opposition to the Burman ethnic group (which makes the ceasefire a fragile one).[46] Although most of the KIA has laid down its arms, a few factions subsist around young combatants of the new generation, less inclined to be co-opted than their elders because they are often excluded from the financial concessions granted by the central authorities.

The Mons. Dwelling east of Rangoon, near Thailand, the Mons make up about 2% of the population (400,000 individuals). They revolted back in 1948 at the instigation of the Karens (even if they are ethnically and culturally closer to the Burmans). After entering into talks with the Ne Win interim government in 1958, when they created their political front, the New Mon State Party (NMSP), they returned to armed struggle sporadically in the 1960s.[47] NMSP activity increased in 1987–88 owing to the economic crisis and the beginning of agitation in the area around Rangoon. Mon territory, hemmed in between the Irrawaddy delta (Burman) and Karen zones, was then rapidly controlled by the *Tatmadaw*, which revived its counterinsurgency operations in the early 1990s. Weakened, the NMSP had to negotiate a ceasefire with the SLORC in June 1995 (which was late by comparison with other insurgent groups) following the junta's successive offensives, and at the urging of Thailand and a few foreign oil companies: access to Mon territory is in fact strategic for these actors (Total and Petronas gas pipelines go through it today). The thousand-strong NMSP, which has refused for ten years to lay down arms despite the truce, still maintains openly strained relations with the military regime.[48]

The 'Sino-Shans' and the case of Khun Sa. Khun Sa (Chang Shi-fu by his Chinese name), of Sino-Shan origin, in 1963 joined one of Ne Win's proxy ethnic militias created in the Shan State to curb the underground activities of the Communist and Shan rebels. Following the betrayal of one of his men in 1969, he was however arrested by the Burmese authorities, which feared his rising local influence. Most of his men then joined the CPB or on the contrary the SSA, which until then they had fought against. Released in 1974, Khun Sa revived the Shan Unity Army (SUA), which he led from Thailand until 1982, when he was expelled by the Thai troops, and then from the south of Kengtung in Burma's northeastern Shan State. Having grown rich through opium traffic, Khun Sa took the lead of one of the most influential militias in the region. Renamed the Mong Tai Army (MTA) in 1987, its troops were made up of rough and ready soldiers from various ethnic groups (Wa, Palaung, Shan, Chinese…), though Khun Sa clearly asserted himself as a "Shan nationalist".

In 1989 the MTA became the UWSA's main rival in terms of drug production and trafficking, but also in its relationship with the central Burmese government. In fact, although the latter was quickly able to take advantage of the ceasefire with the Was, the SLORC's attempt to approach Khun Sa long remained vain, even if he never felt any sympathy towards the Burmese civilian and democratic opposition led by Aung San Suu Kyi since 1988 or ethnic movements such as the Karens or the Kachins. Through clever bargaining tactics, Rangoon then attempted to use the Was against the MTA. By supervising the settlement of Wa communities in the south of Shan State (some of them had migrated there long ago), the junta sought to offset Khun Sa's influence. Today, many Wa settlement areas near the Thai border have become wealthy, particularly those controlled by the local branch of the UWSA led by Wei Xuegang. However, Khun Sa ended up negotiating his surrender to the central Burmese authorities on 1 January 1996. Khun Sa then undertook to gain respectability by switching over to more legal business ventures in Rangoon,[49] where the former drug baron enjoyed his fortune, largely injected into the Burmese economy (hotels, restaurants, transports companies), until his death in 2007.[50]

Altogether, there are about 16 former insurgent movements that have entered more or less dubious ceasefires with the Burmese junta since 1989. Although each maintains control over its territory, these armed groups have (temporarily?) renounced their separatist demands in exchange for more or less extensive political and financial autonomy. Some militias have managed to create true states within the state, such as the UWSA; others, less powerful, have simply become vassals of the central regime. It thus appears that, whether the Burmese junta likes it or not, it has agreed to a form of privatisation of security and dealings along the country's borders, especially in areas that it can only access with difficulty. While exercising strict control over the cities and the country's centre (predominantly Burman), it leaves control of the periphery to ethnic minorities that are no longer hostile to continuation of the central military regime. The junta-controlled transition process delineated by the "road map to a disciplined democracy" and accelerated after the adoption of the 2008 Constitution might however redraw the line of conflicts between those ceasefire groups and the new regime, the ceasefire accords having first been thought as "temporary" and subjected to new bargaining processes once the new Supreme Law is introduced.

Pro-government militias as political and social instruments of the military regime

In addition to insurgent ethnic groups (rebels or ceasefire signatories), there is a third category of militias in Burma, the paramilitary or social groups entirely created and exploited by the Burmese military machine, which "outsources" its order-keeping duties to them—the repression of civilian pro-democracy groups as well as armed struggle against other still insurgent ethnic militias. These Burman or ethnic (Karen, Karenni, Wa, etc.) groups are altogether different from insurgent movements that have signed peace agreements, for they are real military, political and social instruments of the Burmese junta, even if some of them occasionally escape the latter's control.

First are a number of "ethnic" government militias. Like the Burman majority which has been ruling the country since Independence, they are mainly Buddhist and fight alongside the *Tatmadaw*, which allows them to raise funds through various forms of trafficking and arms them against non-ceasefire ethnic guerrilla groups still fighting against the central government. The current military regime's strategy is nothing new. Already in 1963, General Ne Win had set up a "programme" allowing the organisation of local (ethnic) militias in the country's north to fight against the CPB, Shan and Kachin rebellions that were in full expansion at the time. The *Ka Kwe Ye* (KKY) programme gave its name to these private militias which, with Ne Win's blessing, raised funds by transporting opium produced in Shan State to Thailand. Khun Sa (until his arrest in 1969) and Lo Hsing-Han were two of their main leaders until 1973, when Ne Win terminated this programme, the militias having become too independent. Along the same lines, the secret services of General Khin Nyunt (a former Ne Win protégé who was in charge of *Tatmadaw* military intelligence between 1984 and 2004) resumed this policy in the 1990s.

The Buddhist Karens. In October 1994, the Burmese junta managed to co-opt Buddhist elements of the Karen National Union (KNU) to form the Democratic Karen Buddhist Army (DKBA). In exchange for Rangoon's protection and freedom of manoeuvre these Karen Buddhists, which for a long time had fought alongside the leading Christian Karens of the KNU against the central Burmese authorities, were obliged to take part in *Tatmadaw* counterinsurgency operations that began with the dry season offensives of 1994–95. The direct consequence of this split in the Karen movement was the capture of the KNU headquarters located in Manerplaw, in January 1995. Beyond that, Karen Buddhist dissidence has considerably weakened the Karen insurgent movement. The DKBA, on the other hand, has ended up being a victim of its success: with "order" restored in Karen country (at least as far as the junta is concerned), there is no longer any justification for maintaining such a large militia (the DKBA was reported to have 4,000 men), and the Burmese Army now wants to disarm this paramilitary group, which has not agreed. Having constituted a vast contraband network with Thailand since the mid-1990s (mostly in luxury products and drugs), DKBA leaders are not inclined to abandon the arsenal that ensures the security of their trafficking. The question now is what will be the future of this militia: some leaders appear to be prepared to toe the line and continue their commercial activities in civilian life, while some factions do not hide their desire to rejoin their former Christian Karen allies and return to armed struggle.[51]

Following a similar pattern, another, smaller government paramilitary group has been created around a dissident Buddhist section of the Karenni National Progressive Party (KNPP) since the early 1990s. The Karenni National Defence Army (KNDA) was also created and instrumentalised by General Khin Nyunt's services, and since then has been fighting alongside the Burmese army against the KNPP.

The Was. In the early 1990s, the UWSA also acted as a government militia used by the junta against Khun Sa's forces (the Mong Taï Army), particularly in the Thai border zones where a large Wa minority lives, far from its native region near China. Once it had performed this "order-keeping" task, however, the UWSA refused to confine itself to the role of subcontractor and did not hesitate to assert its independence, even defiance, towards the junta. Yet, since the early 2000s, a few UWSA battalions have regularly fought against SSA-South insurgent troops in the eastern part of Shan State. But the stakes for Wei Xuegang's UWSA go well beyond mere subcontracting for *Tatmadaw* counterinsurgency operations. They involve control of the contraband route along the Thai border, mostly in the hands of Colonel Yawd Serk's SSA-S. Furthermore, after years of fierce opposition and terrible fighting between the Shans and the Was, since 2005 the two militias have enjoyed a truce that might end up in closer interaction than the Burmese junta initially imagined.[52]

In addition to ethnic mercenaries, there is a second category of pro-regime militias: civilian political and social movements made up of violent ultra-nationalist Burmans. The well-disciplined Union Solidarity and Development Association (USDA), founded in September 1993 by the military regime and personally backed by the junta head General Than Shwe, is the best example.[53] This movement aims to give the junta the social base that it has lacked up to now. This mass organisation, entirely devoted to the junta and controlled by it, along the same lines as the Indonesian Golkar under Suharto, has rapidly replaced the political party the regime had nevertheless founded in 1989 in order to participate in the elections it organised on 27 May 1990 (the National Unity Party).[54] USDA membership today is reported to run into millions (15 to 18 depending on the source); all civil servants, local notables and soldiers have been forced to join. The organisation is civilian in nature, but that does not prevent it from employing violent methods. It is this group that was behind the events in Depayin, north of Mandalay, on 30 May 2003 during which Aung San Suu Kyi's convoy was fiercely attacked by a crowd armed with pikes, hatchets and knives. The official toll was four dead, but most militant organisations in exile put the number killed during this incident at between 50 and 80. It led to Aung San Suu Kyi's third house arrest as well as a radicalisation of the regime, which has undertaken to marginalise civilian opposition to the great dismay of its Asian and Western partners.

The USDA has thus enabled the junta to distribute a network of militants across the country and to have a base of civilian sympathisers prepared to transform the organisation at any moment into a political force that can ensure the transfer of military power over to civilian rule still controlled by it, especially in the framework of the junta's current road map. Today the influence of the USDA is tending to spread to rural areas: being a card-carrying USDA member means one can avoid being bothered by the military authorities, avoid harassment of all kinds during the constant military checks (on roads, bridges and entrances to villages), be exempt from forced labour "duties" or "requisitions", and take advantage of free Burman language classes (for ethnic minorities) or even English proficiency and computer training courses in the large cities. The USDA has gradually imposed itself as the secular arm of the regime and the direct opponent of Aung San Suu Kyi's National League for Democracy (NLD). In the face of these pro-democracy adversaries, the USDA regularly has recourse to radical methods (counter-demonstrations, disturbance of rallies, harassment of travelling partisans of the democratic opposition, and surveillance and informing on a daily basis, as shown in the aftermath of the repression of Burmese monk demonstrations in September 2007).

Conclusion

Three categories of "militias" can thus be identified in Burma. They have enjoyed various fortunes ranging from economic success (as with the Wa narco-militia's military-financial empires) to the discretion exacted by a suzerain from its vassals (as with marginalised groups such as the Mons) and decline (for example the Karenni and Shan insurgencies running out of steam, disillusionment among the Karens, the isolation of the Naga and Chin rebellions). At the same time, the figures are eloquent: since the SLORC-SPDC came to power in 1988, there have been several thousand people killed (3,000 alone in that very year 1988), 2 million internally displaced persons (particularly Karens, Karennis and Rohingyas), 140,000 people officially listed as displaced persons in Thailand (but some 2 million Burmese "economic migrants" are present on Thai soil), over 40,000 others in India (mainly Chins, but also Kachins and Arakanese), and almost 30,000 cooped up in UNHCR camps in Bangladesh.

The main source of funding for these militia groups, trade in licit goods (timber, precious stones, luxury goods, and automobiles) and illicit goods (drugs, weapons, human beings) continues to develop in the region. For the moment, the junta allows them in practice to grow wealthy through these illegal activities, in particular from cross-border trade and export of synthetic drugs, in which Chinese, Thai and Indian (in the northeast) criminal milieus also participate, increasing Burma's transnational security challenges.

Lastly, the current process of political transition toward "disciplined democracy" in Burma, controlled by the military regime, may well affect the balance that exists between these three types of militias. Although the pro-junta militias are bound to play an increasing role in the country's politics (the USDA is likely to change into a single party in the true sense, while a few weakened ceasefire groups will probably join the process and contest the 2010–planned elections), and the armed insurgencies should not see their nuisance capacity increase, the big unknown factor remains the attitude of the strongest ceasefire groups and other narco-militias that do not at all share the junta's political views. In some cases the junta is obviously incapable of exercising any sort of influence over some of these militias, especially near northern volatile frontiers, and is likely to allow them to organise their counter-states on the periphery of the country as long as they do not threaten the regime. Thus a familiar pattern in Burma would repeat itself, since in the 1950s U Nu's democratic government already only controlled Rangoon and the central Irrawaddy plain, while letting the ethnic organisations rule the border areas.

Furthermore, the sacking of General Khin Nyunt in October 2004 changed the situation and called into question some of the most fragile partnerships between the junta and the ethnic organisations. The surprisingly light sentence handed down on Khin Nyunt (a suspended sentence of 44 years in prison) could thus be explained by the junta's fears of a new ethnic explosion. Whereas he risked the death sentence, Khin Nyunt (the youngest of the historic SLORC leaders) may have had his life spared in order to be used, if necessary, to ensure the precarious balance between the army and the increasingly rich and influential militia groups.

BIBLIOGRAPHY

Egreteau, Renaud, *Instability at the Gate. India's Troubled North East and its External Connections*, New Delhi: CSH occasional paper, 16 February 2006.
Lintner, Bertil, *Burma in Revolt. Opium and Insurgency since 1948*, Chiang Mai, Silkworm Books, 1999.
Meissonnier, Joël and Pierre-Arnaud Chouvy, *Yaa Baa. Production, Traffic, and Consumption of Methamphetamines in Mainland Southeast Asia*, Singapore, IRASEC-Singapore University Press, 2004.
Smith, Martin, *Burma. Insurgency and the Politics of Ethnicity*, Bangkok, White Lotus, 1999 [2nd ed.].
South, Ashley, *Mon Nationalism and Civil War in Burma. The Golden Sheldrake*, London, Routledge-Curzon, 2002.
Takano, Hideyuki, *The Shore beyond Good and Evil. A Report from Inside Burma's Opium Kingdom*, Reno: Kotan Publishing, 2002.

Articles and chapters in edited volumes

Lintner, Bertil, "Drugs, Insurgency and Counterinsurgency in Burma," in John Brandon (ed.), *Burma/Myanmar in the Twenty-First Century. Dynamics of Continuity and Change*, Bangkok: TK Printing, 1997: 207–45.

Ohen, Paul, "Opium and the Karens: A Study of Indebtedness in Northern Thailand," *Journal of Southeast Asian Studies*, vol. 15, n° 1, March 1984: 150–65.

Roy Burman, J.J., "Contours of the Naga Upsurge," *Asia Europe Journal*, vol. 6 n°1, April 2008: 145–56.

Silverstein, Josef, "Civil War and Rebellion in Burma," *Journal of Southeast Asian Studies*, vol. 21, n° 1, March 1990: 114–34.

Steinberg, David, "The Union Solidarity and Development Association: Mobilization and Orthodoxy", *Burma Debate*, vol. 6, n° 1, January–February 1997: 8.

Yawnghwe, Chao-Tzang, "The Political Economy of the Opium Trade: Implications for Shan State," *Journal of Contemporary Asia*, vol. 23, n° 3, 1993: 303–26.

Zaw Oo, Win Min, *Assessing Burma's Ceasefire Accords*, Washington, East-West Centre: Policy Studies No. 39, 2007.

NOTES

1. The terms "Burma" and "Rangoon", more familiar and commonly used, will be preferred here to "Myanmar" and "Yangon", even though these vernacular terms are accepted by the United Nations. By the same token, the "Burmans" will be used to refer to the Bamar ethnic group, not to be confused with the "Burmese", citizens of Burma, who can be of various non-Bamar ethnic groups such as the Karens, Shans, Nagas, etc. Rangoon was the country's capital from 1948 to 2005, when it was transferred next to Pyinmana (in the centre of the country, halfway between Rangoon and Mandalay) and renamed Naypyidaw ("royal city") by the military junta in November 2005.

2. On the ethnic conflicts that have weakened the country since independence, cf. Martin Smith (1999) [2nd ed.].

3. SLORC: State Law and Order Restoration Council, the name of the ruling junta from 1988 to 1997 under General Saw Maung's leadership from 1988 to 1992, and then General Than Shwe from 1992 to 1997. After a discreet "palace revolution" the SLORC was renamed the SPDC (State Peace and Development Council) in November 1997, but despite this purge, General Than Shwe remains at the helm.

4. On the development of insurrection movements in Burma since 1948, see Bertil Lintner's historic analyses (1999) [2nd ed.] and Martin Smith (1999).

5. Precise figures are very difficult to establish; the estimate of 100,000 to 130,000 deaths seems to be the most commonly admitted by the academic community.

6. Josef Silverstein (1990).

7. Interview with the late Padoh Mahn Shah, KNU general secretary, Mae Sot, Thailand, 9 April 2005.

8. Several thousand of them fled Rangoon and the country's large cities through the Karen jungles into exile in Thailand (but also via Kachin and Chin territory into India) between 1988 and 1990. Author interviews with various Burman activists (who prefer to remain anonymous) who went through the Karen jungles in 1988 and 1990 thanks to help from the KNU; Thailand and India (2002–8).

9. Interviews with members of the KNU leadership, Mae Sot, Thailand, September 2008.
10. I shall return to this, the DKBA fitting the description of what I call a "pro-junta militia".
11. "A New Blow to the KNU," *The Irrawaddy-On-Line*, 2 February 2007.
12. "KNU chief's killing a blow for Burma's democracy movement," *The Nation* [Bangkok], 15 February 2008.
13. Between 1996 and 2006, nearly one million people were reportedly displaced in Karen regions: Thailand-Burma Border Consortium, *Internal Displacement in Eastern Burma*, 26 October 2006.
14. Josef Silverstein (1990), p. 121.
15. Paul Ohen (1984), pp. 150–65.
16. Martin Smith (1999), pp. 344–7.
17. Interview with Khu Oo Reh, KNPP Joint-General secretary, Mae Hong Son, Thailand, 15 September 2008.
18. Thus the KNPP for long exploited the "giraffe women" cooped up in paying "tourist" camps on Thai territory, visited by many Westerners, for which part of the admission fee went directly to the Karenni rebels (the "giraffe women" belong to a tribal subgroup, the Padaungs, related to the Karennis).
19. See Chao-Tzang Yawnghwe (1993).
20. Interview with the late Sao Hseng Suk, former Commander in Chief of the SSA (1971–76), Chiang Mai, 24 November 2003.
21. Interview with Colonel Yawd Serk, leader of the SSA-S, Loi Ta Leng, Shan State, September 2008.
22. J.J. Roy Burman (2008).
23. Rahul Bedi (2006).
24. Renaud Egreteau (2008), pp. 18–23.
25. Rangoon was the capital of the country between 1948 and 2005, before the capital was transferred to Pyinmana (in the centre of the country, half-way between Rangoon and Mandalay), renamed Naypyidaw ("royal city") in November 2005.
26. Interview with a member of the Chin National Front in exile in India, New Delhi, 29 March 2006.
27. Interview with Dr Khin Maung, President of NUPA, Chittagong, Bangladesh, 30 October 2007.
28. Interview with a former Major of the Arakan Liberation Army (ALA) living in exile in India, New Delhi, 22 March 2006.
29. Burmese Islam is multifaceted, as it includes the Rohingya, Zerbadis, Chinese (Panthay) and Indian (mainly Tamil and Bengali) communities.
30. Renaud Egreteau (2008).
31. Interviews with KNU, KNPP and SSA-S leaders along the Thai-Burma borders, September 2008.
32. The 2008 Constitution was still not fully implemented at this writing.
33. For further details, see Zaw Oo, Win Min (2007).
34. Regarding the drug production and trafficking run by the Was, see Hideyuki Takano (2002) and Joël Meissonier, and P.-A. Chouvy (2004).
35. Personal observations in Wa areas on the Chinese side, Yunnan, August 2005.
36. None of the insurgent groups still in the field, studied in the previous section, are participating in it. The work of the National Convention ended in September 2007 with a proposed constitutional draft, which was approved by referendum in May 2008.

37. The "southern" Was being led by the Wei brothers: Wai Moe, "Speculation Surrounds Future UWSA Leaders," *The Irrawaddy-On-Line*, 23 July 2008.
38. Bertil Lintner (1997), p. 225.
39. They are indeed often referred to as the "Mong La group". Personal fieldtrip, Mong La, Burma, September 2008.
40. Anthony Davis and Bruce Hawke (1997).
41. Interview with General Sai Khun Noom, leader of SSA-North in charge of economic relations, Ruili (China), 31 July 2003.
42. A billion US$ contract was signed in late 1989, according to Bertil Lintner (1990).
43. Interviews with PSLO cadres, Ruili, China, 30 July 2003 and with Palaung Youth Organisation leaders, Mae Sot, Thailand, 20 September 2008.
44. The British has used the Kachins, like the Karens and the Chins, in the Indian Colonial Army. The Kachins distinguished themselves during World War II, particularly during the reconquest of Burma in 1943–45 (Kachin Rangers, Northern Kachin Levies); the weapon stockpiles left by the Allies and the Kuomintang in 1945 were mostly reused by the Kachin insurgency that gradually developed against Rangoon.
45. Bertil Lintner (1999), p. 395 and Renaud Egreteau (2006), p. 130.
46. Anthony Davis, "Enemy on the Border," *Asiaweek*, 26 (5), 11 February 2000.
47. Ashley South (2002).
48. Louis Reh, "Investigation of New Mon State Party could threaten ceasefire," *The Irrawaddy-on-Line*, 4 October 2005.
49. Interview with Sao Khuensai Jaiyen, former translator of Khun Sa, Chiang Mai, Thailand, September 2008.
50. "Khun Sa, Golden Triangle Drug King, Dies at 73," *The New York Times*, 5 November 2007.
51. Various interviews with KNU leaders, in Mae Sot and Bangkok, Thailand between 2005 and 2008.
52. Interview with Colonel Yawd Serk, leader of the SSA-S, Loi Ta Leng, Shan State, September 2008.
53. David Steinberg (1997), p. 8.
54. In which the NUP suffered a crushing defeat, winning only 10 seats compared to 392 for the NLD, Aung San Suu Kyi's party.

Map 7: Kashmir

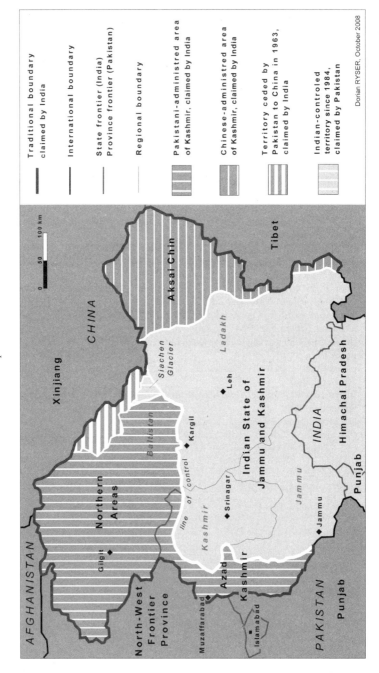

Dorian RYSER, October 2008

Traditional boundary
claimed by India

International boundary

State frontier (India)
Province frontier (Pakistan)

Regional boundary

Pakistani-administred area
of Kashmir, claimed by India

Chinese-administred area
of Kashmir, claimed by India

Territory ceded by
Pakistan to China in 1963,
claimed by India

Indian-controled
territory since 1984,
claimed by Pakistan

0   50   100 km

AFGHANISTAN

CHINA

Xinjiang

Aksai Chin

Tibet

Siachen
Glacier

Ladakh

♦ Leh

♦ Kargil

Baltistan

line of control

Northern
Areas

♦ Gilgit

North-West
Frontier
Province

Kashmir

♦ Srinagar

Indian State of
Jammu and Kashmir

Jammu

♦ Jammu

Himachal Pradesh

Azad
Kashmir

INDIA

Punjab

Muzaffarabad ♦

■ Islamabad

PAKISTAN

Punjab

6

A PATRON-CLIENT PERSPECTIVE ON MILITIA-STATE RELATIONS

THE CASE OF THE HIZB-UL-MUJAHIDIN OF KASHMIR

Amélie Blom

"Militia" is one of the most ambiguous words in the military vocabulary.[1] It veers between two extremes, from a "back-up police force that replaces or reinforces a regular army" to an "illegal formation tasked by a community … with defending its interests through the use of force". The historical trajectory of the Hizb-ul-Mujahidin (Party of the Warriors of God), an armed group that has been fighting to attach the disputed territory of Kashmir to Pakistan from 1990 to the mid-2000s, mirrors the concept's duality: the Hizb operated, all along, as an auxiliary force to the Pakistani army, yet an autonomous one, and was simultaneously a military organisation and a moral police force.

In the mid-1980s, the Pakistani army started to progressively apply to Kashmir a strategy it had previously employed to great effect in Afghanistan: it sub-contracted guerrilla warfare to irregular armed forces. The army confined its role to the supervision and preparation of its proxies' military operations but otherwise allowed them a broad margin of manoeuvre in recruitment, ideological training and financing. These groups, which numbered a dozen in the late 1990s—but more than fifty in the mid-1990s—turned out to be formidable recruiting machines. For almost twenty years, they provided a steady stream of motivated "cannon fodder", militants ready to sacrifice their lives for a cause—the liberation of Kashmir from India—reframed, from then on, as a "*jihad* in the way of Allah".

This model of sub-contracted war amounted to much more than the implementation of a well-tried strategy on a new front: the Pakistani army was also returning to a practice that had been foisted on it, rather than clearly chosen, in October 1947, when it first went to war with India over Kashmir. At that time, after a wave of communal massacres, Kashmiri rebels—principally demobilised soldiers from the Poonch region—joined hands with tribal fighters (*lashkar*) from the areas adjoining Afghanistan to form a loose militia. Its aim was to liberate the Muslim majority territory from the brutal domination of its Hindu ruler and attach it to Pakistan. This force received tacit but modest support from the nascent, beleaguered Pakistani government, but was openly backed by the Chief Minister of North-West Frontier Province (NWFP). Although the army high command, headed by a British general, opposed any form of intervention, dissident officers supervised the delivery of aid to the rebels. Among the dissidents was the then very young general Akhtar Abdur Rahman (1924–88); he is a symbol par excellence of an astonishing historical continuity from the 1947–48 "phoney war" to the 1980s "Afghan *jihad*" that Akhtar supervised, and the post-1987 Kashmiri guerrilla operations that he initially fostered.[2]

The kind of sub-contracted war that the Pakistani army embarked on in the 1990s was somewhat less chaotic than the operations in 1947: faced with another "demand" for it, on this occasion from the Kashmiri separatist groups which had already opted for violence in the 1970s, the high command was united. Moreover, the army controlled the Ministries of Defence and Foreign Affairs and was able to pressurise the first Benazir Bhutto government (1988–90)—as well as all the civilian governments that followed[3]—into supporting the movement.

In its early stage, the policy implemented by the Pakistani strategists fused a mobilising myth—the Afghan "success story"—with a desire to erase the stain of the army's humiliating defeat in 1971 when, with India's military support, East Pakistan seceded to form Bangladesh. As explained by a former head of Pakistan's Military Intelligence, the dominant belief at that time was that once it was "ripe", the "Kashmiri apple" will fall into Pakistan's lap:[4] India, like the USSR in Afghanistan, would be driven away from Kashmir by the *mujahidin* who, like the Bengali rebels in 1971, would enjoy the support of a population that had grown weary of massive electoral fraud (exemplified by the 1987 elections in Indian-administered Jammu and Kashmir) and the excesses of the counter-insurgency. The authenticity of the "two-nations theory" propounded by Muhammad Ali Jinnah, the founding father of Pakistan, would finally be re-established.

The Pakistani army's thirst for revenge might have been slaked by the death of several thousand Indian security forces soldiers during attacks by the *mujahidin*,[5] but the apple, although rotting, refused to fall. Consequently, the delegation of violence to jihadist groups came to encompass, after the mid-1990s, less ambitious goals. While continuously hiding its involvement behind a series of plausible denials, the Pakistani army was now primarily pursuing defensive and diplomatic objectives: (i) protecting Pakistan's territorial integrity by thwarting the drive for independence that Azad Jammu and Kashmir (AJK) was starting to experience as well; (ii) exhausting India, both economically and psychologically, by forcing it to concentrate around 400,000 troops in the zone (thus easing the pressure on the international border); (iii) breathing new life into a territorial dispute that international forums had relegated to the sidelines. The jihadists fulfilled their contract in all these respects.

However, the resource they had once represented became a constraint in the new international context created by the events of 11 September 2001 and in the new regional context arising from the November 2003 cease-fire, which fostered a rapprochement between India and Pakistan (including discreet yet unprecedented anti-terrorist cooperation) that continued until the November 2008 attacks in Mumbai and that might be revived in a near future. These attacks, attributed to the Pakistan-based Lashkar-e-Tayyebah and followed by calls for war in both countries, came as a cruel reminder to the Pakistani authorities that, after twenty years of "authorized privatisation of extraterritorial violence",[6] the greatest danger to regional peace comes from the same jihadist groups that they have promoted. They are now compelled to stigmatise them as "non-state actors"—as Pakistan's President Asif Zardari put it after the Mumbai attack—or "rogue" elements.

The patron-client model, which political scientists have studied extensively but have not yet applied to links between states and irregular armed groups, proves to be a heuristic analytical framework for highlighting the ambiguous relationship between the Pakistani state and the militias to whom it used to delegate the "jihad" in Kashmir. I have selected the Hizb-ul-Mujahidin, the largest jihadist group operating in Kashmir until the mid-2000s,[7] and one that has demonstrated great resilience by maintaining its presence on the battlefield despite the crackdown launched by India in 1989. Despite its longevity, no specific study has been devoted to this organisation so far.

An illegitimate offspring of the "Islamic Movement"
and the Pakistani army

ISI (Inter-Services Intelligence) strategists, encouraged by their successes in Afghanistan, began making overtures to pro-Pakistan political forces in Indian Kashmir in the mid-1980s. Yet they were anxious to avoid a repetition of the errors of the 1965 "Operation Gibraltar"[8] and proceeded with caution: a veteran of the "Azadi movement", arrested by the Pakistani authorities when he clandestinely entered AJK to ask for military aid in 1983, recalled that the aid was not delivered until 1988.[9]

In December 1989, the Hizb-ul-Mujahidin was founded in Srinagar. Its initiators chose this name so as to stress the group's ideological affinity with the *Hizb*-i-Islami led by Gulbuddin Hekmatyar, the Pakistani army's former Afghan protégé, and the Tehrik-ul-*Mujahidin*.[10] The Hizb portrays itself as the "armed wing of the Islamic movement";[11] indeed, it was formed by supporters of the Jamaat-i-Islami (JI), the sub-continent's oldest Islamist movement.[12] Its leader since 1990, Muhammad Yusuf Shah (also known as Sayyid Salahuddin, born 1946), stood as a JI-Jammu and Kashmir (JI-JK) candidate in the 1987 elections. Its ideological inspiration comes from one of the party's most brilliant orators, Sayyid Ali Shah Gilani (born 1929), a member of the JK Assembly until 1989. In Pakistan, it used to be tightly controlled by Abdul Rashid Turabi, *amir* (president) of the JI-Azad Jammu and Kashmir (JI-AJK) and a member of that state's Legislative Assembly.

The Hizb came into existence eighteen months after the outbreak of the insurgency in 1988. This belated foundation may be explained by the ambiguity of its relationship with the Pakistani state, and more precisely with the army. To begin with, the need for a resolutely pro-Pakistan group was not immediately felt by the military, for there was no clear division between pro-Pakistan and pro-independence groups within the Kashmiri "*azadi*" (liberation) movement at that time. For example, members of the Jammu and Kashmir Liberation Front (JKLF), which benefited from weapons, training camps and funds procured for it by ISI, had organised Salahuddin's 1987 election campaign, and had also mobilised for Pakistan Independence Day in 1988. But when the JKLF started to push forward a pro-independence programme, increased its popularity in AJK in 1989–90 and became uncontrollable,[13] marginalising it became a priority for Islamabad. Hence, from the outset, the Hizb functioned as a war machine for weakening and even eliminating the JKLF, which was eventually forced to renounce armed struggle in 1994. Simultaneously, the Hizb was also given the responsibility to rationalise the "*jihad*". Separatist training camps had started to proliferate in AJK and the unchecked activities of mutually hostile splinter groups in JK were detrimental to the "cause". Hence the organisation united various small armed Islamist groups—such as the Zia Tigers, al-Hamza, Ansar-ul Islam, al-Badr, Tehrik-i Jihad-i Islami, Allah Tigers and Hizb-i Islam—which had been struggling for survival since the late 1980s.

Finally, delays occurred because the Pakistan branch of the JI (JI-P) and the JI-JK could not reach agreement on the right moment to launch an armed movement, for their respective positions were determined by different national contexts. The *Jamaati* movement had in fact always maintained a fairly ambiguous position on the Kashmir issue. After supporting the 1947–48 "*jihad*", Maulana Mawdudi adopted an ultra-legalist position (arguing that to continue clandestine operations in Kashmir after the formal agreement of a cease-fire would be a breach of *sharia* law),[14] which exposed him to allegations of treason by the Pakistani political class. These accusations partially determined the party's subsequent positions: taking the lead in the "*jihad* in Kashmir*" campaign in 1989 was therefore a matter of demonstrating its patriotism.[15] It also did everything in its power to ensure that the JK branch mustered recruits for the camps located in Pakistan.

The JI-JK, for its part, feared that opting for armed struggle and operating as Pakistan's military proxy could have very bad repercussions for the party, which risked being ruthlessly suppressed.[16] The JI-JK's own history explains this position. Since its foundation in 1952, it had been guided by a pragmatist policy: although in favour of a merger with Pakistan, it placed more importance on the dissemination of its ideological message through educational activities and participation in elections. This quietist approach enabled it to develop a vast membership network, a vast number of schools and, later, a large student union. Although the leadership of the JI-JK was reluctant to squander its capital, some members had already embraced the armed struggle on an individual basis during the latter half of the 1980s. The party's position changed after the general strike in the Valley on 15 August 1989, a turning point that convinced the JI-JK that there was a significant amount of popular support for the insurgency.

An auxiliary force

The Hizb-ul-Mujahidin's decision-making bodies, defined in its "Constitution" (adopted in June 1990), are highly centralised and modelled on those of all *Jamaati* organisations. Political authority is embodied in the *amir*, who is assisted by a central consultative council (which theoretically "controls" him), and by a representative council which determines political directions. This pyramidal structure is replicated at the provincial level (the Valley of Srinagar and Jammu), and in the districts and cantons. The Hizb also has its own administrator in Pakistan, where the organisation is divided into 32 districts.

But above the *amir* is a post that does not exist in other *Jamaati* organisations: the "supreme guide [or patron]", a position occupied by Sayyid Salahuddin since 1990. There is also a commander-in-chief, appointed by the *amir* with the approval of the supreme guide. Election procedures are somewhat vague: the JI-JK appoints the supreme guide, who himself appoints the *amir* and commander-in-chief. But the former is indeed "supreme", as the latter post has not been filled for some years, while the representative council was dissolved in 1991. And while Sayyid Salahuddin is in principle answerable only to the JI-JK *amir*, it seems that Sayyid Ali Shah Gilani and the Pakistan-based JI *amir* are the only ones he is accountable to. This is a pragmatic arrangement, for Sayyid Salahuddin left the Valley in 1990 and has since resided in Muzaffarabad (capital of AJK), Islamabad and Rawalpindi. The movement is therefore directed from Pakistan.

In JK and AJK, the Hizb-ul-Mujahidin to some extent models its military organisation on the army. Each battalion should contain "313" *mujahidin*,[17] a symbolic figure representing the number of the Prophet's companions at the battle of al-Badr, the historical emblem of divine support for Muslims faced with more powerful opponents. The religious symbolism extends to the companies, some of which are named after the Prophet's companions, while others bear the names of political leaders.[18] The Hizb is known to have run three training camps in AJK and five in NWFP until 2001. It appears to have retained at least one camp in Mansehra (NWFP) and one in Garhi Habibullah, on the NWFP AJK border. However, according to one militant interviewed at Mansehra,[19] the fighters in these camps are disoriented and

139

apathetic and have been "vegetating" ever since General Musharraf placed jihadist organisations under a "regime of supervised liberty" and restricted infiltrations along the Line of Control after 2004. This proves that the Hizb's room for manoeuvre fluctuates in accordance with the changes of direction by Pakistani decision-makers.

The ideological and strategic affinities between the organisation and the Pakistani state are indeed very strong, as attested by the "historic resolution" adopted at the organisation's secret headquarters in Srinagar in October 1990. It is written for instance that because "Pakistan was created in the name of Islam", the organisation fights to "reunify Kashmir and Pakistan".[20] From a strategic point of view as well, the Hizb's "*jihad* of attrition"[21] is serving the Pakistani army's objectives: hence, Indian security forces should be harassed until "their presence in Kashmir became intolerable". To that effect, the armed group will "cultivate within young hearts the passion for jihad and the desire to attain martyrdom by means of spiritual, ideological and physical training". The group claims it uses its weapons only "against the Indian Imperialists and their agents", that is, the Indian security forces and organisations involved in counter-insurgency operations.[22] Besides attacks on Indian troops, "major" Hizb operations have therefore included the destruction of the Lake Wullar dam (February 1990), which the Pakistani government denounced as a crime and a threat to the country's water supply, and the planting of bombs in stadiums (as on Indian Democracy Day in 1995). The group has taken little action outside Kashmir, but claimed responsibility for two attacks in Delhi in 2001.

The Hizb claimed to have killed "770 Indian soldiers" in 2003 alone.[23] However, the pace and scale of its operations diminished drastically after the November 2003 cease-fire.[24] During the course of 2006 and early 2007 for example, as the rapprochement between India and Pakistan was progressing, the group restricted its activities to targeted killings of "informers" and pitched battles with Indian troops during raids on its caches. It condemned the attack on Bombay commuter trains (11 July 2006) and the Delhi-Lahore Samjhota Express (19 February 2007).[25] This chronology is evidence, once more, that the Hizb-ul-Mujahidin is in fact tightly supported, and controlled, by the Pakistani army.

Indeed, without the support of the army and the JI-P, the jihadist organisation would never have survived the numerous reversals of fortune it has experienced since its creation. The most serious setback occurred in 1993–94, with the formation of counter-insurgency groups, "renegades" (often from the Hizb's own ranks) who knew where its caches were located and were likely to carry out reprisals on the families of its recruits. This is precisely the reason why the Pakistani army consequently sponsored less vulnerable groups for guerrilla operations, such as the Harkat-ul-Ansar, the Lashkar-e-Tayyebah and, later, the Jaish-e-Muhammed—groups whose leaders and recruits were almost exclusively Pakistanis. The Hizb has also been destabilised by five splits since 1990, all of which were caused by the overlapping of three types of tension: between local (JK) and external (Pakistan-based) leadership, between military cadres and political bosses, and finally between the various leaders of the armed groups previously absorbed by the Hizb. These leaders had established their authority through their early participation in the armed struggle and found it difficult to accept Salahuddin's authoritarianism and the dominant role of the JI-P.

The patron-client theory

The Pakistani army supported the Hizb because, fundamentally, it is a pro-Pakistan movement and is therefore useful for marginalising pro-Independence, and even autonomist forces. It also serves the army's interests by attempting to rally Kashmiri society to the goal of unification with Pakistan. Indeed, the relationship between the jihadists and the Pakistani army, significantly described as a "marriage of convenience",[26] is above all a clientelist arrangement. Clientelism, defined as a "relationship of dependence... based on a reciprocal exchange of favors between two people, the patron and the client, whose control of resources is unequal",[27] applies well to the relationship between the army and jihadists. It is a relation of exchange, mutually beneficial but fundamentally unequal. It is also an unofficial yet firmly consolidated arrangement that imposes constraints on both parties. This perspective enables us to highlight some of the ambiguities that characterise this partnership.

The ambiguity is, firstly, ideological. The Hizb is perfectly aware of its paradoxical position: while it is duty bound to reject the nationalism of the JKLF, it must also defend Pakistan's nationalist agenda. The task is a difficult one, as implicitly admitted in the group's "resolution in favour of a union with Pakistan" which mentions "the delicate national and religious obligation" that the Hizb has to fulfil in order to make this union possible.[28] The "resolution" devotes a great many pages to demonstrating that attachment to Pakistan can be justified on religious grounds (reunifying the brotherhood of believers) and describes the country's raison d'être exclusively in its pre-1947 formulation, that of the movement for Pakistan. Hence, the Hizb presents itself as the standard-bearer of the "two-nations theory", but says nothing about contemporary Pakistan.

This emphasis on an imagined, and ideally "Islamic", Pakistan needs to be understood in the light of the Hizb's opposition to the JKLF, which is never mentioned but is nonetheless implicitly omnipresent. The entire argument consists of contrasting the impurity of the JKLF's ethnic nationalism with the Islamic (but in reality communalist) nationalism of the Hizb. The pro-Independence programme is rejected as impious, for the concept of a "state formed on the basis of geographic, linguistic or racial nationalities is contrary to the Quran", and because "nationalism" is a "human ideology", an "idol" which "believes it is superior to divine sovereignty".[29] Thus tacitly accused of apostasy, the JKLF becomes a legitimate target.

The ambiguity extends, secondly, to the political sphere, for the clientelist relationship between the Hizb and the Pakistani armed forces is primarily instrumental and leaves little room for emotional issues.[30] The instrumental dimension has been cogently summarised as follows:

ISI provides the arms, funds, infrastructure and communications equipment. But as it cannot recruit directly, the jihadist movements supply the fighters and the indoctrination. It's as if you and me were mounting a 'joint venture'—I'll supply one part, you supply the other—the dependence is mutual.[31]

The division of tasks can also feature in conventional wars, as demonstrated by the Kargil crisis in the spring of 1999: when incursions by the Pakistani army forced Indian troops to redeploy to the northern front, jihadists seized the opportunity to attack previously heavily-guarded military bases in the Valley and extend their activities to rural areas.[32] The patron provided other resources to its jihadist client, including the rear base vital to the continuation of any guerrilla warfare—the Azad or "Free" Jammu and Kashmir state, actually run from Islamabad[33]—and considerable ideological support for the recruitment process. School textbooks, together with the Urdu- and English-speaking press, have thus relayed the jihadist worldview for many years in Pakistan. As a matter of fact, terminology continued to fluctuate after 2001, in accordance with the context. Jihadists are "freedom fighters" and "martyrs" when operating in Kashmir, but "terrorists" in Pakistan; members of the Indian security forces are killed by *mujahidin*, but civilians are attacked by "militants".

The client's task is to convince the population of the legitimacy of the infra-conventional war by appealing for religious solidarity. It also recruits fighters, provides them with ideological training and raises funds. In order to achieve these goals, the Hizb employed a variety of visual and rhetorical tactics in its propaganda material. It aroused anger and indignation in order to immediately suggest ways in which these emotions can be appeased: in its videos, for instance, images of atrociously mutilated corpses are followed by footage of "avengers", *mujahidin* performing physical exercises to a pop music soundtrack. The purpose of such propaganda is threefold: to provoke empathy, to seduce the young and to raise funds, for as Salahuddin has prosaically stated, "those of you sitting at home have a duty to give us money".[34] Indeed, and like other groups, the Hizb-ul-Mujahidin has ensured that the Pakistani army could sub-contract the war at the lowest cost.

The clientelist relationship has an emotional dimension, but it is even more equivocal. The Hizb's pamphlets refer to the "personal relationship or consanguinity" that unites it to "[its] beloved Pakistan", but the attachment is to an idea, the idea of Pakistan (the voice-over to its videos proclaims: "We are Pakistan") rather than to institutions. Consequently, there is no obedience to the army as such, but rather a functional allegiance as long as the army continues to defend the Kashmir "cause" on terms favourable to the Hizb. Therefore, it is not unreasonable to suggest that the organisation's relatively low profile since the 2003 cease-fire is attributable to the Pakistani government's success in persuading it that a pause was essential to the achievement of the ultimate goal: the withdrawal of Indian troops from Kashmir and the territory's restoration to Pakistan. Surely, too, the militarily weakened Hizb also needs a pause and is sensitive to the Kashmiri population's weariness after almost fifteen years of incessant war, repression and curfew. Since 2005, Salahuddin has repeatedly expressed his willingness to accept a cease-fire, combining the unacceptable but unavoidable precondition that India acknowledges the "disputed" nature of the territory with less radical demands.[35]

The one genuine emotional link is to the JI-P, which the Hizb describes as its "mother organisation". This complicates the clientelist relationship by transforming it into a trilateral rather than a bilateral arrangement. The Hizb's policies therefore depend on power relations between the JI-P and the Pakistani government. The JI-P's position on Kashmir is, indeed, greatly influenced by the dynamics of internal politics and it has made regular use of the issue's symbolic dimension in order to counterbalance difficult political choices.[36] Its close link with the JI-P also implies that the Hizb has a wide variety of funding sources at its disposal.[37] In addition to direct voluntary contributions, it can take advantage of the vast fundraising network the JI-P maintains in Pakistan. All party members, for instance, make a monthly contribution to the two main funds for Kashmir. If the figures quoted by the JI-P and the Hizb are accurate, the amount raised in Pakistan and other countries in 2001 by these means approached 700,000 euros (about 56 million rupees).[38]

Leaders and recruits: a sociological profile

While the patron-client framework sheds light on many dimensions of the relations between the Hizb-ul-Mujahidin and the neighbouring state, this does not render the jihadist group a "puppet" of the Pakistani army. The group has a political and ideological trajectory of its own, in JK as well as in Pakistan, as proven by the biographies of its cadres and recruits.

Most of Hizb-ul-Mujahidin's cadres were former professionals of some sort, civil servants or teachers, such as the group's first commander-in-chief, M. Ahsan Dar, who taught in a school run by the JI-JK. Like most *Jaamat* cadres, they represented an educated and recently urbanised middle class. Sayyid Salahuddin was born Yusuf Shah in Badgam district in 1946. Like many first generation militants (including Dar), he came from a family of fruit growers who faced financial ruin as the fruit export market collapsed between 1985 and 1988. Obtaining a degree in political science from Kashmir University (Srinagar) in 1971, Salahuddin joined the student branch of the JI-JK and eventually became its president. He was appointed *amir* of the JI-JK for the Srinagar district in 1986, while continuing to serve as an *imam* in one of the city's mosques.[39] Running as a JI candidate (within the Muslim United Front) in the March 1987 elections, Salahuddin was beaten, arrested and jailed for nine months. A year later, he committed himself to the armed struggle.

Salahuddin belongs to the second generation of JI-JK cadres, one that came to the fore in the 1970s and was greatly influenced by the links established with the Arab world and international Islamist movements.[40] These contacts shaped the perceptions of young Jamaat militants who, having been sensitised to concepts such as "Islamic revolution" and "anti-imperialism", were inspired to move beyond local Islam and adopt a more universalistic approach. Towards the end of the 1980s, some of these activists began expressing opposition to the pacifism advocated by the "elders". To their surprise, they got the support of a veteran member of the party, Sayyid Ali Shah Gilani. His position within the JI-JK stemmed from his oratorical skills and his past association with the party's founder. He had also served for long as the JI-JK representative in the All Parties Hurriyat Conference (APHC).[41] Although he held no post within the Hizb-ul-Mujahidin, Gilani was called the *amir-i-jihad* by the group's followers: he was their spiritual and political leader and the link between the party and the Hizb.

Gilani was born in 1929 in a village located in the Baramulla district (close to the Line of Control) and escaped poverty through the education he received in Lahore and Delhi. His discovery of the ideas of Maulana Mawdudi (who invited him to join the newspaper he was editing) during the crucial period of the first Kashmir War (1947–49) constituted a turning point which, according to him, "defined [his] Islamic identity".[42] Gilani became a teacher and joined the Jamaat in 1953, winning election to the JK Assembly in 1972, 1982 and 1987. Relinquishing his seat in 1989, he threw his weight behind the armed struggle and the Hizb-ul-Mujahidin. Gilani represents the hardliners within the JI-JK, the faction which brooks no compromise over the accession of Kashmir to Pakistan, for it regards the link between the two as almost biological. In his view, a Muslim living in a Hindu majority environment is akin to "a fish trying to survive in the desert".[43]

In one respect, these biographical sketches are strikingly similar. It would be unwise to generalise about all the Hizb's leaders, and even to over-interpret this observation, but one cannot fail to notice that the two key figures of the movement mentioned above are "downgraded" *sayyid*,[44] as both their fathers were manual workers.[45] The Hizb "supreme guide" even changed his name from Yusuf *Shah*[46] to *Sayyid* Salahuddin when he opted for armed struggle: a move that might signify his quest for social revenge and a reclaiming of lost prestige. In accumulating several prestigious titles, he exploited a triple register. Besides Arabising *shah* to emphasise the purity of his lineage (in addition to his legendary Italian cap, he always wears a *keffieh*), he adopted Salahuddin as his *nom de guerre*, thus stressing his allegiance to a chivalrous tradition (Saladin defeated the twelfth-century Crusaders). He also cultivated a link to the Sufi tradition (his followers respectfully and affectionately call him "*pir* sahib").[47] To a certain extent, this may be interpreted as a political version of "ashrafisation", the sociological process whereby an individual achieves social mobility by emulating the norms and cultural ideas associated with the *ashraf* (the "higher" class).[48]

The profile of the Hizb-ul-Mujahidin recruits is very different. It should be noted at the outset that the precise number of recruits is very difficult to determine. According to the Indian authorities, the Hizb fielded 1,234 active combatants in Jammu and Kashmir in 2001.[49] The organisation's own publications put the figure at 12,987 *mujahidin*. If we accept the official Indian figure, and the hypothesis that one militant is sent into combat for every five to ten of those trained for it, total membership would effectively stretch to between 10 and 15 thousand. Estimating the number of "martyrs" is equally difficult. The organisation claims that 27,000 fighters have been "martyred" between 1989 and 2001:[50] this figure is somehow too good to be true as it exactly corresponds to the number of Indian soldiers the Hizb says it has killed during the same period. On the basis of the 585 Pakistani martyrs claimed by the Hizb,[51] and hazarding a guess that the ratio of active members (80% Kashmiri, 20% Pakistani) is identical to the ratio of those killed,[52] the number of Kashmiri martyrs would amount to about 2,400, and the total to about 3,000. Hence, to state that "virtually every village [in Pakistan] has someone who served somewhere [in a militant organization]"[53] seems too far-fetched an assumption—even if recruits from other jihadist and militant organisations were to be included—for a country with a rural population of 120 million.

How do these individuals come to join the Hizb? According to the organisation's cadres, all they require is a "young man in full possession of his faculties who accepts his obligations under the *sharia*, abstains from the commission of mortal sins and is prepared to sacrifice his life and his worldly goods to establish the order of the Prophet".[54] This represents a transfer of the JI's political vision to the military sphere: like the *salihun* (the virtuous), whose vocation is to form the vanguard of the Islamic revolution and supplant the corrupt secular political class at home, recruits form the spearhead in a war to establish Islam as the absolute code of conduct throughout the world.

In reality, young men's motives for joining a jihadist group are not so easy to assess. The propaganda materials published by these groups—in particular their numerous testimonies and biographies of "martyrs"[55]—obviously give a very biased picture, for its aim is to mobilise new recruits. Hence, for instance, parents' approval of their sons' choice to die as a "martyr" in Kashmir is systematically emphasised (while in some cases parents are not even aware of it), as well as their great happiness when hearing that he succeeded in doing so. This hagiographic literature also constructs exemplary and heroic figures of *mujahidin* in order to prove that the organisation can fulfil its moral responsibility: it will pay tribute to the memory of those who died for its cause. Actually, the motives for joining a jihadist organisation can only seriously be investigated through interviews with recruits—or rather former recruits (it is almost impossible to conduct independent talks with those who are still part of the organisation). These interviews not only reveal very distinct individual trajectories that belie the claims of the jihadist propaganda, but also prove how complex and highly personal the reasons to become a *mujahid* can be.

They may include a quest for absolute moral commitment, a desire to escape from an unbearable personal situation, an aspiration to be a hero, a form of opportunism and a "martyropath" passion.[56]

However, at a more general level, three factors distinguish the Hizb recruits from those of other groups. First, most of them were *madrasa*, college and university students.[57] Indeed, the organisation heavily relied on the breeding ground of organisations affiliated with the JI-P, such as the Jamaat-i-Talaba-i-Arabiya (JTA, the association of students in Arabic), which claims to have lost 2,000 of its *madrasa* students in Kashmir.[58] This figure is probably exaggerated, but indicates that the Hizb has attracted an exceptionally large number of students from the JTA, whose anthem is "Allah is our creator, the holy Quran our constitution, jihad our path and martyrdom our destination".[59] The Islami Jamiat-i-Talaba (IJT) claims 500 martyrs. The JI-P's student union (of which Salahuddin himself is a former member) has indeed played a central role in recruiting in both Pakistan and Indian-controlled Kashmir.[60] Several mothers of Pakistani "martyrs" confirmed that their sons had all been members of IJT-Pakistan,[61] an organisation with considerable experience in the matter, having been the source of "seventy-two martyrs in Afghanistan between 1980 and 1990".[62] This suggests that in Pakistan the Hizb had very little need to recruit outside the *Jamaat* network, in striking contrast to other groups—the Lashkar-e-Tayyebah, for example, was unable to draw on the resources of the Jamiat-i-Ahl-i-Hadith's *madrasa* network, and was forced to devote considerable energy to making itself visible in the public arena (hence its high profile in Pakistani cities) in order to attract young men, generally those from poorer backgrounds (small farmers, craftsmen, street traders, house employees, etc.).

Second, there are close family ties between JI-P cadres and Hizb-ul-Mujahidin fighters. Ideological convictions aside, the need to guard against infiltration by Indian secret services and opportunistic militants is an important factor here. The sons of Salahuddin and Gilani may not have taken part in the "Kashmiri *jihad*" (a fact that drew criticism from many of the people I interviewed in Srinagar), but a number of JI-P cadres (at least ten were noted during the course of my research alone) have lost a son, a brother or a nephew in the region. These young men were often introduced to the concept of "*jihad*" at an early age (some of them spent their school holidays climbing with *mujahidin* in the mountains of AJK, for instance). In this case, as proved in the interviews, their mothers, for reasons of political conviction, were unfailingly supportive. The biography of some recruits point to further interesting characteristics: a follow-my-friend attitude, the impact of a jail term, the taste for battle and the frustration of an aborted military career. One mother, the wife of a JI-P cadre, explained why her son, killed in the Valley in 1999, had embarked on *jihad*:

He was a very happy boy and spent more time playing cricket than in study or prayer. But he had been very impressed by the martyrdom of a friend of his, our neighbor's son. Then one day the police arrested him during an IJT demonstration and he spent

21 days in jail. That's where he drew closer to IJT leaders. He was a lot more serious when he came home: he read the Quran all the time, he was a different boy. I already wanted him to go to Kashmir. Of all my sons, he had the strongest passion (*jazba*) for jihad. God had chosen him.[63]

Finally, the Hizb's recruits are of interest in terms of ethnicity. First, Kashmiris constituted up to 80% of the Hizb's fighters (in 2002), as opposed to 20–50% in other jihadist organisations. In Pakistan, most of the group's "martyrs" have come from Punjab (especially Gujranwala, Gujrat, Rawalpindi and Lahore),[64] the most fertile recruiting ground for the IJT, as it is for JI-P-led *madrasas*. In AJK, the Hizb is more highly regarded than other armed groups operating in the region, where the younger members of Harkat and Lashkar in particular often resorted to oppressive measures (extorting money from shopkeepers to fund the "*jihad*", forcing local truck drivers to switch off their radios, etc.). The Hizb's recruitment rate is indeed quite high in a state that still bears the scars of the 1947–48 war. The death of a family member may compel an individual to join up in the hope of wreaking symbolic vengeance, one example being the grandson of a man who was hanged in the prison at Poonch for his part in the 1948 rebellion. Yet the reasons for joining are primarily political. The JI has long been active in AJK, especially in Bagh, a district that has provided many Azad-Kashmiri "martyrs".[65] And jihadist organisations used to maintain close links with the AJK administration, particularly in the late 1980s. For example, pictures of Sardar Sikandar Hayat Khan, the former Prime Minister of AJK (1985–90), featured prominently in pamphlets published by the Hizb in a demonstration held in Lahore in 2000: his "paternal" figure appeared above a photograph of a child dressed like a *mujahid* and armed with a Kalashnikov. Solidarity may also be a family matter: Masud Safraz, head of the Hizb's AJK branch until 2000, is Khan's nephew.

The Hizb-ul-Mujahidin worldview

Studies of the motives that drive jihadist organisations often reflect a reductive economic bias, portraying "Jihad International Inc." as just another type of profit-driven business.[66] While materialism is undoubtedly a factor—the propaganda frequently describes participation in "*jihad*" as a "professional activity"—this reading obscures the historicity and the heterogeneous aspect of jihadist groups. If money were the sole motivation—and if jihadists were mere mercenaries—they could easily be coopted by offers of other paths to enrichment. The numerous instances of re-conversion to "international" *jihad*, the war in Afghanistan and the post-2001 terrorist attacks in Pakistan invalidate this hypothesis. The economic argument tends to influence the way in which jihadist discourse is interpreted: usually, commentators see the religious rhetoric as a cynical exploitation of the discourse of identity. Some, nonetheless, take the actors' convictions seriously. This approach is the least problematic, as long as we bear in mind, of course, the contradictions, the silences and the syntactical, geographical and temporal contexts that illuminate the functions of the discourse. Ideological convictions do matter, as demonstrated by the sociological and political profile of the Hizb's leaders (and of many of their recruits).

Yet, two questions arise: is the accession of Kashmir to Pakistan the logical outcome of the sanctifying of a political struggle? Or does the objective itself determine the manipulation of the religious register? Both hypotheses contain an element of truth. First of all, the reference to military "*jihad*"[67] stems directly from the thinking of Maulana Mawdudi. It formed the basis of his first work (*Jihad in Islam*, 1927), enabled him to conceptualise the fusion of ideology and religion, and justified the break with tradition.[68] According to Mawdudi, Islam is more than a religion of personal salvation; it is supposed to expand universally. Hence, in his view, Islam preaches a violence that is both just and unselfish: the sole aim of "jihad in the way of Allah" is to serve God and to remove the obstacles to the development of Islam. Mawdudi also stresses the reformative dimension of military "*jihad*", for it eliminates both moral corruption (*fasad*) and internal discord (*fitna*). One can say that JI activists implemented the founder's worldview during the persecution of Pakistan's Ahmadi minority in the 1950s, then against Bengali secessionists in the years 1969–71, and finally by the Hizb which focused on eliminating the JKLF "Muslim traitors".

Mawdudi's analysis is worth recalling not only because it inspired leaders like Salahuddin and Gilani, but also because if there is a situation to which it can be "applied", it is surely that of Kashmir. In effect, the tensions in that area are almost identical to those at work when the JI's founder formulated his praise of "*jihad*", which was actually defined implicitly as a communalist struggle against Hindu domination.[69] While Muslims form an overwhelming majority in the Valley, they constitute no more than 64% of the population at the state level (and are a minority in Jammu where, it should be remembered, many of them were massacred during Partition). They are also excluded from many professional positions.[70] This explains why, in keeping with Mawdudi's position, "*jihad*" represents, first and foremost, the abandonment of a conciliatory position in the face of a "cultural domination". As a case in point, the Hizb-ul-Mujahidin pamphlets which repeatedly refer to the rediscovery of dignity through armed struggle: "A great revolution has occurred in the minds of the same Kashmiri Muslims who were once so frightened by imperialism and its agents that their cowardice became the butt of many jokes … the passion for jihad has erased their fear".[71]

The inevitable result of this interpretation is the sanctification of combat. By describing the guerrilla war in Kashmir as a "*jihad*", the Hizb conveys the message that the fighter sacrifices his life not for an ideology, his country or his personal salvation, but for the survival of his religion: his act is therefore one of pure devotion. Yet, besides arousing the fervour essential to all guerrilla operations, this approach is also designed to promote discipline amongst the troops, for "most *mujahidin* are young, inexperienced, inclined to strong emotions, armed to the teeth and prone to acting without thinking".[72] The values of discipline and obedience are glorified and explicitly justified in the name of Islam; insubordination is a "mortal sin".[73] The sacred dimension of military action is, conversely, supported by the militarisation of the faith. This implies that only armed struggle can assure the grandeur of Islam. To this end, the Hizb reformulates the past in a modern idiom:

As long as Muslims were waving the banner of jihad, dignity and victory were theirs; but as soon as they weakened, they began to decline. Through nothing more than the power of their faith and passion for jihad, the believers of the age of the Prophet and the Caliphs defeated two *superpowers*, Rome and Persia, and conquered much of the world.[74]

This statement is followed by a vindication of the *mujahidin* who fought in Afghanistan and renewed the link with a glorious past by defeating a superpower, the USSR, which in this instance stands as India's *alter ego*.

Jihadism also enabled the Hizb to devise a "just war" theory to be applied in Kashmir—"target only the sites and means used by Indians in their imperialist design (garrisons, troop and supply convoys, arms depots, strategic roads and bridges, etc.)" and "avoid attacks on targets that are of public benefit unless the enemy is using them", state its pamphlets.[75] Those who "betray their community and religion should not be spared", although they should be "judged fairly". In this way, interestingly, the organisation also transforms itself into a moral police. It declares, for instance, that "cultural centres, cinemas, video stores, bars and beauty parlours should be priority targets".[76] And indeed, fear and intimidation have resulted in the closure of many such establishments. Besides turning Srinagar into a battleground, the guerrilla war has also reduced the city to a dismal place that offers few distractions for the young. Although the Hizb's puritanical agenda can once again be traced back to the early precepts of the JI (which identified places of entertainment as mediums for the penetration and domination of "Hindu culture"), it surely prepared the ground for the violent treatment of allegedly "non-virtuous" women, including acid attacks on unveiled women, conducted by other jihadist groups in the early 2000s.

Conclusion

This chapter has attempted to clarify the link between a militia force, the Hizb-ul-Mujahidin, and a state, Pakistan. The concept of clientelism has enabled us to shed some light on the mutual dependency that unites the two— unequal—partners. This model helps to explain, as well, the difficulties faced by the Hizb since the Pakistani army was compelled in the mid-2000s, under tremendous international pressure and because of its redeployment on the Afghan front, to "freeze" the Kashmiri "*jihad*". On the other hand, by focusing on the evolution of the organisation, the socio-political characteristics of its leaders and members, and its political *imaginaires*, we have seen that the Hizb is not a simple back-up force. Nor is it enmeshed in a face-to-face confrontation with the army, since its loyalty lies with two parties, the JI-P and the JI-JK, which share the same goals but pursue different paths. The Hizb precisely draws its strength from the fact that although it is a client, its relationship with its patron is not "monogamous".[77]

The clientelist relationship remains a constraining one for the Pakistani state as well. After decades of sub-contracting the war to armed irregulars, it is now confronted with the same dilemma that European states had faced after centuries of indulgence in the "privatisation of extraterritorial violence". Between the 13th and 19th centuries pirates, mercenaries and mercantile companies were allowed to flourish, until the unexpected effects of their activities[78] brought about their prohibition. As shown by Janice Thomson, this resulted from an international and "systematic imperative", rather than from domestic compulsions: states had to ban irregulars in order to avoid being dragged into unwanted wars against each other.[79]

The parallel with Pakistan is striking. First, President Musharraf (1999–2008) banned the jihadist groups not because of any change in the domestic environment but in response to the diplomatic pressure exerted by the US and Indian governments after September 11. Secondly, after having repeatedly used private armies to wage war over the course of 60 years (against India in 1947, 1965, 1971 and 1999; in Afghanistan between 1979 and 1988 in compliance with a request from the US administration; in Kashmir throughout the 1990s), the Pakistani army now faces "unexpected threats" as well. These include, since 2001, Pakistan-based jihadists' interactions with local sectarian groups and the al-Qaeda network, their involvement in attacks against the Pakistan military, the transfer of their fighters to the Pakistani-Afghan border, and their implicit intention to provoke a confrontation between India and Pakistan, as proven by the November 2008 attacks in Mumbai.

It has to be stressed, however, that groups such as the Jaish-e-Muhammad and the Lashkar-e-Tayyebah, but not the Hizb-ul-Mujahidin, are responsible for these unforeseen consequences of the Kashmiri "*jihad* of attrition". The Hizb thus escaped the waves of formal prohibition in 2002, 2003 and 2009,[80] and its infrastructure in Pakistan remains intact. There might be two other reasons for this benign neglect: one, that Indian security counter-insurrection operations have, since the mid-2000s, badly damaged the Hizb's military network in Jammu and Kashmir; another, that it still represents a useful resource for its patron. It is the only group trained for armed struggle, ethnically Kashmiri and solidly embedded in Jammu and Kashmir, that supports a pro-Pakistan agenda. If the dialogue between India and Pakistan ever breaks down, and if the military option once again becomes a priority, the Hizb is ideally placed to apply pressure to India. Although this seems to be a very remote possibility at this stage—given the Pax Americana presently enforced in the region—it can never be excluded.

The client has another symbolic advantage. The current international consensus on the undesirability of "authorised, privatised violence" (especially with regard to Islamist groups), and the legal arsenal against terrorism that has developed from it, expose the Pakistani army to a major problem: how to sever the links with the *mujahidin* in Kashmir when all the propaganda (whether it emanates from universities and research institutes, the media or the army itself) continues to highlight the feeling of insecurity inspired by India and the imperative to liberate Kashmir? How can the army go about cracking down on "miscreants" (the current official term for those who attack national targets) who have sustained far greater losses than the army itself in a "war" conducted largely in the army's interests? In other words, while the Pakistani state might ban, and on a regular basis, jihadist groups, it still has to delegitimate them.

BIBLIOGRAPHY

Amir Rana Muhammad, *Jihad Kashmir wa Afghanistan aur Mazhabi Jamaaton ka ek Jaiza* (Urdu), Lahore, Mashal Books, 2002 [translation: *A to Z of Jehadi Organizations in Pakistan*, Lahore, Mashal Books, 2004].

Behera, Navnita Chadha, *State, Identity and Violence. Jammu, Kashmir and Ladakh*, New Delhi, Manohar, 2000.

Briquet, Jean-Louis and Frédéric Sawicki (eds), *Le Clientélisme politique dans les sociétés contemporaines*, Paris, PUF, 1998.

Davis, Diane E. and Anthony W. Pereira (eds), *Irregular Armed Forces and their Role in Politics and State Formation*, Cambridge University Press, 2003.

Jalal, Ayesha, *Partisans of Allah. Jihad in South Asia*, Cambridge, Mass., Harvard University Press, 2008.

Kepel, Gilles, *Jihad, expansion et déclin de l'islamisme*, Paris, Gallimard, 2000.

Metcalf, Barbara, *Islamic Contestations. Essays on Muslims in India and Pakistan*, Oxford University Press, 2004.

Nasr, Vali Reza, *The Vanguard of the Islamic Revolution, The Jamaat-i-Islami of Pakistan*, London, Tauris, 1994.

Thomson, Janice E., *Mercenaries, Pirates and Sovereigns. State-Building and Extraterritorial Violence in Early Modern Europe*, Princeton University Press, 1994.

Articles and chapters in edited volumes

Blom, Amélie, "Kashmiri Suicide Bombers: Martyrs of a Lost Cause," in Amélie Blom, Laetitia Bucaille and Luis Martinez (eds), *The Enigma of Islamist Violence*, London, Hurst & Co., 2007: 71–88.

Evans, Alexander, "The Kashmir Insurgency: As Bad as it Gets," *Small Wars and Insurgencies*, 11 (1), 2000: 9–81.

Leca, Jean and Yves Schemeil, "Clientélisme et patrimonialisme dans le monde arabe," *International Political Science Review*, 4 (4), 1983: 455–94.

Nasr, Vali Reza, "Communalism and Fundamentalism. A Re-examination of the Origins of Islamic Fundamentalism," *Contention*, 4 (2), 1995: 121–39.

Scott, James C., "Patron-Client Politics and Political Change in Southeast Asia" in Steffen W. Schmidt (ed.), *Friends, Followers and Factions. A Reader in Political Clientelism*, University of California Press, 1977: 123–46.

Sikand, Yoginder, "For Islam and Kashmir: The Prison Diaries of Sayyed Ali Geelani of the Jamaat-i-Islami of Jammu and Kashmir," *Journal of Muslim Minority Affairs*, 18 (2), 1998: 241–50.

———— "The Emergence and Development of the Jamaat-i-Islami of Jammu and' Kashmir," *Modern Asian Studies*, 36 (3), 2002: 705–51.

Hagiographic publications

Aslam, Muhammad, *Sayyed Ali Gilani and the Liberation Movement*, Rawalpindi, Markaz Matbuat-i-Kashmir, 1994.

Suhewardy, Muzamal, *A Decade of Kashmir Struggle 1990–1999*, Lahore, Future Visions Publications, n.d.

Primary sources

Awan Abbas Ahtar, *Karavan-i-Shuhada. Kabul se Kashmir tak* (Urdu) [The Martyrs' Caravan. From Kabul to Kashmir], Lahore, Mohtamim Idarah Matbuat Talebah, 1994.

Bharat se ab larenge ham (Urdu) [Now We Are Going to Fight India], video, Karachi, n.d.

Turabi, Pr. Alifuddin, *Hizb-ul-Mujahidin Jammu-o-Kashmir. Pas-i-Manzar, Nasb-ul-Ain aur Jaddo Jehed* (Urdu) [Hizb-ul-Mujahidin of Jammu and Kashmir. Origins, Objectives and Struggle], Muzaffarabad, Ghulam Muhammad Safi Publisher, February 1991.

Ul-Haq, Shams, *Hizb-ul-Mujahidin. Tarikh, Qeam, Jaddo Jehed* (Urdu) [Hizb-ul-Mujahidin. History, Formation and Struggle], Rawalpindi, Markaz-Matbuat Kashmir, 1994.

Jihad-i-Kashmir, year 1999 (Fortnightly published by the Jamaat-i-Islami Azad Jammu and Kashmir in Muzaffarabad and Rawalpindi).

NOTES

1. André Corvisier, *Dictionnaire d'art et d'histoire militaires*, Paris, PUF, 1988, p. 579.
2. In 1979, Akhtar Abdur Rahman was appointed director general of Pakistan's Inter-Services Intelligence (ISI). See his biography by Brigadier (retd) Muhammad Yousaf, *Silent Soldier. The Man behind the Afghan Jihad, General Akhtar Rahman Shaheed*, Lahore, Jang Publishers, 1991.
3. But when the Prime Minister Nawaz Sharif distanced himself from the army-orchestrated Kargil offensive in 1999, he was ousted from power.
4. Personal interview, Rawalpindi, November 1999.
5. There are no reliable figures: the Hizb-ul-Mujahidin claims to have killed 1,600 Indian officers and 27,000 soldiers between 1989 and 2001 (*Zarb ul-Mujahidin*, October 2001), but according to India's Ministry of Internal Affairs, "no more than" 3,300 regular troops and paramilitaries were killed during this period.
6. Janice E. Thomson (1994).
7. According to Indian government assessments compiled in 2002, more than a third of the 3,400 Islamist guerrillas operating in Kashmir were members of the Hizb-ul-Mujahidin.
8. Special forces units of the regular army attempted to foment an insurrection in Indian Kashmir. The operation was a fiasco owing to the lack of popular support.
9. Personal interview, Srinagar, February 2003.
10. South Asia's first jihadist force, led by Sayyid Ahmed Barelwi (1786–1831). Dubbed the "Mahomet's Crescenters" by the British because of its links with

Wahhabism, this irregular army attempted to "liberate" Punjab from the presence of the Sikhs. Defeated at Balakot in 1831, it arose from the ashes several years later and led the struggle against British rule until 1870.

11. Professor Alifuddin Turabi, (1991), p. 17. At the time of the book's publication, the author was vice-president of the Jamaat-i-Islami of Azad Jammu and Kashmir, and its publisher was the Hizb's *amir*.

12. It was founded in 1941 by Maulana Abul Ala Mawdudi (1903–79). It gave birth, after the 1947 and 1971 Partitions, to distinct political parties in the two Kashmirs, India, Pakistan and Bangladesh.

13. A former director of Pakistani Military Intelligence recalled that when Amanullah Khan (leader of a splinter faction of the JKLF) decided to cross the Line of Control (LOC) in 1992, the Pakistani army was nearly dragged into an escalation of military operations, something it was eager to avoid at the time. (Personal interview, Rawalpindi, November 1999).

14. Vali Reza Nasr (1994), pp. 120–1.

15. Personal interview with a former activist of the Islami Jamaat-i-Tulaba-JK (the student wing of the JI-JK). Srinagar, January 2003.

16. The party's *amir* in fact confirmed that, "2,000 of our members and cadres were killed between 1988 and 1997 because we backed a militant approach" (personal interview, Srinagar, February 2003). The party was outlawed in 1990, and its Srinagar offices are currently located within a police station compound.

17. Muhammad Amir Rana (2002), p. 367.

18. Such as the sections "Zia ul-Haq shaheed" [martyr], "Qazi Hussein Ahmad" and Sayyid Ali Shah Gilani", for instance. See Shams-ul-Haq (1994), p. 13.

19. Zulfiqar Ali, "Back to Camp", *The Herald* (Karachi), July 2005, p. 52. For the situation in the camps in 2006, see Intikhab Amir, "The Waiting Game", *The Herald*, August 2006, pp. 69–82.

20. Professor Alifuddin Turabi (1991), p. 7. Ibid. for all subsequent quotations unaccompanied by footnotes.

21. The expression is used by Gilles Kepel (2000), p. 232.

22. In practice, "agents" included political and religious leaders who rigorously opposed accession to Pakistan.

23. Hizb-ul-Mujahidin spokesman, quoted by Muhammad Amir Rana (2002), p. 68.

24. The only major attacks in Indian Kashmir since that time have been claimed by Al-Badr, the Harkat's loose network and a newcomer to the jihadist scene, Al-Mansurian, which is often described as a front group for the Lashkar-e-Tayebbah.

25. Indian authorities initially attributed the responsibility for this attack to "Kashmiri militants". It was later proved that a pro-Hindutva retired Indian army officer organised it.

26. Personal interview with a ministerial secretary, Muzaffarabad, March 2001.

27. Jean-François Médard, quoted in Jean-Louis Briquet, "La politique clientélaire. Clientélisme et processus politique" in Jean-Louis Briquet and Frédéric Sawicki (eds) (1998), p. 7.

28. Professor Alifuddin Turabi (1991), p. 29.

29. Ibid.

30. For the two dimensions of clientelism, see Jean Leca and Yves Schemeil (1983), pp. 455–94, particularly p. 458.

31. Personal interview (Lahore, August 2004) with an Urdu press journalist who reported the activities of jihadist groups throughout the 1990s.

32. Alexander Evans (2000), p. 76.
33. Through the AJK Council whose president is the prime minister of Pakistan.
34. *Bharat se ab larenge ham* [Urdu], video, Karachi, no date.
35. "Cessation of military operations, release of imprisoned insurgents and establishment of an atmosphere of good-will". See "Hizb Ready for Talks with India", *Daily Times* (Lahore), 17 April 2005. Reports of the jihadist leader's desire to re-enter the political process became increasingly insistent a year later (personal interview with a Kashmiri activist with close links to Salahuddin, Washington, April 2006).
36. For instance, the JI-P justified its temporary alliance with the Benazir Bhutto government in 1990 on the grounds that the latter supported the "liberation movement in Kashmir".
37. Most militant organisations invested their money in land and property, which is the best way of laundering money and keeping it in circulation. This explains why hundreds of houses continue to be built, notably in Srinagar, despite fifteen years of violence.
38. Financing techniques have been modernised. Individual contributions are received in exchange for a coupon bearing the imprint of the "Jihad fi sabil Allah Fund". The coupon is worth 12 euro cents and lists the uses to which the contribution is put.
39. "Muhammad Shehzad's Interview with Syed Salahuddin: We are not Terrorists … We are Freedom Fighters", *The Friday Times* (Lahore), 9–15 May 2003.
40. In 1980, for instance, the junior JI-JK managed to organise an international conference in Srinagar which attracted *imams* from the Medina and Mecca mosques and officials from the Gulf States. On the generational transformation of the JI-JK, see Yoginder Sikand (2002), pp. 705–51.
41. This "all-party conference for freedom" was founded in 1993 on the initiative of the young Mirwaiz Umar Farooq. Its aim is to unify separatist groups and work towards a political and ultimately peaceful settlement with New Delhi.
42. Muhammad Aslam (1994), p. 9.
43. Yoginder Sikand (1998), p. 243.
44. "Sayyid" (fem. "sayyida") is an honorific title given to people said to be descendants of the Prophet Muhammad. The link is often self-proclaimed and unverifiable.
45. Salahuddin is the son of a farmer and Gilani of an irrigation canal maintenance crew's employee.
46. A Persianised version of "sayyid" in the Indian subcontinent.
47. A Persian title which, in the Sufi tradition, also means a spiritual guide or "holy man".
48. In the Indo-Pakistani context, the upper class status of the *ashraf* derives from their claim to foreign ancestry, which thus sets them apart from later converts to Islam. See Barbara Metcalf (2004), p. 176.
48. This is the figure advanced by Praveen Swami (a correspondent for the Indian daily *The Hindu* in Kashmir), who established it from sources given by the Indian Ministry of Internal Affairs. Personal interview, New Delhi, February 2003.
50. 12,000 "devout" and 15,000 "supporters". *Zarb-ul-Mujahidin* (one of the Hizb's fortnightly magazines), October 2001.
51. Muzamal Suhewardy (no date), p. 31. This estimate is plausible, though inflated, given that 364 families are looked after by the JI-P's Martyrs of Islam Foundation (the Shuhada-i-Islam Foundation) in Lahore.

52. According to official Indian sources, of the 12,500 militants killed between 1990 and 1999 only 15–20% were classified as "Pakistanis/foreigners".

53. Christine Fair, "Militant Recruitment in Pakistan: Implications for al-Qaeda and Other Organizations", *Studies in Conflict & Terrorism*, 27, 2004, pp. 489–504, p. 494.

54. Professor Alifuddin Turabi (1991), pp. 19–20

55. Such as the biographies of the 27 "martyrs" of the Hizb published in Abbas Akhtar Awan (1994).

56. Amélie Blom (2007), pp. 71–88.

57. See Abbas Akhtar Awan (1994), pp. 244–5.

58. Muhammad Amir Rana (2002), p. 365. The IJT claims 1,115 members in Pakistan and 13,000 supporters; the JTA 218 members and 1,400 supporters.

59. The organisational overlap reveals the extent to which the two groups are linked: the Hizb's deputy supreme guide is none other than M. Javed Kasuri, the former head of the JTA.

60. Personal interviews with a member of IJT-P (Lahore, September 2003) and a former member of the IJT-JK (Srinagar, February 2003).

61. Personal interviews, JI-P headquarters, Lahore, October 2002.

62. Vali Reza Nasr (1994), p. 69.

63. Personal interview, Lahore, September 2002.

64. Of the 364 families looked after by the Shuhada-i-Islam Foundation, 300 are from Punjab.

65. Personal interview with a resident of Bagh, August 2004.

66. For an example of this approach, see Jessica Stern, "Pakistan's Jihad Culture", *Foreign Affairs*, 79 (6), November-December 2000, pp. 115–26.

67. *Jihad* is by no means confined to armed struggle. Besides assisting the *mujahidin* and families of martyrs, the JI-P's "Jihad-fi-sabil-Allah Fund" also builds hospitals and provides aid to students from poor families and victims of natural disasters.

68. This paragraph draws on a seminar conducted by Marc Gaborieau: "Islam in the Indo-Pakistani Sub-Continent: The Origins of Muslim Fundamentalism 1912–1979", Centre d'Etude de l'Inde et de l'Asie du Sud (EHESS/CNRS), 1999–2000.

69. In the 1920s and 30s, Mawdudi was haunted by the fear that the Muslim community—understood as both a cultural and a political force—could be annihilated. The ulema's allegiance to the Congress Party and the secularist positions adopted by the Muslim League convinced him of this danger. See Vali Reza Nasr, "Communalism and Fundamentalism: A Re-examination of the Origins of Islamic Fundamentalism", *Contention*, 4 (2), winter 1995, pp. 121–39.

70. In 1989, they made up only 1.5% of directors in the state banking sector and 30% of the administration. See Navnita Chadha Behera (2000), p. 154.

71. Professor Afhuddin Turabi (1991), p. 4.

72. "Commander" Ahsan Dar, quoted in Mohammad Amir Rana (2002), p. 367.

73. In order to maintain discipline, the Hizb refers to a *hadith* attributed to the Prophet: "He who obeys his leaders, obeys me. He who obeys me, obeys God".

74. Professor Aliffudin Turabi (1991), p. 5. Emphasis added.

75. Ibid., p. 19.

76. Ibid., p. 19.

77. The term used by Jean Leca and Yves Schemeil (1983), p. 458.

78. Pirates functioned as quasi-states, mercenaries threatened to plunge their home states into unwanted inter-state wars, and mercantile companies waged war on each other, etc.
79. Janice E. Thomson (1994).
80. The ban included the Lashkar and Jaish-e-Muhammad. Both had overtly supported Osama bin Laden. The Hizb was careful to avoid such mistakes.

Map 8: Pakistan

This map is based on *Le Pakistan*, Christophe Jaffrelot (ed.), Paris, Fayard, 2000

7

THE SSP

HERALD OF MILITANT SUNNI ISLAM IN PAKISTAN

Mariam Abou Zahab

In the context of Pakistan, "sectarianism" denotes the conflict between the Sunni and Shia communities, which make up about 80% and 20% of the population respectively. South Asia has a long tradition of sectarian violence between Sunni and Shia Muslims, especially in the form of isolated incidents during the Moharram processions.[1] Until recently, doctrinal differences were largely confined to theological arguments and concerned a relatively small segment of the population. In general, Sunni and Shia[2] co-existed peacefully, and marriages between the two communities were frequent.

The latent tensions between Sunni and Shia were exacerbated by the Islamisation policy introduced by General Zia ul-Haq (1977–88), an approach based on a narrow interpretation of Hanafi Sunni Islam[3] and favouring the Deobandi school of thought.[4] However, numerous external factors also contributed to the radicalisation of religious identities: the Iranian revolution (which reinforced the Shia identity and triggered a religious and later political mobilisation of the community);[5] regional rivalry between Saudi Arabia and Iran; the war between Iran and Iraq (which was perceived in Pakistan as a war between Sunni and Shia); and the launch of *jihad* in Afghanistan. This context was conducive to the emergence of sectarian movements that maintained ambiguous links with traditional religious parties and were often accused of conducting a proxy war on behalf of foreign powers, from whom they received money and arms. In the 1990s, these groups launched a violent campaign to protect the interests of their respective communities. Some 4,000 people, most of them Shia Muslims, were killed; thousands were injured during targeted assassinations and indiscriminate attacks on mosques and processions.

Is the often quoted theory of outside interference enough to explain the scale of sectarian violence? Or should we accept the interpretation advanced by the International Crisis Group (ICG)–"Sectarian conflict in Pakistan is the direct consequence of state policies of Islamization and marginalization of secular democratic forces"[6]–and attribute the conflict to purely internal factors?

While acknowledging the importance of external factors, one of the arguments advanced in this chapter is that the scale and intensity of the violence owe much to the exploitation of sectarian movements by two elements: social groups competing for local power, and successive governments pursuing short-term domestic and regional political goals.

What is the historical and ideological background of these groups? What goals do they hope to achieve? What constitutes their support base? What forms of violence do they employ? What is their relationship to the Pakistani state? We shall attempt to answer these questions through an examination of the Sipah-e-Sahaba Pakistan (SSP, Army of the Prophet's Companions), a Sunni extremist movement created in Jhang, a town in central Punjab, in 1985.

The origins of the SSP

The SSP appeared in Punjab in 1985 in the context of an Islamisation policy which, by identifying the version of Islam promoted by the state as the "true Islam", institutionalised religious discrimination and paved the way for the politicisation of religion.

The SSP has often been described as a reaction to aggressive, Iranian-backed Shia militancy. In reality, outside interference had a catalytic effect on one of the most fertile areas in Pakistan at a time when politico-religious entrepreneurs had grasped the power of anti-Shia rhetoric as a means of mobilising communities.

The social structure particular to Jhang was highly conducive to the emergence of the SSP. In this specific context, the conflict between Sunni and Shia may be interpreted as the outcome of a struggle for political power between rural Shia feudal landlords and an emergent urban middle class adhering to the Deobandi school of Sunni Islam.[7]

The SSP sprang from the Jamiat-e-Ulema-e-Islam (JUI), a Deobandi Sunni party founded in 1945 by pro-Pakistan ulema who had broken away from the Jamiat-Ulema-e-Hind (JUH), which opposed religious nationalism. Formally established as a political party in Lahore in 1968, the JUI fielded candidates in the first national elections in 1970, taking 25% of the vote in North West Frontier Province (NWFP), where it formed a short-lived coalition government (1972–73) with a Pashtun nationalist party, the National Awami Party (NAP). The JUI, also firmly embedded in the Pashtun regions of North Baluchistan, had access to a vast network of *madrasas*, seminaries which played a major role in the Afghan *jihad* and the subsequent emergence of the Taliban.

Like other Deobandi groups, the JUI participated in the anti-Ahmadi movement,[8] which in 1974 culminated in the adoption of a constitutional amendment that reclassified the Ahmadiyya community as a non-Muslim minority. The anti-Ahmadi movement was particularly active in Jhang, for at Partition the community had established its headquarters at Rabwah, near the city of Chiniot, in the same district. The anti-Ahmadi controversy fuelled the development of sectarian discourse and was thus a key factor in the rise of the anti-Shia movement.

Precursors of the SSP also include the Majlis-e-Ahrar, a less well-known movement founded by a group of reformist Punjabi ulema in 1929. The Ahrar, which recruited its members from Punjab's urban lower-middle class, campaigned against British rule, the feudals[9] and the Ahmadiyya. In the early 1930s, it launched a movement for the defence of Islam in Kashmir. The Ahrar became notorious for its participation in anti-Shia activities in the late 1930s, notably in Lucknow, where its Punjabi members took part in violent clashes between Sunnis and Shias in 1937 and 1938. The movement went into decline after Partition and its members (followed by their sons) were "reconverted" to violence, first against Ahmadis and later against the Shia. This trajectory explains the sectarian education received by many SSP members, who continued a family tradition that the teaching in Deobandi *madrasas* simply reinforced.

Finally, in Karachi, there was a predecessor of the SSP in the Sawad-e Azam Ahl e-Sunnat (the Sunni Majority), a virulently anti-Shia organisation created by Pashtun clerics in the early 1980s. This group, believed to have been set up by the martial law authorities, also counted Haq Nawaz Jhangvi, founder of the SSP, as a member, and was the first to call publicly for Shia Muslims to be classed as *kafir* (infidels).

The SSP has always maintained ambiguous relations with the JUI, skilfully playing off the rivalry between the Maulana Fazlur Rehman and Maulana Sami ul Haq factions. Interaction is very strong at *madrasa* level. The links with the JUI have never been broken; the party's leaders claim to agree with the SSP's ideas, but differ as to its methods.

Haq Nawaz Jhangvi was born in Jhang district in 1952. A fine orator, he attended a *madrasa* in Multan and, like other SSP leaders, launched his career during the anti-Ahmadi agitation in 1974. He also denounced the beliefs and practices of the Barelvi school[10] and the influence of Shia Islam on the rural Sunni population through the agency of Shia landowners, most of whom, in Jhang district, claimed a spiritual power derived from their status as the descendents of saints. Haq Nawaz was vice-president of the Punjabi branch of the JUI when the SSP was created.

The SSP's founders, almost all of whom were shopkeepers, local residents and Mohajirs,[11] held meetings in a mosque in the Piplianwali quarter of Jhang. Aware of the possibilities afforded by anti-Shia propaganda, they recruited and manipulated a number of extremist mullahs, notably Jhangvi.

The Zia regime, anxious to counter Shia activism triggered by its attempts to impose Hanafi Sunni Islam and punish the community for its defiance of martial law and successful resistance to the state collection of *zakat* (alms tax), encouraged the SSP's formation. Zia also saw it as a way to break the Pakistan Peoples Party (PPP), with which many Shias identified. The anti-PPP strategy also gave rise to the Mohajir Qaumi Movement (MQM), created in Karachi in 1984. It should be noted that both movements emerged shortly before the lifting of martial law (1 January 1986), and that Jhangvi—or at least his mentors—clearly nursed political ambitions despite the SSP's insistence that it was a non-political, purely religious movement. Jhangvi himself always referred to separation between politics and religion as a plot devised by the enemies of Islam.

Furthermore, Saudi Arabia, concerned by Iran's eagerness to export its revolution and the level of Shia activism in Pakistan, was inclined to provide financial support for movements like the SSP. The United States, whose relations with Iran had deteriorated considerably following the embassy hostage crisis, made no objection. Iraq, competing with Iran in the massive dissemination of sectarian literature in Pakistan, also contributed to the SSP's coffers.

During the 1980s, SSP activity was generally confined to the denunciation of "Shia heretics" and the large-scale production of sectarian literature, most of which was authored by Zia ul Rehman Farooqi, a Mojahir scholar employed at the Ministry of *awqaf* (endowments, a key Islamic institution).

The SSP seeks to combat the Shia by any means, have them declared a non-Muslim minority and, ultimately, transform Pakistan into a Sunni state. It advocates the defence, through constitutional and legal measures, of the honour of the *Sahaba* (*namus-e-Sahaba*, Companions of the Prophet), and the death sentence for anyone who insults them. This is aimed at the Shia, who are accused of cursing the first caliphs (*tabarra*) during their mourning ceremonies. The organisation calls for the restoration of the caliphate system of government (*Khilafat-e Rashida*, which is also the title of its monthly journal) and for the anniversaries of the deaths of the first caliphs—particularly one Moharram, the death of Caliph Omar—to be declared public holidays. In order to eliminate sectarian violence, it demands a ban on Shia public mourning ceremonies (essentially the processions involving flagellation and other physical manifestations of mourning), which are judged offensive to Sunnis. Other demands include an end to Iranian interference in Pakistan's domestic affairs, and the prohibition of Shia sectarian literature distributed with the support of Iranian cultural centres and the Iranian embassy in Pakistan.

The SSP and the electoral process

In 1988, Haq Nawaz stood as a JUI candidate against Abida Hussain, the dominant Shia figure in Jhang. He obtained 38,995 votes, but Abida Hussain was elected with 47,374 votes. Note, however, that during non-partisan elections in 1985, Sheikh Yusuf—a local industrialist and member of the Sheikh caste[12] who would later become the SSP's principal source of local financial support and exploit it to break the monopoly in municipal politics of his rival Sheikh Iqbal[13]–had won a seat on Punjab's Provincial Assembly. Yusuf was backed by the same people who would go on to form the SSP a few months later.

Haq Nawaz's successor as head of the SSP, Maulana Isar ul Qasmi (born in 1964), came from an Ambala Mohajir family which had settled in the Samundri district. Educated at three *madrasa*s in Lahore, he abandoned an unsuccessful business career to become *khatib* (preacher) in an Okara mosque, where his reputation owed more to his clashes with the police than to erudition concerning religious matters.

A JUI cadre, Qasmi joined the SSP in 1986 and was elected as a JUI representative to the National and Provincial Assemblies in 1990, defeating Sheikh Iqbal. Abida Hussain did not stand in this election but supported Sheikh Iqbal against the SSP. Iqbal, however, was unable to attract the Shia vote. Qasmi was assassinated in January 1991. In a move that revealed the competition between the SSP and local Sunnis for the same electoral base, the SSP, despite the lack of evidence, chose to accuse Sheikh Iqbal's family of the murder rather than attribute it to Shia elements. For security reasons, the authorities did not organise a by-election until April 1992. In the meantime, outbreaks of sectarian violence in Jhang claimed many lives.

The 1992 election, successfully contested by the SSP candidate Maulana Azam Tariq, signalled the movement's emergence as a political force. For the first time in Pakistan's history, a sectarian organisation had won an election. The campaign unfolded in a climate of terror; the SSP announced that it would not accept defeat, and participation was around 40%.[14]

In the context of Jhang, Azam Tariq was an outsider. Born in 1962 to a Mohajir family which had settled in a village near Chichawatni, he attended the celebrated Binori Town Deobandi *madrasa* in Karachi, obtaining a "double MA" in Arabic and Islamic studies. He was an outstanding orator—it was said that he could "ignite water"—and his teachers advised him to use language as a weapon. He taught in a Karachi *madrasa* before joining the SSP in 1987. Shortly afterwards he travelled to Afghanistan, where he displayed little aptitude for combat but inspired the fighters with his preaching. Returning to Pakistan, he became imam of the Siddiq-e-Akbar mosque in north Karachi (still an SSP bastion), where he was spotted by Haq Nawaz and Zia ul Rehman Farooqi, the SSP ideologue, and invited to take over the Jamia Mahmudia *madrasa*, the organisation's base in Jhang.[15] He was re-elected to the National Assembly in 1993, obtaining 55,004 votes as opposed to the 36,278 votes garnered by the independent candidate Sheikh Iqbal.

From the time of his arrival in Jhang and the SSP's formal entry into politics, Azam Tariq devoted considerable energy to creating a respectable image for the movement and distancing it from the thugs it attracted in large numbers. During the 1993 election campaign he stressed the need to maintain law and order in Jhang, denounced unemployment as a cause of disorder and claimed to have furthered the town's economic development, notably by securing its connection to the gas network. These campaign themes won him a number of Shia votes. Two SSP members, natives of Jhang, also won election to the Punjab Provincial Assembly in 1993: Sheikh Hakim Ali, who in 1995 would become Fisheries Minister in the pro-PPP provincial government of Sardar Arif Nakai, and Riaz Hashmat Janjua, who would be appointed adviser to Manzoor Wattoo, the head of the provincial government. Manzoor Wattoo, whose father was Ahmadi, was susceptible to pressure from the SSP, which partly explains the impunity enjoyed by militants at that time.

However, the SSP's political influence in Jhang began to decline in 1997. Azam Tariq, defeated in the National Assembly elections by Amanullah Sial, a Shia feudal landlord, succeeded in winning a seat on the Punjab Provincial Assembly. He took over the leadership of the SSP that same year, after sustaining serious injuries when the group was attacked in Lahore (Zia ul Rehman Farooqi died in this attack). A Shia, Mehram Ali, was subsequently convicted of these crimes and executed.

The SSP's social base in Jhang

Jhang is the only district in which sectarian strife and class conflict (between landowners and other social categories) coincide to the extent that they structure the political dimension. Anyone seeking to enter the political arena but lacking the necessary capital—land, a modern education or family networks—uses religion as a lever.

A number of Mohajir entrepreneurs, middlemen and businessmen with interests in pesticides, fertilisers, leather, textiles, flour, sugar, vegetable oil and transport saw their wealth increase considerably in the 1980s under the economic liberalisation policy implemented by General Zia. This group formed a new middle class; it existed on the margins of the traditional urban middle class (many of whom had enriched themselves at Partition by seizing the wealth of Hindus and Sikhs in Jhang) and lacked representation in the traditional political parties. Unable to influence the local population, which was locked into a clientelist relationship with the landowners, Mohajir business communities began funding religious movements. Their initiative coincided with the development of clientelist arrangements between the state and clerics and *madrasas*, a network facilitated by the *zakat* and *ushr* (a religious tax on crops) committees, inspired by Zia's policy of Islamisation. The rising business elite realised the potential benefits of this ideological resource and supported the exploitation of Islam for political ends.

The Mohajir middle class was quick to grasp the advantages of joining—or at least supporting—the SSP: the movement had the potential to further its interests. Mohajirs who could not obtain the endorsement of the Pakistan Muslim League (PML) ran on the SSP ticket and attracted bloc votes. Local mullahs, for their part, secured votes for the SSP in return for services, and especially for jobs. Thus people who felt no particular hostility towards the Shia community were elected on the SSP ticket. When the organisation was outlawed in 2002, some of its cadres, clerics included, joined the pro-Musharraf PML-Q, a clear indication that their allegiance to the SSP had been determined more by access to power than by religious ideology.

The organisation also attracted the support of local Sunnis, Deobandis and even Barelvis, who owned modest estates and sought to contest the hegemony of the big Shia landowners.

Apart from Haq Nawaz, whose family was indigenous to the area, all the SSP's leaders were Mohajirs. Although educated in prestigious *madrasas*, they were "peripheral" and indeed *lumpen* rather than traditional ulema. All had taken part in the Afghan *jihad*, and many belonged to the Arain caste which, while occupying a fairly low ranking in the Punjabi hierarchy, had become economically dominant in the province after Partition. The caste continued its social ascent under the regime of Zia ul Haq, who was himself Arain.

Most grassroots activists were recruited from the *madrasas* which proliferated in southern Punjab and constituted an almost inexhaustible pool of recruits. One striking aspect of the demonstrators fielded by the SSP was their youth; this was particularly noticeable the day after 11 September and during the riots that followed the funeral of Azam Tariq in 2003. Despite abundant evidence to the contrary, the SSP constantly denied its links to the *madrasas*, although Mohammad Amir Rana counted 34 affiliated seminaries.[16] Apart from central and south Punjab, the SSP was particularly well embedded in Karachi, where it recruited Punjabi and Pashtun students from the *madrasas*. The SSP maintained a much lower profile in north Punjab, especially in the "army belt" districts,[17] where sectarian loyalties were not as relevant in political terms.

The organisation also attracted the urban young who had attended Urdu-medium state schools, a group characterised by its poor education, lack of qualifications, inability to find work and vulnerability to indoctrination. These third-generation Mohajirs resented graduates of the English-medium private schools, had no prospects and were eager for an identity and a cause to fight for. They were ready to follow anyone who blamed an "other" for their predicament—Shia Muslims in this instance—and offered them a way out of it. Moreover, by claiming to speak in the name of Islam, they could compensate for their social marginality.

The SSP also recruited criminals, a practice that began before 1992. Such people—especially drug traffickers—were quick to grasp that the SSP provided the perfect cover for their activities. The arrangement was mutually beneficial: criminals gained political protection and were able to operate with impunity, while the SSP used them to maintain a certain level of mobilisation in the streets and intimidate its rivals.

Drug traffickers used the SSP to conduct their business. This was the case in Jhang and also in Karachi in 1995, where the SSP formed an alliance with the MQM-Haqiqi[18] in order to share the benefits of the drug and arms trades with mafia syndicates.

In sociological terms, the similarity to the MQM in Karachi is striking. But whereas the MQM offered the youth of Karachi a substitute ethnic identity, the identity on offer in Punjab was that of a Sunni militant. Ethnic identity was not a viable option for the Mohajirs of Punjab. In fact it was irrelevant, as most Punjabis accepted their identity as Pakistanis. Moreover, Punjabi Mohajirs refused to be defined as such and referred to themselves as Pakistanis. On the other hand, the local population, many of whom spoke Siraiki, had not fully accepted the presence of settlers (*abadkar*) from northern Punjab, the people who had migrated south in the late 19th century when the Canal colonies were opened, and still regarded Mohajirs as outsiders.

Like some other social categories, Mohajir traders sought to break the stranglehold on the structures of power maintained by feudal landlords and local Sunni businessmen. They supported the SSP but kept their distance from it. The Jhang Chamber of Commerce also used SSP activists as an alternative police force. When crime rates increased, businessmen paid more to buy security.

Having consolidated its presence in Jhang, the SSP extended its activities to other towns in central and south Punjab. Faisalabad, the largest industrial city in the province, the centre of Sunni extremism and home to a large number of Mohajirs, soon became an SSP bastion.

In Pakistan, the state is perceived as illegitimate and institutionally weak, and is thus widely distrusted. The SSP attracted people who were looking for protection from corruption and nepotism. The organisation responded to this demand by setting up a form of patron-client relationship that functioned in the same way as traditional networks.

Haq Nawaz adopted a different approach to the *madrasa-* and mosque-centred activities of traditional ulema. He became involved in social work, attempted to resolve the population's material difficulties, arbitrated in conflicts between neighbours and found jobs for the unemployed. Within a very short period, he had established himself as a credible alternative to the feudals for purposes of protection and the distribution of wealth. He was also more accessible and more efficient, and was thus able to reach beyond the Sunni community and extend his electoral base. Azam Tariq adopted a similar approach, as we were able to observe when spending a day at his home in Jhang. By 6 a.m., a crowd had gathered outside his door to request a variety of favours. He stage-managed the event, sitting cross-legged on his bed, flanked by telephones and a fax machine. He listened patiently, offering advice, writing job references and helping to fill in hospital admission forms and applications for financial assistance. A single telephone call secured the release of a young man the police were holding in custody. His visitors, impressed by his charisma and effectiveness, insisted that the lot of the poor had improved considerably since his arrival in Jhang. The SSP was much more accessible than the feudal landlords, who had to be approached through an intermediary who would arrange an appointment and then keep the supplicant waiting; the setting in which the supplicant was received was designed to intimidate, and everything was done to ensure that he felt obliged to the feudal landlord. The SSP had also set up a mutual aid fund to look after prisoners and their families. It was located in the Piplianwali mosque, next door to Azam Tariq's modest house.

In order to spread its message and mobilise its recruits, the SSP relied on local mosques and Deobandi *madrasas*. The function of these establishments was twofold: they provided the manpower which kept the conflict alive, and also reproduced the ideology behind it through a brand of teaching that focused on denouncing the "other", and the production of sectarian literature. The SSP was the first movement to fully exploit sectarian literature as an instrument of mobilisation. Besides the monthly *Khilafat-e Rashida* published in Faisalabad, it distributed pamphlets and booklets containing extracts from Shia texts attributed to anonymous Iranian authors. For the most part, these texts concerned the allegedly dissolute life of the wives of the Prophet and the *Sahaba*, and were intended to arouse hatred towards Shia Muslims. The young men who read this literature were horrified, and felt duty-bound to defend the honour of the *Sahaba* and of Aisha, the Prophet's favourite wife. Zia ur Rehman Farooqi produced a compilation of some two hundred Shia works entitled *Tarikhi Dastawez* (Historic Documents). In 1991, this was presented to Nawaz Sharif, then head of the Punjab provincial government, with a view to securing a ban on such material. The introduction to the collection contained anti-Shia quotations from Sunni texts as well as *fatwas* approved by 400 ulema from the various branches of Sunni Islam.

Audio and video cassettes were also used extensively to recruit new members, as we were able to note when we asked militants about the circumstances that had led them to join the movement.

In January 2001, as electoral support declined, Azam Tariq changed tactics and announced a five-point programme for the application of *sharia* law in 20 Punjabi towns. The programme was primarily aimed at re-mobilising activists and keeping them occupied. The militants would ensure that shops closed for half an hour for prayers and boycott those that did not comply. Shops would also close on Friday and open on Sunday. Other targets included satellite and cable TV stations; establishments involved in this "immoral" culture would be boycotted. Finally, militants were to urge the population to reject courts that applied the British-based judicial system and turn to ulema and mosques which meted out justice in accordance with Islamic law. As Azam Tariq was imprisoned once again in February 2001, the programme was not launched.

Funding

The SSP's principal financial backer in Jhang itself is Sheikh Yusuf, a local small businessman who amassed considerable wealth in the 1960s. Based in Lahore and very well connected in military circles, Yusuf owns the Hasnain Construction Company, which won the contract to build the Peshawar-Islamabad motorway.

Some of Faisalabad's leading Mohajir industrialists have also funded the movement. The main task of the 17 branches the SSP claims to maintain overseas—in countries such as the United Arab Emirates, the United States and Britain—is to raise money from the businessmen of the Punjabi diaspora. Grassroots members contributed very little money. Like other religious movements, the SSP collected the hides of animals sacrificed at Eid (the festival of sacrifice) and sold them to the tanneries at auctions. Criminal activities—armed robbery, kidnapping and ransom, *qabza* operations (groups seizing land by force and very often staking their claim to it by erecting a mosque), and even drug trafficking—provided another source of income.

Finally, the SSP is said to have received Arab funding (from sources known as the "powerful external godfathers"), although this cannot be verified.

Anyway, the SSP had considerable financial resources at its disposal. Large sums were spent on bailing out militants or bribing the police to release those under arrest. In 2001, Azam Tariq offered the family of Sadiq Ganji[19] a large sum in blood money in order to prevent his murderer's execution. The rifts and infighting that followed the assassination of leaders were usually triggered by arguments over the control of the group's financial assets. This was notably the case in 2001, when one of the sons of Zia ul Qasmi (director of the Qasmia *madrasa* in Faisalabad), a member of the SSP Supreme Council, joined the JUI's Qadri faction and denounced Azam Tariq, accusing him of stealing the proceeds from the sale of hides as well as donations from other countries. The recurrent and often violent conflicts between Azam Tariq and the sons of Haq Nawaz—one of whom was murdered in 2002 in Karachi in unexplained circumstances—were also about financial matters. The power struggles that followed Azam Tariq's murder revolved around the distribution of the movement's funds.

Violence and the Lashkar-e-Jhangvi

Membership of the SSP provided young Sunni Muslims with a refuge in the form of a different identity. Their parents had envisaged Pakistan as a Muslim paradise on earth, a land free of injustice and oppression. Having suffered rejection and humiliation when looking for work, they realised that the SSP, which blamed Shias for their predicament, offered them a way to defend their interests. These young people were eager to acquire social status and saw membership of the SSP as a means of inspiring respect, even if only through the fear the organisation aroused. In a society which regarded violence as a legitimate way to settle differences, considerable power accrued to those prepared to use it. Moreover, the militants regarded violence against the Shias as a perfectly legitimate activity, since the aim was to purify the religion. They believed in the rightness of their actions, and the encouragement they often received from their families reinforced their conviction that nothing could stop those who acted in God's name.

Sectarian violence is often seen as an acceptable way of expressing discontent. The police do nothing to stop militants rampaging through the streets after the funerals of murdered leaders. In October 2003, we witnessed the riot that followed the funeral of Azam Tariq in Islamabad: militants, many of them very young, attacked and looted shops, set fire to a cinema, smashed the windows of hundreds of cars and stole trunks containing the gifts of worshippers from a nearby Shia sanctuary. The police made no attempt to intervene. The Ministry of the Interior subsequently stated that as the young people had been enraged by their leader's murder, it was natural for them to express their anger. The disorder and the targets selected strongly suggested a revolt by the have-nots against a Westernized urban middle class.

The violence began in 1986, with anti-Shia riots in Lahore. In 1987 Ehsan Elahi Zaheer and Habib ul Rehman Yazdani, leaders of Ahl-e-Hadith, the Pakistani advocates of Salafism, were assassinated. Ehsan Elahi Zaheer was the author of *Khomeini and the Shia*; translated into many languages, the book is still popular in Saudi Arabia, where it is distributed to pilgrims in Mecca and Medina. In 1987, clashes between Deobandis and Barelvis in Jhang resulted in the deaths of two Barelvis. Twelve SSP cadres, including Haq Nawaz, were arrested and later released on bail. Haq Nawaz retained bitter memories of the humiliating treatment he received while in police custody.

A turning point was reached in Peshawar in August 1988, with the assassination of Allama Arif Hussaini, a Parachinar Pashtun and leader of the Shia party Tehrik-e-Nifaz-e-Fiqh-e-Jaafriya (TNFJ), which became Tehrik-e-Jaafriya Pakistan (TJP) in 1993. Allama Hussaini acted as Khomeini's *wakil* (representative) in Pakistan. His activities aroused great concern in Saudi Arabia and Iraq. Among those implicated in his murder was a close colleague of General Zia and a native of Jhang, which indicated that Inter-Services Intelligence (ISI) had played a part in the affair. Haq Nawaz Jhangvi himself was assassinated in February 1990, probably at the instigation of Sheikh Iqbal. However, the SSP attributed the crime to Shia elements, a tactic that enabled it to mobilise the Sunni community in Jhang. Sheikh Iqbal and his family were targeted by SSP militants, and Sheikh Iqbal himself was killed by members of the organisation in March 1995.

In December 1990, the murder of Haq Nawaz was followed by that of Sadiq Ganji, the Iranian consul general in Lahore. The diplomat was killed by a man who was a member of the SSP at the time and who was allegedly accompanied by a junior air force officer seconded to the ISI.[20] Another SSP member, a resident of Jhang who had changed his name to Haq Nawaz, was convicted of the murder and executed in February 2001.

During the 1990s, the SSP spawned numerous dissident splinter groups, many of which were led by local mullahs and served the interests of the feudal lords. The most violent of these groups, Lashkar-e-Jhangvi (LeJ, Army of Jhangvi), emerged in 1994, soon after the SSP's entry into politics. The LeJ's founders criticised SSP leaders for having abandoned Haq Nawaz's mission, and were committed to its continuation through violence.

The LeJ developed into the armed wing of the SSP and carried out attacks that would have been too costly for the SSP in political terms—the murder of Iranians and Shia dignitaries, and reprisals for the killing of Sunni dignitaries, SSP leaders and militants. Azam Tariq told us that the LeJ was created by

SSP militants who had suffered at the hands of the police during the violence in Jhang in 1992 and had subsequently been forced to go underground. These claims were repeated by other SSP leaders, who maintained they had expelled extremists like Malik Ishaq, a LeJ ideologue and member of the SSP supreme council, for their espousal of armed violence following the government's persecution of militants. They also pointed out that those expelled for indiscipline had been trained by the SSP and shared its values; it was therefore hardly surprising if they reacted whenever sectarian violence claimed the life of an SSP militant.

In public, Azan Tariq's statements were far more categorical: he totally denied the existence of any link between the SSP and the LeJ, and condemned members whose opposition to the peaceful campaign for the application of Islamic law had created the rogue organisation.

The LeJ's founder, Riaz Basra (born in 1967), came from a poor family in the Sargodha region and attended a *madrasa* in Lahore before joining the SSP in 1986. Rising to become the movement's head of information, he stood for election in 1988 in the same Lahore constituency as Nawaz Sharif, obtaining 9,000 votes. Arrested in 1992 for the murder of Sadiq Ganji, he escaped in 1994 when being transferred from prison to court. "Influential friends" (the ISI) are alleged to have facilitated his escape. Basra fled to Afghanistan, where he established his own training camp, although he often quarrelled with the Taliban. LeJ militants, who probably never exceeded 100 in total, used Afghanistan as a sanctuary until November 2001, entering Pakistan to stage anti-Shia operations and returning immediately. The LeJ specialised in the murder of Iranian diplomats, leading Shia officials, lawyers, doctors, wealthy businessmen and high-ranking police officers, including Ashraf Marth, the brother-in-law of Chaudhry Shujaat, the Interior Minister at the time. Marth had conducted a detailed investigation of the attack on the Iranian cultural centre in Multan, and had revealed the LeJ's links with foreign elements. The group also attempted to assassinate Nawaz Sharif in January 1999. Riaz Basra regularly crossed the border into Pakistan and even attended a Tabligh rally in Raiwind. In telephone calls and faxes to newspapers, he claimed responsibility for the attacks carried out by LeJ militants.

In Afghanistan, the LeJ took part in the massacres of Hazara Shias and Iranian diplomats at Mazar-e-Sharif in 1998. The movement was outlawed in August 2001. Riaz Basra, whose links with the intelligence service were notorious, fled Afghanistan and was arrested in the tribal zone in December 2001. He was handed over to the intelligence services, which eliminated him in May 2002. The Pakistani government subsequently portrayed the LeJ as the Pakistani branch of al-Qaeda and blamed it for every attack on foreigners and religious minorities, although many of these claims were scarcely credible. By 2000, the group was torn by arguments, notably over the management of funds and the appropriateness of continuing sectarian attacks under a military government. This last point demonstrates, if need be, how the relationship between the group and certain sections of the army was at least ambiguous.

The attacks on Shias in Quetta in 2004 may have been the work of the LeJ, although the leaders of its two main factions—Akram Lahori and Qari Asadullah alias Qari Abdul Hai—had been arrested in 2003. The LeJ benefited from rifts in the SSP following the assassination of Azam Tariq: grassroots militants, disillusioned by the arguments, were inclined to join a group that remained loyal to the ideals of Haq Nawaz and Azam Tariq.

The Jaish-e-Muhammad (JeM, Army of Muhammad), founded (with ISI support) in February 2000 by Maulana Masood Azhar, a graduate of the Binori Town *madrasa* and a close confederate of both Haq Nawaz and Azam Tariq, emerged as the jihadist façade of the SSP. In October 2000, Masood Azhar addressed a conference on *jihad* and declared: "We march hand in hand; the SSP pursues *jihad* alongside the JeM".

The social base remained unchanged, and many activists shifted from one movement to the other. Moreover, the JeM maintained close links with the SSP. From the outset, the JeM not only competed with the Lashkar-e-Tayyebah in Kashmir, but took part in sectarian attacks, particularly against Christians.

Tools of the state

Each successive Pakistani government has used the SSP to achieve short-term goals. The Zia regime backed it in order to combat ethno-nationalism, strengthen Muslim identity in Pakistan and bring down the PPP, which had been attracting Shia votes since the 1970s.

Following the country's return to democratic rule in 1988–and particularly during the second Benazir Bhutto government (1993–96)–the PPP, a party which lacked Islamic legitimacy and sought to defeat the PML, formed two alliances: one with the JUI at the federal level[21] and another with the SSP in Punjab. In return, the SSP was allowed to pursue its violent activities with impunity.[22]

The government took no firm action against sectarian movements—especially the SSP–until 1998, when the PML held a majority in Punjab and in the federal parliament. The antiterrorist unit within the Special Branch of the Pakistani police had been transformed into a separate service and given the task of combating sectarian terrorism in April 1995, but it did not begin to function until the appointment of Tariq Pervaiz as its head in 1997. By 1998, it was clear that anti-terrorist laws had failed, and that threats against police officers and politicians were on the rise. Given the impossibility of obtaining guilty verdicts in the courts, the police in Punjab were ordered to eliminate "terrorists" instead of trying to arrest them. As a consequence, 37 alleged "terrorists" were eliminated in Punjab. But not all police officers approved of the policy. Some believed it actually exacerbated the situation, for militants were prone to even greater violence when they knew they would be killed even if they surrendered. In addition, their deaths denied the police the opportunity to elicit information concerning their networks. The policy had yet another perverse effect: extremists formerly shunned by the religious parties were welcomed back into the fold when the manhunt began.

The fact remains that many policemen, including some high-ranking officers, were sympathetic to the SSP[23] and therefore susceptible to bribery and intimidation. Junior officers often complained that they were unable to arrest SSP militants, or were forced by their superiors to release those in custody.

In the mid-1990s, the police discovered that collaborating with SSP militants was generally more lucrative and less dangerous than the alternative. The antagonists arrived at a tacit understanding: if the police did not delve too deeply into SSP affairs, they would not be targeted. They also received large sums of money from businessmen in return for releasing SSP militants in their custody.

The policies adopted by Nawaz Sharif's government had very little impact, however, for the country's leaders could not stem the support the SSP received from abroad, notably from the Taliban. Moreover, during the 1990s the army ceaselessly exploited the instability bred by the violence, pressurising democratic governments by claiming that they were incapable of maintaining law and order. Both Benazir Bhutto and Nawaz Sharif were forced to appeal to the army when violence reached a critical level.

The 1999 military coup did little to alter the situation. General Musharraf outlawed the LeJ in August 2001, a measure that would probably have come to nothing had it not been for the events of 11 September. The SSP then came under strong pressure from the government. President Musharraf accused it of training its militants in Afghanistan and destroying Shia property in Peshawar during anti-American demonstrations, charges that Azam Tariq was hard put to deny.

On 12 January 2002, President Musharraf banned the SSP. The organisation maintained a low profile for several months, then resumed its activities under the name Millat-e-Islamia Pakistan (MIP). Azam Tariq, placed under house arrest and later transferred to prison, was elected as an independent in October 2002 and immediately declared support for President Musharraf. He refused to join the Muttahida Majlis-e-Amal (MMA), the alliance of religious parties, on the grounds that it tolerated the presence of Sajid Naqvi, leader of the Shia party Tehrik-e-Jaafria (TJP), which had resurfaced as Tehrik-e-Islami after being banned in January 2002. Once elected, Azam Tariq played by the establishment's rules, obtaining the release of SSP militants and a lenient approach to the movement's activities in return for his support. The authorities seemed interested in using it to create a religious alliance to rival the MMA. The SSP then adopted a new charter which laid great emphasis on unity between Muslims and harmony between the Sunni and Shia of Pakistan.

Azam Tariq was assassinated in Islamabad on 6 October 2003, in circumstances that will probably remain shrouded in mystery. There are indications that the killing, ostensibly a result of strife within the movement, was approved at the highest level of government.[24] The MIP was banned in November 2003, but as in the past, prohibition appeared to have no effect.

Since 2004, the tribal areas and the Kohat district of the NWFP have been a sanctuary for members of the SSP, and sectarian attacks have become commonplace in Kurram and Orakzai tribal agencies as well as in Peshawar and

Dera Ismail Khan, notably after the assault on the Red Mosque in Islamabad in July 2007, which had a strong sectarian dimension as the Red Mosque had long been an SSP stronghold.

Meanwhile, restrictions were relaxed and in April 2006, the SSP organised a rally in Islamabad; the participants, under police protection, chanted anti-Shia slogans with impunity. Once again, it seemed that rather than crack down on the SSP, the authorities preferred to hold it in reserve.

In 2008, the SSP was active again in Karachi. It organised a public demonstration in March against the Danish cartoons, and two other meetings in June and August, at which weapons were displayed. It was believed that the government was using it to exert pressure on the MQM.

Conclusion

The dynamics of sectarian strife demonstrate that religion is nothing more than a pretext. Above all, the conflict is the reflection of the socio-economic tensions that pervade a society in transition, and an expression of the complex trajectories of modernisation. Emergent categories have used the SSP as a vehicle for social change; they have exploited the claims of the disaffected to further their own interests, a strategy not dissimilar to those employed by Hindu nationalist movements. Moreover, state exploitation of the SSP and other jihadist movements has led to an increase in the level of violence against Shia Muslims, which intensified after the invasion of Iraq in 2003.

Pakistanis appear to have understood the ambivalent role played by the state. Shias do not blame Sunnis for the violence—their anger is directed at the state. Mobs do not target Sunni houses and establishments after attacks on Shia Muslims—they target public buildings and the symbols of the state.

Sectarian organisations have therefore failed to radicalise the population. Nor has the conflict between Sunni and Shia Muslims ever reached the scale of the violence between Hindus and Muslims in India. But the Talibanisation of the tribal zones, encompassing as it does the entire North West Frontier Province and even parts of Punjab, indicates the extent to which sectarian groups constitute a threat to both state and society. The authorities' insistence that the violence is the work of hostile foreign elements is a convenient way to divert attention from their inability to put an end to it. Measures such as banning movements will not solve the problem, for they offer the disaffected young, the very people who feel excluded from society, no alternative. Pakistan is faced with a challenge to its survival. In order to combat religious extremism effectively, the government must revive the economy, restore political parties to their rightful position and strengthen its own institutions. These are the only means by which the tendency can be reversed.

BIBLIOGRAPHY

Abbas, Hassan, *Pakistan's Drift into Extremism*, New York, Sharpe, 2005.

Amir Rana, Mohammad, *Jihad Kashmir wa Afghanistan. Jihadi Tanzimon aur Mazhabi Jamaaton ka ek Jaiza* (Urdu) (An A to Z of Jehadi Organizations in Pakistan), Lahore, Mashal, 2004).

Friedman, Yohanan, *Prophecy Continuous. Aspects of Ahmadi Religious Thoughts and its Medieval Background*, Berkeley (Calif.), University of California Press, 1989.

Iqbal, Afzal, *Islamisation in Pakistan*, Lahore, Vanguard Books, 1986.

Journals and chapters in edited volumes

Abou Zahab, Mariam, "The Politicization of the Shia Community in Pakistan in the 1970s and 1980s," in Silvia Naef and Farian Sahabi (eds), *The Other Shiites, From the Mediterranean to Central Asia*, Berne/New York, Peter Lang, 2007: 97–112.

Abou Zahab, Mariam, "The Sunni-Shia Conflict in Jhang (Pakistan)," in Imtiaz Ahmed and Helmut Reifeld (eds.), *Lived Islam in South Asia*, Delhi, Social Science Press, 2004: 135–48.

Kennedy, Charles, "Islamization and Legal Reform in Pakistan, 1978–1989," *Pacific Affairs*, 63 (1), 1990: 62–77.

Nasr, Syyed Vali Reza, "Islam, the State and the Rise of Sectarian Militancy," in Christophe Jaffrelot (ed.), *Pakistan. Nationalism without a Nation?*, Delhi, Manohar, 2002: 85–114.

Qasim Zaman, Mohammed, "Sectarianism in Pakistan: The Radicalization of Shi'i and Sunni Identities," *Modern Asian Studies*, 32 (3), 1998: 689–716.

Reports

International Crisis Group, "The State of Sectarianism in Pakistan," *Asia Report*, 95, 18 April 2005.

NOTES

1. The first month of the Islamic calendar, during which Shias commemorate the martyrdom of Hussain (grandson of the Prophet Mohammed) and his companions at Karbala in the year 680.
2. There is little statistical evidence regarding adherence to religious groups, but it is estimated that Shia Muslims make up 15–20% of the population. In 2007, this amounted to between 25 and 30 million people, making Pakistan's Shia community the second largest in the world, Iran having the largest.
3. Afzal Iqbal (1986); Charles Kennedy (1990).
4. The reformist school of thought associated with the *madrasa* founded in Deoband (northern India) in 1867. The original aim of the Deobandi school was to purify Indian Islam by discarding "non-Islamic" practices such as the cult of saints and the rites and practices adapted from Hinduism.
5. S. Vali Reza Nasr (2002), pp. 85–114; Mohammed Qasim Zaman (1998); Mariam Abou Zahab (2007), pp. 97–112.
6. International Crisis Group (2005).
7. Mariam Abou Zahab (2004), pp. 135–48.

8. Founded in Punjab in the late 19th century by Mirza Ghulam Ahmad who claimed that he had received a revelation and that he was the promised Messiah and a prophet without a book. The Ahmadi movement advocates a defensive *jihad*; its members also engage in peaceful proselytising. Most Muslims consider the Ahmadis as outside orthodox Islam. The Ahmadiyya have been subjected to persecution throughout the Indian subcontinent. See Yohanan Friedman (1989).

9. In Pakistan, the term "feudal" denotes the owners of large landed estates who consolidated their power under colonial rule and continue to dominate the political life of the country.

10. Also known as Ahl-e-Sunnat, disciple of Ahmed Raza Khan (died in 1921), originally from Barcilly. The Barelvi movement embodies the Sufi traditions of the subcontinent. Barelvis are particularly devoted to the Prophet Mohammed and believe in the intercession of saints and martyrs.

11. Muslims who left India in 1947 and settled in Pakistan.

12. The Sheikh caste is composed of alleged descendents of the Qureshi Arab clans, and therefore occupies a high position in the subcontinent's Muslim caste hierarchy. In reality, most of its members are Hindu converts.

13. For details on Jhang and the SSP's exploitation of local rivalries, see Mariam Abou Zahab (2004).

14. A relatively high turnout for elections in Pakistan.

15. All assassinated SSP leaders are buried within the walls of this seminary.

16. Mohammad Amir Rana (2004).

17. The non-irrigated areas from which the army has been drawing recruits since the colonial era.

18. A dissident faction of the MQM created in 1992 with the support of the intelligence agencies.

19. The Iranian consul in Lahore assassinated in December 1990.

20. Hassan Abbas (2005), p. 207.

21. Maulana Fazlur Rehman was appointed president of the Parliamentary Foreign Affairs Commission by Benazir Bhutto.

22. S. Vali Reza Nasr (2002).

23. Police officers who were also SSP members participated in attacks against Shias in Karachi. One of them was killed in May 2004 in a suicide attack on a Shia mosque.

24. The fact that the SSP has never called for a detailed investigation or the conviction of those responsible tends to support this theory.

Map 9: Bangladesh

8

THE ISLAMIST MILITIAS OF BANGLADESH
SYMPTOMS OF A WEAK STATE?

Jérémie Codron

The militia phenomenon is intrinsically bound up with the history of the Bangladeshi nation-state. Even today, the events it recalls in public opinion are the 1971 war of independence, or the Bangladeshi "war of liberation". In the collective memory, the militias epitomise the armed groups of volunteers (*razakar*) recruited by the Pakistani army to fight the nationalist forces (*mukti bahini*, or liberation forces). Students played a key role in the recruitment process, and this remains one of the main features of the Bangladeshi militia scene. One of the two branches of the *razakar*—Al-Badr—was directly supplied by militants of the Islami Chatro Sangho, the Jama'at-e Islami student front at the time. The other militia—Al-Shams—was composed of fighters mostly belonging to the Urdu-speaking community from Bihar, who decided to align themselves with the Pakistani army in order to defend their interests.

In a state as young as Bangladesh, this dialectic between liberators and collaborators is still extremely vivid in people's memories. Whereas the *mukti bahini* were immediately promoted to the rank of "army of liberation", the pro-Pakistani combatants were accused of collaborating with the enemy, betraying the Bengali nation, and perpetrating the most serious abuses against the civilian population. We thus find the same pattern as in post-war France, a history that Bengali nationalists have in fact drawn on widely to impart a moral cast to their discourse.[1] Grafted onto this is the ideological dimension: one of the pillars of the state at its birth being "secularism"—that is, the authorities' neutrality towards all religions—the *razakar*, inspired by Islamic ideology and, in some cases, by the spirit of *jihad*, are all the more stigmatised as internal enemies of the Bengali nation.

Islamism still suffers in the national *imaginaire* from the stigmas of collaboration and war crimes, especially in so far as a fringe of the Islamist movement has opted for radicalism and violence as its mode of political action. On the post-9/11 international scene, and in the context of the "war on terror", the Islamist militias present in the country are regarded as threats in that they call into question the image of Bangladesh as a "moderate, democratic Muslim country"—an image it seeks to defend in order to appear as a model in the contemporary Muslim world.

At the same time, however, since the October 2001 electoral victory of the coalition comprising the National Party of Bangladesh (BNP) and two Islamist organisations—the Jama'at-e Islami Bangladesh (Jama'at) and Islami Oikyo Jote (IOJ)—assertion of the nation's Islamic identity has become an essential political instrument, while the Islamists have emerged as powerful allies. This contradictory situation forced the government of Khaleda Zia (2001–06) to adopt an ambiguous attitude towards the phenomenon of Islamist militias. Indeed, she used them to fight her political opponents (the Awami League (AL) and left-wing parties), while continually denying their existence to foreign donors—at least until the spectacular bombings of 17 August 2005. When more than 450 small bombs exploded simultaneously nationwide, and responsibility for the attack was formally claimed by the Jama'at-ul-Mujahidin Bangladesh (JMB), burying one's head in the sand became impossible. The determination of the armed Islamist groups to destabilise a fragile Bangladeshi democracy was obvious, and their nuisance capacity was demonstrated in the autumn of 2005 by the series of attacks on the judicial apparatus, marked by the first suicide-bombings in the country's history.

Radical Islamism: a new type of political violence?

The targets and operational modalities of the attacks attributed to the "Islamic movement" since 1999, as well as the damage inflicted, indicate that this Islamist violence is profoundly different from the political violence of the past. Violence has always been an important feature of the handling of political conflict in Bangladesh, but the earlier form and circumstances of such incidents were significantly different from what we find today. Thus, in the years that followed independence, armed Maoist groups struggling against the "bourgeois" government of Sheikh Mujibur Rahman targeted representatives of the state and public institutions (prefects, police stations, etc.); their main objective was to procure weapons. Moreover, traditional struggles between political parties, or between different factions of the same party, served precise aims: settling scores, wresting control over a district, or assassinating election candidates. These actions were generally targeted and restricted to actors belonging to the circle of "armed politics".

Hence the unprecedented character of the incidents that have occurred since 1999. For the first time, people outside that circle have been targeted. And even when what is involved are political assassination attempts, like those directed at the leaders of the AL on 21 June and 21 August 2004 and 27 January 2005, the "collateral damage" is extremely serious. Thus, although Sheikh

Hasina, chairman of the AL, emerged unharmed from the attack of 21 August 2004, the casualty figures were 22 dead and more than 100 wounded, and a climate of general panic developed in the capital over the next few days. In short, it is a form of violence that operates in accordance with terrorist methods and is structured around the idea of "internal *jihad*"—a *jihad* directed not against a foreign enemy but against society itself.

Until the series of attacks carried out by the JMB in 2005, no responsibility for such actions was claimed—a contrast to the various armed communist groups carrying out attacks. According to a former activist of the Islami Chatro Shibir, the student wing of Jama'at-e Islami, who was active in the movement for 16 years but has now withdrawn from political life, this involves a conscious strategy:

Those who work for jihad in Bangladesh are like ghosts, like shadows. You don't hear anyone shouting that they are for jihad in our country. Activists receive instruction, they read a lot of books on jihad, but they remain concealed. It is not as if our country has been invaded by foreigners, like Afghanistan or Iraq. There the *mujahidin* are heroes. Here they prefer to act while saying nothing. In that way, you don't know who is responsible, everyone accuses everyone else, and that helps destabilize the country. Their goal is not to make people aware of some particular organization, but to create confusion and chaos. That allows them to continue operating without naming leaders. And in the end it's the Islamic movement that emerges strengthened.[2]

Notwithstanding this ambiguity, two facts allow us to attribute these actions to Islamist groups. The first is the geographic zones where the attacks have occurred, which are also strongholds of political Islam. It was in the districts of Khulna, Jessore, Sylhet, Bagerhat and Satkhira that some of the Jama'at's 17 deputies were elected in 2001. The north and the region of Sylhet, over-represented in the list of attacks, are also regions where Deobandi and Ahl-e-Hadith *madrasa*s, known for their fundamentalist teaching, are very widespread. Finally, the campuses of the universities of Rajshahi, Khulna and Sylhet are recruitment centres for Islamist youth.

Symbolic targets. Selection of the sites, events and people targeted forms part of the overall project of the "Islamic movement" referred to by the former Shibir militant quoted above. It is a decentralised movement comprising the set of organisations, whether armed or not, that advocate a renewal of Islam and a struggle against all social and cultural practices deemed contrary to a pure vision of the Muslim religion. The members of the political and intellectual elite who remain attached to the ideals of liberation, and in the first place to the separation of religion and politics, are identified as the main enemies. Hence the attacks on leaders of the AL (especially the most eminent of them, those likely to obtain office in the event of victory in the next elections) and on communists, whose materialism and atheism are violently assailed in Islamist literature.

Traditional practices of Islam also find themselves under attack. The tombs of Sufi saints, and the cult devoted to them, are favourite targets. The following remarks, taken from an interview with Maulana Delwar Hussain Sayeedi, known for the radicalism of his positions within the Jama'at, illustrate this tension between traditionalism and fundamentalism:

Most Bangladeshis are not genuine Muslims. They venerate gurus, *pirs*,[3] they kneel before tombs, they worship idols like Hindus… All this is contrary to *Tawhid*, the oneness of God and the Muslim faith. Our work consists in Islamising this society and teaching everyone what *la ilaha il'Allah* means.[4]

Q: Does that mean it's necessary to destroy the tombs of the saints and build mosques instead?

A: We are not against tombs in and of themselves and the Muslims buried in them are honourable men. But Muslims have a duty to struggle against the anti-Islamic activities that occur on these sites. Did you know there are drugs and alcohol there? The people who sully Islam must be expelled, so that these sites become places of prayer.[5]

Other targets privileged by the armed groups are cultural activities pertaining to "Bengali folklore", which is very far removed from a strict conception of the Muslim religion. In this category, the bomb attacks on several popular theatre festivals in January 2005 followed the same pattern: the explosions occurred at the precise moment when a female dancer came on stage during a musical interlude or when actors began to play cards in the context of their theatrical piece. They aimed to make an impression by pinpointing the most profane aspects of the entertainment.

The final component of the Islamist project is a struggle against certain powerful NGOs (BRAC, Grameen Bank), which are regarded as pro-Western because of their sources of funding and the projects they deliver in rural areas, particularly education and micro-credit for women. A JMB activist offers a sophisticated argument to justify the struggle against these NGOs: "Many years ago, the East India Company seized our country to make profits from it; the NGOs are a new incarnation of the Company. They sponsor anti-Islamic activities and alienate people from religion. We must prepare ourselves mentally and physically to confront them".[6]

It should be noted that the strategic dimension of these acts is often as crucial as the ideological concerns: the attacks are motivated by a desire to expel organisations that are perceived as foreign agents so as to replace them in the social arena, in the knowledge that these actors exercise a decisive influence on rural communities, especially at election time.

New ways of operating. As regards modes of action, the procedures employed for these attacks can be divided into four categories overall. In "classical" bomb attacks, like those that targeted the offices of the BRAC and Grameen Bank NGOs in the region of North Bengal, the explosive devices were manufactured locally. The team tasked with the operation was small: a maximum of three people arrived by motorcycle at the site of the attack, threw bombs and immediately made their escape. The predominant aim was intimidation, since this kind of action is insufficiently precise to inflict significant human casualties.

Then there are the attacks that struck theatrical festivals or meetings of the AL or the Communist Party, which were more sophisticated and, above all, more devastating. The bombs were concealed on the site of the event and exploded at a precise moment, which required collusion with certain organisers. Moreover, the explosives were sophisticated: investigating officers revealed that the products used were RDX and C4 (plastic) and the bombs contained a radio receiver making it possible to trigger explosion by remote control, rather than using a timer.

In the case of the grenade attacks of 21 May 2004, 21 August 2004 and 27 January 2005, targeting high-ranking figures and much more murderous, the mode of action was very different. In these three operations, the weapons used were ARGES grenades, initially designed in Austria, but also manufactured in China and Pakistan. As emphasised by a member of a parallel commission of inquiry into the 21 August 2004 attack set up by the Supreme Court Bar Association, they were "designed to kill, and not to exert psychological pressure".[7]

Furthermore, the way in which these attacks were conducted invited comparison with a commando-style operation, involving a larger number of people (ten to twenty) and a sophisticated plan of action. Thus, the police estimate that four teams, positioned in different places, were used in the attack on Sheikh Hasina. At the moment of the attack that killed the former minister Shah Kibria, the electricity was briefly cut in order to create surprise and increase the sense of panic in the crowd. Given this, it is reasonable to believe that the attacks benefited from collusion on the part of some of the personnel responsible for security, or even from local police authorities. In any event, this raises the issue of the role played by the state in handling the militants' violence.

The final category of Islamist violence involves the suicide attacks of the autumn of 2005, for which the JMB claimed responsibility. These actions raise a certain number of issues. The tactic of suicide attacks was completely unprecedented in Bangladesh and such actions imply the presence within the JMB of highly ideologically motivated cells in which the death of the combatant is glorified: this is the case, in particular, of the Shahid Nasrullah al-Arafat Brigade. Finally, this tactic reveals the implementation of an Islamic concept developed in the JMB's literature—that of *qital*. This involves a narrower, exclusively bellicose vision of *jihad*, which justifies struggle against a state threatening Islam and makes it illegitimate to serve the ungodly state or even to obey its laws. In this vision, there is no such thing as "innocent civilians", but simply two camps: those who serve the state and who, for that reason, are regarded as infidels; and those who opt for battle—whence the general invitation to join the JMB found in all its tracts.

From student movement to jihadist groups

Bangladeshi Islamist movements do not all conceive recourse to violence in the same way. While the concept of *jihad* forms part of the ideology of most of the armed groups, it does not always have the same function and is not always the central element in their project. Some movements aim to conquer the state through a process of infiltration and work in close collaboration with legal Islamist parties; an example is the Islami Chatro Shibir, which will be studied here. Others act more as pressure groups outside the government, making demands concerning specific issues. The third category contains organisations characterised as "jihadist", for which violence is central to their strategy for Islamising society.

Islami Chatro Shibir: matrix of the armed groups? The Islami Chatro Shibir (Student Islamic Camp) is the student front of the Jama'at-e Islami and is the oldest Islamist group active in Bangladesh. It was created in 1976 by former members of the Al-Badr militia who had not fled Bangladesh and who escaped the purges directed against "collaborators". When it was founded, it was still independent of the Jama'at, which at the time had no legal existence in the country, and developed theses that were much more radical than those of its future parent organisation.

As Ahmed Abdul Quader, chairman of the Central Committee in 1981–82 prior to becoming a dissident, explains:

At a time when Jama'at was still illegal and regarded as the party of the collaborators of 1971, our movement was the spearhead of the Islamic revolution. ... After 1979, there were tensions between the students and Jama'at, because we supported the Iranian revolution, whereas Jama'at followed Saudi Arabia. And when I was elected chairman of the movement, the conflict became serious, above all on the issue of the Shibir's autonomy. We wanted to remain independent and keep our distance from politicking. But ultimately, the leaders of Jama'at took control of the central committee thanks to some ambitious students; and those who were for revolution, like Khomeini's, were forced to leave the movement.[8]

This was the context in which the Shibir became the student wing proper of the Jama'at and placed itself at the service of its strategy of Islamising institutions, which is set out in full in the party's literature. According to Kamruzzaman, assistant general secretary, this involved a "silent revolution", a gradual change in the mentality of those who formed the nation's elite—particularly through political activity in the educational sphere.[9] Contrary to what one often reads, it is not in the *madrasa*s that the Shibir is most influential, but in public institutions, especially those of higher education: colleges, universities, medical faculties, engineering and business schools. The aim is to bring about a transformation of society from above, not solely by conquering government in the classical sense, but through a process of infiltrating every locus of power, from the Secretariat (the core of the civil service), via financial institutions, to the Islamic Foundation.[10]

The Shibir has a paramount role in this strategy. Its internal structure is geared towards this long-term goal. There are several levels of activism. In the first instance, a student has the role of an observer, which does not allow him to participate directly in the organisation's activities. He must undergo a phase of training, in which small group meetings, intensive reading of internal literature and of ideologues like Maududi or Syed Qutb, as well as daily prayers, aim to create personal discipline and a group spirit. Then he becomes a *shathi* (sympathiser), which involves more duties, in particular keeping a diary of activities that is regularly inspected by leaders, making financial contributions and recruiting new students. Finally, the highest level is that of *shodoshyo* (member), and this is the group from which unit heads are recruited. At this stage, militants are trained in the management of human resources and leadership. As a still-active militant explains:

When you join the Shibir, you need a lot of patience. It sometimes takes years before you become a leader. Moreover, to pass from one stage to the next, there are exams to check your knowledge. It's a long process; you mustn't be too ambitious. Whereas in other student organisations, you can make it to the top very quickly, you just have to know the right people, in the Shibir you first learn to serve the organisation and Islamic movement before thinking of yourself.[11]

The movement's transition to armed action dates back to the beginning of the 1980s, which saw the Shibir seeking to establish itself on the campuses of Chittagong and Rajshahi. According to a former militant, the rectors of the two universities, appointed by the governments of General Ziaur Rahman and then General Ershad, were close to the Islamists and gave Shibir students free rein to pursue their activities. The object was to establish a force in these institutions capable of rivalling the other student organisations, especially the AL branch at Chittagong University and that of the Communist Party at Rajshahi.

Armed cadres are not recruited randomly. They belong to the highest circle of activism and are selected for their individual discipline. Training sessions in small groups are organised, whose programme is both physical (martial arts and handling locally manufactured light arms) and psychological. As regards the latter, the instructors develop the concept of martyrdom. But it assumes a different meaning from that attributed to it by jihadists, for in this instance martyrdom does not necessarily involve the death of the fighter. Instead, it is a question of sacrifice on behalf of the organisation. Weapons must not be used for personal ends. On the contrary, militants must accept that they are merely the armed wing of the movement. This discipline is precisely what differentiates it from other Bangladeshi student organisations, where possession of weapons increases the power of those who carry them and makes them more autonomous vis-à-vis the group. Given its specificities (ideology, discipline, group spirit), the Shibir takes on certain features of a militia, even if the use of arms is in fact restricted to a minority.[12]

During the police operations that led to the arrest of JMB activists, particularly in August 2003 and in 2005–06, investigators revealed that a number of them had been active in the Shibir.[13] These discoveries raised the question of the links between the student movement and jihadist groups: Can the Shibir be regarded as the matrix of the armed groups? Some jihadists did indeed belong to the Shibir in their youth, but involvement in the more radical groups came at the cost of breaking with the student organisation.[14] The latter no longer recognises those militants as belonging to the Islamic movement and refuses to support their new activities. This attitude is determined by the current strategy of the Jama'at-e Islami, which is seeking a new legitimacy. Keen to appear a moderate party of government, the Jama'at systematically denies the existence of any link with Islamist militias.

Disavowal of the jihadists by the organisation does not mean that all connections have been severed. According to the former militant quoted above, militants from the armed groups who once belonged to the Shibir strive to preserve personal links with the Jama'at leaders. This is possible in so far as active members of the Shibir are always taken under the wing of an older leader, who then acts as mentor. When a militant chooses the clandestine path of *jihad*, these personal links enable him to keep one foot in traditional political life, which can prove a valuable aid. Thus, after the arrest of several activists suspected of involvement in the attack on Kibria on 27 January 2005, police officers were pressured by local leaders of the Jama'at, who "advised" them to release certain suspects.[15]

Fundamentalist pressure groups: the example of the anti-Ahmadi movements. The second type of organisation corresponds to the fundamentalist movements. They must be distinguished from organisations which, like the Jama'at and Shibir, have their own ideology, one certainly inspired by the Koran and the Sunnah, but whose free interpretation serves to fashion a political project adapted to the requirements of modernity. Here the term "fundamentalist" refers to actors who reject modernity and have no specifically political ideology. Their action is restricted to the religious sphere and their discourse derives from a literal interpretation of the foundational texts of Islam.

Of particular interest among these movements are organisations that fight the Ahmadiyya sect, because they have recently gone over to armed action to attain their objective: compelling the government to declare the Ahmadi minority non-Muslim. There are two main groups: Amra Dhakabashi (We Dhakians), founded in 2003 and based in several of the capital's mosques; and Khatme Nabuat Andolon Bangladesh (Movement of Bangladesh for the Seal of the Prophecy), which is the Bangladeshi branch of a transnational network based in Pakistan, the Almi Majlis-e Tahaffuz-e Khatm-e Nabuat (World Committee for the Defence of the Seal of the Prophecy), whose creation dates back to the 1950s.

The initial actions launched by these movements date from the late 1990s, with the murderous attack on the Ahmadiyya mosque of Khulna in 1999 and the explosion of a bomb in the sect's central mosque in Dhaka in 2000. However, from October 2003 a change in strategy can be observed. Rather than carrying out occasional attacks for which no responsibility was claimed, the anti-Ahmadi groups opted for more regular and open actions that have earned them notoriety. The stated objective is to mobilise the population of "genuine Muslims" living around the main Ahmadi centres of Bangladesh to out pressure on the Ahmadiyya and to raise public awareness of the issue through media coverage of their actions.

"Shock" operations follow the same pattern. The target—generally a mosque, sometimes the district of a town where Ahmadis live—is designated a few days in advance via the press and by imams of mosques affiliated to the movement. Attacks occur on Friday, the day of congregational prayer, after a sermon in which the imam motivates the faithful and calls for violence. Firearms are not used—at most one finds truncheons—and it is numbers that count. Thus, during the days of agitation organised at Satkhira (North Bengal) from 16 to 20 April 2005, Khatme Nabuat managed to assemble 15,000 people.[16] The goals vary: from symbolic acts (demonstrators tear off the mosque's plaque and replace it by a sign reading: "Qadiani place of worship,[17] not to be confused with a mosque"), to the destruction of religious centres, as at Brahmanbaria in October 2004.[18]

The success of such mobilisations cannot be explained solely by the organisational capacity of movements like Khatme Nabuat. In fact, the latter presents itself as a Muslim cultural and theological association; it has very few members and a simple manned office in Dhaka. But its leaders, particularly its emir Mufti Noor Hossain, have links with several high-ranking religious figures. Among them, we find the Khatib of the national mosque, Maulana Obaidul Haque, the editor of the daily newspaper *Inquilab*, Maulana Abdul Mannan,[19] as well as the leader of the Islami Oikyo Jote party, Mufti Amini. These religious leaders are at the head of a dense network of Deobandi *madrasas* distributed throughout the country and linked to the Lalbagh mosque at Dhaka, whose imam is Mufti Amini.[20] On the one hand, this loose set-up makes it possible to mobilise a pool of militants using *madrasa* students. On the other, it prevents the movements being proscribed or subjected to legal action in the event of violence or clashes with the police.

Because of the support given by these religious figures who are extremely influential in Dhaka, the government of Khaleda Zia found itself in an uncomfortable position over the "Ahmadi problem". This can be inferred in particular from the attitude of law and order forces, who perform their role and protect the minority in incidents heavily covered by the media, when those forces' actions are liable to be denounced by human rights groups or foreign diplomats, but turn a blind eye in other instances or, even worse, ally with the rioters, as on 17 April 2005 in Satkhira.[21]

These fundamentalist movements, which have found their hobbyhorse in the anti-Ahmadi struggle, represent a force with which the BNP has had to deal throughout its mandate, and play a role at election time. Brandishing this threat, Khatme Nabuat issued two ultimatums for the Ahmadiyya to be declared non-Muslim. The first was successful, since it led the government to ban Ahmadi publications on 8 January 2004. Announced in January 2005, the second gave the authorities a year to meet the movement's main demand. However, with the series of attacks carried out by the JMB and the repression initiated by the government in 2005, the anti-Ahmadi groups have been compelled to keep a low profile so as not to attract the hostility of a population that is increasingly aware of the threat of radical Islam.

The jihadist movements: from local violence to transnational network. The third category of militias, characterised here as "jihadist", comprises organisations that conceive the Islamic revolution as a necessary phase of violence against society in order to transform it, and which therefore find themselves in a situation of open conflict with the authorities. Two types of jihadist group can be identified: those who have only a local base and whose objective is restricted to Bangladesh, and those who possess a network extending throughout the country and also have contacts with foreign figures or movements.

Among local jihadist groups, two in particular began to attract attention in the early 2000s. The first, Hizbut Tawhid (Party of the Oneness of God), was originally an intellectual movement. Founded by Bayezid Khan Panni, a charismatic figure from Dhaka famous for having participated in virtually all anti-state clandestine movements since 1971, Hizbut Tawhid is an organisation composed of laypersons and its militants do not come from the *madrasa* milieu. Its ideology is drawn from Panni's philosophical writings, which might at first sight be characterised as an ecumenical system of thought. The organisation operates as a sectarian group, active in the region of Kushtia (western Bangladesh), where Panni comes from. Its objective is the creation of a network of religious schools to compete with the local Deobandi *madrasas*. Hizbut Tawhid's real enemies are the ulema and mullahs of the rural areas, who are regarded as corrupt Muslims. But over and above this spiritual and pietistic discourse, the organisation also spreads a subversive message, denouncing the use of religion by the state and the political parties in power. In one of its pamphlets, it actually defines itself as "the only party on Earth chosen by Allah". Outside this "chosen" community, two groups are identified: the "ignorant", who are to be invited to follow the true Islamic way through the teaching of Hizbut Tawhid, and the "hypocrites", whom militants must fight through *jihad*.[22]

In accordance with this dual strategy, Hizbut Tawhid militants receive a theoretical education in one of the organisation's local branches. Then some of them follow training courses in *jihad* in a camp located in Tangail, north of Dhaka. At present there are supposedly 1,200 activists trained for combat, including 200 women, divided into nine districts (out of 64).[23] Several violent clashes have broken out between militants of Hizbut Tawhid and students from the *madrasas*, as in September 2003 at Narayanganj, when the casualty total reached 70 wounded and one dead. In the latest operation, in March 2005, activists besieged a *madrasa* in the Bhola district (in the south of the country), drove out the pupils and burned 200 copies of the Koran, which prompted a protest movement by the ulema of Bangladesh, who demanded that the government proscribe the sect.[24]

The second local jihadist organisation studied here, Shahadat-e al-Hiqma (Testimony of Wisdom), is active in the Rajshahi region. It made its existence known through the voice of its head, Kawsar Siddiqui, a young activist aged 24 who was active in the Islami Chatro Shibir in his adolescence. After the victory of the coalition led by the BNP in 2001, it came into conflict with the Jama'at-e Islami, whose entry into government it regarded as a betrayal and an abandonment of the revolutionary ideal. However, according to a journalist from Rajshahi, the rise to power of this local jihadist leader was due to a struggle for influence inside the Jama'at, one of the leaders of the Islamist party having taken Siddiqui under his wing in order to exert influence in the Rajshahi region by means other than traditional politics.[25] Shahadat-e al-Hiqma is therefore a typical example of an armed group arising from the matrix of the Shibir referred to above. Moreover, its ideology, which can be characterised as "Islamo-nationalist", is close to that of the Jama'at: the Islamic revolution must first of all occur inside the country and serve to defend the sovereignty of Bangladesh against "political, economic and cultural aggression from abroad".[26]

The only difference with the Jama'at, though certainly an important one, is the emphasis on armed struggle to attain that end. The numerous provocations directed at the government since 2002, as well as violent actions against public buildings in Rajshahi, have earned Siddiqui several terms of imprisonment for sedition, as well as the banning of his organisation on 9 February 2003. Nevertheless, the fact that he has always been released after a short period, and then imprisoned again, as well as the media coverage of these police operations organised by the authorities, makes it reasonable to think that Shahadat-e al-Hiqma and its "boss" have served as a scapegoat for a government seeking to divert attention from other, more dangerous jihadist organisations.

The groups that we are now going to discuss have more extensive influence, local support bases in numerous districts and, above all, a capacity for significant action that can be explained by the substantial financial sources they tap. The first is an emanation of the Pakistani jihadist organisation Harkat-ul-Jihad al-Islami (Movement for an Islamic Holy War, HUJI). On the face of it, this is not a structured group, but rather a network of former religious students who have passed through Deobandi *madrasa*s and established contacts with the radical Islamist movements of India, Pakistan and/or Afghanistan. Thus, the arrest in September 2003 of 18 activists suspected of involvement in the attacks on cinemas in Mymensingh enabled the police to apprehend a local Islamist leader, Maulana Abdur Rauf, who claims to have studied in the Deoband seminary in 1982 alongside one of the main suspects in the attempted assassination of Sheikh Hasina in Gopalganj in 2000. During his interrogation, he claimed that Mufti Hannan had allegedly organised meetings between several Bangladeshi religious authorities and HUJI militants in Pakistan. In 1989, Abdur Rauf was himself trained in Karachi, before going to fight in Afghanistan from 1989 to 1992. On his return to Bangladesh, he once again met Mufti Hannan and then founded the Jamiatul Islamia Nurul Alum Qaumi Madrasa in Mymensingh in 1997, as well as the Tanzim-e Tamir-ud-Din Bangladesh group, which began to recruit students and to provide them with training in *jihad* in the *madrasa*. Altogether, 150 students were trained between 1997 and 2002, all of them originating from districts other than Mymensingh.[27] This last point encapsulates the difference from the groups studied above, for which geographic proximity or links established at college or university underlie the process of recruitment. Here the militants are few in number, but selected from an expanded network of *madrasa*s or religious associations.

So there have definitely been contacts between several Bangladeshi religious figures and foreign jihadist movements, whether the HUJI in Pakistan or the Taliban in Afghanistan. No serious lead indicates that Bangladeshis have been recruited into international terrorist movements. But it is clear that the jihadist ideology has been imported into Bangladesh via these contacts and that it is being spread there today from certain *madrasa*s, like those of Mymensingh, Chittagong or Sylhet.

The second organisation studied here clearly reflects the links between the local and the international that characterise some Bangladeshi jihadist movements. From April 2004, the Jagrata Muslim Janata Bangladesh (Awakened Muslim Masses of Bangladesh, JMJB) group made its appearance with so-called "vigilance" armed operations in the districts of northern Bengal. Its commander-in-chief, nicknamed "Bangla Bhai" (Bengali Brother), was active in the Chatro Shibir during his studies at Rajshahi University, and then he became a teacher in a private education centre run by the Jama'at in Dhaka, before being dismissed in 2000 for having neglected party activities and begun to develop overly radical ideas.[28]

From 1 April 2004, the JMJB announced a *jihad* against the communist activists of the region, known by the name of Shorbohara (the destitute), members of the Communist Party of East Bengal banned by the government. A quotation from Bangla Bhai clearly illustrates the aims of these armed operations: "Our goal is to eliminate members of the Shorbohara and the corruption of society, to seize illegal weapons, and to establish the ideal of the prophet Hazrat Mohammad". At the outset, the movement sought the support of village populations, showing them that it was in their interest to supply information on communist militants because the latter were subjecting the peasants to a protection racket. Bangla Bhai presented himself to the villagers as a righter of wrongs and was cast as such by the local press, at least at the start of his operations.

However, the JMJB very soon adopted a strategy of terror to intimidate the local population. One of these punitive expeditions, targeting a communist leader sought by the police, offers a glimpse of the methods used. Bangla Bhai's men went through the villages around Rajshahi and, loudhailers in hand, urged the population to come and watch the sentencing and public execution of the arrested leader. He was hung up by his feet and beaten to death and then his corpse was displayed for several days to impress the inhabitants. Such psychological pressure is all the more effective in that the *razakar* militias used the same methods during the Bangladesh war of independence. During these vigilante operations, 50 murders were carried out and more than 500 people were kidnapped to be interrogated in the Vitigram camp, near Rajshahi, which also served as a training centre for JMJB militants.

Along with these violent actions, Bangla Bhai sought to enforce a strict conception of Islam. In the villages where it exercised influence, men were obliged to let their beards grow, women had to wear the *burqa*, music was banned together with the sale of cigarettes in village stalls, and men had to go to the mosque to pray five times a day. In addition to the terrorist methods described above, the JMJB developed its propaganda via frequent speeches, through which activists aimed to prove themselves omnipresent in the public space. Squads of three or four armed men regularly patrolled the villages to enforce this simplistic vision of *sharia*. A quotation from Bangla Bhai illustrates his perception of his activity: "People say we are part of al-Qaeda, that we are Taliban, or an armed Islamist organization. But we aren't. We want to serve the people and serve them in accordance with the teachings of Hilful Fuzul [a famous trade agreement between Arab families in the time of the Prophet, based on morality in economic relationships]".[29]

To fund itself, the JMJB used ransoms derived from kidnappings and also required villagers to donate a proportion of their income in the form of *zakat* (Islamic tax), in exchange for the security the organisation is supposed to offer them. In reality, the militia used the same methods as the Shorbohara— i.e. a protection racket—demonstrating that in this specific instance there is a fine line between a jihadist group and a criminal gang.

According to local journalists in Rajshahi, the JMJB is in fact a local emanation of a much larger and older movement, the Jama'at-ul Mujahidin Bangladesh (Party of the Mujahadin, JMB), led at the time by Maulana Abdur Rahman, spiritual master of Bangla Bhai. Born in the Bogra district, Rahman grew up in a religious milieu. His father, Abdullah Ibne Faizal, was one of the leaders of the Jamiyatul Ahl-e-Hadith organisation, and had fought in the Islamist militias alongside the Pakistani army in 1971. During his studies, Rahman was active in the Shibir and then joined the Jama'at-e Islami, before leaving for Saudi Arabia, where he studied at the Islamic University of Medina. On his return to Bangladesh, he worked for the Saudi Embassy in Dhaka from 1985 to 1990 and then founded a *madrasa* in his district of origin, with the support of the NGOs Rabita-ul-Alam al-Islami (Saudi) and Islami Oytijho Sangstha (Bangladeshi). This school, the Al-Madina Islamic Cadet Madrasa, was one of the JMB's main education centres. In 2005, the movement had a training centre in each of the country's six administrative divisions and mustered around 5,000 activists.[30]

According to a militant arrested in January 2005 following attacks on several traditional theatre performances, the particularity of the JMB is that it has formed bomb squads ready to attack "anti-Islamic" targets identified by the organisation's leaders. In each of these teams, some militants are tasked with procuring explosives while others specialise in manufacturing bombs. They have no contact with the militants who actually carry out the attacks, which prevents any trail from being followed. Dealing in explosives is an important feature of the organisation, as suggested by the seizure of combat equipment in JMB centres in the border districts of Chapainawabganj and Joypurhat, and the discovery by the police of 200 kg of plastic explosives in Bogra in 2003.

The JMB has an extensive network thanks to its relations with Ahl-e-Hadith Andolon Bangladesh (Ahl-e-Hadith Movement of Bangladesh, AHAB), led by Asadullah al-Ghalib, a professor of Arabic at Rajshahi University. Until his arrest in February 2005, Ghalib was a key figure in the funding and recruitment of jihadists in Bangladesh. His organisation, created in 1994 with the financial aid of two foundations, one Saudi (Hayatul Igaccha) and the other Kuwaiti (Society for the Renaissance of the Islamic Legacy), set up a network of 700 *madrasa*s belonging to the Ahl-e-Hadith tendency and spread over 42 districts, which represents around 50,000 students. The latter are divided into three branches: children (up to twelve years of age), young men, and girls. It is from the youth branch that candidates for *jihad* were selected for special training in one of the JMB's centres.[31]

Over above this educational infrastructure, Ghalib's influence stemmed from his network of personal contacts in the region and beyond. It was through the intermediary of the Indian jihadist leader Maulana Abdul Matin Salafi that he obtained the initial Saudi funds to finance AHAB. Thanks to his Pakistani and Arab contacts, he enables young graduates to go for training in one of the major Ahl-e-Hadith *madrasa*s and to return and teach in the AHAB network. According to the former general secretary of the movement, Rezaul Karim (who was dismissed in 2001), Ghalib also received several activists in his Rajshahi *madrasa*, like the Pakistani jihadist leader Maulana Abdullah Nasser Rahmani or the Kashmiri *mujahid* Gazzali. While these allegations should be treated with caution, various pieces of evidence, like the arrest in 2000 of four Kashmiris on the Indo-Bangladeshi border, make it reasonable to suppose that there have indeed been visits from foreign militants in this network of *madrasa*s.[32]

Government and parties: Between laissez-faire and instrumentalisation

Since the incidents of 1999, the problem of Islamic activism has never been tackled head-on by the authorities. Rather than being regarded as a threat liable to destabilise the state, it has become a component of the conflicts that characterise Bangladeshi party politics. After each attack or discovery by the police of subversive Islamic activities, the parties accuse one another of sponsoring extremist groups. These party quarrels, which take precedence over *raison d'état* and national security, have greatly contributed to the development of the phenomenon. To take the example of the 20 January 2001 attacks on the AL and the Communist Party, according to a member of the Central Investigation Department (CID) who was forced into early retirement, investigators made no serious attempt to apprehend the real culprit, but followed the instructions of an "influential figure" in the Interior Ministry who demanded the arrest of a BNP leader, a candidate in the October 2001 legislative elections.[33] Likewise, after the grenade attack of 21 August 2004, one of the first hypotheses suggested by the BNP was that the AL had itself organised the operation to increase its popularity, which would explain why Sheikh Hasina was able to escape unharmed.

Police weakness and collusion with the Islamist militias. Added to this problem of political interference, which is certainly not restricted to handling of the militia phenomenon, is the lack of preparedness of the law and order forces and the problems they experience in confronting the new actors. The episode of 15 August 2003, which saw police forces unleash an assault on JMB activists suspected of preparing a series of attacks in the Joypurhat region (North Bengal), is revealing of this lack of resources, as illustrated by the testimony of an officer who took part in the operation:

With only 11 officers, including me, we had the upper hand over a group of 100 *mujahidin*, who approached the entry gate of the house we had surrounded and who suddenly attacked us with machetes, bamboo sticks and firearms, shouting *"Allahu Akhbar"*. ... The Joypurhat police station had been informed that Montezar Rahman, a former leader of Jama'at-e Islami in this district, was organizing a meeting of the main cadres of JMB at his house that night. My superior officer was warned by the superintendent of police and we had to act immediately, without preparation. The reinforcements we requested didn't arrive until 7 a.m. ... The *mujahidin* were very disciplined and attacked us fearlessly, while we had only pistols.[34]

There has even been collusion between police forces and the Islamist militias. Thus, during the "vigilance" operations organised by Bangla Bhai, the local authorities offered it their complete support. Even though JMJB militants were already suspected of several murders, the jihadist leader organised his first public meeting on 23 May 2004 in Rajshahi under police protection. The city's superintendent of police officially received a delegation of activists and declared to them in front of journalists: "We salute you because you are helping us to eliminate the Shorbohara of Rajshahi. We shall have to cooperate with you in the future so that people can live in peace". Subsequently, the JMJB, thanks to its armed force and above all its reign of terror over the region's villages, took charge of apprehending communist militants, lists of whom were supplied by the police, and then handed them over to law and order forces.[35]

At the outset, the JMJB was thus regarded not as an Islamist militia, but as a group of "ordinary people who have taken up arms in order to protect themselves" Encouraged by this attitude, the JMJB's leaders sent a memorandum to the Minister of the Interior that clearly set out their motivation:

"Stopping terrorism is not a matter solely for the government. The brave people of Bagmara have united against the terrorists and are helping law and order forces to eliminate the outlaws, because none of the parties in power or opposition is capable of resisting these organized outlaws".[36]

With the media coverage of the violent actions of Bangla Bhai from mid-May 2004 onwards, and foreign pressure that compelled the central government to take measures against the movement, it was the Prime Minister Khaleda Zia who demanded of her Interior Minister, Lutfozzaman Babar, the immediate arrest of Bangla Bhai, who then disappeared. He was only apprehended in March 2006, when the government was forced to admit that the JMB's transition to terrorist activity was a direct threat to it. Lutfozzaman publicly acknowledged that arresting Bangla Bhai was made extremely difficult by the political support he enjoyed. During a telephone call to a local newspaper, Bangla Bhai had denounced the government's hypocrisy and claimed that his operation had received the support of three cabinet members and representatives of the Rajshahi region. According to a journalist from *Prothom Alo*, it was the former Land Minister, Ruhul Kuddus Taluker, who had given his support to the JMJB in launching operations against clandestine communist leaders, responsible (according to him) for the killing of four of his relatives and close friends.[37]

Heads in the sand

The official position of the government, which for a long time refused to acknowledge the existence of armed Islamist groups on its soil, greatly contributed to those groups' development. This state of denial can be explained in two ways. On the one hand, since 2003 foreign donors have made "maintenance of law and order" and an improvement in security their main requirement, which rules out government recognition of any form of private violence and, all the more so, any possibility of cooperation between the militias and the regular units of the security forces. On the other hand, Bangladesh is anxious to preserve its image as a "moderate Muslim country" and is above all concerned not to appear as a potential source of Islamist terrorism in the post-9/11 context.

However, at the end of February 2005, when a conference was being held in Washington at the initiative of the European Union and the World Bank to discuss problems of governance in Bangladesh, the latter not being invited to attend, the government finally decided to act and proceeded to arrest 100 Islamist leaders and activists, before banning the JMB and the JMJB. These measures remained limited and seem to have been predominantly motivated by the Washington meeting (the first militants were released in April). It was only in 2006, under the combined pressure of the "international community" and the jihadists themselves, who were now engaged in a campaign of suicide attacks, that the government of Khaleda Zia decided to react. In the space of a few months, all the leaders of the JMB and the JMJB were captured and sentenced to death (Bangla Bhai, Abdur Rahman and four of their henchmen were eventually executed on 30 March 2007). For the government, however, they were nothing more than "local bandits", accused of a series of murders, robberies and bomb attacks. In the official version, the Interior Ministry explained that these movements had tried to foment serious social unrest by leading a group of young people astray and using and abusing their religious convictions. The term "terrorist network" was carefully avoided in speeches and the groups' ideology was not subject to analysis; at most, reference was made to "using Islam". Finally, the social base of these organisations—that is, the network of Ahl-e-Hadith *madrasas* which trained the militants—and their sources of funding were not considered in the investigations. As in Pakistan, these Islamist militias will therefore be able to rise from their ashes under a different name, when national and international pressure has eased.

Conclusion

Study of the militia phenomenon has produced two main hypotheses, confirmed by fieldwork. The rise to power of the Islamist militias at the end of the 1990s first of all reveals an increasing dissemination of violence, in as much as private armed groups developed autonomously and even emerged in certain regions as the principal depositories of a violence that they alone conceived as legitimate. Furthermore, ambiguous relations between the militias and the state demonstrate not so much a failure of the latter[38] as the instrumentalisation of the armed groups by political figures in the BNP-Jama'at coalition in power from 2001 to 2006, which used them in the context of local party conflicts.[39]

What the Islamist militias of Bangladesh ultimately lack is a *cause célèbre* such as the Indian occupation of Kashmir, the Soviet invasion of Afghanistan, or the American intervention in Iraq. The discourse of the jihadists, who want to transform Bangladesh into an Islamic state, pertains more to utopia than a genuine political project. This is clear from the slogan launched by the Islami Oikkyo Jote party: "*Amra shobai hobo taliban, Bangladesh hobe Afghanistan*" ("We shall all be Taliban and Bangladesh will become Afghanistan"). This is first and foremost a provocation, designed to secure a hearing on the international stage, not a genuine programme; and the Islamist parties themselves are utterly ignorant of the realities of the Taliban regime or the social environment in which that political movement developed.

Consequently, rather than serving a great cause that seems doomed in advance, the Islamist militias are caught in a double game. On the one hand, their aim is to make Bangladesh a state of strategic importance for the great powers—in particular, by presenting it as a new source of international terrorism. On the other hand, they are seeking to influence national political life as much as possible. Given the existence on the political stage of parties that are Islamist in allegiance, it is towards them that they turn to find allies at government level. In this case, the problem stems from the fact that the militias risk losing their specificity, rather than appearing to be a new force. At best, they can succeed in weakening the tendency that will be characterised here as progressive or secular, by engaging in assassinations or attacks on the politicians or intellectuals who compose it. At worst, they become tools in power games between the parties, as Bangla Bhai and his gang temporarily became. In this case, the parties use them as they previously used armed cadres of a criminal kind, before discarding them when they become too much of an embarrassment. An organisation like the JMB clearly understood the impasse into which this second strategy was leading it, when it decided on 17 August 2005 no longer to attack the secular opposition but to attack state institutions, so as to destabilise its former allies.

BIBLIOGRAPHY

Books

Ali, Shawkat A.M.M., *Faces of Terrorism in Bangladesh*, Dhaka, University Press, 2006.
Kabir, Bhuian Md. Monoar, *Politics and Development of The Jamaat-e-Islami Bangladesh*, New Delhi, South Asian Publishers, 2006.
Kamaruzzaman, Mohammad, *Adhonik Juger Islami Biplob* (Bengali) (The Islamic Revolution Today), Dhaka Islamic Publications, 2002.
Karlekar, Hiranmay, *Bangladesh, The Next Afghanistan?* New Delhi, Thousand Oaks (Calif.) and London, Sage Publications, 2005.
Menski, Werner and Biswajit Chanda (eds), *Cancer of Extremism in Bangladesh*, Centre for Ethnic Minority Studies, SOAS, Bangladesh Conference Steering Committee, London, 2005.
Riaz, Ali, *God Willing. The Politics of Islamism in Bangladesh*, Lanham (Md.), Oxford, Rowman and Littlefield, 2004.

Articles and chapters in edited volumes

Bhattacharya, France, "Le Bengale oriental entre islam et identité régionale," in Christophe Jaffrelot (ed.), *Le Pakistan*, Paris, Fayard, 2000: 71–107.
Hakim, Muhammad A., "The Use of Islam as a Political Legitimization Tool: the Bangladesh Experience, 1972–1990," *Asian Journal of Political Science*, 6 (2), December 1998: 98–117.
Hours, Bernard, "De la croyance religieuse à l'action politique. Comment devient-on fondamentaliste au Bangladesh?" in Gérard Heuzé and Monique Selim (eds), *Politique et religion dans l'Asie du Sud contemporaine*, Paris, Karthala, 1998: 25–40.
Rashiduzzaman, Mohammad, "The Dichotomy of Islam and Development: NGOs, Women's Development and Fatawa in Bangladesh," *Contemporary South Asia*, 6 (3), November 1997: 239–46.
Selim, Monique, "Les politiques de l'islamisme au Bangladesh: entre libération et collaboration," in Gérard Heuzé and Monique Selim (eds), *Politique et religion dans l'Asie du Sud contemporaine*, Paris, Karthala, 1998: 41–75.

NOTES

1. See Monique Selim (1998), pp. 60–1. The line defended by the main representative of this secular tendency, the so-called "Committee for the elimination of the collaborators and murderers of 1971" is that of a genocide committed by the Pakistani army against Bengalis.
2. Interview with a former leader of Shibir, Chittagong, 24 March 2005.
3. *Pirs*, who claim to be descendants of Sufi saints, are emblematic figures in South Asian popular Islam. They are charismatic spiritual guides reputed for their miraculous powers.
4. Part One of the Muslim profession of faith: "There is no god but God".
5. Interview with Delwar Hussain Sayeedi, Dhaka, 10 March 2005.
6. Interview published in *Daily Star*, 4 February 2005, after the arrest of this activist.
7. Interview with a member of the Supreme Court Bar Association, Dhaka, 2 April 2005.
8. Interview with a former member of Shibir, Dhaka, 11 October 2003.
9. Mohammad Kamruzzaman (2002).
10. This para-public foundation (it is "autonomous" but placed under the supervision of the Ministry of Religious Affairs), established in 1975, has the mission of supervising the functioning and funding of mosques and religious educational establishments, as well as promoting knowledge of Islamic history and values in Bangladeshi society.
11. Interview with a Shibir militant, Dhaka, 10 November 2003.
12. Interview with a former leader of Shibir, Chittagong, 24 March 2005.
13. *Daily Star*, 16 August 2003 and 3 February 2005.
14. Interviews with journalists from *Daily Star*, Dhaka, 12 March 2005, from *Prothom Alo*, Dhaka, 15 March 2005, and from *Bhorer Kagoj*, Chittagong, 23 March 2005.
15. *New Nation*, 1 February 2005.
16. *Daily Star*, 21 April 2005.
17. Qadiani is the other name for the Ahmadis and refers to the geographic origin of the sect in the eastern Punjab.
18. Interview with one of the leaders of the Ahmadi community, Dhaka, 6 April 2005.
19. *Inquilab* is the second highest-selling daily in Bangladesh. It often acts as a spokesman for the Islamist parties, especially the Islami Oikyo Jote.
20. Interview with a member of Khatme Nabuat, Dhaka, 18 March 2005 and with Mufti Amini, Dhaka, 24 August 2003. It should be remembered that the Islami Oikyo Jote was part of the majority coalition from 2001 to 2006, but did not obtain any ministerial portfolios.
21. *Daily Star*, 28 April 2005.
22. Interview with a Hizbut Tawhid militant, Kushtia, 28 March 2005.
23. *Daily Star*, 15 September 2003.
24. *Daily Star*, 28 March 2005 (column).
25. Interview with a *Prothom Alo* correspondent, Rajshahi, 17 October 2004.
26. Interview with Kawsar Siddiqui published in *Prothom Alo*, 5 November 2003.
27. *News Today*, 21 September 2003. Mufti Hannan was arrested on 1 October 2005 and sentenced to life imprisonment for sedition and attempted murder.

28. Information about the JMJB is drawn from interviews with a *Daily Star* journalist and a correspondent of *Prothom Alo* in Rajshahi, as well as newspaper articles on the subject published since 2004.
29. Interview with Bangla Bhai published in *Daily Star*, 13 May 2004.
30. *Daily Star*, 31 January 2005.
31. Interview with a journalist from *Prothom Alo*, Dhaka, 15 March 2005.
32. *Daily Star*, 18 February 2005.
33. Interview with a former CID inspector, Dhaka, 16 April 2005.
34. Interview published in *New Age*, 20 August 2003.
35. *Prothom Alo*, 17 May 2004.
36. *Prothom Alo*, 24 May 2004.
37. Interview with a *Prothom Alo* journalist, Dhaka, 15 March 2005.
38. This idea of a "(quasi-)failed state", brandished by agents of the "international community" present in Bangladesh, has been disproved by the success of the repression undertaken by the government of Khaleda Zia in 2006 (even if, as we have seen, that policy has not tackled the phenomenon of radical Islamism at its roots) and, above all, by the provisional government which succeeded it. In fact, when the members of the BNP-Jama'at had no choice but to abandon the protection they were offering to the radical Islamists, the action of police forces, combined with that of the army and intelligence services, proved extremely effective.
39. It should be stressed that this instrumentalisation does not only involve the BNP and Jama'at. In its time, the AL used clandestine communist groups in identical fashion.

Map 10: The Hindi Belt

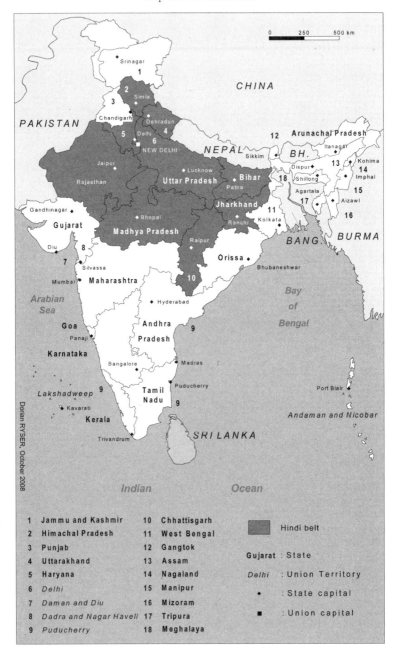

1	**Jammu and Kashmir**	10	**Chhattisgarh**
2	**Himachal Pradesh**	11	**West Bengal**
3	**Punjab**	12	**Gangtok**
4	**Uttarakhand**	13	**Assam**
5	**Haryana**	14	**Nagaland**
6	*Delhi*	15	**Manipur**
7	*Daman and Diu*	16	**Mizoram**
8	*Dadra and Nagar Haveli*	17	**Tripura**
9	*Puducherry*	18	**Meghalaya**

Hindi belt

Gujarat : State
Delhi : Union Territory
♦ : State capital
■ : Union capital

9

THE MILITIAS OF HINDUTVA

COMMUNAL VIOLENCE, TERRORISM AND CULTURAL POLICING

Christophe Jaffrelot

As mentioned in the introduction to this volume, a militia can be broadly defined as an organisation engaged in some form of violence—physical and/or psychological—whether this organisation is in open confrontation with the state or conducts underground operations for the state. Hindu nationalism, one of the oldest ideological streams in Indian politics, has developed a deep-rooted culture of violence. Ashis Nandy argued that it harks back to one of the "warrior-cultures" in India, that of the Chitpavan Brahmins of Maharashtra.[1] Certainly, the peculiar culture of this caste and its historical trajectory were conducive to forms of radicalism,[2] but there was nothing automatic about its promotion of a culture of violence.[3] In fact, the advent of modern politics during the late 19th century saw the emergence, among the Poona-based Chitpavans who joined the Indian National Congress, of moderates—like M.G. Ranade and G.K. Gokhale—who promoted a non-aggressive brand of nationalism, as well as extremists like B.G. Tilak, who played a pioneering role in the invention of a Hindu nationalist culture of violence.[4]

Tilak, a resourceful political entrepreneur, reinterpreted his Chitpavan legacy to build a new ideology of proto-Hindu nationalist *Realpolitik* justifying violent means. His pro-Hindu and anti-Muslim leanings were evident from the way he politicised traditional festivals such as Ganesh Chathurthi (which gave birth to processions in the form of mass demonstrations) and introduced an equally militant yearly celebration of Shivaji's birthday. Regarding violence, he presented the *Bhagavad Gita* as a sacred text legitimising the use of violence in the anti-British freedom struggle.[5] He argued that *Karma*

Yoga (the Yoga of action) was the most valuable discipline to resort to in this context, and that one should follow the teaching of Krishna to Arjuna in the *Gita*:[6] every act, even a violent one, was legitimate, according to him, if it was executed for the well-being of the World and without attachment to its fruits.[7] Tilak also justified political violence independently of the rules of combat. For instance, he approved of Shivaji's killing of General Afzulkhan, an emissary of Emperor Aurangzeb, although it was Shivaji himself who had invited the General to negotiate. It was on these very grounds that the major controversy between Tilak and Gandhi broke out in 1920. Not only did Tilak's Hindu revivalism contrast with Gandhi's ecumenism and syncretism, but he also strongly opposed the notion of *ahimsa*. Gandhi portrayed him as a leader for whom the ends justified the means and might was right.

While Tilak endowed his Chitpavans caste fellows with a new political repertoire mixing Hindu militancy, violence and *Realpolitik*, Savarkar—and other Tilakites—not only gave a more distinctly anti-Muslim shape to Hindu nationalism, but also built the first militias of this school of thought. Many others were to develop over time—always against Muslims—, including the Rashtriya Swayamasevak Sangh (RSS). However, the Savarkarite tradition differed from the RSS. The former was much more interested in direct violent action by militias propagating an explicit anti-Muslim martial ethos, whereas the latter—which shared the same anti-Muslim ideology—focused on a longer term agenda aiming at transforming Hindu society and was careful to avoid attracting too much attention from the state, in order to pursue this objective. Things changed to some extent in the 1980s when the RSS, by creating the Bajrang Dal, revisited the Savarkarite tradition. Like the Savarkarite militias, the new offshoot of the Sangh Parivar started to exert violence over Hindus as well. And when they exerted communal violence, both schools of thought did not hesitate to use the state—in its colonial or post-colonial incarnations—and tended to resort to terrorist means in a similar way.

A tale of two traditions of Hindu militias?

Savarkarism: from Abhinav Bharat to the Hindu Rashtra Dal. Vinayak Damodar Savarkar is probably the best example of the Tilakite brand of politics of violence (incidentally his father, a small landowner-cum-moneylender of Nasik district[8] used to read him Tilak's articles in *Kesari*).[9] Already during his high school years, Savarkar started a secret society called Mitra Mela which organised the political festivals introduced by Tilak in honour of Ganesh and Shivaji.[10] At Fergusson College, a prestigious institution he joined in 1901, Savarkar transformed the Mitra Mela into an Abhinav Bharat (Young India) Society in 1905, which drew its name and inspiration from Mazzini's "young Italy" but was also influenced by Frost's *Secret Societies of the European Revolution (1776–1876)*, a book dealing mostly with the Russian nihilists.[11] Interested in Western forms of nationalism and revolution, Savarkar applied to the

London-based India House established by S.K. Verma in order to learn the techniques of terrorism with European revolutionaries.[12] He obtained the required scholarship thanks to a letter of recommendation by Tilak in 1906.[13] Indeed, he got in touch with Sinn Fein members[14] and an old Paris-based Russian terrorist from whom he procured via two emissaries a handbook on how to make explosives.[15] He sent this manual to India where it was used extensively. In 1909 Vinayak's brother, Ganesh—who was in charge of Abhinav Bharat since his departure for London—was arrested for "seditious writings"[16] and sentenced to life imprisonment in the Andamans. In order to avenge his brother, Savarkar had Curzon Wyllie, one of the advisers of the Secretary of State for India in London, assassinated. Arrested in 1910, he was tried and sent to the Andamans as well.

Savarkar became the father of Hindutva ideology in jail. In 1923, he wrote the charter of Hindu nationalism that his book, *Hindutva, Who Is a Hindu?* was to become, and then founded a Hindu Sabha through his brother Ganesh when he left the Andamans for Ratnigiri, where he remained in custody between 1924 and 1937. Immediately after his release he became president of the Hindu Mahasabha, the first Hindu nationalist party, and he remained so until 1943.

As early as 1937, Savarkar sought to join hands with Keshav Baliram Hedgewar, the founder of the RSS and a great admirer of his. In December of that year, Hedgewar took him to Nagpur, Chanda, Wardha, Akola, Umred and other places in order to meet members of the movement who were enthralled by his speeches.[17] He took part in the RSS Officers Training Camp which took place in Poona in 1940[18]—the RSS had already agreed to handle security for the Hindu Mahasabha session that had taken place in Nagpur in 1938.[19]

However, V.D. Savarkar's brand of Hindu nationalism and his expectations of the RSS were not compatible with the latter's agenda, especially after M.S. Golwalkar took over from Hedgewar in 1940 at the helm of the organisation. The militarisation of the Hindus was Savarkar's top priority since he feared that otherwise Muslims would attack the majority community throughout India.[20] For him, the RSS was the emerging Hindu army he longed for while the Hindu Mahasabha was their political instrument. However, neither Hedgewar nor Golwalkar was willing to fit into these plans. First, they had their own road map, which focused on socio-psychological work in a long-term perspective; they not only wanted no distraction from this agenda, but in addition were anxious not to attract British repressive measures at a time when, because of World War II, paramilitary movements were watched closely. Second, the RSS leaders were not prepared to play second fiddle to Hindu Mahasabha politicians for whom they had no great respect, Savarkar excepted. An anonymous Hindu Sabhaite from Nagpur wrote in early 1940: "RSS has not (*sic*) connection with the Hindu Sabha. They openly say so and do not make the secret of the fact that their indifference towards Hindu Mahasabha (*sic*). They say that there is no difference between the Hindu Mahasabha and the Congress".[21]

The RSS disapproved of the agitations started by the Hindu Mahasabha—for instance the one that was launched in the late 1930s in the Muslim state of Hyderabad in order to protect the Hindus—and dissuaded its members from taking part in them. When they did, it was in a personal capacity and they took the risk of being expelled by RSS leaders.

As a result, the Hindu Mahasabha decided to create its own Hindu Militia, a movement also known as the Ram Sena (the army of Ram). This movement, which took shape in December 1939 during the Calcutta session, was the brainchild of B.S. Moonje who argued then that such a body was necessary in case the British lost the war and "Muslim nations beyond the North-West frontier could invade India and the Muslims here may help them".[22]

Moonje, a rather unknown character, played a very important role in the making of the Hindutva movement in Maharashtra, and especially of its militarist mindset. Of all Tilak's lieutenants, it was Moonje who most consistently insisted that Hindus should be inducted into a martial ethos. A Deshastha Brahmin from Nagpur, a milieu that retained some nostalgia for the Maratha Empire and continued to profess loyalty to the Bhonsle kingdom,[23] B.S. Moonje was an eye surgeon who rose to the very apex of the Congress Party in the Central Provinces after World War I and founded the Nagpur unit of the Hindu Mahasabha in the 1920s. Although he was a Brahmin, he was not a vegetarian[24] and even proclaimed the virtues of eating meat.[25] He liked to refer to himself as a "Maratha Brahmin"[26] and to introduce himself as "a Brahmin by caste and by temperament perhaps a Kshatriya",[27] particularly because he used to hunt. In 1920, in fact, he started shooting clubs. Moonje was resolutely opposed to *ahimsa*. "In our religion," he claimed, "violence in the defence of one's rights is not condemned".[28] This drove him to add that he "like[d] the Muslims for the virile vigilance with which they protect their racial interests [...], which, alas, is visibly lacking in the present-day Hindu race".

The Hindu Militia members wear a highly codified uniform—khaki shorts, khaki shirt, saffron cape—and wield a spear. Its missions were listed by Moonje as follows:

1. All must assemble daily at some place, 2. Military Drill, 3. Lathi, Kathi, Sword, 4. P.T. [physical training], 5. Ideology, 6. Pamphlets and booklets with particular reference to past History, 7. Sunday and holidays: touring villages in batches of ten or twenty for mass organization, 8. Rifling, shooting, riding, cycling, motoring, etc., 9. Camp in Puja, Diwali or Summer vacation.[29]

These activities call to mind those of the Prabhat Pheris started by the Congress in the 1920s, except for the emphasis on rifling and shooting which became part of a truly paramilitary discipline. Moonje, who had been elected president of the Ram Sena for five years by the Hindu Mahasabha's Working Committee, inaugurated it on 17 March 1940. But in August the British, who were alarmed by the proliferation of militias in each community, banned military exercises and uniforms.

The Hindu Mahasabha then began a twofold strategy of collaboration with some princely states and with the British. In the 1940s, a few Maharajas were prepared to cooperate with the Hindu Mahasabha in order to have their community militarised. In Alwar, the Mahajarah worried about the growing mobilisation of Muslim Meos. He welcomed the development of a Hindu Mahasabha-sponsored militia, the Arya Veer Dal, in 1945, whose volunteers came from all over North India.[30] Two years later, in July 1947, he appointed as Prime Minister N.B. Khare, a former Congress man who—like so many other Chitpavan Brahmins—had developed affinities with Hindu nationalism and its paramilitary dimensions. When he was Chief Minister of the Central Provinces in 1938, Khare had already passed a law making it legal to bear arms under certain conditions, a decision strongly supported by Savarkar[31] who also requested that military training be introduced at school.[32]

However, in military matters, the key man in the Hindu Mahasabha was still Moonje, who had designed the project for a military school as early as 1929 and who, when in Europe to take part in the First Round Table Conference, seized this opportunity to visit the military academies of France, Germany and Italy. There he met Mussolini, who was very pleased to learn that an Indian should want "to see his army and institutions dispensing military education".[33] Moonje went also to see the working of the Ballila movement.[34] On his way back he decided to start a military school in Nasik and began raising funds to this end. Maharajas who were warriors by avocation were the most willing to contribute. The Bhonsle of Nagpur—after whom the school was named—were among the most generous, but the Maharajah Holkar (from Indore),[35] the Maharajah Gaewkad (from Baroda) and the Maharajah Scindia (from Gwalior) who inaugurated the building in 1938,[36] followed, like the rulers of Dewas, Dhar,[37] Bikaner, Patiala,[38] etc. The school was supervised directly by Moonje, who moved his residence to Nasik. But its appeal was limited to Maharashtra, most of the teaching being in Marathi.[39]

In addition to Maharajahs, the Hindu Mahasabha leaders approached the British to request military training for their coreligionists. Moonje had already lobbied so much in the 1920s that the British had created a selection committee for inducting Indians into Sandhurst for officer training.[40] He had been appointed to this committee in 1925.[41] During the Second World War, Savarkar put even more pressure on the British in order to "militarize Hindudom". As soon as the war began in 1939, the Hindu Mahasabha Working Committee emphasised that war offered an opportunity for the general militarisation of the Hindus that should not be missed.[42] By 1940, the Hindu Sabhas of Bengal, Central Provinces and Bombay Presidency were taking part in regional War Committees in which the British had started to recruit Indian soldiers—and which the Congress naturally boycotted.

After the Muslim League officially declared in favour of a separate Pakistan in March 1940, Hindu Mahasabha-sponsored militias multiplied in the perspective of the coming Partition as self-defence private armies. In Bengal, for instance, Shyam Prasad Mookerjee started a Hindu Shakti Sangha[43] while criticising Savarkar for collaborating with the British so openly that he undermined the party's nationalist credentials. Mookerjee's alternative strategy consisted in militarising the Hindus but opposing the British, too—especially after the Congress launched the Quit India Movement. This strategic line became dominant in 1943 when Mookerjee became President of the Hindu Mahasabha, replacing Savarkar, who wanted to resign for health reasons and had already launched the Hindu Rashtra Dal (HRD) in May 1942, whose leaders were Nathuram Godse and N.D. Apte, two Chitpavan Brahmins from Poona.

Launching the HRD, Savarkar explained that it was intended to meet the need for "a secret organization of volunteers for secret operations".[44] He rallied to the movement RSS members who, like Nathuram Godse, thought that the RSS's strategy contented itself with "organization for the sake of organization".[45] However, few of the RSS' members left it, dual membership being the rule.[46] The HRD made some progress when the Tilakite notables of the Kesari group started to support the organisation after the unleashing of violence in Bengal and Punjab.[47] Having raised some money, the HRD organised a training camp in Ahmedanagar in May 1943 for 70 volunteers from Maharashtrian-speaking districts of British India and princely states.[48] In March 1944, the Bombay Provincial Hindu Sabha could rely on 300 HRD members.[49] At that time, the movement emphasised weapons training. The volunteers learned how "to manufacture bombs and to use guns from bicycles and cars and how to use pistols and revolvers".[50] The key instructor in these techniques was N.D. Apte, who had served in the army as Assistant Technical Recruiting Officer. In this capacity, he could use the War Service Exhibitions—which were intended to attract young Indians to the army—for initiating HRD members into the art of modern arms. In 1945 he organised a parallel Dal Shibir (training camp) in Poona in order to train a group of Savarkarites.[51] In May 1947 Tilak's grandson, Jayantrav, joined the HRD,[52] which made also inroads in princely states like Gwalior where a Hindu Rashtra Sena took shape as a subsidiary.

The terrorist agenda that the HRD had set for itself culminated in the 1948 assassination of Gandhi, who had already been the target of the Savarkarites before. In 1934, they had thrown a bomb at the Poona Municipal Town Hall where Gandhi by Godse was making a speech against Untouchability in the course of his Indian tour against this social curse.[53] In 1947–48 the two main architects of the plot against Gandhi, Godse and Apte, decided to kill him not only to punish him for his appeasement of Muslims to which they attributed Partition, but also to get rid of a man who had obliged the Indian government to give Pakistan "its due" in financial terms. But the assassination of the Mahatma meant the end of Savarkarism. Not only were Savarkar and his colleagues arrested and Godse as well as Apte executed, but this stream of Indian politics lost the little legitimacy it had acquired in the context of Partition.

Displays of strength and persuasion, the RSS' preferred strategies. The political marginalisation of Savarkarism gave the RSS more leeway. It had already become the dominant Hindu brigade after two decades of steady growth. As mentioned above, the Rashtriya Swayamsevak Sangh (National Volunteer Association, RSS), founded in 1925 by Keshav Baliram Hedgewar, concentrated on a long-term endeavour to transform the Hindu community. Convinced that the latter was made vulnerable by its pacifism and its divisions in the face of a united and aggressive Muslim minority, the RSS set itself the goal of galvanising the community both physically and morally.

The allegedly defensive nature of the RSS can be better understood by looking into the circumstances that spawned the movement in the 1920s, those created by the Khilafat movement, which quickly turned its attacks on the Hindus in places where the latter had conflictual relations with the Muslims, sometimes over purely economic matters. For example, on the Malabar Coast (today's Kerala), the Moplahs (Muslim peasants) rose up against their Hindu landlords in 1921. The result was a wave of communal riots that swelled all the more since reports of the incidents from one town to the next were distorted in such a way as to generate the wildest rumours.

In this context, Hedgewar decided to create the RSS in Nagpur to defend the Hindus. Replicating a deeply entrenched stereotype in Indian psychology, he considered the Muslims to have greater strength because of their meat diet and their religious unity symbolised by Friday's congregation in which everyone, poor and rich alike, prayed together at the mosque, whereas Hindus were frail—partly because of the food taboos observed by the upper castes, all strictly vegetarian—and they were divided into countless castes and sects.

From that time on, the RSS presented itself as a self-defence movement and criticised Mahatma Gandhi's method advocating nonviolence. Against Muslims, whom they viewed as potential aggressors, RSS members believed that strong-arm tactics were the only effective method. The Hindu body and mind thus needed to be reformed to bring about the advent of a new man. To achieve this, Hedgewar designed a special system of which the basic unit is the *shakha*. *Shakha* means "branch", and in fact this entity is the fundamental building block of the network that Hedgewar hoped to spread across India. A *shakha* is both a place and a social group: every day at sunrise and/or sunset, the members of a *shakha* meet for physical training sessions and ideological lectures. The main RSS target was young people who were more energetic and malleable and embodied tomorrow's India. The organisation attracted them to the *shakha*s by practicing games of their age. How many *swayamsevak*s say they joined the movement to play *khokho* or *kabaddi*? Gradually, the games turned into physical training, including practice in handling the *lathi* (a baton also used by the police).

At the same time, the *swayamsevak*s learn what amounts to military discipline. Even today, each session begins and ends by saluting the saffron flag, considered as the movement's inspiration. In addition, RSS members wear uniforms imitating those worn by the British police during colonial rule: white shirt, black cap, khaki shorts and leather boots. As for the ideological propaganda conveyed by the *shakha*s, it is systematically based on bygone Hindu grandeur and hatred of the Muslim invaders, whose abuses committed in the Middle Ages are described in gory detail. The Hindu nationalists also hold them responsible for the decline of the Hindus that made way for British colonisation.

From a sociological standpoint, the *shakha*s have a vocation to welcome all Hindus without distinction of caste or class (hence the need for a uniform) and to serve as the crucible for a new national sentiment: the RSS likes to see itself as the microcosm of the *Hindu Rashtra*, a Hindu nation in miniature. To achieve this, Hedgewar early on devised a specific method to train cadres to be above social status and distinctions. These *pracharak*s or preachers, in the very front lines of the movement, were to devote their lives to the RSS, renouncing any professional career or family life. Constituting an itinerant elite corps, they were assigned the mission of founding new *shakha*s throughout India. They eventually formed the heart of the "brotherhood in saffron", to use the expression coined by Walter Andersen and Shriddhar Damle.[54] Their sacrifice to the cause gave them an aura of prestige in the eyes of the *swayamsevak*s, who often saw them as *karma yogi*s, world renouncers transcending castes and classes.

Through the devotion of the *pracharak*s, the network of *shakha*s fanned out quickly from its epicentre in Nagpur. Northern India was the first area of expansion, but others followed suit. In 1939, the RSS counted 40,000 members divided into approximately 500 *shakha*s, and in 1943, 76,000 of them—including 35,000 in the Central Provinces, 20,000 in Bombay Presidency, and 14,000 in Punjab.[55] In 1948, there were 600,000 *swayamsevak*s, mainly in northern India.[56] This upsurge was naturally due to the circumstances created by Partition.

In the late 1940s, while Partition was approaching, the RSS adopted features of a private army, like Savarkar's HRD at the same time. In Punjab, RSS members armed and trained themselves in order to protect Hindus who were in a minority in the province, but also in order to eliminate Muslims from districts that they claimed even though they were not in a majority there, or not in a very large majority. A circular by the RSS of Lahore explained, "The problem therefore is to arrange things that (*sic*) districts of Lahore, Sheikhpura, Lyallpur, Montgomery and part of Multan have to fall in with India".[57] To achieve this, the RSS prepared explosives and killed in a fairly organised manner. K.D. Jhari, who was to leave the RSS afterwards, remembered in the 1970s "with feelings of sheer abasement, that the hand-grenades we had made in large numbers were used at several places like Samballkha to attack and destroy the Muslims and their households".[58] Taking stock of the situation in Delhi as well as Punjab, *The Statesman* considered in March 1948 that during Partition "The Sangh was the best organized in each town and as is well known did not lag behind in the use of bombs, hand-grenades and fire-arms".[59]

Similarly, the RSS attacked Muslims in a logic of ethnic cleansing in places where they formed more or less influential pockets. The states of Alwar and Bharatpur, which had very substantial Meo populations, are cases in point. In Alwar the Prime Minister, N.B. Khare, declared twenty years later that, with the help of the RSS, "The state became non-Muslims (*sic*). 50,000 were converted to Hinduism by the Hindus, not a joke. About 15,000 might have been slaughtered".[60] The Maharajah of Alwar had allowed the RSS to set up training camps to resist "separatist" demands from the Meos, a group of Muslims among whom the Tabligh-e-Jamaat conducted active propaganda.[61]

These developments at the time of Partition show that the RSS was perfectly able to resort to violent means the same way as the Savarkarite militias—and indeed did not "lag behind" as regards the use of arms and explosives. However, in less exceptional circumstances than the Partition, the RSS cultivated a quietist discourse. It did not adopt a discourse legitimating violence, for two reasons. First, because its preferred method remained persuasion, in keeping with its deep-seated conviction that its ethos inherited from Brahminical values was superior to any other, and if it could not persuade, the RSS preferred to dissuade its potential aggressors by displays of strength of which no other Indian organisation today was capable; this is the purpose of immense rallies where tens of thousands of uniformed *swayamsevaks* march in time, taking over towns for the duration of their endless military-like parades. A second reason, of course, was that such violence would have placed it outside the bounds of the law, whereas its priority remained the expansion of its network of *shakhas* through groundwork at the grassroots level and in a long-term perspective. This endeavour has been constant and the growth of the movement linear, except during the dark spots in the movement's history: the ban on the organisation after Gandhi's assassination, and the Emergency. In 2004, the RSS *shakhas* numbered 33,758 and the *up-shakhas* (the real units of the movement) 48,329.[62] From 10,000 *shakhas* in the 1970s to 30,000 in 2000, the RSS network virtually tripled in size, whereas the Indian population had merely doubled.

This *shakha*-based *modus operandi* naturally does not rule out recourse to violence. Some RSS members of course perpetrate violent acts, particularly against Muslims during riots. But their wrongdoings often concern the movement only indirectly, not only because violence can then be attributed to individuals, but also because the primary affiliation of the people charged may not the RSS, but one of its offshoots. Thus the commission in charge of investigating the riots in Jamshedpur in 1979 had to conclude that it was a local leader of the Bharatiya Mazdoor Sangh, the workers' union founded by the RSS, who was responsible for these incidents.[63] After independence in 1947, the RSS in fact set up a myriad offshoots that enabled it to reach new social milieus and diversify its *modus operandi*, concerning among other things the use of violence, as is evident from the creation of the Bajrang Dal, which represented a real shift in the RSS perspective.

The Bajrang Dal or the outsourcing of violence

The RSS had already established one offshoot prior to independence, without altering its method. Founded in 1936, the Rashtra Sevika Samiti was none other than the female counterpart to the RSS. Hedgewar, loath to mix the sexes, had come up with this solution to allow women to take part in the Sangh's work. The other components of the "family" (*parivar*), all founded after 1947, each adopted its own specific *modus operandi*.

The first of them, the Akhil Bharatiya Vidyarthi Parishad (ABVP), was created in 1948 on the model of the communist student union, so as better to resist the latter on university campuses. In 1951 Golwalkar, Hedgewar's successor, finally resigned himself to supporting the creation of a political party, the Bharatiya Jana Sangh, in order to have a voice in the political arena, having grasped the importance of this resource in 1948–49 when the RSS had been banned by Nehru and was not able to find any regular backers among the political personnel. The BJS merged with the Janata Party in 1977 and was reborn under the name of Bharatiya Janata Party in 1980. In 1955 came the turn of the Bharatiya Mazdoor Sangh (BMS), the workers' union.[64] In 1964, the RSS founded the Vishva Hindu Parishad (Universal Hindu Association), whose stated mission was to federate the various sects that divided Hinduism into countless rival currents.[65]

These groups, which form the backbone of the Sangh Parivar,[66] all have the same organisational pattern: the RSS sets them up by sending one or more experienced *pracharak*s having an affinity with the sector of activity involved. The organisations thus created enjoy considerable autonomy. But the heads of RSS offshoots and the RSS leaders consult one another and meet regularly to coordinate their efforts. In the 1980s, their actions took on a new, explicitly violent dimension with the formation of a new subsidiary group, the Bajrang Dal.

The Bajrang Dal, a by-product of the Ayodhya movement. The Bajrang Dal was founded in the spring of 1984, not under the auspices of the RSS but under those of the VHP, thus adding an additional degree of mediation and concealment of the link between the Bajrang Dal and the RSS. The Bajrang Dal was created to help the VHP accomplish the mission the RSS had just assigned it: to increase the strength of Hindu mobilisation in the Ayodhya movement. For many Hindus, Ayodhya in Uttar Pradesh is the former capital of the god Ram, one of Vishnu's most popular avatars in northern India. According to a widespread but unverifiable belief, there once stood on top of Ram's birthplace in Ayodhya a temple that the Muslims supposedly replaced by a mosque in 1528. This building is called Babri Masjid (Babur's Mosque), after the name of the first Mughal emperor who had it built. In 1949, Hindu nationalist movements such as the Hindu Mahasabha laid claim to the site, a Ram idol having mysteriously appeared there, placed in all likelihood by them. Incidents there prompted the government to place seals on the building to stave off communal violence.[67] The controversy resurfaced in 1984 when the RSS saw the restitution of this site to the Hindus as a potentially mobilising issue. The VHP was then instructed to orchestrate a campaign in favour of building a temple to Ram in Ayodhya. In April 1984 the Dharma Sansad (Parliament of the Hindu religion) unanimously adopted a resolution to "liberate" the site of the Babri Masjid.[68] It was in this context that it set up an armed branch in May, the Bajrang Dal.[69] The VHP website moreover specifies that the Bajrang Dal was founded "with the temporary and localised objective of awakening youth of Uttar Pradesh and get their involvement in the Ramjanmabhoomi movement (literally "land of Rama's birth").[70]

The name of this organisation proves that the VHP was seeking to create shock troops: the word "*bajrang*", meaning "strong", is in fact associated with Hanuman, for it designates the club that he is often depicted as brandishing.[71] The Bajrang Dal's first mission in 1984 was to provide a security service for the Ram Janaki Yatra, a procession that left from Sitarmahi in Bihar with Ayodhya as its destination, in which the "pilgrims" carried images of Ram and Sita whom they claimed to want to "liberate".[72] The Yatra continued its route towards Delhi to put pressure on the political authorities for whom Indian citizens were about to cast their votes in the general elections scheduled for January 1985. But the assassination of Indira Gandhi in October radically altered the political agenda.

The first leader of the Bajrang Dal, Vinay Katiyar, was naturally a former RSS *pracharak*; after having embraced this career in 1972, he had become ABVP secretary. But he contrasted strongly with the Brahminical archetype attached to such a function: he was not from an upper caste but from a caste of cultivators, the Kurmis. These origins are revealing of the rather plebeian nature of the Bajrang Dal, an organisation that was not designed to cultivate the RSS ethos and *samskars*. Moreover, it did not claim to have the same degree of discipline. Its members were not required to meet daily like the *swayamsevaks* in the RSS *shakhas*, but simply to take part in training camps where they were supposed to learn "how to be bold".[73] Until 1993, the Bajrang Dal did not even have a uniform. Uniforms do not seem to have particularly caught on since then; the Bajrang Dalis still recognise one another by one sign only, the saffron-colored headband marked "Ram" that they wear on their forehead. The Bajrang Dalis that I interviewed in the Hindi belt were for the most part jobless and involved in semi-illegal activities, gambling and especially lotteries. They were a reserve force that the Hindu nationalist movement could mobilise at any time to do its dirty work. Katiyar in fact one day declared in a press interview: "Might is the only law I understand. Nothing else matters to me. In India it is a war-like situation as between Ram and Ravana".[74]

If one of Manjari Katju's informers is to be believed, routine Bajrang Dal activities at the local level went from watching over (and protecting) Hindu girls in the neighbourhood to preventing cows from being slaughtered in the abattoirs (at the hands of Muslims for the most part), and included systematic spying on the local Muslims, especially when they were immigrants from Bangladesh.[75]

But the biggest matter involving the Bajrang Dal was of course the Ayodhya movement, in which its militants were constantly at the forefront of the agitation. In 1990, there were many of them among the *kar sevak*s who stormed the Babri Masjid and were the first to be put down by the Uttar Pradesh government. On 6 December 1992 they were again in the front lines, actively participating in the demolition of the Ayodhya mosque and the building of a makeshift temple (Ram Mandir) on its ruins. At the same time, the Bajrang Dal was also involved in countless riots pitting Hindus against Muslims all over India. In Bhopal, for instance, where rioting following the demolition of the Babri Masjid left 161 dead—most of them Muslims—the Bajrang Dalis played a key role. One of the protagonists in the riot recalls, "We received the order from the Sangh Parivar not to go to Ayodhya [on 6 December 1992] because there was the premonition [*purvabhas*] that a fight might happen here [in Bhopal]. Therefore, a few people stayed here in alert. [...] We took part in the riot. Muslim people killed policemen and looted the people. Therefore we took part [in the riot] and then scared the Muslims away".[76]

The Bajrang Dal was banned by the Narasimha Rao government, as was the RSS and the VHP, after the Babri Masjid was demolished. However, the Bajrang Dal was legalised again the following year on 4 June 1993. But it was not in a position simply to revert to its prior activities because the RSS and the rest of the Sangh Parivar—starting with the BJP–wanted to exert better control over an organisation that had exhibited its lack of discipline during the Ayodhya movement. Although there is no doubt that demolition of the Babri Masjid was part of the Sangh Parivar's plans, the way things occurred might have made its leaders afraid of being unable to cope in the long run with elements that had such a modus operandi. The Bajrang Dal—some members of which who joined in the mosque's demolition went so far as to pose for the cameras with a knife between their teeth—especially needed to be called to order.

The RSS thus established a constitution by which to frame its activity. On 11 July 1993 the Bajrang Dal—which at that time only existed legally in a handful of states—became a nationwide organisation as the VHP's official youth wing.[77] It was provided with a uniform (blue shorts, white shirt and a rust-coloured scarf) and a handbook aimed mainly at those in charge of training in some 350 camps the Bajrang Dal ran all over India.[78] In the preface to this little book written in strongly Sanskritised Hindi, Acharya Giriraj Kishore, second in command of the VHP, paid tribute to the heroes of 6 December 1992: "On that day the force of youth, escaping its leaders, and despite their repeated injunctions, went forward to accomplish its mission—a mission aimed to erase the shameful scar [that was the Babri Masjid]".[79] But this was immediately followed by "Whether it is an individual or a nation, the entire society or an organization, only one who knows discipline can achieve success, awareness and excellence. Without discipline there can be no success. Discipline comes from training and exercise. And if a disciplined man is also brave, what more can you ask for?!"

Giriraj Kishore's emphasis on discipline was translated in the 1990s by the establishment of a rigorous new system. First, the Bajrang Dal adopted the specific RSS technique of sermons (*baudhik*) delivered by a local official so that each member would know what he was supposed to think. Secondly, Bajrang Dal officials at the block level were now to meet on a weekly basis to coordinate their activities; meetings would be monthly for those officiating at the district level and quarterly for the state-level officials. In addition, the organisation began holding two or three plenary sessions per year at the national level. This routine was supplemented by another, marked by a cycle of commemorations which all differed from those observed by the RSS.[80] In April, Hanuman Jayanti is celebrated as Balupasana Diwas or "Worship of Strength Day". Next comes Valmiki Diwas, for Valmiki, the Untouchable saint celebrated in a spirit of promoting social harmony (*samajik samrasta*), a formula that aims to conceal the conflicts inherent in the caste system. On 14 August, Pakistan's national holiday—as a way of emphasising that it was Muslims, not Hindus who divided India—the Bajrang Dal celebrated All-India Memorial Day, during which it reasserted its commitment to a reunified India *(Akhand Bharat)*, aiming to erase the Partition. On 2 November came Martyrs' Day to mark the anniversary of the repression of 1990, during which a dozen Bajrang Dalis were killed by the police as they made their first assault on the Babri Masjid. Finally, 6 December, National Glory Day, commemorated the demolition of that mosque.

From lathis to firearms: emulating the threatening Islamist Other…and its Israeli enemy. Starting in the 1990s, the Bajrang Dal set up training camps where its militants received extremely rigorous physical conditioning. They practice a mixture of martial arts (judo, karate and ju-jitsu) specially designed by their trainers. They also learn to climb ropes, to leap through blazing hoops and, especially, to shoot with rifles and pistols. This training is reminiscent of what some Islamists undergo as shown in televised reports of the al-Qaeda camps in Afghanistan after the fall of the Taliban. In fact, when interviewed by Smita Gupta in 2004, the organisation's president justified such physical training by mentioning threats which all stem from Muslims: for him it was merely "to defend society and the social fabric against abductors and molesters of women, thieves, Pakistan's Inter Services Intelligence agents and Bangladeshi infiltrators".[81]

In fact, a camp head in Ahmedabad explained in one of the rare interviews published on the subject: "The jehadis have no fear of death. They learn this at an early age in the madrassas. We must also end our fear of death".[82] All available interviews on the subject show that the physical training activists undergo aims to counter a perceived rise in Muslim threats due to the appearance of suicide attacks in the region—in Indian Kashmir to begin with. Hence the idea mentioned by Bal Thackeray, the leader of Shiv Sena, another Hindu nationalist organisation, to set up Hindu suicide squads.[83]

This discourse shows to what extent the Bajrang Dal camps fit within a logic of strategic mimesis of supposedly threatening Others. Such an approach has already led Hindu nationalists to draw inspiration from the Western idea of a nation so as better to fight the British, and invent a Hindu proselytism inspired by the work of Christian and Muslim missionaries so as better to resist them:[84] Hindu nationalists thus also strive to imitate the methods of those they perceive as threats to their identity, even to their survival. But here the process results in a twofold imitation: on the one hand the Bajrang Dalis emulate the threatening Islamist Other, on the other hand, they draw their inspiration from those who have already fought these Muslim militants. Indeed, certain leaders of the Bajrang Dal claim that they are importing Israeli techniques. One of them from the Ayodhya camp thus explained in the year 2000 that Hindu nationalists actually drew their inspiration from Israeli society, for the Israelis make an effort to inculcate the Art of War in all of their citizens to enable them to defend themselves against a hostile environment. And the same man added: "India's [situation is] even worse. Israel has threat only from outsiders while India faces threat from even those inhabiting it".[85] Another Bajrang Dali in this camp added just as significantly: "I am of the secret service of Bajrang Dal. Israel's Mossad is my inspiration".

Some 30 Bajrang Dal camps were thus created throughout India in the 1990s, to which of course must be added those of the Durga Vahini. These "Durga brigades" (Durga being one of the terrible forms of Devi), which cropped up in the 1990s to bring together the female "youth" of Hindu nationalism, have adopted a *modus operandi* similar in all respects to that of the Bajrang Dal, even if here the accent is placed more on defence (and even self-defence) of Hindu girls. Female Hindu nationalist militants practice the same physical and paramilitary exercises as the Bajrang Dalis, including learning how to use firearms.[86]

Even if the use of firearms appeared in the Bajrang Dal starting in 1996, it is the wielding of other deadly weapons that has become more important. The group's favourite instrument is the *trishul* (trident), a weapon associated with Shiva which for that reason, like the Sikh *kirpan* (dagger), is not covered by the Indian Arms Act. The oath taken by Bajrang Dalis when they join attests to the importance of this trident: "With God as my witness, I pledge I will always be ready to rise to the defense of my country, religion and society while promising that I will not misuse this *trishul*". Although the organisation presents the object as a mere religious symbol, the blades are still over 10 cm long, and many victims of riots in which Bajrang Dal has been involved have fallen under its blows. Altogether, the movement estimates it distributed over 500,000 of them between 1986 and 2004.[87] It is true that in the early 2000s, the Bajrang Dal boasted twice as many members. In 2001, according to its president, its membership numbered 1,250,000.

Thugs in charge of doing the RSS' dirty work. What does the Bajrang Dal use its strike force for? Although the logic of strategic mimesis that spawned it recalls the traditional *modus operandi* of the RSS, it differs from that organisation in its relationship to violence: although subjected to greater discipline, it displays an aggressiveness that the RSS, believing in the techniques of persuasion and shows of strength, has always shied away from in order not to attract too much attention. The Bajrang Dal cultivates this ethos because it must perform the Sangh Parivar's dirty work. In 2004 its new president, Prakash Sharma, told Smita Gupta: "Just as Hanuman was always ready to help Ram in times of emergency, so the Bajrang Dal is in constant readiness to assist the VHP and the *sadhus* [Hindu renouncers of the world]. The youth power of the Bajrang Dal can be mobilized at any time for conflict situations".[88] And Prakash Sharma concluded by saying the Bajrang Dal was the Sangh Parivar's "problem solving organization".

To begin with, the Bajrang Dal kept the Ayodhya issue alive by mobilising its activists in the street. In January 2000 the organisation announced that discussion of the timetable for a new attempt to build the temple would be on the agenda of its convention in Bhopal. Since the Chief Minister of the Congress government in Madhya Pradesh, Digvijay Singh, had forbidden access to the capital of his state to Bajrang Dal militants, a confrontation ensued with the police forces, which demonstrated Bajrang Dal's determination. Nevertheless, the Ayodhya issue was put on the back burner: first, the government in New Delhi, led by the BJP since 1998, did not want to have to deal with a new wave of confrontation between Hindus and Muslims, and secondly, the judges made sure the *status quo* was maintained. The Bajrang Dal thus redeployed its forces.

A self-defence militia in Kashmir. The Bajrang Dal sent a large number of its militants to Jammu and Kashmir to protect Hindus who they claimed were victims of abuse at the hands of separatists. This measure came in reaction to the exodus of many *pandits* (Kashmiri Brahmins) in the Srinagar valley who found refuge in Delhi or in Jammu, the only part of the state where Hindus were a majority. There, in the Poonch, Doda and Rajouri districts, according to its former president, Rajendra Jain, Bajrang Dal cadres infiltrated government-sponsored village safety committees. It is naturally impossible to verify this, but the same idea cropped up again in a press conference held by the VHP international general secretary, Praveen Togadia, on 26 March 2000, and during Narendra Modi's reelection campaign as Chief Minister of Gujarat in 2002.[89] Each time, these Hindu nationalist leaders announced the deployment of private armies along the Pakistani border to prevent infiltration, not only in Kashmir but also in Punjab, Rajasthan and Gujarat.

The Christians, a substitute target? The Bajrang Dal also partly redirected its guns towards Christians. Missionaries were an age-old Hindu nationalist target (particularly for the VHP, which was created on the occasion of a visit from the Pope to India, to oppose the Catholic church's proselytising). The

Bajrang Dal attacked not only missionaries but also the faithful, with unprecedented violence. In January 1999, in Orissa, one organisation member, Dara Singh, murdered an Australian missionary, Staines, and his son by burning them alive in their car. In Madhya Pradesh, the violence targeted priests as much as it did worshippers, most of them tribals that the Hindu nationalists were seeking to convert. However, it was in Gujarat—the only state governed by the BJP at the time—that the new repertoire of action was systematised in the second half of the 1990s. From 1997, every Christmas was the occasion for anti-Christian persecution by VHP offshoots, the Bajrang Dal or the Hindu Jagaran Manch (Front to Awaken Hindus). In the Dangs district, a predominantly tribal area where Christian missionaries and Hindu nationalists vie to win the allegiance of the tribals, some 30 churches were attacked—most of them entirely or partly burned down—in 1998. A similar scenario was repeated the following year in the same district of Gujarat.[90]

This unprecedented unrest directed against Christians came at a time when Sonia Gandhi agreed to lead the Congress, a party then in the process of remobilisation that could once again pose a threat to the Hindu nationalist movement. The latter moreover began denouncing her foreign origins—she was born in Italy, but had acquired Indian citizenship in 1985—and her Christian roots. Katiyar, then head of the Bajrang Dal, consequently justified its newborn hostility toward Christians: "Christians have become aggressive ever since Sonia Gandhi took over as Congress president. Christians feel they have the perfect protector… to convert Hindus".[91]

Bajrang Dal activists attacked Christians in Orissa on a more massive scale in 2008. The situation had already worsened in December 2007 when tribal Christians had decided to erect a Christmas Gate in front of a Hindu place of worship in a village called Brahmanigaon. The local Hindus, a minority, alerted the VHP leader, Swami Laxmananda Saraswati, who rushed to the place. His car was attacked by Christian tribals and the clashes left ten dead. Six months later, on 23 August 2008, the Swami's *ashram* was celebrating Janmasthami when about 30–40 assailants wearing masks attacked the place with revolvers and four AK-47s. They killed the Swami and four of his aides and disciples. The VHP and the Bajrang Dal orchestrated the retaliation which resulted in the killing of nine people, the demolition of 30 churches and orphanages,[92] the burning of 300 villages and the destruction of 4,104 houses of Christian families. About 50,000 Christians left their place to find shelter in relief camps in cities.[93] The Hindutva forces then declared that only refugees who converted to Hinduism would be allowed to return to their villages.[94]

A cultural police in the service of Hindu orthodoxy and orthopraxy. In addition to pursuing violent action against Christians as well as Muslims in the 1990s and 2000s, the Bajrang Dal developed a new method—although still relying on violence—whose targets this time were Hindus, and which can only be described as a form of cultural policing. In India the notion of cultural policing is usually associated with the Muslim or Sikh communities, whose fundamentalists have indeed sought to enforce a code of good conduct ranging from deploying a form of moral brigade to use of strong-arm tactics.[95] Hindu nationalists have rarely attacked their coreligionists the same way before. This rule has however suffered from two major exceptions that must not go undiscussed: Gandhi, as mentioned above, and the Communists.

The RSS and the Communists often clash violently in Kerala, a state where the BJP has not met with great success at the polls, but where the RSS has many *shakhas*. The densification of this network following the Emergency was thus accompanied by an upsurge in violence between these two groups: between January 1978 and March 1979, 164 violent incidents were recorded.[96] As regards other Hindus, the RSS has always preferred to use persuasion, as noted above. In stark contrast, the Bajrang Dal devotes its efforts to repressing all those it considers deviant.

Defending the Hindu gods against the "erring ways" of art. The Bajrang Dal's primary targets are artists who, it believes, lack due respect towards Hindu culture. Historically, this is the initial target it chose by attacking the famous painter Maqbool Fida Husain in 1996. That year, Bajrang Dal militants attacked the Herwitz gallery where this painter was exhibiting in Ahmedabad (Gujarat). They destroyed canvases and wall hangings worth 15 million rupees representing the Buddha, Hanuman and Ganesh. But the real cause of their fury was something else, a canvas dating from 1976 that depicted the goddess Saraswati far too scantily clad to their taste.[97] Three days earlier the Maharashtra authorities had recorded a complaint against Husain which accused him of encouraging inter-community hatred through his work and insulting a religion. Husain was again a victim of the Bajrang Dal on 2 May 1998 when militants ransacked the painter's apartment in Mumbai in protest against his canvas "Sita Rescued", which portrayed the famous scene in the *Ramayana* showing Sita freed from the claws of Ravana. Officially the vandals said they were attacking the liberties the artist had taken in representing Sita so scantily dressed; in private they did not conceal their indignation that a Muslim artist had dared to reproduce a moment in Hindu mythology.[98] Eight years later, in March 2006, the Hindu Jagaran Manch, a Sangh Parivar offshoot closely linked to the VHP, lodged a complaint in Haridwar—one of the Hindu holy cities—against Husain for promoting ill will among religious groups, selling obscene work and perturbing national harmony. The court in Haridwar issued a warrant for the painter's arrest—he was 91 years old at the time—and ordered the seizure of his properties. His lawyer obtained the referral of the case before the Supreme Court, which on 9 May stayed the Haridwar court decision. Husain moved to Dubai in 2003, but publicly apologised for a canvas representing India in the form of a naked goddess in 2006. He offered to give it to the Mumbai police force to be put up for auction, the proceeds to go to the families of police officers who were victims of the July 2006 terrorist attacks that had left nearly 200 dead. In a recent judgment (May 2008) the Delhi High Court rejected the criminal proceedings being carried out against M.F. Husain. However, he has not yet returned to India.

Hindu artists have also been the target of Bajrang Dal wrath for their "immoral" treatment of Hindu deities. On 29 January 2004, a gang of militants attacked the Garden Art Gallery in Surat and destroyed eight canvases not only by M.F. Husain, but also by K.H. Ara, N.S. Bendre and Chittrovanu Mazumdar. The instigators of this act of destruction gave no justification for their deed: such gratuitous violence is aimed at art considered as deviant by its very nature, it seems.[99]

In February 2004, militants from the movement filed a complaint against a Hindu artist, Shail Choyal, for canvases he had painted for an information campaign of the NGO "CARE" about nursing newborn children. They in particular criticised the painter's depiction of Hindu deities such as Ganesh and Krishna. On 10 February their complaint was admitted by the police who, in the company of some 50 Bajrang Dal activists, searched the offices of the director of the Udaipur Lok Kala Mandal, the art centre where the canvases were stored, seized the paintings and put the director and the painter behind bars. They were later released on bail, but the Bajrang Dal organised a protest march during which their effigies were burned.[100]

This cultural policing is not only directed against famous painters, it also even hunts down amateur artists. For instance, in Gwalior, an employee of the Indian Institute of Tourism and Travel Management was accused by the Bajrang Dal and the Durga Vahini of having staged a play, *Kal, Aaj aur Kal (Yesterday, Today and Tomorrow)*, that showed disrespect for Sita, Ram and Laxman. On 14 March 2004 members of these two organisations burst into her home to blacken her face in public as punishment. Her father as well as her brothers and sisters stepped in. They were beaten and thrown out of their house while their home was ransacked, all this under the passive gaze of police officers.[101]

In May 2007, Hindu nationalists burst into the fine arts department of a university in Vadodara (MS University, which has one of the best art departments in India) where the best student works of the year were exhibited. They attacked one of them, S. Chandramohan, who was 23 years old, accusing him of making obscene pictures using religious subjects. One of his canvases represented a goddess giving birth to a man and another penises forming a Christian cross—which the local church also criticised. The young man was arrested and thrown into prison. The faculty dean was requested to shut down the exhibition, which he refused to do. He was then suspended by the university president, Manoj Soni, and the exhibition was cancelled.[102]

Defending Hindu society traditions against iconoclastic creators. The blasphemous nature of certain works of art is not the only motive for cultural policing that the Bajrang Dal indulges in. Attacks made on Hindu social traditions are another. Faithful to the social conservatism of Sangh Parivar, the Bajrang Dalis are easily angered by vehement challenges to the caste system. *Ponga Pandi*, a play denouncing the condition of the Dalits, was their target in 2004. On 18 August Bajrang Dal activists prevented the director, Habib Tanvir, from performing the play in Gwalior (and this while the local Superintendent of Police and the District Magistrate were in the audience). The reasons given by the troublemakers had to do with transgressing sacred taboos—for instance the fact that the play showed a man entering a temple with his shoes on.[103]

Portrayal of the role of women in society is another issue that gives rise to Bajrang Dal strong-arm tactics, as can be seen in the controversies around Deepa Mehta's films. In 2000, this Indian-Canadian director chose to do a film about the life of Hindu widows in Benares in the 1930s, *Water*. At that time these women were condemned to remaining single and to begging, even prostitution, bearing in mind they were sometimes still very young when their husband died. They often regrouped in "homes" or "shelters" where they lived on public charity and eked out a living by making fuel out of cow dung. The screenplay showed an "illicit" relationship between a Brahmin widow and a Dalit, and the rape of another. The President of the VHP, Ashok Singhal, immediately declared that this film would be an insult to "ancient Indian culture and traditions"[104] and threatened "more violent protest" if Deepa Mehta tried to shoot her film in India. She did so nevertheless after having secured all the required authorisations from the central government and the authorities of Uttar Pradesh. The set that was constructed on the banks of the Ganges was totally ransacked by Bajrang Dal activists. Deepa Mehta then decided to continue shooting in Madhya Pradesh where she was warmly welcomed by the Chief Minister, Digvijay Singh. But there again, the Bajrang Dal resorted to force to prevent the shooting from taking place.

One of Deepa Mehta's previous films, *Fire*, had already ignited the anger of the Hindu nationalists, for it portrayed a lesbian relationship between two housewives neglected by their husbands. The same theme was taken up by *Girlfriend*, a "Bollywood" film that sparked an even more violent Bajrang Dal campaign in 2004: posters were torn down and screenings were prevented in most of Mumbai's theatres, a sign that the organisation was playing the role of a moral police in defence of the most conservative Hindu values.

Combating the Westernisation of customs. In his indictment against *Water*, Singhal indicated very significantly that he saw it as "a conspiracy by the votaries of western culture to tarnish the image of widowhood in India"—probably because Deepa Mehta was based in Canada. But opposition to the Westernization of customs is in itself part of the repertoire of the Hindu nationalists' cultural police.

This part of the repertoire is mainly manifested in violent protests during celebrations or holidays assimilated with the West because they are Christian in origin (such as Christmas) or not corresponding to the "national" calendar (such as New Year's Eve).[105] The event that focalises the most attention is St Valentine's Day. This celebration of romance is criticised every year by the Bajrang Dal as a symbol of Western depravity and gives rise to physical violence perpetrated by its activists: young people who get together to celebrate the day together are beaten up, shops selling Valentine's Day iconography or decorated with it are ransacked, etc. The other embodiment of Western decadence that Hindu nationalists readily attack is none other than the pageant held to elect Miss India—not to mention the male variants of this big media circus.

The various aspects of cultural policing conducted by the Bajrang Dal all reflect the same univocal perspective that can hardly be called characteristic of Hinduism. The religion can certainly not be dissociated from the most rigid form of orthopraxy, embodied by the caste system, but the dogmatism and prudish moralism expressed by the puritans have never been among its more salient features. As evidence of this, the statues of goddesses that adorn the temples are not only scantily clad, but on top of that, their eroticism is legendary. If Hussain's Saraswati is naked, this is because the divinity has often been shown this way, as many sculptures, some of which date as far back as the 12th century, attest.[106] Far from being in sync with the tradition they claim to defend, the Hindu nationalists are adding notes to a purely ideological score.

The relationship to the state

In contrast with the Hindu Mahasabha, which aspired to win power, and Savarkar's HRD, which collaborated with the colonial authorities and princely states, the RSS from the start tried to keep its distance from the state. The organisation viewed it as an artificial entity, in contrast to society, the true anchor for Hindu civilisation—and thus the nation. The RSS's mission was precisely to regenerate society to restore the nation's vitality. Division was the worst of all the ills it suffered from. That is why the *pracharaks* worked to get beyond social divisions of class and caste, and the *shakhas* were supposed to be the crucible for newfound unity. The state only interested the RSS in that it could help the organisation to achieve its long-term societal objectives. Hence the function the movement attributed itself as *Raj Guru*, the prince's counsellor.

The RSS especially began to show an interest in state power when the latter attacked it after Gandhi was assassinated and also during the Emergency, two major crises during which the movement was banned. The other two periods during which the RSS took an interest in political power were, in contrast, those where ministers from its ranks took part in government, 1977–79 and 1998–2004. It was in fact counting on this new political situation to play its role as *Raj Guru* to the fullest. Each time it was disappointed, because the Hindu nationalists in government had to compromise with partners who did not all share their ideas.

The situation with the Bajrang Dal was altogether different. Given the movement's violent nature, its legal standing was much more precarious and the need for some official custodians even greater. The BJP protected the movement when it was in power from 1998 to 2004. The Vajpayee government resisted the urgings of Congress states that came out against the Bajrang

Dal. In July 2001 Digvijay Singh and Ashok Gehlot, Chief Ministers of Madhya Pradesh and Rajasthan respectively, asked the Vajpayee government to ban the Bajrang Dal. The former wrote a long letter to this effect, recounting the movement's various doings in his state, to conclude that the organisation's members repeatedly provoked Muslims and Hindus. The second did the same in a letter stating: "The language and tone of the proclamations made by Bajrang Dal in its public meetings sharply reflect the non-secular and fundamentalist nature of its ideology which will undoubtedly lead to disruption of peace and tranquility of our country... [The] distribution [of *trishuls*] has all the potential of creating a dangerous situation in the country".[107]

The Vajpayee government nationally took no measures against Bajrang Dal. Its support for the organisation moreover became clear with the arrest of Dara Singh, who murdered the missionary Staines in 1999. When Singh was imprisoned in January 2000 after being on the run for a year, a BJP MP who would become a minister in the Vajpayee government, Dilip Singh Judeo, offered to handle his defence; he only withdrew the offer after receiving a reprimand from the BJP President.

But the Rao government itself showed great restraint in its repression after the demolition of the Babri Masjid. The number of arrests was fairly limited, 1,500 in Uttar Pradesh, about 1,000 in Madhya Pradesh and fewer than 4,000 in the rest of India. And on the top of that, the people imprisoned were released shortly afterwards. By the same token, the ban on the Bajrang Dal was lifted less than a year after it had been issued. Such clemency reflected Rao's effort to win the Hindu vote and thus curb the BJP's rise. That is not the only explanation, however.

First, Hindu nationalists enjoyed the benefit of a number of court decisions. The outlawing of the RSS, the VHP and the Bajrang Dal was declared under the Unlawful Activities (Prevention) Act of 1967, which requires approval by a tribunal. On 4 June 1993, the tribunal presided by P.K. Bahri of the High Court of Delhi cancelled the bans on the RSS, the VHP and the Bajrang Dal, finding that their leaders had no intention of causing harm to the Babri Masjid. Such an order attests both to the pernickety legalism of the judges, who constantly require irrefutable evidence that in this case was impossible to produce, and certain ideological affinities. It recalls the decision handed down by the Supreme Court in favour of Shiv Sena leaders accused of bringing religious considerations into their election campaign; they were finally cleared by the judges on the pretext that Hinduism was not a religion but "a way of life", precisely the definition used by Hindu nationalists. The Bajrang Dal again benefited from this combination of factors in the Dara Singh case. The commission of inquiry appointed by Vajpayee—a one-man show, since it was made up of a single Supreme Court judge, D.P. Wadhwa—cleared the organisation of all suspicion.[108]

Furthermore, the authorities—especially those low on the chain of command—seem to be far from systematically disapproving of the Bajrang Dal's schemes. The study of its cultural policing in the previous section has shown that in most of the incidents described, the movement performed its dirty work in the presence of police forces that were either passive or in collusion. This is because for the administration, particularly at the local level, the Bajrang Dal is credited with a certain capacity for enforcing order, while the dominant community often approves of the inspiration for this action. In some respects, the Bajrang Dal is both a vehicle for disseminating or privatising violence and one more state agency at the local level.

In this regard, the RSS's original plan might well be under way: it is working, particularly via the Bajrang Dal, towards the advent of a Hindu nation based less on the state than on social structures drawing on the wellspring of Hindu orthodoxy and orthopraxy. The *Hindu Rashtra* is thus in progress. This expression moreover reflects perfectly the ambivalence of the process: it first refers to a community of civilisation, a *Gemeinshaft*, but also to a political structure. It is at once a society and a state. In this regard, the Sangh Parivar is involved in shaping a new state. The Indian state was built around a bureaucracy inherited from the British. But its formation—in the sense meant by Berman and Lonsdale that we reviewed in the introduction to this volume—remained to be accomplished. The Sangh Parivar is working towards it in its own way, by instituting social regulations that shape a collective body, but also by forms of authority that hold the whole thing together. Such a transformation is especially obvious in the case of Gujarat.

Gujarat, a laboratory for Hindu nationalism. The state of Gujarat—which has so far only been mentioned in passing—illustrates better than any other the argument that has just been made. Gujarat warrants separate consideration for two reasons. First, it has been governed by the BJP for over ten years, a record, without the party needing to form a coalition with one or more partners. Second, it is the only state to have a former RSS *pracharak*, Narendra Modi, as Chief Minister. These two factors are decisive in that they have enabled the Hindu nationalists to appoint to the administration, and in particular the police, trusted associates in league with such controversial organisations as the Bajrang Dal.[109] In fact, the borderline between police forces and these movements has become extremely blurred, to the point of fostering the enrolling of Bajrang Dalis in the police and vice versa. The paramilitary Home Guards, a force made up of civilians used by the authorities to keep order at the local level, have filled their ranks with RSS and Bajrang Dal members. A high-ranking police officer admits that the district commanders of the Home Guards began to change as soon as the BJP came to power in Gujarat.[110] When he was Chief Minister of Madhya Pradesh and arrested Bajrang Dal militants as mentioned earlier, Digvijay Singh noted that among the individuals taken in for questioning were four Gujarat police officers.[111]

The Bajrang Dal strike force, and the state protection it enjoys in Gujarat, were clear to see in the 2002 riots. These began on 27 February in Godhra, a district headquarters bordering Rajasthan, following the death of 57 Hindus burnt alive in two train carriages which had allegedly been set on fire.[112] The train was carrying back from Faizabad (the district in which Ayodhya is located) Hindu nationalist activists—some of them members of Bajrang Dal—who had travelled to Ayodhya to build the famous temple dedicated to Lord Ram on the ruins of the Babri Masjid. Modi immediately declared that it was a "pre-planned, violent act of terrorism"[113] and had the bodies taken to Ahmedabad, the largest city in Gujarat. The arrival of the bodies at Ahmedabad station was broadcast on television, causing considerable upset among the Hindus. The following day, the VHP organised the shutdown of the city, which soon degenerated. In Ahmedabad, an armed horde of several thousand people attacked Muslims' houses and shops, killing 200. Three other districts, Vadodara, Gandhinagar and Sabarkhanta, were the scene of comparable violence. The next day, 1 March, mainly rural districts were added to the list of hotspots: Panchmahals, Mehsana, Kheda, Junagadh, Banaskantha, Patan, Anand and Narmada. On 2 March Bharuch and Rajkot, which had yet to be affected by communal violence, were hit in turn. On the 4th, riots broke out in Surat, a town that had been the theatre of extensive Hindu-Muslim violence in the 1990s.

The violence was thus propagated by Bajrang Dal activists, squads of whom generally arrived in the Muslim neighbourhoods by the truckload. They wore a basic uniform—the RSS khaki shorts and a saffron headband—and carried daggers and tridents. Their favourite targets were Muslim women, of whom great numbers were raped and killed.[114] In Naroda Patiya, a Muslim neighbourhood in Ahmedabad, one of the Bajrang Dal ringleaders allegedly cut the foetus out of the belly of a woman nine months pregnant, threw it into the fire and then burned her alive. This heinous crime was attributed to a local thug both by the survivors of Naroda Patiya[115] and by the Hindus for whom he is "the hero of Naroda Patiya".[116]

The riots of 2002 spread to the surrounding villages and thus in many cases to localities where few Muslims resided.[117] The agents of this spread were mainly Bajrang Dalis from the city or nearby villages. These *tolas* (groups), whose members were wearing saffron-coloured headbands and chanting anti-Muslim slogans, entered the villages on tractors or in jeeps. They were divided into three categories, *todwavalla* (those who were destroying), *lootwavalla* (those who were looting) and *baadwavalla* (those who were burning). Altogether, over 1,200 villages were affected, particularly in the districts of Panchmahals, Mehsana, Sabarkantaha, Bharuch, Bhavnagar and Vadodara. 2,500 Muslims from 22 different villages were evacuated and moved to refugee camps.[118]

All in all, the violence of 2002 probably claimed over 2,000 victims and thousands of wounded. It was a pogrom along the lines of ethnic cleansing.[119] This massacre was the work of all those that the Bajrang Dal could mobilise, with the state's blessing. In each neighbourhood, a "Bajrang Dal convenor" coordinated the riots, coordination that was ensured by some of Modi's ministers from the police control posts. But the troops thus activated turned out to be extraordinarily diverse. A report filed by one of the NGOs active in the field indicates that among the criminals identified by the survivors, there were a large number of Dalits—usually drawn to the riots by the lure of gain as long as they are ensured that any looting will go unpunished—but also Brahmins, Sindhis and others. There were also politicians as well as bus drivers, craftsmen, etc. This has led an NGO official based in Ahmedabad to consider that the Bajrang Dal is "a myth". In Ahmedabad it is indeed an evanescent entity, an organisation with no headquarters or durable structure, which forms, disappears and forms again according to circumstance. This elastic group crystallises with mobilisation movements and even more so with outbreaks of violence.

Such a mode of functioning does not prevent it from demonstrating extraordinary efficiency. After the riots of 2002, for instance, the Bajrang Dal made sure that witnesses to the violence did not have recourse to the law. Some of them defied the taboo as long as the authorities guaranteed them police protection,[120] but most of them gave up the idea. Recourse to intimidation is not limited to the victims of 2002. In 2006, Babu Bajrangi informed the owners of theatres throughout Gujarat that he was against the screening of a film entitled *Parzania* that recounted the riots of 2002 through the true story of a Parsi family whose child has been missing ever since. All of the theatres yielded to pressure, and the film was not shown in the very state that served as its backdrop. A citizen of Mehsana district, N.K. Acharya, a retired civil servant, took legal action. He in turn was a victim of intimidation, kidnapped and held for two weeks in March 2007.[121]

Beyond that, Babu Bajrangi has extended his "parallel government"—to borrow N.K. Acharya's terms—to moral issues. He suddenly started showing up on the campus of Gujarat University in Ahmedabad to beat up young Muslims who were looking at female Hindu students too intently for his taste. Then he went on a crusade to "rescue" girls of his caste—Patel—who had married a Muslim or a man of a different caste. One of his pamphlets explained that love marriages harmed Hindu traditions, and that rescuing a Hindu girl was equal to saving 100 cows.[122] In the space of a few months, over 700 girls were thus "rescued", forced to abort when they were pregnant, and remarried to a man of the caste—an additional sign of the orthopraxic obsession that plagues Hindu nationalists. Sometimes parents whose daughter has "married beneath her station" without their approval and run away, usually to Mumbai, use Babu Bajrangi's services to find her and bring her back home. Some husbands have brought actions before the courts of Gujarat and Maharashtra—the state of which Mumbai is the capital—but to no avail, and the police refrained from carrying out an inquiry on Bajrangi. Once again the Supreme Court had to step in. It initiated an inquiry that finally prompted the Bajrang Dal to expel him from its ranks in February 2007. He immediately called a press conference to state that he would remain a member of the organisation.[123]

Besides the Supreme Court, certain associations and NGOs came to the aid of Bajrang Dal victims. In April 2007 members of Anhad, Sanchetna, Aman Samuday and Safar demonstrated in front of a police station in Ahmedabad to support the complaint lodged by a woman, Mausami Shah, who had been kidnapped by Bajrangi's shock troops, brought home and forced to resume living with her husband, a Hindu, whom she had left for a Muslim. Mausami Shah was lectured by a police inspector and Bajrangi on the Ellisbridge police station premises—they both advised her to return to her marital home. She obeyed, then ran away before being caught by Bajrang Dalis. [124]

Although Gujarat remains the Indian state where the rule of law is the most seriously challenged, Madhya Pradesh—also governed by the BJP since 2003—has seen similar developments. In April 2007, a delegation of representatives from Hindu nationalist organisations—RSS, VHP and Bajrang Dal—submitted a memorandum to the Governor of the state in protest against the trend of marriages between Muslim men and Hindu women that they claimed to have noted. Their leader, the local RSS chief Uttamchand Israni, stated to the press on this occasion: "Everyone talks of the children's right to marry but what about the parents' rights?"[125] Among the demonstrators in the procession were members of the Hindu Kanya Suraksha Samiti (committee to protect Hindu girls), an offshoot of the Sindhi Panchayat—the committee that had assigned itself the task of regulating the life of the Sindhi community, a big group in Bhopal area since Partition. They claimed that state officials should not have the power to issue marriage certificates, which should be the prerogative of community organisations.

In fact, the state retreated in Madhya Pradesh under pressure from the Sindhi Panchayat in the "case" that served as a backdrop for the demonstrations of April 2007. What sparked a protest was the marriage of a young Sindhi, Priyanka Wadhwani—22 years old and thus of age—and a young Muslim, Mohammad Umar, who ran away to Mumbai to marry. The police immediately arrested the groom's brother and illegally held him at the police station for one week. His wife, a senior official in the Indian Administration Service, an elite civil service corps, could do nothing other than visit him every day. A police team from Madhya Pradesh then went to Mumbai to question the couple. The young woman was instructed to return to Bhopal to declare before the courts that she had chosen to marry freely. She preferred to do so before the tribunal of Mumbai. As Priyanka's parents had had no objection to their daughter's choice, they were the targets of intimidation from the Bajrang Dal, which still hoped to bring the young woman back into the Hindu fold. Once again, only court judges and a few human rights organisations were able to resist the pressure, as well as young Sindhi women who rise up against the diktat of Sindhi Panchayat that forbids them from using cell phones so as to keep better track of them. [126]

To sum up, the activities of the Bajrang Dal pertaining to cultural policies—which are forms of psychological-cum-physical violence—contribute to the making (or "formation") of an authoritarian state with the protection of officials. Its activities against the Muslims in the framework of communal conflicts are also conducted in conjunction with the state apparatus when the BJP is in office, as is evident from what happened in Gujarat. A recent development suggests that in addition to the police and other state agencies, the Indian army might be affected too, as officers—serving or retired—display some active sympathy for Hindu nationalism. This new development took shape in the context of the convergence between the Sangh Parivar and Savarkarite organisations that had already worked with the regular army during the British Raj.

From militia to terrorism: the Sangh Parivar back to Savarkarism?

In the early years of the 21st century, segments of the Sangh Parivar returned to the Godse pattern of the late 1940s when members of the RSS distanced themselves from an organisation they found too passive in the context of the Partition and followed the Savarkarite strategy of terrorism. Nathuram Godse epitomised this strategy since he not only joined the HRD Savarkar had just created to fight Muslims, but was also the main architect of the plot leading to the assassination of Gandhi. In the 2000s, the context of the crisis was not on the same scale as Partition, but was still due to Muslim activism.

Since the turn of the century, India has become one of the countries most severely affected by Islamist attacks. Every six months or so a commando operation or a major explosion occurs in a big city—or, more rarely, in a mid-sized town—killing dozens, sometimes hundreds, of people. Between 2001 and 2008, they caused the deaths of about 800 people. The Indian government often attributed this violence to neighbouring countries until 2006–07, and the November 2008 Mumbai attack, once again, has been attributed to a Pakistani commando by the Indian police. According to this official discourse, local citizens were not responsible for such misdeeds for which the guilty parties were allegedly from Pakistan and Bangladesh. But Indian investigators have shown that Indian Muslims are increasingly taking part in these terrorist activities in revenge for the Ayodhya movement-related riots and the Gujarat pogrom. These local Islamists may work in close connection with foreigners, but they are not only informers facilitating actions planned by outsiders; they take the initiative for attacks as well, as is evident from the bomb blasts in 2008 in Jaipur, Ahmedabad and Delhi which were all claimed by a new organisation, Indian Mujahidin.

As a result, Hindutva-minded people, usually members of the Sangh Parivar, have created or joined new militias, which have actually turned out to be terrorist groups, whose main aim was to take revenge on the Indian Muslims. This new development became clear during the inquiry into the Malegaon blast that killed six people in front of one mosque of that city in September 2008, just after Ramadan.

The first person to be arrested by the police in this case, Pragya Singh Thakur, was a *sadhvi* (a female world renouncer), who had been an ABVP leader in Ujjain and Indore until 1997,[127] before becoming member of the National Executive of the ABVP and embracing *sannyas*.[128] Pragya Singh was arrested along with Shamlal Bhavar Sahu, a commerce graduate from Christian College in Indore who owned a mobile phone shop but also acted as a real estate broker, and Shiv Narayan Singh, a BSc graduate from New School College in Indore who was an electrician and an insurance agent.[129] These electronics experts were involved in the making of the bombs that exploded in Malegaon.

A second group of accused was made of army men, some retired, who were connected with the Bhonsle Military School (BMS), which had developed in Nasik and established a branch in Moonje's home town, Nagpur. Major Ramesh Upadhyay, a former military officer, was arrested first, and immediately admitted that he had taken part in three meetings with Pragya Singh and her accomplices on the Nasik BMS premises to plan the Malegaon blast. Ajay Misar, the public prosecutor, declared, "Upadhyay, who was posted in the artillery department while working with the Indian military, is suspected to have guided the arrested accused on how to assemble a bomb and procure RDX".[130] Another key figure of the group was another serviceman, Lt Col Prasad Purohit, who had approached Upadhyay when he was posted at Nasik as liaison officer. Purohit and Upadhyay imparted military training to young activists—including bomb making—and were instrumental in procuring arms and explosives. Purohit forged documents during his stint in Jammu and Kashmir—where he was posted in 2004–05—to obtain arms licences for others. After shifting to Panchmarhi (Madhya Pradesh) in July–August 2008, Purohit organised training camps in which 54 people took part and were taught the handling of arms and explosives. He had organised similar camps in Pune. However, most of the training camps took place in the BMS,[131] which had been directed between 1973 and 1988 by Rtd Major P.B. Kulkarni, associated with the RSS since 1935.[132] In fact, the Bajrang Dal organised training camps in the BMS (Nagpur) as early as 2001.[133] Two years later, the school started to provide firearms training to the students in the 10–15 age group.

The five accused were all members of Abhinav Bharat, a Pune-based movement apparently initiated by Purohit in June 2006,[134] whose acting president was Ramesh Upadhyaya[135] while the president was none other than Himani Savarkar, the president of the Hindu Mahasabha and the daughter-in-law of V.D. Savarkar.[136] The movement of the same name, founded by the Indian revolutionary that Savarkar was then, had been dissolved in 1952. Purohit recreated it at a time when he badly felt the need to defend his community against the Muslims. According to one press report:

The interrogation of Purohit establishes him as a man with forthright views on Hindu extremism. He was extremely frank in expressing his concerns about Hindus getting killed by jihadi terror groups and strongly felt that something had to be done about it. He had shared such views—that Hindus needed to retaliate—on several occasions with his colleagues in the Army. Of course, none of these colleagues realised the seriousness of his opinion or that it would lead him to plot real revenge attack. […] Purohit was the key man behind Abhinav Bharat, building its cadre by drawing 'extremist' elements from VHP and RSS. An expert at liaisoning, Purohit had a unique sixth sense in identifying radical members of the right wing outfits like VHP and then motivating them to join Abhinav Bharat.[137]

This picture recalls the way Savarkar attracted Godse, an RSS man, into his own HRD; Godse then shifted from one militia to another. Another common element between the HRD and Abhinav Bharat—in addition to the fact that both organisations were based in western Maharashtra and led by Brahmins (mostly Chitpavans)—pertains to their relationship to the military institution. Savarkar tried to have Hindus recruited in the army and Apte taught the HRD members what he had learned as a soldier. Similarly, Abhinav Bharat relied on (ex-) army men who were, in a way, armed violence professionals. This strategy was well in tune with the manner in which the Sangh Parivar had initiated some rapprochement with ex-army men since the late 1980s. In fact, Upadhyay once headed the BJP's Mumbai unit of the party's ex-servicemen cell.[138] The BJP was indeed the first to bring in ex-army men. In 1989–91, at the time of its electoral takeoff, the party had welcomed into its ranks two Rtd Air Marshals, six Rtd Lieutenant Generals, four Rtd Major-Generals, four Rtd Brigadiers, four Rtd Colonels, two Rtd Majors, three Rtd Captains, two Rtd Wing Commanders, one Rtd Air Commodore, one Rtd Lieutenant-Colonel, one Rtd Squadron Leader and one Rtd Flying Officer.[139] Some of them were appointed to the BJP National Executive and at the helm of the party's Defence cell. Examples were Rtd Lt Gen. K.P. Candeth and Rtd Lt Gen. Jack Frederick Ralph Jacob—who was to be appointed Governor of Goa by Vajpayee in 1998—, two heroes of the 1971 war, and B.C. Khanduri, who became MP in 1989,[140] a minister in Vajpayee's government in 2000–04 and Chief Minister of Uttarakhand since 2007. After the BJP came to power in 1998, two dozen more ex-servicemen joined the BJP.[141] This inflow of ex-army men reflects the increasingly communal atmosphere of the military institution. In December 2003, a survey by the Centre for the Study of Developing Societies for *Tehelka*, one of the first among army men—and probably the most comprehensive one—showed that for 19% of the soldiers interviewed the army practiced some religious discrimination; 24% of Muslims among them thought so.[142]

Indeed, the Sangh Parivar, after some hesitation, supported those who had been accused in the Malegaon case and therefore did not consider them as rivals whose extremism was misplaced. The Bajrang Dal chief, Prakash Sharma, declared that "policymakers should be worried if the Hindus were taking to arms because of the government's skewed approach to war on terror" and admitted that the Bajrang Dal was running training camps also "to boost their morale [of the Bajrang Dal's members]. The country wouldn't get its Abhinav Bindras if there were no armed training for the youth".[143]

Such comments suggest that, in contrast to the 1940s when the Savarkarites and the RSS leaders followed two different routes, there are more affinities between the two now. This convergence has largely been due to the Bajrang Dal, an RSS affiliate which operates like Abhinav Bharat so far as violent actions are concerned. During the 2006 inquiry into the Nanded blast,[144] a retired Navy Officer hailing from Pune, S.R. Bhate—associated with the RSS since 1996—declared to the police that as early as March-April

2000 he had been asked by the local Bajrang Dal leader "to train his activists in the use of gelatine sticks at a camp in the city"[145] and then at a larger one in the BMS (Nasik). "Bhate told the ATS [Anti-Terror Squad] investigators that the camp had been organised by the RSS and about 115 activists from across the country were trained in karate, ground obstacles and firing of revolvers. Two retired ex-servicemen and a senior retired officer from the IB [Intelligence Bureau] were also present he stated".[146] This *modus operandi* calls to mind that of the RSS in 1947 when the movement organised training camps in Alwar state. In a way, the RSS, with the Bajrang Dal, has created a buffer organisation which endows the Sangh Parivar with an organisation doing the dirty work the Sangh was once obliged to do for itself—tasks similar to those of the Savarkarite organisations, be they called HRD or Abhinav Bharat.

Conclusion

While Hinduism is known throughout the world for its non-violent tradition, the culture of political violence has been nurtured by Hindu nationalist ideologues and activists from the late 19th century onwards. This repertoire— which was especially strong among Maharashtrian Brahmins—translated into the creation of two kinds of militias. The Savarkarite variety resorted to terrorism considering it as a legitimate mode of action and openly supported the militarisation of the Hindu community. The RSS, in spite of its paramilitary style, adopted a more quietist *modus operandi* situating the movement's work in a virtually messianic long term: its objective was to transform Hindu society into a *Hindu Rashtra* and its favourite methodology to achieve that aim relied on the *shakha* technique. Its strategy was muscular to impress others—mainly Muslims—by demonstrations of strength (massive drills and parades etc.). Both patterns—the Savarkarite one and the RSS one—converged, however, at the time of Partition. When Swayamasevaks were heavily involved in the Partition massacres, it became clear that the RSS model in no way ruled out recourse to violence. But such violence was exceptional because the RSS was anxious to remain within the law perimeter in order to achieve its long term agenda. Also, the RSS was reluctant to use its strike force against Hindus—except communists, of course—, their preferred *modus operandi* being persuasion, even seduction, cloaked in civilisational language.

The RSS changed in the 1990s with the rise of the Bajrang Dal, the new brigade of Hindu nationalism whose techniques call to mind those of the Savarkarites but result also from emulation of the Islamists. Not only was this militia trained for far more systematic physical violence than that practiced by the RSS, but its self-appointed role as the new cultural police saw it using violence against Hindus as well. The Bajrang Dal has thus introduced an additional factor into the spread of violence in India. In addition, in many respects it appears as an unofficial instrument of the state, not only because its deeds receive the tacit approval of local authorities, but also because on a number of occasions, the courts have cleared it of all suspicion. In this regard it contributes to shaping the state in the sense meant by advocates of the *Hindu Rashtra*. Gujarat under Narendra Modi constitutes a laboratory for Hindu nationalism that provides a spectacular illustration of this evolution.

Although the violent methods of the cultural police set up by the Bajrang Dal contrast with the quietist ethos of the RSS, they are perfectly in sync with the Savarkarite tradition, which has been reinvigorated in reaction to the spread of Islamist attacks. As some of these have been attributed to Indian Muslims, Hindu nationalist groups started to target local mosques (like in Malegaon), following a terrorist *modus operandi* that calls to mind the HRD's techniques in the 1940s—all the more so as (ex-) servicemen have been involved, as in the HRD. The rise of the Bajrang Dal thus reflects a certain convergence of two currents of Hindu nationalism, a scenario that the Shiv Sena, which drew also from the RSS but advocated violence in a more open way, had already begun to exemplify since the late 1960s.

These trajectories are systematically implemented through emulation of the threatening Islamist "other", as is evident from the Shiv Sena's project of initiating Hindu suicide-squads. The Hindu nationalist culture of violence, therefore, combines a partly autochthonous repertoire, including the Chitpavan legacy, and external influences such as jihadist techniques. This is a perfect illustration of the partly mimetic ideology-building process of Hindu nationalism at large.[147]

BIBLIOGRAPHY

Books

Anand, V.S., *Savarkar, A Study in the Evolution of Indian Nationalism*, London, Woolf, 1967.

Andersen, Walter and Sridhar Damle, *The Brotherhood in Saffron. The Rashtriya Swayamsevak Sangh and Hindu Revivalism*, New Delhi, Vistaar, 1987.

Baker, D.E.U., *Changing Political Leadership in an Indian Province—The Central Provinces and Berar, 1919–39*, Delhi, Oxford University Press, 1979.

Bathval, Dr Harichandra, *Rashtriya Swayamsevak Sangh. Ek Parichay (Hindi) (The Rashtriya Swayamsevak Sangh. An Introduction)*, Delhi, Suruchi Prakashan, 1998.

Chitragupta, *Life of Barrister Savarkar*, Bombay, Acharya Balarao Savarkar, 1987 [First edition: 1926].

Curran, Jean A., *Militant Hinduism in Indian Politics. A Study of the RSS*, New York, Institute of Pacific Relations, 1951.

Dharmaveer, B.S., *Moonje Commemoration Volume*, Nagpur, Birth Centenary Celebration Committee, 1972.

Deshpande, B.V. and S.R. Ramaswamy, *Dr. Hedgewar, the Epoch-Maker. A Biography*, Bangalore, Sahitya Sindhu, 1981.

Jaffrelot, Christophe (ed.), *Hindu Nationalism. A Reader*, Princeton University Press, 2007.

Jaffrelot, Christophe, *Hindu nationalism and Indian Politics*, London, Hurst, 1996.

Jaffrelot, Christophe (ed.), *The Sangh Parivar. A Reader*, Delhi, Oxford University Press, 2005.

Katju, Manjari, *Vishva Hindu Parishad and Indian Politics*, Hyderabad, Orient Longman, 2003.

Laine, James W., *Shivaji. Hindu King in Islamic India*, Delhi, Oxford University Press, 2003.

Nandy, Ashis. *At the Edge of Psychology*, Delhi, Oxford University Press, 1980

Ray, B. (ed.), *Gandhi's Campaign against Untouchability, 1933–34. An Account from the Raj's Secret Official Reports*, New Delhi, Gandhi Peace Foundation, 1966.

Shrivastava, H., *Five Stormy Years: Savarkar in London*, New Delhi, Allied Publishers, 1983.

Yajnik I., *Shyamaji Krishnavarma*, Bombay, Lakshmi Publications, 1950.

Articles and chapters in edited volumes

Bhatia, Bela, "A Step Back in Sabarkantha," Seminar, 513, http://www.india-seminar. com

Gupta, Smita and Christophe Jaffrelot, "The Bajrang Dal: the New Hindu Nationalist Brigade," in Mushirul Hasan (ed.), *Living with Secularism. The Destiny of India's Muslims*, Delhi, Manohar, 2007: 197–222.

Jaffrelot, Christophe, "Militant Hindus and the Conversion Issue (1885–1990): From Shuddhi to Dharm Parivartan. The Politization and the Diffusion of an 'Invention of Tradition'," in Jackie Assayag (ed.), *The Resources of History. Tradition and Narration in South Asia*, Paris, EFEO, 1999: 127–52.

———— "The BJP at the Centre: A Central and Centrist Party?" in Thomas Hansen and Christophe Jaffrelot (eds), *The BJP and the Compulsions of Politics*, Delhi, Oxford University Press, 2001: 315–69.

———— "The Visva Hindu Parishad: A Nationalist but Mimetic Attempt at Federating the Hindu Sects," in Vasudha Dalmia, Angelika Malinar and Martin Christhof (eds), *Charisma and Canon. Essays on the Religious History of the Indian Subcontinent*, Delhi, Oxford University Press, 2001: 338–411.

———— "The 2002 Pogrom in Gujarat: The Post-9/11 Face of Hindu Nationalist Anti-Muslim Violence," in J. Hinnels and R. King, *Religion and Violence in South Asia*, London and New York, Routledge, 2006: 173–92.

———— "Opposing Gandhi: Hindu Nationalism and Political Violence," in Éric Meyer, Gilles Tarabout and Denis Vidal (eds), *Violence/Non-violence. Some Hindu Perspectives*, Delhi, Manohar, 2003: 299–324.

———— "La stigmatisation et l'imitation de l'autre dans l'invention du nationalisme: le cas de l'Hindutva en Inde," in Bertrand Badie and Yves Deloye (eds), *Mélanges en l'honneur de Pierre Birnbaum*, Paris, Fayard, 2007: 141–52.

Jayaprasad, "The Impact of Hindu Nationalism on Kerala Society and Politics. A Case Study of the RSS," doctorate thesis in political science, University of Kerala, Trivandrum, 1989: 207–41.

Jhari, K.D., "Creating the Urge to Kill," *Secular Democracy*, July 1970.

Madhok, B., *RSS and Politics*, New Delhi, Hindu World Publications, 1986.

Qureshi, Ishtiaq H., "A Case-Study of the Social Relations between the Muslims and the Hindus, 1935–1947," in Cyril H. Philips and Marie D. Wainwright (eds), *The Partition of India*, London, Allen and Unwin, 1970, p. 366.

Rudolph, Lloyd and Suzanne, "Cultural Policy, the Textbook Controversy and Indian Identity," in A.J. Wilson and D. Dalton (eds), *The States of South Asia*, London, Hurst, 1982: 131–2.

Tilak, B.G., *Srimad Bhagavadgita Rahasya*, Poona, Tilak Bros., 1936.

Van Der Veer, Peter, "'God Must be Liberated!' A Hindu Liberation Movement in Ayodhya," *Modern Asian Studies*, 21 (1), 1987: 283–303.

Reports

Citizen's Initiative, *How has the Gujarat Massacre Affected Minority Women? The Survivors Speak*, Ahmedabad, 2002.

Government of India, *Report of the Commission of Inquiry into the Conspiracy to Murder Mahatma Gandhi*, New Delhi, part I, 1966.

Government of Punjab, *Rashtriya Swayamsevak Sangh in Punjab*, Lahore, Government Printing Press, 1948.

People's Union of Civil Liberties (PUCL), "Cultural Policing by Bajrang Dal and the Rajasthan Police" (http://www.pucl.org).

Report of the three-Member Commission of Inquiry Headed by Shri Jitendra Narain Former Judge, Patna High Court, to Inquire into the Communal Disturbances that Took Place in April 1979, in and around Jamshedpur, 1981.

NOTES

1. Ashis Nandy, "Final Encounter—The Politics of the Assassination of Gandhi," in Ashis Nandy (1980), p. 78.
2. The Chitpavans served in large numbers in the armies of Shivaji and the Maratha Empire during the 18th century. As a result, they absorbed aspects of the Kshatriya ethos, the caste of the Kshatriyas being absent in western India. Then they came to occupy every rung of the administration in the Maratha Confederation after one of them, Balaji Vishvanath Rao, became the Peshwa (Prime Minister). Subsequently Poona, the capital of the Peshwas, became associated with the Chitpavans although many of them continued to live in the coastal Konkan districts.
3. To be fair to Nandy, he mentions the decline of the Chitpavans' social status during the British Raj as an important factor of their political radicalisation.
4. See Christophe Jaffrelot (2003), pp. 299–324.
5. The first Marathi edition of this book on "the secret of the Gita" compiles texts and speeches going back to 1902. I have used the first English edition, B.G. Tilak (1936).
6. Ibid., pp. 424, 478 and 645.
7. This is a (partial) re-interpretation for, while Krishna refers to the duty of the Kshatriyas, since violent action is part of the *dharma* of this *varna*, Tilak applies his message extensively to all men and with the nation's "salvation" in mind.
8. V.S. Anand (1967), p. 19.
9. Chitragupta (1987) [First edition: 1926], p. 11.
10. Home Department (Political), *Proceedings for the Year 1911*, P/8713, April 1910 Pro No.47, India Office Library and Records (London).
11. Ibid.
12. I. Yajnik (1950).
13. S.K. Verma had just started this home in 1905 in order to house—and train— Indian students with "extremist" leanings.
14. Home Department (Political), *Proceedings for the Year 1909*, P/8153, April 1909, p. 1033, India Office Library and Records (London).

15. H. Shrivastava (1983), pp. 72–4.
16. Home Department (Political), *Proceedings for the Year 1909*, P/8713, Oct. 1909 Pro No.215, India Office Library and Records (London)
17. B.V. Deshpande and S.R. Ramaswamy, (1981), p. 160.
18. Ibid.
19. Savarkar Papers, Reel no.3, File no. 8, 12/11/1938, Nehru Memorial, Museum and Library.
20. Similarly, in the late 1930s, the Secretary General of the Hindu Mahasabha, Ganpat Rai, considered that: "What the Hindus require at this juncture is a regular army [for] when communal riots break out in the cities of India, Hindus cry out for rescue force to relieve them from the clutches of the aggression". Ganpat Rai's letter to Moonje, dated 03/04/1939, Savarkar Papers, Reel No.4, File No.8.
21. "What should be the attitude of the Hindu Mahasabha towards the RSS?" (Anonymous note), M.G. Chitnavis Papers, File no. 19, Nehru Memorial Museum and Library.
22. *Indian Annual Register*, Calcutta, 1939, vol. 2, p. 340.
23. D.E.U. Baker (1979), p. 16.
24. *Tribune*, 9.11.1927 in Jayakar Papers, National Archives of India, File no. 741.
25. B.S. Dharmaveer (1972), p. 5.
26. Letter dated 23/04/1932 to Maharaja Scindia, Moonje Papers, NMML (Microfilm Section), Reel No. 7.
27. Moonje's letter to Raja Ichalkarang, dated 18/05/1936, ibid., Reel No. 11.
28. *The Maratha*, 18/06/1922.
29. "Hindu Militia (Ram Sena)," M.G. Chitnavis Papers, file No. 91, NMML.
30. Hindu Mahasabha Papers, P-72, NMML.
31. Savarkar Papers, Reel no. 1, File no. 2, Letters by V.D. Savarkar to N.B. Khare, 1 July 1938 and 21 September 1938.
32. Ibid., "Memorandum" (September 1938).
33. V.G. Deshpande, in B.S. Dharmaveer (1972), p. 25.
34. M.N. Ghatate, "Dr. B.S. Moonje—Tour of European Countries," in *Dharmaveer Dr. B.S.* (1972), pp. 68–9.
35. *Moonje Papers*, Reel no. 11, NMML (microfilm section), Moonje's letter to N.C. Kelkar, dated 10/04/1936.
36. *Hindu Outlook*, 30/03/1938, p. 1.
37. *Moonje Papers*, NMML (Microfilm Section), Reel no. 10, Moonje's letter to Appasahib Kelkar, dated 25/02/1936.
38. Ibid., Reel no. 11, Moonje's letter dated 16/06/1936.
39. *The Maratha*, 31 March 1939, p. 2.
40. V.C. Ulabhaje, "Organisation for Conversion," in *Dharmaveer Dr B.S.* (1972), p. 45.
41. B.S. Moonje, "Speech on Indianization of Armed Forces," ibid., p. 110.
42. Hindu Mahasabha Working Committee meeting, 21–22 September 1940. L/P&J/8/683 Coll 117/D1, IOLR
43. "Annual Report of the Bengal Provincial Hindu Sabha for the Year 1943–44," in S.P. Mookerjee, *Awake Hindusthan*, Calcutta, 1944, p. 5.
44. *Report of the Commission of Inquiry into the Conspiracy to Murder Mahatma Gandhi*, part II, New Delhi, Government of India, 1966, pp. 66–7.
45. Hindu Mahasabha Papers, p.51, "The Provincial Hindu Sabha—January 1945," p. 45, NMML.

46. Interview with Balarao Savarkar, 4 December 1988, New Delhi. Balarao Savarkar, who had become the assistant secretary of the HRD in 1942 was one of the few who left the RSS to join the HRD. He was to become V.D. Savarkar's private secretary soon after.

47. *Report of the Commission of Inquiry into the Conspiracy to Murder Mahatma Gandhi*, Part I, (1966), p. 168 and p. 300.

48. Ibid., Part II. p. 67.

49. Hindu Mahasabha Papers, P-29. Letter from K.V. Bodas date 13/03/1944.

50. *Report of the Commission of Inquiry into the Conspiracy to Murder Mahatma Gandhi*, Part II (1966), p. 321.

51. Proceedings of Ministry of Home Affairs, File no. 28/7/45 Poll (I), National Archives of India.

52. Interview with Balarao Savarkar.

53. B. Ray (ed.) (1966), p. 191.

54. Walter K. Andersen and Shridhar D. Damle (1987).

55. "Note on the Volunteer Movement in India," Intelligence Bureau, 27 January 1940; ibid., August 1940, in L/P & J/Coll. 17–C18 India Office Library and Records, London.

56. J.A. Curran (1951), and Walter K. Andersen and Shridhar D. Damle (1987), p. 50.

57. *The Rashtriya Sawayam Sevak Sangh*, Lahore (1948), pp. I–IV.

58. K.D. Jhari (1970), p. 28. See also B. Madhok, *RSS and Politics* (1986), p. 36.

59. Cited in *The Rashtriya Sawayam Sevak Sangh* (1948), p. 3.

60. "N.B. Khare Life history transcript," New Delhi, NMML, p. 72.

61. *Report of the Commission of Inquiry into the Conspiracy to Murder Mahatma Gandhi*, Part I (1966), pp. 242–3.

62. *The Hindu*, 13 March 2004.

63. *Report of the Three-Member Commission of Inquiry Headed by Shri Jitendra Narain, Former Judge, Patna High Court, to Inquire into the Communal Disturbances that Took Place in April 1979, in and around Jamshedpur*, 1981, p. 41.

64. See http://www.rss.org.parivar

65. Christophe Jaffrelot, "The Visva Hindu Parishad: A Nationalist but Mimetic Attempt at Federating the Hindu Sects" (2001), pp. 338–411.

66. For further detail, see Christophe Jaffrelot (ed.) (2005).

67. Christophe Jaffrelot (1996), chapter 2.

68. *The Organiser*, 22 April 1984, pp. 1–2.

69. Regarding the circumstances surrounding its founding, see *Hindu Vishva*, 21 (7), March 1986.

70. See http://vhp.org/

71. This leads Manjari Katju to the mistaken conclusion that Bajrang Dal means "The Army of Monkeys". See Manjari Katju (2003), p. 51.

72. On this foundational episode, see Peter van Der Veer (1987).

73. Interview with Acharya Giriraj Kishore (senior general secretary of the VHP) on 11 February 1994 in New Delhi.

74. Vinay Katiyar, "It is a war-like situation," interview published in *Frontline*, 24 April 1992, pp. 9–12.

75. Manjari Katju (2003).

76. Interview in Bhopal with a local Bajrang Dal leader, son of a police officer, who only agreed to speak on condition of anonymity.

77. Interview with Vinay Katiyar quoted by Smita Gupta and Christophe Jaffrelot, "The Bajrang Dal: the New Hindu Nationalist Brigade," in Mushirul Hasan (ed.) (2007), p. 202.

78. Interview with Acharya Giriraj Kishore in New Delhi.

79. Acharya Giriraj Kishore, "Preface" to R.P. Sharma, *Shikshak Margdar-shaka*, Delhi, Bajrang Dal, 1993.

80. Regarding the RSS calendar, see Christophe Jaffrelot, *The Hindu Nationalist Movement*, op. cit.

81. Quoted by Smita Gupta and Christophe Jaffrelot (2007), p. 204.

82. Quoted by Dionne Bunsha, "At a Hindutva Factory," *Frontline*, 7–20 June 2003.

83. This idea, which was formulated in 2002, gave rise to some very instructive exchanges on the discussion forum of *Outlook* magazine, http://www.outlookindia.com

84. Christophe Jaffrelot, *The Hindu Nationalist Movement* (2007), chap. 1 and "Militant Hindus and the Conversion Issue (1885–1990): From Shuddhi to Dharm Parivartan. The Politization and the Diffusion of an Invention of Tradition," in Jackie Assayag (ed.) (1999), pp. 127–52.

85. Quoted by Smita Gupta, "Desi Mossad is Getting Ready at Bajrang Dal's Ayodhya Camp," *Indian Express*, 30 June 2000.

86. Hubert Vaz "Empowering Women. The VHP Way," *Indian Express*, 21 May 2003 and P. Bhattacharya, "Hindu Nationalists Give Martial Arts Training to Girls to Protect their Faith," *Neapolitan* (Naples), 7 June 2003.

87. Interview with Surendra Jain, former Bajrang Dal president, by Smita Gupta, quoted in Smita Gupta and Christophe Jaffrelot, (2007).

88. Interview with Prakash Sharma, ibid.

89. Christophe Jaffrelot (2006).

90. For further details, see Christophe Jaffrelot, "The BJP at the Centre: a Central and Centrist Party?" (2001) (see the section entitled "Gujarat, a Laboratory for Hindu Nationalism," pp. 356–63).

91. Interview quoted by Smita Gupta and Christophe Jaffrelot (2007).

92. *The Times of India*, 28 August 2008.

93. *The Statesman*, 7 September 2008.

94. *Indian Express*, 8 October 2008.

95. Thus India became one of the major countries of Muslim mobilisation against liberties that Salman Rushdie had taken in his description of the Prophet in *The Satanic Verses*, and Khalistani militants went on a campaign against places where liquor was sold in Punjab in the 1980s.

96. K. Jayaprasad (1989), pp. 207–41.

97. Praveen Swami, "Predatory Pursuit of Power," *Frontline*, 23 May 1998.

98. See "BJP–The Saffron Years," Sabrang Alternate News Network, http://www.countercurrents.org and K.S. Narayanan, "When Might is Right," *Deccan Herald*, 1 July 2001.

99. Ranjit Hoskote, "The Mob as Censor," *The Hindu*, 11 February 2004.

100. PUCL, "Cultural Policing by Bajrang Dal and the Rajasthan Police," http://www.pucl.org.

101. P.S. Tripathi, "A Law unto Itself," *Frontline*, 23 April 2004, p. 41.

102. See Madanjeet Singh's article "Cultures & Vultures: Wake-up Call from Vadodara" in *The Hindu*, 18 May 2007.

103. A. Herdenia, "Sentimental intolerance," *Deccan Herald*, 31 August 2003.
104. Quoted in *The Hindu*, 5 February 2000.
105. Intimidation by the Bajrang Dal and another RSS offshoot, the Hindu Jagaran Manch, in 2000 did not succeed in discouraging Hindus from participating in New Year festivities: A. Tripathi, "Saffron Threat Fails to Dampen Spirits," *The Times of India* (Lucknow), 31 December 2000.
106. Praveen Swami, "Predatory Pursuit of Power," 1998.
107. Interview quoted by Smita Gupta and Christophe Jaffrelot (2007).
108. See http://www.vhp.org/wadhwa.htm
109. For further details, see Christophe Jaffrelot, "The BJP at the Centre: a Central and Centrist Party?" (2001) (see the section entitled "Gujarat, a Laboratory for Hindu Nationalism," pp. 356–63).
110. Interview with a former Ahmedabad police officer under the cover of anonymity.
111. Interview with Digvijay Singh on 7 April 2007 in New Delhi.
112. The utmost caution is required in relating this incident that has sparked heated controversy, and legal investigation has yet to clearly establish the sequence of events.
113. Quoted in *Communalism Combat*, 8 (77–78), March-April 2002, p. 12.
114. *How has the Gujarat Massacre Affected Minority Women? The Survivors Speak*, Ahmedabad, Citizen's Initiative, 2002.
115. Interviews conducted in Naroda-Patiya on 6 April 2007.
116. To borrow the terms of N.K. Singh, editor-in-chief of *Indian Express* (Ahmedabad) (interviewed on 5 April 2007 in Ahmedabad).
117. Bela Bhatia, "A Step Back in Sabarkantha," *Seminar*, 513; http://www.india-seminar.com
118. These figures come from a confidential report of the National Human Rights Commission following its March 2002 investigation in Gujarat.
119. Christophe Jaffrelot (2006), pp. 173–92.
120. Five years after the events, police are still stationed in neighbourhoods where clashes occurred and their trucks patrol refugee camps still in operation.
121. See *Indian Express* (Ahmedabad), 3 January 2007, 8 February 2007 and 22 March 2007.
122. Syed Khalique Ahmed, "From Naroda-Patiya to Parzania, He's the One Calling the Shot," *Indian Express* (Ahmedabad), 18 February 2007.
123. Ibid., February 21, 2007 and *Times of India* (Ahmedabad), 22 February 2007.
124. See "Civil Society Organisation Demand Bajrangi's Arrest," *Indian Express*, 26 April 2007.
125. Quoted in "Hindu Organisations Call for Bhopal Bandh," *The Hindu*, 14 April 2007.
126. Badal Saroj, "Communal Goons Turn Marriages into Nightmares," *People's Democracy*, 29 April 2007.
127. Before then she was a member of the Madhya Pradesh Executive Council of the ABVP (*The Times of India*, 26 October 2008).
128. According to some press reports she was also the president of the national executive of the Durga Vahini for a considerable time (M. Hafeez and S. Sonawane, "Malegaon Blast: Lt-Col Purohit held," ibid., 6 November 2008).
129. Ibid., 27 October 2008.
130. Ibid., 31 October 2008.

131. *The Indian Express*, 7 November 2008.
132. Ibid., 2 November 2008.
133. V. Ganjapure, "We love our country and aim to produce all-round leaders," *The Times of India*, 2 November 2008.
134. Another source gives June 2008 as the foundation date. It also says that the movement was founded at Jabalpur on the premises of a Sindhi organisation (Sindhu Shakti Parishad). Mayaram Jeswani, the president of this association and the vice-president of the Madhya Pradesh branch of Abhinav Bharat, is a former activist of RSS and VHP: S. Bose, "Sindhi body under scanner for terror links," *The Times of India*, 4/11/2008.
135. *The Indian Express*, 4 November 2008.
136. *The Indian Express*, 14 November 2008.
137. Bharti Jain, "I masterminded Malegaon blast: Lt Col", *The Economic Times*, 7 November 2008.
138. M. Hafeez, "Retd Major trained Sadhvi in bomb-making: Prosecutor," *The Times of India*, 31 October 2008.
139. These newcomers joined the BJP after several other ex-army men, including Major Jaswant Singh and Capt. Jagat Vir Singh Drona, who became the RSS Sanghchalak of Kanpur after he retired and the city's MP in 1989. In addition to ex-servicemen, ex-policemen joined the BJP in the late 1980s and early 1990s, including S.C. Dixit, former DGP of Uttar Pradesh who became Vice-President of the VHP and Varanasi MP on the BJP ticket in 1991, as well as B.P. Singhal (former DGP of Uttar Pradesh as well), and Ashok Singhal's brother.
140. In addition to Drona, Khanduri and Jaswant Singh, Rtd Maj. D.D. Khanoria was elected MP of Kangra (Himachal Pradesh) in 1990.
141. *Radiance*, 22–28 March 1998.
142. *Tehelka*, 14 February 2004.
143. *The Indian Express*, 30 October 2008.
144. In that incident, two Bajrang Dal activists were killed while they were allegedly assembling a bomb in a Nanded home (*Indian Express*, 9 November 2008).
145. "A 2006 probe had also thrown up ex-servicemen, Bhonsala school links," *Indian Express*, 1 November 2008.
146. Ibid.
147. See Christophe Jaffrelot, "Stigmatising and Emulating 'Threatening Others'–The Formation of Hindu Nationalism", *The Hindu Nationalist Movement and Indian Politics*, 2007, pp. 11–80.

Map 11: Punjab

JAMMU AND KASHMIR

PAKISTAN

Gurdaspur

6

Amritsar

1

1

Jalandhar 2

Firozpur

3

5 Moga

Ludhiana

4

Muktsar

Sangrur

Bathinda

Patiala

Mansa

HIMACHAL
PRADESH

HARYANA

RAJASTHAN

1 Kapurthala   4 Fatehgarh

2 Nawanshahr   5 Faridkot

3 Rupnagar   6 Hoshiarpur

Dorian RYSER, October 2008

10

THE KHALISTAN MILITIAS

SERVANTS AND USERS OF THE STATE

Laurent Gayer

The government has done more for me in a week than what I could have achieved by myself in ten years.

Sant Jarnail Singh Bhindranwale, shortly after his release from prison,
October 1981.

The Sikh insurgency that shook the Indian Punjab between 1984 and 1995 was rooted in the religious militias which rose up between 1978 and 1984 and came to challenge the Indian state's monopoly on legitimate violence by drawing from both the theological and the epic "cognitive stock"[1] that structure representations of violence in the Sikh community. This movement, led by Sant Jarnail Singh Bhindranwale, a preacher, initially enjoyed Congress party patronage as well as that of the federal authorities after Indira Gandhi returned to power. In its second phase, after the final break between Sikh militants and the Indian state, it was in Pakistan that the radical Sikh movement found its principal state support. Sikh militia members, and later insurgents, were however wary of becoming mere subcontractors for the Pakistani secret services, both to preserve their room for manoeuvre and to avoid alienating their social base. Rather than the Indian and later Pakistani states' instrumentalisation of the Sikh militias, the phenomenon discussed here is rather one of "collusive transactions" between actors operating in originally different spheres. And rather than leading to stabilised strategic partnerships, these collusive relations have produced precariously balanced power configurations that are always on the verge of disintegrating.[2]

Contrary to what the title might suggest, this chapter will contain little discussion of Khalistan.[3] It is not so much the ideological dimension of the Sikh separatist movement as its means of deployment that is of interest here. The aim is therefore not to take stock of the political and social significations of the Khalistan movement, already studied in detail elsewhere,[4] but rather to reveal the relations, at the same time intimate and conflictual, between Sikh militants that gave rise to the Khalistan movement and their partners within the Indian and Pakistani states.

'Collusive transactions' between Sikh religious militias and the Indian state

The development of "collusive transactions" between Sikh militants and certain sectors of the Indian state dates back to the late 1970s. At that time, Indira Gandhi used Sikh fundamentalist groups[5] to sideline the moderate factions of the Shiromani Akali Dal (SAD),[6] which challenged Congress political hegemony in the province and had come to the fore during the State of Emergency (1975–77) by demonstrating pugnacity contrasting with the silence of other opposition parties. Although it is certain that Indira Gandhi approved their strategy to marginalise the SAD, it originated from her son Sanjay and especially the Sikh Congress leader Zail Singh.

State policy or personal policy? Zail Singh and the Sikh radicals. Born into the intermediary cast of carpenters (Ramgarhias), Zail Singh (1916–94) received a religious education at the Shahid Sikh Missionary College in Amritsar, which earned him to the end of his life the nickname *giani* (guardian of the books in the Sikh religion), even though he failed his final exams. In the late 1930s he joined the Indian National Congress and was jailed for five years for having defied the Maharaja's authority in the princely state of Faridkot. Upon independence, he entered the Punjab government and then the Senate before becoming the first non-Jat[7] Chief Minister of Punjab in 1972. In 1980, after Indira Gandhi returned to power, he became Home Minister and two years later President of India.

Zail Singh's support for the Sikh radicals stemmed first from a personal initiative: this veiled strategy aimed to marginalise his main rivals in the province, whether they were Sikh nationalists in the SAD, a party dominated by the Jats, or opponents within his own party (and particularly Darbara Singh, who became Chief Minister of Punjab in 1980). This strategy, however, met with Indira Gandhi's approval and that of her entourage. It predated the return of Zail Singh to power, as he encouraged a group of Sikh fundamentalists who, like himself, belonged to a different caste from the Jats[8] to band together to challenge the SAD's hegemony within the governing body for the main Sikh places of worship, the Shiromani Gurdwara Prabandhak Committee (SGPC). Zail Singh apparently paid the bill for the meal during which the Dal Khalsa was formed on 20 April 1978.[9]

This Amritsar-based organisation took the name taken by the confederation of Sikh militias that fought against the Mughals and later the Afghans in the 18th century (the *Misl*) and established a protection system (the *Rakhi*) on which Ranjit Singh's empire was built. Ranjit, son of the commander of one of these militias *(misldar)*, conquered Lahore in 1699, and then went on to build a state that stretched as far as Afghanistan and Sindh. Although Muslims and Hindus occupied nearly half the leadership positions in the state and Ranjit Singh had established a "secular" system prefiguring that of contemporary India,[10] the Sikh nationalists who appeared at the turn of the 19th and 20th century reinterpreted this political structure as a "Sikh state". The most radical of them have been calling since 1940 for the creation of a "state of the pure"—Khalistan—that would revive the "kingdom of Lahore".[11]

As soon as it was founded, the Dal Khalsa took a separatist stance by demanding the creation of Khalistan. Despite Zail Singh's support (he had no qualms about personally telephoning provincial journalists to request that they publish front-page stories about the Dal Khalsa),[12] the organisation never managed to break onto the Sikh political-religious scene. As early as 1981, it escaped control of its mentor (later Home Minister), by organising a sensational aircraft hijacking.[13] Zail Singh was more fortunate with another of his protégés, *Sant* (saint) Jarnail Singh Bhindranwale, who was allegedly selected by the *giani* and Sanjay Gandhi from a list of 20 potential "clients" drawn up by Sanjay's advisers after a field mission in Punjab.[14]

Sant Jarnail Singh Bhindranwale's militia career. Born in 1947 into a family of small Jat landholders, Jarnail (General) Singh was the youngest of seven children and was sent to the prestigious Damdami Taksal seminary founded in the 18th century by one of the most famous Sikh "saint-warriors" *(Sant-Sipahi)*, "Baba" Dip Singh, whose career strongly influenced Bhindranwale.[15] Having curried favour with the seminary principal Sant Kartar Singh, Bhindranwale succeeded him in 1977 and rose to fame the following year when a dozen of his partisans were killed by the guns of a Sikh schismatic movement, the Sant Nirankaris, that had considerable backing in the state and federal bureaucracy.[16] Bhindranwale, vehemently criticising the slackening of moral standards in the Sikh community after the Green Revolution,[17] took on the role of *Sant-Sipahi* in both speech and posture. Decked in a turban wrapped in the style of Nihangs, Sikh ascetics who practice martial arts, Bhindranwale always sported a revolver and an ammunition belt slung across his shoulder, and liked to be surrounded by young, heavily armed men. Under his leadership, the Damdami Taksal seminary became a centre for military training as well as religious education that was the primary recruitment pool for the Sikh militia movement.

The movement shifted into political violence in the early 1980s, first with the murder of the Sant Nirankaris' leader on 24 April 1980, then with the slaying of the biggest Hindu press tycoon in the state, Lala Jagat Narain, on 9 September 1981. Killings of "deviant" Sikhs, policemen and Hindu civilians increased in the following year (the police listed nearly 200 between 1982 and 1984), and there was no doubt about Bhindranwale's direct involvement in some of them. According to one member of his entourage, Kanwar Singh Dhami, "it was Bhindranwale himself who ordered these murders and his men perpetrated them".[18] The cleric had even allegedly drawn up a "blacklist" of personalities to be slain, and this document, regularly updated according to rumour, was the object of great speculation in Punjab. Far from doing him harm, such rumours lent Bhindranwale an aura of power and invulnerability, as did his regular tours in neighbouring states—as far as Delhi—during which he paraded with his heavily armed combatants. Seeking to rekindle the Sikhs' martial sentiment, especially among the younger generation, the *Sant* called on every village in Punjab to form a commando made up of three young baptised Sikhs equipped with a motorcycle and three revolvers.

The religious militia that gradually took shape around Bhindranwale had no political ambition, at least not officially. Its outward vocation was religious in nature, since it aimed to fight against "deviant" Sikh heretics like the Sant Nirankaris, or simply lax ones such as Sikhs who trimmed their beards (a real obsession with Bhindranwale, facial hair being a recurrent motif in his speeches) or indulged in drink or drugs. Despite his repeated claims that he had no political agenda, Bhindranwale backed three Congress candidates in the 1980 general elections and in 1982 was cooperating with moderate factions of the SAD in their agitation movement against the federal authorities, symbolically described as a *dharm yudh* ("just war").[19] But the political role Bhindranwale gradually took on should be sought not in these fragile collusions with institutional and political actors at the state and federal level, but in the protection system he set up, inspired directly by the *Rakhi* system practiced under the *Misl*, in which landowners paid one-fifth of their annual income in exchange for protection of their property and lives by Sikh warlords.[20] Far from discrediting him, as has been suggested, the wave of killings and planned murders attributed to Bhindrawale, combined with the impunity his state patronage lent him, made him a feared and respected figure. A growing number of Sikhs from all social classes turned to him for help in land tenure disputes, the search for a job, and so on. The *Sant* honoured all of these requests (even if he demanded payment for his services from the wealthiest) and his combatants' muscle (or weaponry) worked miracles for his clients. Bhindranwale not only took money from those who requested his protection, he also imposed it on those who would have happily gone without it. He addressed his requests for "donations" by mail to large shopkeepers and entrepreneurs, who generally paid up promptly.

This protection system, recalling Sikh history, is at the crux not only of the process of state formation,[21] but of the militia phenomenon as well, which should not come as a surprise. Is not the state basically a successful militia, and does not every militia hope to create a state within the state, even its own state? In the case at hand, Bhindranwale clearly had the ambition of constituting a parallel authority that was both political and religious, and although he may have played the game of instrumentalisation for a while, it was mainly in his own interest. Bhindranwale was never an undercover state agent. He mainly sought to divert state resources to private ends, to "form the state for himself" to use Bruce Berman and John Lonsdale's expression.[22] The theory of Bhindranwale's gradual autonomisation from his state mentors is thus not entirely convincing. Even when he seemed remote-controlled by Congress leaders, Bhindranwale always had his own agenda. The increase in his military capability and, proportionally, his popular support only gave him the means to openly assert his autonomy. This naturally did not leave the Indian state indifferent.

The first state actor to react to Bhindranwale's provocations was the Punjab police. On 13 September 1981 police sought to interrogate the preacher, whom they suspected of involvement in the murder of Lala Jagat Narain. But when they arrived in the village in Haryana (a neighbouring province of Punjab) where Bhindranwale had been invited to give one of his firebrand sermons, the *Sant* and his partisans had already left the premises, apparently in haste, because they had abandoned the vehicles in which was found the collection of sermons the cleric took wherever he went. In fury, the police set fire to the vehicles. This incident was a decisive moment in Bhindranwale's militia career,[23] leading him to reassess not only his relations with state institutions but also his mission and historic role. As Mark Tully and Satish Jacob, two BBC correspondents who closely followed Bhindranwale, clearly understood, "it was the immortal words of Bhindranwale that went up in flames at Chando Kalan and the preacher never forgave the government for that". According to the two journalists, it was actually the burning of his sermons much more than his arrest (which finally occurred on a date and place he himself set, 20 September 1981) that hastened the break between Bhindranwale and Zail Singh. "What would you do if someone killed your nearest and dearest? They have insulted my Guru by burning my papers", Bhindranwale declared shortly after the incident.[24] The change in Bhindranwale's outlook, once he was convinced his vocation was to confront this state that was denying him a place in history, seems to not have been perceived by Zail Singh, who continued to defend the *Sant*, particularly by claiming before Parliament, less than a month after Lala Jagat Narain's murder, that Bhindranwale had nothing to do with the incident. The *Sant* was immediately released, which reinforced his aura, since he was able to boast of a symbolic victory over the Indian federal government.

The disintegration of a "collusive transaction". The rift between Bhindranwale and the government was triggered in July 1982 by the arrest of his right-hand man, the son of his predecessor at the head of the Damdami Taksal, Amrik Singh. Fearing a police offensive, Bhindranwale hid out in a pilgrim hotel near the Golden Temple in Amritsar before moving his headquarters to the Akal Takht[25] at the heart of the complex the following year. Fortification was then started, coordinated by a former Indian army general, Shabeg Singh, who had joined Bhindranwale after leaving the army in disgrace (a hero of the Bangladesh liberation war during which he had formed the Bengali *Mukhti Bahini* guerrilla force, he was banished from the army for corruption just before retiring). Several hundred armed Sikhs settled into the Golden Temple with their leader and prepared to confront security forces. Indira Gandhi finally decided to act after the massacre of Hindu bus passengers by Sikh militants in Punjab on 5 October 1983. The next day, the Prime Minister announced the imposition of president's rule in Punjab, which involved suspending Darbara Singh's Congress government and placing the state under supervision of the Indian central government. This measure hardly impressed Bhindranwale and his militia and on 18 November, four Hindu passengers on a bus were murdered. Killings of Hindu civilians increased during the following month until the army was finally called in on 30 May 1984, and started deploying itself around the Temple complex in the following days. Given Bhindranwale's refusal to surrender, the army was ordered to "clean out" the complex on 5 June. This decision was made by Indira Gandhi alone, and Zail Singh was not informed of it.

The symbolism of this attack, which Bhindranwale may have sought to provoke to radicalise the Sikhs, was twofold. The irruption of tanks and soldiers within the walls of the Golden Temple, as well as the massacre of hundreds of unarmed pilgrims,[26] reminded the Sikhs of "holocausts" (*gallughare*) of which they had been victims in the 18th century.[27] This attack, which coincided with the celebration of the first Sikh martyr, Guru Arjun, who died under torture in 1606, also sharply revived the memory of major figures in Sikh history who had chosen death rather than submission to an authority they believed iniquitous. And in the months that followed, the Sikh religious militias gave way to an all-out insurgency.

Diplomatic collusions: relations between the Pakistani state and the Sikh insurgency

In the weeks following Operation Blue Star, a few hundred Sikhs decided to leave for Pakistan, believing that there they would find support against the Indian state. These militants were nevertheless to be disappointed: the Pakistani state initially denied them military aid and imprisoned them so as to control their movements better. It was not until the Sikh insurgency truly began to organise in 1986 that the Pakistani secret services considered supporting the insurrection in earnest. And it was not until after a platform of fundamentalist groups controlled by Islamabad was created that such military support took on a significant dimension, leading to more intense violence in Indian Punjab in the late 1980s.

From the start of the Sikh insurgency in 1984, relations between the rebels and representatives of the Pakistani state were fraught with tension. The Pakistanis in fact sought to satellise these foreign protesters, who long resisted those attempts. Accounts by militants present in Pakistan during the years

1984 to 1995 present a very different picture from the fanciful analyses hawked by the Indian press regarding the functioning of the Pakistani secret services, depicting instead an image of Pakistan's "diplomacy of disorder"[28] marked by pragmatism, iterative methods, racialism, and devotion to the policy of divide and rule. Most of these features of Pakistan's parallel diplomacy are rooted in the security policy implemented in India under British colonial rule.[29] Interviews with commanders or even the rank-and-file of the Khalistani guerrilla movement at the same time attest to the irreducible autonomy of these insurgents, who learned to exploit the Pakistani state and operate at the interstices of its sovereignty.

The birth of a virtual guerrilla force. The young Sikhs who travelled to Pakistan in the summer of 1984 had diverse profiles. Some had belonged to Bhindranwale's militia or the All India Sikh Students Federation (AISSF) led by Amrik Singh, and had escaped from the Golden Temple just before the Indian army offensive. Others were active in the Babbar Khalsa, a fundamentalist organisation formed in 1978 to fight against the Sant Nirankaris and later quarrelling with Bhindranwale—even though some members of his entourage today claim that these tensions were a pretence aimed at dissociating the *Sant* from the murders of Nirankaris perpetrated by the Babbars, who actually had his total approval.[30] Along with these seasoned militants who over the preceding years had moved in Bhindranwale's entourage were a few police officers and young men with no prior militant experience, who were shocked by the profanation of the Golden Temple. Although most of these young men belonged to the Jat caste, and more specifically to small landowning families from the districts bordering Pakistan (Gurdaspur and Amritsar) who scarcely benefited from the Green Revolution, some Khatris (usually shopkeepers) and Mazhabis (literally "the pious", meaning Sikh "Untouchables") also joined the movement. The movement was not homogeneous in terms of class either: although most insurgents were from the small and middle peasantry,[31] some sons of good families with a high level of education also took part in the armed struggle, such as Daljit Singh Bittu (see below).

The rebels always crossed the border in small groups of three to ten people, usually swimming. Crossing the Ravi River posed difficulties for those who did not know how to swim. But Pakistani villagers often came to their aid, especially by offering them the use of their water buffaloes so that the Sikh insurgents could hang onto their tails to make it across.[32] Once on the Pakistani side, the illegal immigrants were escorted to the nearest border post where the Rangers[33] then took the responsibility of informing the secret services (Inter-Services Intelligence, ISI). Initially, the Pakistanis decided to regroup the Sikh militants in an isolated quarter of Faisalabad prison in Punjab. The insurgents, numbering nearly 500 at the end of 1984, were given special treatment, but their movements were tightly controlled. A handful of them, identified as potential leaders, were housed in villas in Lahore, Sialkot or Narowal. These were actually gilded cages. ISI was quite familiar with the

Sikh militia circles, having planted informers in Bhindranwale's entourage (to the point of knowing in detail the task assigned to each combatant entrenched in the Golden Temple on the eve of Operation Blue Star). But the agency long hesitated as to what strategy to adopt with regard to the Sikh rebels whose ardour was equalled only by their lack of discipline. Punjab was not Kashmir, whose status was a fundamental issue in the history of the process of Pakistani state formation, and the Pakistani army was not prepared to trigger another war with India out of sympathy for the Sikh cause or even out of pure opportunism. The Pakistani wait-and-see attitude surprised the Sikh "insurgents" whose status as "freedom fighters" (*azadi ghulatiye*, as they like to be called) was still very theoretical. As months went by, surprise turned into resentment and then open hostility when the Pakistanis not only refused the would-be insurgents their military backing, but also denied them the possibility of returning to India to fight. In January 1986 the Faisalabad "prisoners" tried to escape, but this attempt ended in bitter failure: most of the fugitives broke limbs jumping from the prison wall and one was shot down by the Pakistanis. Some of them were later roughed up by the prison wardens, and officials of the Pakistani Interior Ministry had to intervene to protect the wounded.[34]

Attempts to satellise the Sikh insurgency by its Pakistani patrons. As a former Babbar Khalsa combatant points out, "the Pakistanis wanted all the combatants to be members of an organization",[35] and it was not until the first Sikh political-military structures were formed in 1986 that ISI really began to back these insurgents' war effort. On 26 January 1986, a group of pro-Khalistani activists organised a meeting of the *Panth*[36] under the auspices of the Akal Takht, the highest seat of Sikh religious authority. It was after this *Sarbat Khalsa* that the first "Panthic Committee" in charge of coordinating Sikh resistance came into being. According to the Sikh tradition of the *Panj Pyare* (the "five beloved") established by the last Guru, Gobind Singh,[37] this committee was made up of five men: Gurbachan Singh Manochahal, a former soldier struck from the ranks for indiscipline, Wasson Singh Zaffarwal, a former trade union activist close to the Akali Dal, and three Damdami Taksal members, Gurdev Singh Usmanwala, Dhara Singh and Arun Singh. From the start, the Panthic Committee had both a political and military mission: in collaboration with the AISSF, it was to coordinate not only the Khalistan movement's legal arm—the movement having been launched officially with the "Declaration of Independence" adopted by the Panthic Committee before the Akal Takht on 29 April 1986—but also organised armed struggle. This was to be conducted by the Khalistan Commando Force (KCF), which came into being following the *Sarbat Khalsa* in 1986.

The KCF's 400 combatants were officially commanded by a general, seconded by lieutenant-generals and area commanders. As the anthropologist Cynthia Keppley-Mahmood suggests, these ranks served more as a symbolic gratification attributed for heroic *faits de guerre* than to reproduce the discipline in the resistance that some of its members had known in the army.[38] Between 1986 and 1988, KCF leaders strived to establish a central command structure. But the centralisation of military operations and arms supply facilitated infiltration of the KCF and elimination of its combatants (200 of them were reported killed between 1986 and 1988).[39] Drawing lessons from this failure, Zaffarwal restructured the organisation in 1990, this time giving it a cellular structure: each group was to operate independently, developing its own source of arms supply in connivance with local smugglers and Indian border guards.

Zaffarwal, who settled in Pakistan in 1987,[40] became the military commander of the KCF the following year, after Lab Singh's death. The task befell him to coordinate KCF actions, supply his combatants with arms and supervise their military training in coordination with the Pakistani "agencies" which the former insurgent leader still to this day refuses to identify—less out of caution, in truth, than because he does not believe the matter has any importance: "Did the people who were involved with us belong to the ISI? [laughter]. Perhaps... Call them ISI or whatever you want... For us they were Khans or Chaudhrys..."[41] The secret service agents supplied Zaffarwal with arms for the KCF combatants. These were then illegally transported into India, by 15–20 kg loads per "mule". Each KCF combatant staying in Pakistan (it was rare for more than 20 to be present in the country at any one time, according to Zaffarwal) was thus to return with his consignment to India. During their time in Pakistan, these combatants sometimes received rudimentary military training. During the sessions, emphasis was naturally placed on guerrilla techniques, but according to Zaffarwal, the Pakistanis never sought to replicate in Punjab the field methods used in Afghanistan.

Zaffarwal's relations with his Pakistani "patrons" were fraught with tension: "We disapproved of their strategy. We were asking for substantial aid, but they were pushing us to kill civilians, like bus passengers, and set bombs. We were absolutely opposed to such actions". But any open opposition to ISI directives was severely punished, even when it came from insurgent leaders. Thus Zaffarwal was subject to six months' imprisonment for having protested one day against the way Pakistani Secret Service agents wanted to use his men in an operation in Indian Punjab.[42] Gradually sidelined by fundamentalist groups represented in the second Panthic Committee (see *infra*), Zaffarwal ended up leaving Pakistan in 1996. He then escaped to Zurich, where with the help of a Sikh attorney with contacts at the UN, he was granted political asylum. He finally turned himself in to the Indian authorities in 2001 after negotiating the conditions of his surrender with Prakash Singh Badal's Akali government.

In the Pakistanis' eyes, the KCF had a number of failings. Its combatants were deemed too undisciplined, too political (making them less easily controllable than fundamentalist militants for whom the creation of Khalistan was not the primary goal of armed struggle) but also, and this is not merely anecdotal, too "scrawny". Dominated by Punjabis and, to a lesser extent, Pathans, the Pakistani army remained under the influence of stereotypes that guided security policy under colonial rule. One of these was the myth of "martial races", of which the Punjabis and Pathans believe themselves to be the region's finest exemplars. The interiorisation of these racial stereotypes was reflected in ISI's relations with its Sikh protégés. The latter were selected on the basis of their caste and their physique, the Pakistanis displaying a clear preference for well-built Jats, supposedly less well represented in the KCF than among its rival organisations. For instance, an ISI officer quoted by the anthropologist Joyce Pettigrew claimed that "Zaffarwal's boys were so skinny...," whereas rival groups of the KCF that joined their forces to form the second Panthic Committee in 1988 "were the real fighters coming through, strong and healthy".[43] According to Pettigrew, another factor explains the Pakistanis' outward preference for the second Panthic Committee: the ability of these armed groups to fund themselves (via extortion or armed robbery) and their willingness to remit a portion of the sums collected to their Pakistani mentors. In other words, it is alleged, Pakistani intelligence officers simply extorted from the Sikh insurgents and preferred those who were more generous to them (these kickbacks being made to individuals and not in the form of a tax for state protection).[44]

The second coalition of armed groups included the Babbar Khalsa as well as dissident KCF (KCF Panjwar) and AISSF (AISSF Bittu) factions, which a new armed group, the Khalistan Liberation Force, soon joined. The tutelary figure of the second Panthic Committee, also known as the *char jhujharu jathebande* (the four groups of liberators), was Dr Sohan Singh, a doctor who had been superintendent of Punjab hospitals and who struck up a special relationship with the Pakistanis even if he claims to have spent most of his seven years (1986–93) underground in Indian Punjab and Nepal, where he was finally arrested in 1993 (denounced, according to him, by the KCF).[45] Another salient figure of the second Panthic Committee was Daljit Singh Bittu, a former veterinary student at the Punjab Agricultural University in Ludhiana, son of an entomology professor at the same university. Bittu converted to armed struggle in the aftermath of Operation Blue Star, being convinced that all other methods of resistance to oppression by the central authorities had failed. Advocating a merger of the AISSF into the armed resistance movement, he himself went underground in July 1985, where he remained for over ten years until his arrest by Punjab police. Bittu recalls his years in the resistance in eloquent terms:

The faction that I led was entirely devoted to armed struggle. We organized operations against the security forces, their informants, against trains, the media and bureaucrats responsible for so many murders. [...] Life underground was a truly unique experience; it was a very intense period in my life, full of emotion... It was really an exciting period. It can't be rationalized; it's beyond words. Our entire being was absorbed by the struggle. It was war. Life only had meaning in death. We had to go through it, as individuals, as a nation and as religion, to learn what real life meant. This feeling came to us through Guru Nanak, Guru Gobind Singh, and Sikh history. It was the same struggle. The *Khalsa* spirit, the teachings of the Gurus and the forces of history offered ordinary people an opportunity to become heroes. During this period, the nation rose up through a purer and stricter life.

According to Bittu, the Pakistanis played a minor role in Sikh insurgent military training: "We never got any serious military training from the Pakistanis. And the use of weapons is part of our history. With each operation, I learned to handle a new weapon. I really learned by doing. Actually, I can't say that the Pakistanis helped us in any decisive fashion. The truth is, they looked the other way".

Rather than directly supply weapons, the Pakistanis allegedly allowed the second Panthic Committee combatants to obtain arms in the country, particularly in the "tribal areas",[46] which were also the preferred supply channel for the Afghan *mujahidin*. ISI apparently did deliver weapons to the *char jhujharu jathebande*, but such deliveries were "insignificant", according to Bittu.[47] That does not mean he did not always maintain cordial relations with his Pakistani protectors. He depended on them for his political survival in that his social base, like that of all the "commanders" affiliated with the second Panthic Committee, was narrower than that of the KCF which, in the early years of the insurrection, enjoyed widespread popular support in rural Punjab, especially in the districts of Amritsar and Gurdaspur. By seeking to impose a strict religious orthopraxy via a series of social reforms (a ban on alcohol and drugs, change in dress code, abolition of the dowry, etc.), the armed groups affiliated with the second Panthic Committee, especially the Babbar Khalsa, alienated themselves from the Punjab population just as they diverted the Sikh insurgency from its political goals.

The "underlife" of Sikh insurgents. Although the leaders of Sikh armed groups seem to have enjoyed a fair amount of freedom of movement in Pakistan starting in 1986, especially to secure arms, this was not the case for the rank-and-file militants (the *munde*, or "kids"). Under close surveillance by Pakistani Secret Service agents and having limited relations with the Pakistani population as well as among themselves, these combatants—who after being moved from Faisalabad prison[48] usually found themselves housed in deserted Sikh temples *(gurudware)*—were subjected to stifling social control.

Pakistani control over the Sikh insurgents, by way of incarceration and then their burdensome patronage, helped to transform the Khalistan movement into a "total" institution, whose members live "all the aspects of [their] life on the premises in the close company of others who are similarly cut off from the wider world".[49] Although psychiatric asylums studied by Erving Goffman, or even prisons, provide the most compelling examples of "total" institutions, Goffman himself points out that "radical movements", especially when they are based in religious values, can be placed in the same category: in such organisations, "the member is expected to place himself at the disposal of the current needs of the organization. In telling him what he should do and why he should want to do this, the organization presumably tells him all that he may be". Yet no "total" institution, however effective it may be, is able to impose total social control on its members. In the wings of these institutions or the interstices of their social control, more or less conscious and more or less radical resistance to the institutional order develops. That is the "underlife" of the institution, which, to use Goffman's enlightening analogy, is "to a social establishment what an underworld is to a city".[50]

This theoretical framework is worth applying to relations between Sikh insurgents and their Pakistanis "patrons": it prompts one to take a look at the strategies of circumventing the rules of the total Khalistani institution used by its militants. The most spectacular but also the most widespread of these forms of "underlife" was voluntary death in combat. As I have already shown elsewhere,[51] the Khalistani martyrs differ from their jihadist or Tamil counterparts by the non-strategic aspect of their voluntary death. Unlike al-Qaeda or LTTE militants, the Khalistani insurgents never developed a "sacrificial ideology"[52] glorifying death in combat. It was of their own accord, and often against the advice of their "commanders", that they engaged in missions of no return. Zaffarwal himself agrees, even if he tends to put his combatants' lack of discipline into perspective: "It's true that a lot of young men wanted to die. We tried to hold them back, but to no avail. I wouldn't say they disobeyed us, but rather that the number of martyrs exceeded all expectations…"

A close associate of Zaffarwal who was with him in Pakistan and involved in training and arming the KCF combatants, does not bother with such subtleties: "The problem [with the Sikhs] is that, like the Iranians, we have this f… tradition of martyrdom. You had to be there [in Pakistan] to understand. We had gone mad. Because you got to live, man, you got to live. Me too, I was like hypnotized and my wife was afraid I wouldn't come back [to London]. Because it's so easy to cross the line…"[53]

In the first years of the Sikh insurgency, this quest for martyrdom that expressed the combatants' desire to escape the all-encompassing framework of their movement often involved a practice called *wanggar*. It consisted in informing and defying an adversary on a strictly individual basis to provoke him to a duel. The young rebels usually went directly in front of a police station and heaped insults on their target before informing him at what time he would be attacked. This chivalrous behaviour was probably in part a game, but also enabled Sikh rebels to escape control of their Pakistani protectors and refute the accusations of their Indian adversaries who presented them as terrorists in the pay of Islamabad.[54]

The quest for martyrdom, however, cannot be reduced to a strategy of individual resistance to the all-encompassing framework of the Khalistani movement. It was also fuelled by death wishes that show similarity between the early Sikh insurgents and Iranian "martyropaths".[55] Beyond these deadly callings, and from a more original angle, the quest for martyrdom also fits in with the symbolic competition among combatants for stakes involving access to posterity. This is pointed out in no uncertain terms by Zaffarwal's deputy quoted above: "The problem with martyrdom is that everyone wants to achieve it and that it winds up being a matter of individual prestige".[56] The theological and historical framework in which Sikh combatants situated their armed struggle was conducive to these individual sacrifices. But it is actually the symbolic competition among members of the resistance that led the combatants to carry out suicidal missions, rather than those cultural repertoires. The practice of *wanggar*, which was very costly in terms of human lives, gradually gave way to operations involving less risk-taking for the combatants. How can this evolution be explained? Should it be taken as a sign of more effective social control on the part of armed group leaders and their Pakistani mentors? Or should the explanation be sought in a change of strategy among the combatants themselves who had more or less given up the idea of dying? These two hypotheses are not necessarily mutually exclusive. Even if the "terrorist" strategy of the Pakistanis, who in the early 1990s convinced the Sikh insurgency leaders to abandon the guerrilla campaign in favour of bombings, stirred controversy among the pro-Khalistan circles, it had the merit of presenting a coherent line of action that spared human lives. The Khalistani combatants remained to be converted to this new form of armed struggle. And if that was possible, it was because a profound change occurred within them. The hypothesis I will formulate here is that there was a renewal of combatants in the late 1980s. The first generation of "martyropath" militants, guided by a death wish, died out (largely eliminated by Indian security forces) and their place was taken by more "opportunistic" insurgents[57] who found in the Khalistani movement a "career" in the trivial sense of the term. Whereas the first Sikh insurgents often entered the resistance fully intending to die, their successors joined armed groups to live better—to be able to acquire, via extortion and armed robbery, consumer goods (televisions, electrical appliances), tools of trade (trucks) or else property (land, houses) that had become signs of success and modernity in Green Revolution Punjab, but had remained inaccessible to the small and middle peasantry.[58] It would be misleading to reduce this dynamics of social change within the Khalistani resistance to a mere matter of criminalisation or ideological dilution. The main reason lies elsewhere, in the immanent or transcendent nature its participants saw in armed struggle. Did these insurgents fight to escape the torments of this world or on the contrary to cure them, even through very idiosyncratic methods of personal enrichment? It was the purpose that each combatant invested in his own radical engagement, in interaction with his militant environment, that oriented his relation to violence and the inherent risk of carrying it out.

After collusion: re-sectorization and reconversion of Sikh insurgents

Collusion between Sikh militias and their state patrons, Indian and Pakistani alike, has always been fragile. As explained above, the events of 1984 led to the disintegration of "collusive transactions" between Sikh religious militias and the Indian state. Then there was an initial trend of "re-sectorisation" of the insurgents, that is, their banding together in a new autonomous social sector: an underground nationalist movement. This process remained incomplete, however: despite their apparent break with the Indian state, some insurgent leaders maintained ties with the police and especially members of the Border Security Force (BSF) which were prepared to help the Sikh rebels cross the border until it was closed in 1993, in exchange for weapons or money. But these ties may sometimes have gone beyond an exchange of favours, or simple family solidarity in the case of combatants informed of security force movements by relatives in the police or military. Several leading figures in the pro-Khalistani movement were "turned" in this way by Indian intelligence agencies. According to Joyce Pettigrew, most of the second Panthic Committee leaders (Sohan Singh and the leaders of the Babbar Khalsa, in particular) were thus in the pay of the Indian state, which gave them discreet support via its intelligence service in order to sideline more political groups such as the KCF.[59] This analysis tends to take at face value the rumours circulating in rural areas of Punjab and KCF accusations against its rivals; but the very existence of these rumours is enough to confirm that the "re-sectorisation" of Sikh insurgents into an underground movement was not yet complete, if only in the eyes of the insurgency's social base and its combatants. And it is indeed because it was always plausible that the accusation of compromise with the Indian state was so often used by the movement cadres to discredit their adversaries.

However incomplete, at least in the minds of its actors and their audience, the re-sectorisation of Sikh militants on Indian soil went along with a new form of collusion with state actors, this time the Pakistani military elite. Earlier I discussed the conditions in which this "collusive transaction" was able to emerge in the field of parallel diplomacy and the tensions woven into its process of institutionalisation. The "underlife" of Sikh combatants already expressed, in an informal and individual manner, a desire to recover a margin for manoeuvre and place themselves outside the state authorities' reach. Exile was another form of escape, as in Zaffarwal's case. In this precise case, his leaving Pakistan was tantamount to defection, since Zaffarwal renounced political activities after being granted political asylum in Switzerland, even if he placed a plaque on the door to his Zurich residence proclaiming "Khalistan House".[60] Hence the break with the state did not systematically lead the pro-Khalistani militants to pursue their struggle in a new independent social sector, but at times accompanied demobilisation and professional reconversion on their part. For instance, the former KCF chief today works as a homeopath in his native village of Zaffarwal (Gurdaspur district) in the heart of what was Sikh insurgency territory from 1984 to 1995. After negotiating his surrender with Prakash Singh Badal's Akali government, the former warlord served a two-year prison sentence (2001–03). Since his release, he has retired from politics but does not rule out starting his own party someday. For the moment, he prepares mysterious mixtures in the family home and, given the number of villagers lining up at his door, this startling reconversion seems to have been fairly successful.[61]

Most of the Sikh insurgency cadres and militants were killed by the Indian security forces (according to most estimates, at least 30,000 people lost their lives in the conflict between 1984 and 1995). Among the survivors, a handful chose to remain in Pakistan to continue their rearguard battle.[62] Most of the survivors of the Sikh insurgency have nevertheless pursued their struggle by democratic means, like the Naxalite leaders who have been tempted by the parliamentary route (see Nicolas Jaoul's chapter in this volume). These veterans hope to draw politically on the social capital they believe they have acquired through their participation in armed struggle. But those who have decided to enter the legal political arena have usually been disappointed. At the height of Indian state terror, relatives of major martyr figures (notably Bimal Kaur, widow of Beant Singh, Indira Gandhi's assassin, who was elected MP in 1989) and a few Khalistan movement leaders managed to get elected to the lower house of the Indian parliament, especially when they had done prison time (like Simranjit Singh Mann and Atinder Pal Singh in 1989). But such electoral success was short-lived: the parliament was prematurely dissolved in 1991 and the candidates with ties to the insurgents never managed to repeat the triumph of 1989,[63] though S.S. Mann recovered his seat in 1999 before losing it again in the following election in 2004. The gradual return to normal in Punjab beginning with the 1992 elections, and the population's desire to turn its back on the "dark years",[64] deprived the Khalistanis of popular support, as they themselves agree: "Many people feel respect for us, but most of them are afraid. They're demoralized", Daljit Singh Bittu believes.[65]

Beyond the martyrs' family circle, those who took part in the elections were generally "leaders" on the fringe of the insurgency whose fleeting popularity had more to do with their political prisoner status than their military experience. For example, Simranjit Singh Mann, a former police officer who was drawn in by Bhindrawale, never took part in any armed operation against the Indian state, even if he is suspected of having helped Bhindranwale procure arms and—much less plausibly—of having been involved in Indira Gandhi's assassination. Atinder Pal Singh, for his part, was active in the ranks of the AISSF and took up the Khalistan cause following Operation Blue Star. But this intellectual from a wealthy family ruined by Partition never took part directly in the armed struggle.[66]

As for the former combatants who joined political parties, they have refused to run for elected office, such as Kanwar Pal Singh (who today is active in the Dal Khalsa, relaunched as a political party in 1998) and Daljit Singh Bittu (who became a member of SAD-Amritsar, headed by Simranjit Singh Mann, before breaking with him in 2007 to launch his own political party). These veterans of the armed struggle cast a nostalgic gaze on their past ("armed struggle is something wonderful and much easier than democratic politics", declared Daljit Singh Bittu) that is allied with a certain scorn for institutional politics. Going into politics means agreeing to "wallow in the mud", says Daljit Singh Bittu. In the Indian context it also means settling for "small and trivial democratic arrangements" that lack the "dazzle" of underground action and violence.[67]

Conclusion

Like most militia organisations in South Asia, Sikh irregulars placed themselves under the patronage of state actors while offering protection to their social base. In the Sikh case this protection offer, which joins together on the same continuum organised crime, "terrorists" and the state,[68] drew its inspiration from the contractual security system (the *Rakhi*) set up by the first Sikh militias (the *Misls*) in the 18th century. Using his collusion with the Indian federal government, Sant Jarnail Singh Bhindranwale gradually took on the role of a *misldar* (militia commander), dispensing his protection in exchange for moral and sometimes financial support. Until Operation Blue Star, the misdeeds attributed to his men only reinforced the aura of this controversial character and lent credibility to his protection offer. This system ended up being challenged, however, by the disintegration of collusive transactions between Sikh religious militias and the Indian federal government.

The Khalistani insurgents attempted to reproduce this protection system, especially in rural areas, by threatening retaliation against police suspected of abuse or becoming involved—sometimes against their will—in land tenure conflicts and family vendettas. However, the rise and intensity of the repression directed at individuals as well as harvests (since the police systematically destroyed crops in areas with strong insurgent presence) helped to devalue the Khalistanis' protection offer. Alongside this external devaluing of the protective function of the Khalistanis, its cost rose sharply in the late 1980s owing to internal factors following the second Panthic Committee's undertaking of social reforms, which alienated its main social base by seeking to impose a puritanical moral order in rural areas. The criminalisation of the insurgency after it was hijacked by "opportunistic" militants also contributed to raising the cost of the Khalistani militants' protective function—now literally, because the appearance of these new actors on the local "protection market"[69] placed increased financial pressure on the peasant population. This rise in the cost of protection was all the more poorly perceived by its clients since it came at a time when doubt was cast on the racketeers' (*lutere*) actual protection capacities.

Taken in isolation, the success of repression and the criminalisation of Sikh insurgent groups are therefore not enough to explain their political and military failure. It is the combination of these factors that is at the root of this failure, in that they both contributed to undermining the protection system that the Sikh religious militias had managed to set up in the years 1978–84, with the active support of the Indian federal state, or at least some of its most eminent agents.

BIBLIOGRAPHY

Books

Berman, Bruce and John Lonsdale, *Unhappy Valley. Conflict in Kenya and Africa*, volume 1: *State and Class*, London, James Currey, 1992.

Briquet, Jean-Louis and Gilles Favarel-Garrigues, *Milieux criminels et pouvoir politique. Les ressorts illicites de l'État*, Paris, Karthala, 2008.

Crettiez, Xavier, *Violence et nationalisme*, Paris, Odile Jacob, 2006.

Dal khalsa, *Jun 84 ke Shahid* (Punjabi/English) (The Martyrs of June 84), Amritsar, 2nd ed., 2007.

Dhillon, Kirpal, *Identity and Survival. Sikh Militancy in India, 1978–1993*, Delhi, Penguin, 2006.

Dobry, Michel, *Sociologie des crises politiques*, Paris, Presses de Sciences Po, 1986.

Duggal, Kartar Singh, *Secular Perceptions in the Sikh Faith*, Delhi, National Book Trust, 1992 [1st ed. 1982].

Gayer, Laurent, "Les Politiques internationales de l'identité. Significations internationales des mobilisations identitaires des sikhs (Inde) et des Mohajirs (Pakistan), " PhD thesis in political science, Paris, Sciences Po, 2004.

Goffman, Erving, *Asylums. Essays on the Social Situation of Mental Patients and Other Inmates*, New York, Doubleday Anchor, 1961.

Grewal, Manraj, *Dreams After Darkness. A Search for a Life Ordinary under the Shadow of 1984*, Delhi, Rupa, 2004.

Kapur, Rajiv A., *Sikh Separatism. The Politics of Faith*, London, Allen & Unwin, 1986.

Keppley-Mahmood, Cynthia, *Fighting for Faith and Nation. Dialogues with Sikh Militants*, Philadelphia, University of Pennsylvania Press, 1996.

Pettigrew, Joyce, *The Sikhs of the Punjab. Unheard Voices of State and Guerrilla Violence*, London, Zed Books, 1995.

Puri, Harish K., Judge, Paramjit Singh and Jagrup Singh Sekhon, *Terrorism in Punjab. Understanding Grassroots Reality*, Delhi, Har-Anand Publications, 1999.

Singh, Bhagat, *A History of Sikh Misals*, Patiala, Punjabi University Press, 1993.

Singh, Gurharpal, *Ethnic Conflict in India. A Case Study of Punjab*, Basingstoke/New York, Macmillan/St. Martin's Press, 2000.

Tully, Mark and Satish Jacob, *Amritsar. Mrs Gandhi's Last Battle*, London/Sydney, Pan Books, 1985.

Articles and chapters in edited volumes

Bhogal, Balbinder Singh, "Text as Sword: Sikh Religious Violence Taken for Wonder," in John R. Hinnells and Richard King (eds), *Religion and Violence in South Asia. Theory and Practice*, London, Routledge, 2006: 107–35.

Gayer, Laurent, "Le Pakistan: un État en formation dans un contexte de turbulences internes et externes," *Annuaire Français de Relations Internationales*, Paris/Bruxelles, La Documentation française/Bruylant, 2004: 395–416.

————— "Le "jeu de l'amour": trajectoires sacrificielles et usages stratégiques des martyrs dans le mouvement pour le Khalistan," *Cultures & Conflits*, 63, Autumn 2006: 113–33.

————— "La privatisation de la politique étrangère en Asie du Sud: modes populaires d'action diplomatique et pratiques de sous-traitance stratégique en Inde et au Pakistan," *Transcontinentales* (Paris), 3, 2nd semester 2006: 119–20.

Juergensmeyer, Mark, "The Logic of Religious Violence," in David Rappoport (ed.), *Inside Terrorist Organizations*, London, Frank Cass, 1988: 172–93.

Khosrokhavar, Farhad, "Le modèle Bassidji," *Cultures & Conflits*, 29–30, 1998: 59–118.

Oberoi, Harjot, "Sikh Fundamentalism: Translating History into Theory," in Martin E. Marty and Scott Appleby (eds), *Fundamentalisms and the State. Remaking Politics, Economies and Militancy*, University of Chicago Press, 1993: 256–85.

Pettigrew, Joyce, "In Search of a New Kingdom of Lahore," *Pacific Affairs*, 60 (1), Spring 1987: 1–25.

——— "Martyrdom and Guerrilla Organisation in Punjab," *Journal of Commonwealth Politics*, 30 (3), November 1992: 387–406.

Schalk, Peter, "Resistance and Martyrdom in the Process of State Formation in Tamililam," in Joyce Pettigrew (ed.), *Martyrdom and Political Resistance. Essays from Asia and Europe*, Amsterdam University Press, 1997: 61–83.

Shah, Alpa, "Markets of Protection: the "Terrorist" Maoist Movement and the State in Jharkand, India," *Critique of Anthropology*, 26 (3), 2006: 297–314.

Tilly, Charles, "War Making and State Making as Organized Crime," in Peter Evans, Dietrich Rueschmeyer and Theda Skocpol (eds), *Bringing the State Back In*, Cambridge University Press, 1985: 169–191.

NOTES

1. If there are indeed "remnants of the past" in certain protest movements, it is less for reasons of historical determinism than due to a strategic positioning imposed on social actors in a political crisis situation; these "critical junctures" in fact deprive the actors of "the routine methods of anticipating and gauging situations" and lead them to turn to the past to find answers to their uncertainties; cf. Michel Dobry (1986), p. 289.

2. Michel Dobry views such disintegration of collusive transactions as mainly affecting state sectors, but it seems to me that a similar threat hangs over the collusive relations between state and social actors, ibid., pp. 276–85.

3. Khalistan (literally, the "land of the pure") was a project for a sovereign Sikh state that was conceptualised in the 1940s.

4. Laurent Gayer (2004), chapter 4, pp. 613–30; Rajiv A. Kapur (1986); Harish K. Puri, Paramjit Singh Judge and Jagrup Singh Sekhon (1999); Gurharpal Singh (2000).

5. On the origins and discourse of the Sikh fundamentalist movement, see Harjot Oberoi (1993), pp. 256–285.

6. This party, founded in 1920, has since been the main Sikh political organisation.

7. The Jats are landholders who have dominated Sikh politics since the 18th century. They dominated the militias that fought the Mughals and the Afghans, then in Ranjit Singh's court. Since it was founded in 1920, the Akali Dal has basically been a Jat party and Bhindranwale, like most of the insurgents in the 1980s and 90s, belonged to this caste.

8. Dal Khalsa activists all belonged to the caste of Khatris, the group to which Sikh Gurus belong. Members of this caste hold a wide variety of functions: shopkeepers, businessmen, civil servants and military personnel.

9. Mark Tully and Satish Jacob (1985), p. 60.

10. All religions (Sikhism, Islam and Hinduism) were considered equal in Ranjit Singh's Khalsa Raj, and the personal status of the Maharajah's subjets differed according to their religious affiliation. Even if it is hard to establish a direct relationship between this secular system and contemporary India, the analogies are striking; cf. K.S. Duggal (1992 [1ˢᵗ ed. 1982]).

11. Joyce Pettigrew (1987), pp. 1–25.

12. Mark Tully and Satish Jacob (1985), p. 60.

13. This hijacking, inspired by the Palestinian example and aiming to secure the release of Sant Jarnail Singh Bhindranwale, who had recently been arrested, took place on 29 September 1981. Shortly after take-off from Delhi, five Dal Khalsa members took command of an Indian Airlines aircraft bound for Srinagar by waving fake grenades (actually oranges painted black). They diverted the aircraft to Lahore, where the Pakistani authorities neutralised the hijackers after they had asked to be allowed to perform their ritual ablutions in the airport. Two of the hijackers were arrested coming out of the bath, and the other three captured by a commando disguised as maintenance personnel; interviews with one of the hijackers, Tejinder Singh, and the "brain" of the operation, Harsimran Singh, Punjab, May 2001.

14. Mark Tully and Satish Jacob (1985), p. 57.

15. According to legend, Baba Dip Singh, decapitated by the Afghans, managed to reach the Golden Temple to die there, holding his sword in one hand and his head in the other. Shortly before Bhindranwale died during Operation Blue Star, he declared: "Baba Dip Singh had to carry his head several kilometers to deposit it here, whereas I have the privilege of offering mine right here".

16. Kirpal Dhillon (2006), p. 69.

17. For an analysis of Bhindranwale's speech, see Mark Juergensmeyer, "The Logic of Religious Violence," in David Rappoport (ed.) (1988).

18. Interview, Palsora (Punjab), 24 January 2007.

19. Regarding Sikh theology of violence and its "Dharmic" justification, presented as a form of restoring social and cosmic order, see Balbinder Singh Bhogal (2006), pp. 107–35.

20. Bhagat Singh (1993), pp. 46–51.

21. Charles Tilly (1985), pp. 169–91.

22. Bruce Berman and John Lonsdale (1992) vol. 1, p. 38.

23. Regarding this notion, see the general introduction to this volume.

24. Mark Tully and Satish Jacob (1985), p. 68.

25. The Akal Takht (The Throne of the Timeless One), built in 1606, stands facing the Golden Temple (Harimandir Sahib, or "Holy Temple of God"), the most revered of Sikh shrines, located in Amritsar. In the mind of its designer, Guru Hargobind, who began the militarisation of the budding Sikh community, the Akal Takht was supposed to symbolise the Gurus' temporal power (*miri*), whereas the Harimandir Sahib incarnated spiritual authority (*piri*). It has always been reserved exclusively for religious ceremonies, whereas the Akal Takht soon become the Panth's main political institution where Gurus meted out justice and the nascent Sikh community gathered in an assembly (*Sarbat Khalsa*) to make collective decisions (*gurmata*) that had the power of law.

26. The number of casualties of Operation Blue Star cannot be ascertained. It included about 400 Sikh combatants, a hundred soldiers (83 according to official figures), and probably hundreds of civilians trapped in the Temple complex during the assault. Since most of the bodies were disposed of by the army at the end of the operation, and burnt in secrecy, the exact figure of Bluestar's casualties remains open to question. As far as the Sikh militants killed in the assault are concerned, evidence collected over the years by the Dal Khalsa for 388 of them suggests that the vast majority of them were baptised Sikh men (only two female fighters are recorded to have died in the operation) who belonged to the Damdami Taksal; cf. Dal Khalsa, *Jun 84 ke Shahid* (Punjabi/English) (The Martyrs of June 84), Amritsar, 2nd ed., 2007.

27. During the 18th century, the Sikhs were subject to an outright extermination campaign by the Mughal authorities and later the Afghan invaders. This campaign culminated with the "small holocaust" (*chota gallughara*) of 1748 and especially the "great holocaust" (*vada gallughara*) perpetrated by the Afghans led by Ahmed Shah Abdali in 1762.

28. Laurent Gayer, "Le Pakistan: un État en formation dans un contexte de turbulences internes et externes" (2004), pp. 395–416.

29. Regarding the colonial antecedents of parallel diplomacy and privatisation of war in Pakistan, see Laurent Gayer, "La privatisation de la politique étrangère en Asie du Sud: 'modes populaires d'action diplomatique' et pratiques de sous-traitance stratégique en Inde et au Pakistan" (2006), pp. 119–20.

30. Interview with Kanwar Singh Dhami, Palsora, 24 January 2007.

31. As Joyce Pettigrew points out, large landholders were too much in league with the state, and landless peasants too busy fighting for their everyday survival, to take part in the insurgency; Joyce Pettigrew (1995), p. 57.

32. Interview with Kanwar Singh Dhami, Palsora, 24 January 2007.

33. Regarding this paramilitary force in charge of protecting Pakistan's borders, cf. Laurent Gayer, "Les Rangers du Pakistan: de la défense des frontières à la 'protection' intérieure," in Jean-Louis Briquet and Gilles Favarel-Garrigues (eds) (2008), pp. 23–55.

34. Interview with Kanwar Singh Dhami, Palsora, 24 January 2007.

35. Interview with Kanwar Pal Singh, Amritsar, 21 January 2007.

36. Literally meaning "the way", this term refers to the Sikh community as a whole, made up of "baptised" Sikhs (*amritdhari*) and "latitudinarians" (*sahajdhari*).

37. The *Panj Pyare* were the first members of the Khalsa, the "community of the pure" founded by Gobind Singh in 1699.

38. Cynthia Keppley-Mahmood (1996), p. 55.

39. Joyce Pettigrew (1995), p. 84.

40. According to the journalist Manraj Grewal, Zaffarwal's first visit to Pakistan dates back to 1984. It was during this first journey that he is supposed to have got in touch with ISI and discussed the launching of the KCF with its officials; cf. Manraj Grewal (2004), p. 118.

41. Names of Muslim upper castes, symbolising the two major ethnic components of the Pakistani army: the Pathans (symbolised by the surname Khan) and the Punjabis (symbolised by the surname Chaudhry).

42. Manraj Grewal (2004), p. 122.

43. Quoted by Joyce Pettigrew (1995), p. 188.

44. Ibid.

45. Interview with Dr Sohan Singh, Mohali (Punjab), 24 March 2001.

46. One of the main sources of weapons procurement for these Sikh combatants was Darra Adam Khel, in Khyber Agency.

47. Interview with Daljit Singh Bittu, Ludhiana, 22 January 2007.

48. After the first Panthic Committee was formed, the Pakistanis allowed the Khalistani *munde* to leave Faisalabad prison to take refuge in *gurudware*.

49. Erving Goffman (1961), p. 203.

50. Ibid., pp. 180 and 199.

51. Laurent Gayer, "Le "jeu de l'amour"…" (2006), pp. 113–33.

52. Peter Schalk (1997), p. 67.

53. Interview, London, 22 July 1999.

54. Joyce Pettigrew (1992).

55. Farhad Khosrokhavar (1998), pp. 59–118. Regarding the Sikh "martyropaths", cf. Laurent Gayer, "Le 'jeu de l'amour'" (2006).
56. Interview, London, 22 July 1999.
57. Here we borrow Farhad Khosrokhavar's categories in "Le modèle Bassidji" (2006).
58. Laurent Gayer, *Les Politiques internationales de l'identité* (2004), pp. 310–12.
59. Joyce Pettigrew (1995).
60. Manraj Grewal (2004), p. 123.
61. Personal observations, January 2007.
62. Among the last Sikh insurgency leaders in Pakistan, whose extradition is demanded by India, are Gajinder Singh (leader of the Dal Khalsa), Lakhbir Singh Rode (leader of the International Sikh Youth Federation), Wadhwan Singh Babbar (chief of the Babbar Khalsa), Ranjit Singh Neeta (commander of the Khalistan Liberation Force) and Paramjeet Singh Panjwar (chief of one of the KCF factions); these insurgency leaders mostly live in Lahore; cf. "India's 42 Most Wanted," *Outlook* (New Delhi), 21 January 2002.
63. The Shiromani Akali Dal (United), close to the Khalistani militants, won ten out of Punjab's 13 seats in the lower house of the Indian parliament.
64. This desire to put violence behind them was already apparent in the late 1980s; the Prime Minister V.P. Singh was thus given a triumphant welcome upon his visit to the Golden Temple in 1989.
65. Interview, Ludhiana, 22 January 2007.
66. On the career of Atinder Pal, who became a taxi driver in the United States after his release, before returning to Punjab to go into business, see Manraj Grewal (2004), chapter 7.
67. Xavier Crettiez (2006), p. 92.
68. Alpa Shah (2006), p. 299.
69. Ibid.

CONCLUSION

Laurent Gayer and Christophe Jaffrelot

Until recently, the spectre of war between states seemed to have been entirely warded off in South Asia. India and Pakistan, which were engaged in a "composite dialogue" between 2004 and 2008, at least temporarily renounced resolving their disputes through violence. That represented remarkable progress for two states involved in structural rivalry since the Partition in 1947, which led to four open conflicts in the past decades (in 1948, 1965, 1971 and 1999). Following the Mumbai attacks of November 2008, India suspended this dialogue process. Rumours of troops mobilisation and possible "surgical strikes" against jihadist camps in Pakistan once again made headlines, with the head of the Hindu nationalist organisation Rashtriya Swayamsevak Sangh (RSS) even calling on Indian citizens to prepare themselves for nuclear war.[1] The future will tell whether this was mere pre-electoral gesturing on the part of the Indian political class or whether the two countries are truly on the verge of a new military confrontation. However, the latter possibility would expose them to an unbearable risk of escalation.

Even if there has been a fragile and incomplete pacification of interstate relations at the regional level, a reverse phenomenon is observed within states. All South Asian societies, whatever the nature of their political regimes, are confronted with the rising power of militia organisations that are as violent in their discourse as in their physical deeds and whose targets are the state, religious communities, rival castes and classes, as well as "domestic enemies", "deviants" and "traitors" in their community.

The impact of such militia violence on societies in the region cannot be measured only using the death toll as a yardstick. More fundamentally, the foothold that militia groups have taken in South Asian countries partakes of the "brutalisation" of their societies. This notion, originally formulated by the historian George Mosse in his study of interwar European societies,[2] is highly useful for the analysis of contemporary South Asia. It invites us to work on the genealogies of political violence and not restrict scrutiny to practices

259

alone, but to take into consideration the full extent of hate discourse that authorises recourse to violence by providing it with a moral, cultural or theological justification.

The brutalisation of societies does not involve only a legitimation of recourse to violence in resolving political disputes. It exceeds the political field to perturb the full range of social relations via a process of routinisation of violence, which spreads to most spheres of activity, from the economy to family relations.

In fact, the violence mirrored by the state and private armed groups not only causes "collateral damage" among civilian populations: it sinks in deep, calling into question, if not redefining, the rules of life and society. This rupture is not always obvious and the passing visitor would have trouble perceiving it. The trivialisation of violence in fact produces situations that appear to be normal—after all, life goes on even in the deadliest war zones on the planet. The growing insensitivity of societies to violence undoubtedly contributes to this illusion of normalcy. Yet on closer examination, this apparent "normality" is extremely fragile. In a context where violence can break out at any moment, people learn to remain constantly on the alert. As Linda Green suggests, fear becomes a way of life.[3] Initially developed in the Latin American context,[4] this research agenda is beginning to develop in South Asia via in-depth field studies in regional conflict zones, especially among the most vulnerable populations.[5]

The development of militia organisations affects all South Asian political systems, from democracies to military regimes. It levels out differences, and in this regard India—as Christophe Jaffrelot shows in his chapter—displays striking similarities with countries in the region with less deep-rooted democratic traditions.[6] First of all, militias embody a form of social violence that unfolds at the local level where individual liberties have never really been guaranteed for all. Next, the state's representatives at this level sometimes see the militias as intermediaries that can help them enforce a form of order—that of the well-established social balance of power and hierarchies.

Analysing the lasting effects of militia violence on societies does not preclude the need for a parallel investigation into the conditions in which they are absorbed. The case studies brought together here supply valuable lessons in this regard. As the Bangladesh and Pakistani examples stress, studied here by Jérémie Codron and Amélie Blom, countries that are tempted to privatise violence—for domestic or diplomatic purposes—have sometimes managed to reverse the trend by successfully delegitimising and crushing violence that was previously tolerated or even encouraged. In this regard, the apparent weakness of some states—Pakistan under General Musharraf and Bangladesh under Khaleda Zia—is sometimes closer to a strategic fiction in which the loss of control displayed by officials enables them to dissociate themselves from illegitimate violence while justifying exceptional practices. And when this fiction ends up proving untenable or counterproductive in the face of pressure from an "international community" increasingly preoccupied by the "terrorist threat", these supposedly weak states prove surprisingly effective in the repression of private operators of violence. The case of Bangladesh is exemplary in this regard, since it only took Khaleda Zia's government and the Transition Authority that succeeded it a few months to close down two jihadist organisations, the Jama'at-ul Mujahidin and the Jagrata Muslim Janata Bangladesh, which had been terrorising the country for several years. The Pakistani example, however, suggests that it is not always easy to get the genie back into the bottle. Certainly, as Amélie Blom shows in this volume, the Pakistani jihadists operating in Indian Kashmir are in total disarray now that their state backing has dried up. But in recent years their organisations have broken free of their "patrons", and they will probably survive any interruption of such sponsorship. Similarly, as Mariam Abou Zahab suggests, the Sunni sectarian movements originally sponsored by the army have gradually taken their distance from it, first placing themselves in the service of more local interests before turning against their former protectors after September 11, 2001 and the ensuing strategic about-face in Islamabad.

Some of these conflicts are lasting longer than others because of outside support. The conflict in Indian Punjab in the 1980s and 90s, studied here by Laurent Gayer, is revealing of the role of outside actors in the spread of militia violence. The Indian state was thwarted in its effort to rein in the Sikh militias that it had patronised until then, owing to the attitude of the Pakistani authorities, who provided support—albeit moderate and fairly belated—for the Sikh insurgents. Nevertheless, the Indian state managed to normalise the situation in Punjab by using the military stick and the democratic carrot.

Outside support for private armed groups is not limited to the sponsorship of foreign states, always fragile because of its reliance on the diplomatic context. Militias in South Asia have also drawn support from their transnational, business and diaspora networks. The case of the LTTE, studied by Chris Smith, is particularly eloquent in this regard. The LTTE war machine, which until recently was matched by none in the region and perhaps in the world, had been fuelled by a huge transnational arms supply network coupled with a closely-knit Tamil diaspora. But however transnational it may be, this world-wide LTTE network did not escape the control of the states over which it was spread. The recent changes in the attitude of France, Britain and even Thailand towards LTTE activities on their soil, in the direction of greater vigilance, had dealt a heavy blow to the Tamil separatist organisation, which has thus lost the bridgeheads of its transnational network. More importantly, the state of Sri Lanka has been able to win the war—or at least a key battle—against the LTTE in the spring of 2009.

The cases of Nepal and Burma, studied here by Gilles Boquérat, Marie Lecomte-Tillouine and Renaud Egreteau, highlight the broad range of solutions at the state's disposal to end, or at least regulate, militia violence. Beyond repression, it can envisage several modes of co-optation. The first and most controversial involves the *incorporation* of private practitioners of violence by integrating them into the state security forces. Such an undertaking is always lengthy and a source of new conflicts between professionals of legitimate violence—the military or the police—and their former adversaries. The case of Nepal, where the army is hardly eager to open its ranks to the former Maoist combatants,[7] is particularly eloquent in this regard. In May 2009, this issue even led to the resignation of the Nepalese Prime Minister and former head of the Maoist insurgency, "Prachanda", thus striking a blow to the peace process that had started in 2006.

Along with incorporation, *contractualisation* constitutes another possible mode of co-optation of former combatants or insurgents. In this case, the state officially acknowledges private armed groups' role in controlling a given territory. This is the case of ethnic militias allied with the Burmese junta, described by Renaud Egreteau. In exchange for their loyalty to the central government, these private violence entrepreneurs are often allowed to extract economic resources from their area of influence, which range from perfectly legal production activities to smuggling of illicit goods.

As Nicolas Jaoul and Laurent Gayer show here, demilitarisation of former combatants can also occur through their political reconversion via legal political parties. However, the example of the Bihar Naxalites tempted by the parliamentary route and that of former Sikh combatants in Indian Punjab illustrates the obstacles that lie in the way of these political reconversion strategies, both at the group level of the organisation and at the individual level of former combatants. The process of demilitarising the members of Liberation was thus hindered by strategic factors (ongoing armed opposition from caste militias and rival Naxalite factions) as much as by political dilemmas (what meaning and form can mass radicalism take?). The disenchanted remarks made by former Khalistan movement combatants on their legal political activities within the framework of India's parliamentary democracy underline for their part the social and psychological cost of decommissioning, which is experienced not only as an ideological compromise, but also, more deeply, as the abandonment of an exciting way of life.

Although some militias die out with the passage of time, failing to renew their cadres and militants or voluntarily disbanding, others transform themselves. Thus, in addition to the persistence of old militias such as the Naxalites, India may see the development of existing Hindu militias and the emergence of new ones in the context of increasingly numerous Islamist attacks. Whether these attacks are perpetrated by Pakistan-based jihadist groups or by local radicalised Muslims, their actions have already led some Hindu militias to turn to terrorism as well in a logic of strategic mimesis. This new development is all the more worrying since military personnel (serving or retired) happened to be involved in operations such as the blasts in front of a mosque in Malegaon in 2008.

NOTES

1. Javed Naqvi, "RSS chief says India should be ready for nuclear war," *Dawn, online edition*, 13 December 2008.
2. George L. Mosse, *Fallen Soldiers. Reshaping the Memory of the World Wars*, Oxford University Press, 1991. The author studies the process of routinisation of violence that led up to the Second World War via procedures of " trivialisation" (through dissemination in both the public and private sphere of images, songs and games referring to war) and "brutalisation" (by extolling military virtues and more simply brutality with respect to inflexible social orders).
3. Linda Green, *Fear as a Way of Life. Mayan Widows in Rural Guatemala*, New York, Columbia University Press, 1999.
4. An outline of research into the routinisation of violence in Latin America can be found in Kees Koonings and Dirk Krujit (eds), *Societies of Fear. The Legacy of Civil War, Violence and Terror in Latin America*, London, Zed Books, 1999.
5. Gender studies are in this regard way ahead of the rest of the social science literature devoted to South Asia. Feminist authors were indeed the first to perceive and take an interest in the routinisation of violence in the region; cf. Anuradha Chenoy (ed.), *Militarism and Women in South Asia*, Delhi, Kali for Women, 2002; Neloufer de Mel, *Militarizing Sri Lanka. Popular Culture, Memory and Narrative in the Armed Conflict*, London, Sage, 2007.
6. India's democracy, however, continues to offer certain guarantees—legal ones in particular—against militia development. On 31 March 2008, for instance, the Supreme Court ruled against the Chhattisgarh government, declaring unconstitutional the military aid this state gave the Salwa Judum anti-Naxalite combatants.
7. The reluctance of regular armed forces to integrate former Maoist combatants is not only rooted in ideological motives but also in corporatist logics, in that the Maoists want their combatants to be incorporated into the army at the same rank, which would certainly upset the military hierarchy.

INDEX